In the Name of Humanity

In the Name of Humanity

THE GOVERNMENT OF THREAT AND CARE

ILANA FELDMAN
& MIRIAM TICKTIN,
EDITORS

Duke University Press DURHAM & LONDON 2010

Designed by Jennifer Hill
Typeset in Garamond Premier Pro
by Achorn International

Library of Congress Cataloging-in-Publication Data
appear on the last printed page of this book.

Duke University Press gratefully acknowledges the
University of Michigan Women's Studies Department,
which provided funds toward the publication of
this book.

CONTENTS ∽

ACKNOWLEDGMENTS vii

Introduction 1
GOVERNMENT AND HUMANITY
  Ilana Feldman & Miriam Ticktin

When Humanity Sits in Judgment 27
CRIMES AGAINST HUMANITY AND THE
CONUNDRUM OF RACE AND ETHNICITY
AT THE INTERNATIONAL CRIMINAL
TRIBUNAL FOR RWANDA
  Richard Ashby Wilson

Children, Humanity, and
the Infantilization of Peace 58
  Liisa Malkki

Narrative, Humanity, and Patrimony in
an Equatorial African Forest 86
  Rebecca Hardin

Inhumanitas 115
POLITICAL SPECIATION, ANIMALITY,
NATALITY, DEFACEMENT
  Allen Feldman

"Medication is me now" 151
HUMAN VALUES AND POLITICAL LIFE IN
THE WAKE OF GLOBAL AIDS TREATMENT
  João Biehl

Environment, Community, Government   190
    Arun Agrawal

The Mortality Effect   218
COUNTING THE DEAD IN THE CANCER TRIAL
    S. Lochlann Jain

Inequality of Lives, Hierarchies of Humanity   238
MORAL COMMITMENTS AND ETHICAL DILEMMAS
OF HUMANITARIANISM
    Didier Fassin

The Politics of Experimentality   256
    Adriana Petryna

Stealth Nature   290
BIOMIMESIS AND THE WEAPONIZATION OF LIFE
    Charles Zerner

BIBLIOGRAPHY   325

CONTRIBUTORS   359

INDEX   363

ACKNOWLEDGMENTS ᕲᕲ

THE ORIGINS of this volume lie in our experience teaching a class together called "Government and Humanity" while we were in the Columbia Society of Fellows in the Humanities from 2002 to 2004. We are grateful for opportunities this fellowship provided. We are also indebted to the wonderful students whose thoughtful and generous engagement with the course made us want to spend many more years pondering the relationship between government and humanity. The first step in developing our ongoing conversations into a collection of essays was the convening of a workshop in April 2005 at the Kevorkian Center for Near Eastern Studies at New York University. We thank the center's staff for their generous assistance with all the logistics. We also thank the NYU Humanities Council, the University of Connecticut Human Rights Institute, and, at the University of Michigan, the Office of the Vice Provost of Research, the International Institute, the Women's Studies Program, and the Department of Anthropology for crucial financial support for the workshop and the book project. If a great class made us first think of compiling a book, a fantastic workshop convinced us that this project was worth pursuing. We are tremendously grateful to all the participants for such stimulating discussions. In addition to the contributors to this book, paper givers and discussants included Samera Esmeir, Tom Keenan, Emily Martin, Timothy Mitchell, and Hugh Raffles.

As we have worked to develop the volume, we are indebted to Rob Blecher and Andrew Zimmerman for helpful comments on the introduction. A number of research assistants have provided invaluable assistance in pulling together the volume. Our deepest thanks go to Julienne Obadia, Carol Wang, Emily Sekine, Giovanna Fischer, and Marie Cour. We also thank Jake Kosek and two other reviewers for Duke University Press for their careful readings and tremendously helpful comments on the entire manuscript. Without Ken Wissoker's interest, there would be no book. Also at Duke, Courtney Berger, Leigh Barnwell, and Tim Elfenbein were always helpful and patient.

INTRODUCTION ⟳

Government and Humanity

Ilana Feldman &
Miriam Ticktin

WHAT DOES IT MEAN to claim "humanity" as your political constituency? What is it to govern, fight, and care in the name of humanity? These are the questions that this volume grapples with. Surveying the contemporary political scene one finds humanity mobilized in a remarkable array of circumstances. Whether considering the challenge of global environmental destruction, the ethics of scientific research on stem cells, or the identification of genocide and other atrocities, activists on all sides of the issues know that a claim to speak on behalf of humanity stakes out a powerful position. It is one of the few categories that is meaningful across political, religious, and social divides. While people may disagree on the source of its power, almost everyone agrees that humanity should be considered sacred. As a universal subject, the claims of humanity should, it seems, be paramount—and to speak on its behalf should bring discussion to a close, permit action to begin, and enable lives to be saved. And yet, the meaning of humanity is not as clear as its widespread appearance in political and ethical discourse might suggest. The call to humanity often does not have the intended clarifying effects.

There are simply too many understandings of humanity for it to be the final word.

When everyone speaks in the name of humanity, no one can monopolize its meaning. In the debate over stem cell research, for instance, both advocates and opponents speak of saving lives and of protecting the sacredness of humanity. Opponents argue that research on stem cells derived from human embryos violates the sanctity of human life in the name of research; supporters argue that refusing to allow such research condemns humanity to further disease, suffering, and death. This debate remains unsettled, though recent technological advances suggest that the issue may be resolved by the possibility of creating stem cells without humanity. Humanity not only means many different things, its meanings are often contradictory. Environmental conservation efforts can, by displacing people and constricting their livelihoods, clash with the rights claims of local populations, and each can claim to pursue the good of humanity (Veit and Benson 2004; Alley and Meadows 2004). In other words, by identifying certain peoples as the source of environmental degradation, and by understanding environmental degradation as a threat to the future of humanity, conservationists may—in the name of humanity—threaten the basic human rights of local populations to live and to choose their own livelihood.

Similarly, human rights and humanitarian perspectives on how best to protect human life can mandate conflicting courses of action. This conflict is abundantly clear in the debate about what to do about the profoundly tragic—and highly contested—situation in the Darfur region of Sudan. After the outbreak of conflict in 2003, human rights activists called for military intervention to "save Darfur," to stop what they identify as genocide. Humanitarian workers, in contrast, warned of the catastrophic effects of military action on their ability to deliver relief.[1] They believed that more lives would be lost in the intervention because it would render the presence of humanitarian workers impossible, threatening humanitarian neutrality and aid workers' lives. All parties to this debate, and many others like it, speak for humanity.

Faced with what sometimes seems a cacophony of competing voices it is tempting to dismiss humanity as an empty signifier—a category that claims universal relevance and to encompass all human beings, but which in fact is so historically, geographically, and politically situated as to have no meaning beyond its particular instantiations. In this volume, however, we take a different approach. In exploring the importance of universalist claims in making humanity an effective category, we are not principally interested in proving that such claims are in fact particular. While such debunking work is often important, and claims to encompass every person and experience should not be simply accepted at face value, our project here is to explore the effects of the claim-making itself. In so doing, we consider what Anna Tsing (2005: 6) has termed the "sticky engagements" of universal categories. It is through such engagements, through "friction," Tsing suggests, that "universals become practically effective" even as they "never fulfill their promises of universality" (8). The capacity of humanity to govern so much of the contemporary political and ethical imaginary, and to have such demonstrable and significant effects on people's lives, is the product of a deployment of universals.

In this collection we bring together essays that consider the configurations of humanity in three different arenas—humanitarianism and human rights, biological technologies, and humans and nature—each of which offers a distinct perspective on this problem. We choose these sites not only to highlight the diversity of spaces and scales at which humanity is articulated but to show that humanity gains its power in the intersection of these different areas. The chapters illuminate the range of governing practices that have been crucial to the production of humanity across a global field. The universalist claims and practices—about justice, about bodily integrity, and about the meaning of the natural world—that fill out the category of humanity are given concrete expression in governmental arrangements that rely on notions of humanity as their foundation.

By looking at the intersections of human rights, environmentalism, and biotechnology we can begin to disentangle the multiplicity of referents in humanity. The domain of human rights and humanitarianism—an area that is marked by an internal tension between rights and needs, between legal forms and ethical practices—offers direct insight into political and legal genealogies of humanity as a universal category that takes the commonalities of human beings as its ground. For practitioners, this "anthropological minimum" (Mehta 1999: 52) serves as the starting point for elaborating the political and social obligations that humans have to each other—the humanitarian connection. Both biological technologies and work on humans and nature elucidate not just human connection but the nature of human beings. Biotech works on the "interior" of humanity—on the bodies of human beings. These interventions at an often microscopic scale shape human possibility, not first as political beings (though clearly that, too) but as living entities. Environmentalists insist that we recognize the entanglements of humanity—that human life is only possible in and through the broader environment of which it is a part. At the same time, the government of nature—which requires at once the regulation of human behavior and resource management—illuminates how both guarding and effacing apparent boundaries between the human and its outside have been crucial to the formation of this category.

Understanding the category of humanity also requires attention to its complicated relationship with its various cognates. The human, the humane, the humanitarian, and the inhumane are clearly all at play in the elaboration of humanity and they just as clearly lend sometimes contradictory meanings to this category. Thomas Laqueur (1989, 2009) describes the emergence of humanity as "sentiment," a process he links to a conjoining of the human and the humane. He argues that in the late eighteenth century the human began to be conceived not as a matter of physiological fact but as "the ethical subject—the protagonist—of humanitarian narrative" (2009: 38). Humans, that is, became humane—compassionate, sympathetic, ethical. Humanity is, he suggests, the sensibility that emerges from this development. It was the enlarging circle of moral inclusion, of obligation to treat fellow humans as connected, which made possible the exercise of humanity as ethical sentiment.

In the genealogy that Laqueur traces, humanity as object—a biological fact—is superseded by its elaboration as a category of universal solidarity. We suggest, however, that the continuing life of this category as an object is also crucial to understanding its contemporary operations. As we have already noted, debates about developments in biotechnology are frequently concerned with the fate of humanity as object. Questions about whether it is ethical to intervene in ways that might fundamentally transform the biological conditions of human being exist in the same field of thought that defines humanity as ethics, but the two senses of humanity are distinct in important ways. In both cases, ethics are a matter of crucial importance, but in one case humanity poses ethical questions and in the other it is an ethical answer to problems such as cruelty and the inhumane.

The inhumane is not only a threat *to* humanity, however. Sometimes it is a threat that defines humanity. Humanity is frequently "defined by its breach" (Teitel 2004), as when cruelty shapes understandings of the humane or when the "essence" of human being is clarified by some people's subjection to the most degrading and devastating conditions. The inhumane has also been central to the universalist reach of humanity. Part of the reason that human rights, for instance, are so widely seen as globally relevant and important is the horror that violations of these rights evokes in people. To a certain extent, then, humanity is less about a claim to global connection (though it is that also) and more about the identification of universal threats. One of the paradoxes of the centrality of threat to defining humanity is that it is most often other human beings who are identified as the source of this threat. Humanity is linked to sentiments not only of sympathy and compassion but also of fear and insecurity.

GOVERNING THROUGH HUMANITY

How do these competing aspects of humanity find concrete expression? In part through the governing work that operationalizes these ideas to produce order, prosperity, and security. Humanity is not a new concern for governance to be sure. In the contemporary moment it has been especially important to the emergence of new forms of "transnational governmentality" (Gupta and Ferguson 2002) in which nongovernmental organizations (NGOs), corporations, and other international actors are crucial to the government of localities and even states. Rather than focusing on the decline in state power that such governance seems to indicate—a decline that has been clearly overstated—we highlight how it has been made possible precisely by the resurgence of universalist categories such as humanity.[2]

Inserting humanity into the conversation helps move it beyond the impasse around the state of the state that has characterized some of the literature on globalized governance (Appadurai 2001; Wallerstein 2004; Sassen 1998, 2006; Ong 1999; Hall 1991). Aihwa Ong (2006: 198) has called attention to the ways that NGOs, for instance, become "practitioners of humanity" who identify and make claims on behalf of "different categories of excluded humanity." It is not just changes in state power that opens the space for NGOs to operate more expansively but also the articulation of their constituency as humanity. Humanity does not replace, but rather sometimes bypasses, other ways of dividing up government (Mitchell 1999; Gupta 1995; Feldman 2008a).[3] Nations, states, and borders all continue to exist and to shape government. And yet, the appeal to humanity—the claim to govern or to intervene on behalf of a universal humanity—permits the growth of governing technologies that operate at a different scale and with different targets.[4]

The emerging global networks of NGOs that operate "without borders" (Redfield 2005; Ticktin 2006a), legal institutions that claim universal jurisdiction (Borneman 2004; Teitel 2005), forms of citizenship that do not appear to match territorial configurations (Ong 2006; Benhabib 2007; Sassen 2006), and varieties of political and security practices that claim humanity as their constituency (Collier, Lakoff, and Rabinow 2004; Masco 2006) are all part of the latest expression of this global category. James Ferguson and Akhil Gupta (2002) suggest that transnational governance constitutes a challenge to the spatial relations and hierarchies on which states depend. Just as important, transnational governance also reconfigures the object of governing work. Not exactly citizen, subject, or even population, it is a resurgent humanity that is the target of these practices. In reinvigorating humanity for the global scene, these new forms of governance are also transforming it.

So what is humanity as an object of governance? It appears as both sentiment and threat—an object of care and a source of anxiety—though the latter often seems more pressing. Claims that humanity is being threatened—whether by environmental catastrophe, moral failure, or political upheaval—provide a justification for the elaboration of new governing techniques. At the same time, humanity is also identified as itself a threat—to nature, to nation, to global peace—which governance must contain. These apparently contradictory understandings of the relation of the threat to the category of humanity coexist and remain in persistent tension. This state of ambiguous yet ever present threat helps maintain the dynamic coproduction of governance and humanity.

HISTORIES OF HUMANITY

Humanity has a long history as a foundational principle for politics and ethics. The question of whether certain sorts of people—slaves, Native Americans—should be considered human and therefore deserving of particular rights and protections was long debated (Aristotle 1998; Sepúlveda 1892; Casas 1972). Humanity, that is, marked a dividing line between those to whom politics and ethics pertained and those to whom they did not. What distinguishes this older history of humanity from its modern incarnation is precisely the notion of universality. While these earlier modes of distinction have not entirely disappeared—in fact they periodically reappear in discussions about how to deal with "terrorists," "insurgents," and other modern "savages"—the discourse of humanity since the Enlightenment proceeds from the assumption that this category has universal valence.

The French Revolution's Declaration of the Rights of Man and Citizen is one of the most frequently cited examples of this new belief. The first article of the declaration states the principle: "Men are born and remain free and equal in rights. Social distinctions may be founded only upon the general good." Distinction, in other words, is a social product rather than a natural condition. Many people have noted, as Hannah Arendt did, that in the Declaration the category of *man* (*human* in our terms) is immediately dissolved into that of *citizen*. Even as humanity is declared a universal status, and a universal basis of rights, its applicability is immediately constrained by the need for other characteristics (national, citizen) to make those rights effective (Arendt 1951; Balibar 2004). Nonetheless, the significance of the claim to universality should not be underestimated. In fact, Arendt suggests that it is precisely universality—specifically the universal organization of humanity into nations—that makes being "merely" human such a vulnerable position. When you are only human and nothing else, then, and only then, can you be expelled from humanity itself.[5]

The philosophical ideal of a universal humanity has been intimately connected to ideologies and practices of governance. Representative government and popular democracy, as declared by the American and French revolutions, both derived from a belief in universal human capacity and were meant to actualize this possibility. This mode of government did away with the privileges of birth in the name of instituting equality between all human beings. It promised—among other equalizing measures—universal suffrage. That the "Rights of Man" proclaimed by the French Revolution were by no means universally applied is often noted to critique this "advance" in human dignity. And it was not only in hindsight that these problems were recognized. Shortly after the issuance of the Declaration of the Rights of Man, Olympe de Gouges answered with a "Declaration of the Rights of Woman and the Female Citizen." In her point-by-point response to the original declaration, de Gouges both offers women a way into the political body in a manner similar to men—demanding that women be seen as equal before the law, that they have the opportunity to speak in public, and that they be subject to criminal procedures just as men—and highlights the distinctiveness of what she calls "the sex that is superior in beauty as it is in courage during the suffering of maternity." This tension in her approach—what has in years since been described as the tension between sameness and difference in feminist thought (Scott 1996, 2001; Weedon 2001; Riley 1988; Ang 2001)—illuminates some of the challenges of responding to exclusions within a universalist frame. Joan Scott calls this the paradox of feminism: exclusion was legitimated by the different biologies of men and women, yet when feminists argued for inclusion in the name of "women" they reproduced the very sexual difference they sought to eliminate.

Just as women responded immediately to their exclusion from the universalism of the French Revolution, slave insurgents in what was the French colony of Saint-Domingue (now Haiti) reacted in the early 1790s by demanding their inclusion in the new National Assembly. Here, colonialism as form of government shaped the production of the category of humanity in different exclusionary and inclusionary ways. Laurent Dubois (2000) argues that the slaves not only demanded inclusion in republican citizenship but in their insurrection and demands for racial equality universalized the idea of rights. Indeed, Dubois suggests that their struggle against exclusion is what produced the political idea of universal rights we inherit today—universality was the product of exclusion. Their ideas "actually outran the political imagination of the metropole" (22), and out of alliances between slave insurgents and republican officials in the Antilles a new colonial order emerged in which universalism took on more concrete meaning, making those in the colonies subject to the same constitution as those in metropolitan France.

We should also remember that although the language of universal humanity provided a way for colonial subjects to make claims for a different political reality, it was also part of colonial logics of governance. The idea of a "civilizing mission," of colonialism as a humanitarian endeavor, relied on a universal conception of humanity that suggested everyone was in some way part of a shared community. It also relied on a hierarchical understanding of that human community which suggested that European powers and populations had an obligation to assist the colonized in developing their human capacity (Spivak 1988; Colonna 1997; Stoler 1997; Conklin 1997). The idea of humanity was crucial to both the operations of colonial empire and to resistance to that empire, to both the elaboration of nation-states and their apparent decline.

One effect of humanity's universal claim is that, if it is now presumed to encompass every person, then new sorts of work—discourse, technologies—are required to expel people from this category. To be treated as less than fully human—as *homo sacer* as Giorgio Agamben puts it (1998)—people might, for instance, be first denaturalized (Arendt 1951). In the aftermath of the Second World War, which confirmed that people remained willing, even eager, to do the work of expelling people from humanity, new efforts were made to expand the global reach of this universal category. Even as realization of the 1948 Universal Declaration of Human Rights (UDHR) remains constrained by the United Nations' commitment to state sovereignty, the UDHR set forth a vision of a global order in which all persons would have access to the same "rights and freedoms . . . without distinction of any kind." In practice, the application of these universal rights requires making all sorts of distinctions within humanity, as categories of vulnerability are identified and proper subjects of human rights are produced.[6] Talal Asad (2003: 150) argues that this subject is a specific sort of person—one who possesses bodily integrity, expresses him- or herself freely, and chooses his or her own beliefs. He suggests that as a production—not just a recognition—of similarity, human rights have to be seen as a "mode of converting and regulating people, making them at once freer and more governable" (157).

If the first elaborations of universal humanity required a rethinking of relations among people, humanity is increasingly called on to consider its connections with the wider sentient and nonsentient world. The UDHR outlines universal human "rights," while more recent documents such as the United Nations Framework Convention on Climate Change and the corresponding Kyoto Protocol describe universal human "responsibilities." The responsibility for the environment invoked in these treaties suggests that the universalism of the category of humanity both reaches outward beyond its boundaries (though, of course, care of nonhuman nature has clear benefits for human beings) and intersects with other universalist claims.

THE PROBLEM OF HUMANITY

Humanity—its boundaries, its possibilities, and its politics—is widely recognized to be a problem, but how that problem is understood varies considerably. From a humanist perspective, the fundamental question that surrounds humanity is one of justice. The question of justice, in turn, is frequently understood to require some response to hierarchy and inequality. Karl Marx (1978a, 1978b), for instance, identified the problem of humanity as one of material inequality—he felt there could be no emancipated category of humanity in a system of capitalism, where inequalities are produced by unequal relationships to the means of production. He argued that inequalities grounded in the commodity form keep individuals alienated from each other, from themselves, and, hence, from their very essence, their "species-being" or social nature. Human emancipation, then, requires the abolishment of private property, which will restore the social relations rendered invisible by the commodity form. Marx argued for a collapse of the distinction between civil society and political society, so that human beings are not divided into public (abstract) and private (substantive but egoistic) selves but become a fully materialized, horizontally equal, humanity. Here the production of a real, emancipated humanity involves abolishing private differences, including, ultimately, the nation-state.

If Marx thought the problem of humanity was one of material inequality grounded in capitalist relations of production, postcolonial scholars and activists have further identified the problem as one of the racial exclusions that have accompanied colonialism, what Partha Chatterjee (1993: 18) has called "the rule of colonial difference." The exclusionary and dehumanizing practices that took place in the name of the colonial civilizing mission are now well known (Elkins 2005; Hochschild 1998; Lazreg 2007; Shepard 2006). To some, the argument against colonialism required exposing the category of humanity itself as exclusionary and racist. As Frantz Fanon writes in *Wretched of the Earth* (1963: 312), "When I search for Man in the technique and the style of Europe, I see only a succession of negations of man, and an avalanche of murders." While Fanon argued for replacing this restricted colonial humanity with a new and better version, others have rejected humanism altogether and abandoned any hope in the category of humanity. For instance, Louis Althusser (1969) used the term "antihumanism," by which he and other structural Marxists implied a rejection of the bourgeois individualism that informed humanism. The problem of humanity for him—and, more broadly, for other postcolonial antihumanists—is precisely the imperial attempt to render humanity a universal ethical and political subject, as history shows us that this can result in the monopoly of the category by a few, and the denial of the humanity of others who do not conform. The solution to the problem of humanity in these terms is a project to recognize radical alterity, to do away with universality, and to analyze these forms of difference looking at both structures and subjects, and not simply assuming a universal human subject.

So, on the one hand, a Marxist approach might argue for the abolition of the private differences between people in order to forge a coherent humanity; on the other hand, postcolonial scholars and activists argue for the recognition of difference, rather than its extermination, and some have argued for the abolition of the universal political category of humanity altogether, assuming humanism will always be a failed project. Still others call into question the boundaries of many debates about humanity, arguing that the problem of humanity is not simply—or for some even primarily—about relations between people. Jacques Derrida (2008) disrupts the privileging of humanity over animality, not by attributing to animals those capacities they supposedly lack—such as reason, intelligence, language, and sympathy—but by questioning the underlying notion of transcendence that justifies the valuation of human rights above all other concerns. Science and technology studies has been fruitful ground for "posthumanist" inquiries (even as some would reject this label). Donna Haraway (1991, 2007) proposes the cyborg—a hybrid being that transgresses essentialized identities and bounded categories of nature and culture—as a way to decenter the human subject. In her more recent work on companion species, Haraway emphasizes how humanity is constituted through contingency and relatedness. In a similar vein Bruno Latour (1987), Michel Callon (1986), and John Law and John Hassard (1999) offer actor-network theory, which considers humans and nonhumans alike as actants who participate in "networks" that are constantly assembling, falling apart, and reforming. Scholars working in this area reframe the position of the human subject as an integral but not privileged part of a complex web of dependencies between other active organisms, objects, technologies, and landscapes (Strathern 1991; Mol 2003; De Landa 2006; Helmreich 2009; Raffles 2002).

Also seeking to disrupt boundaries, though not necessarily the same ones, are writers who argue in favor of cosmopolitanism as a response to the problems of humanity. The cosmopolitan project recognizes that there are many ways to deal with difference: one can be universalist or relativist; one can divide people up into units based on ethnicity, nationalism, or multiculturalism. Cosmopolitanism tries to make sense of these other understandings of the problem of humanity, bringing them together in a world in which the nation-state is no longer the primary political unit. Authors reinvoking theories of cosmopolitanism (Cheah and Robbins 1998; Breckenridge et al. 2002; Beck and Sznaider 2006) do so precisely because they are responding to the blurring of the global and local, the national and the international, in the contemporary world. Ulrich Beck and Natan Sznaider (2006) identify an increasing set of interdependencies and potential crises associated with them: economic, moral, ecological, and the risk of terrorism. While looking to Immanuel Kant's philosophical notion of "world citizenship," the literature on cosmopolitanism nevertheless responds to the earlier critiques of universalism and humanism by arguing that many global public spheres may exist. There can be many cosmopolitanisms, many universalisms, which could transform risk into possibility and make of our increasing interdependencies new forms of political cooperation. Furthermore, cosmopolitanism need not be the abstract idea that Kant proposed; it is actually being filled out increasingly by habits of thought and feeling. Cosmopolitanism is attentive to threat but optimistic about the possibility of transforming humanity to respond to that threat.

From another perspective, the problem of humanity is neither that it is exclusionary nor that it is incompletely realized but rather that it has successfully become a means of organizing global community. Carl Schmitt, whose ideas have recently been taken up by some on the political Left even though Schmitt supported Nazism in the early 1930s, articulated this view of humanity as fundamental threat particularly clearly. He argued that the replacement of a European law or order (*nomos*) by an international order whose subject was humanity actually leads not to world politics but to a world policing power (Schmitt 1996). Rather than have an order which identifies friends and enemies ("just enemies"), the new international order leads to situations where justice and morality are defined a priori as being on one side of a conflict (the side of humanity), with injustice and immorality on the other (Koskenniemi 2002). Politics is replaced by moralism, which, perhaps paradoxically, removes all limits from international violence. Wars fought in the name of humanity actually "usurp a universal concept against its military opponent" (Schmitt 2007: 54; cf. Koskenniemi 2002: 433), using humanity as a tool for imperial expansion. With humanity identified as the only just cause for war, enemies are denied the quality of being human. Indeed, to be an enemy is to be an outlaw of humanity. It is the claim to fight "in the name of humanity," Schmitt argued, that permits the most extreme acts of inhumanity in war.

Even as the political meaning and effect of humanity is evaluated quite differently in these various literatures, all concur that it is a category with import—whether as a "solution" or a "problem." The chapters in this volume make clear that humanity not only is perceived as a problem by scholars but is central to debates among actors in each of the fields considered here. Humanitarian workers, environmental activists, doctors, and engineers each grapple with how to understand humanity, what obligations identification of this category may entail, and where the limits of its reach may be. The chapters in the volume let us see these debates in action.

The chapters describe the ways that humanity has been filled out as a category, and how government is intimately involved in this operation. The authors suggest that, rather than being always "too weak a force in itself to generate sufficient solidarity" (Robbins 1998: 4), humanity is sometimes too strong to permit other ways of imagining connection to proliferate. As an object of government, humanity does make new forms of global connection possible, but these connections can be debilitating as well as liberating, threatening as well as a source of protection. Sites explored in the chapters show how, in the name of global peace and security, certain people and political positions are identified as threats to humanity. Although in this introduction we identify the chapters by their thematic areas, this is only one way of seeing their connections. The different order of presentation in the volume is meant to open up other readings as well.

HUMAN RIGHTS AND HUMANITARIANISM

Human rights and humanitarianism are areas of practice, law, and discourse that have obvious fundamental connections to ideas about humanity. They have equally significant, though often vexed, relationships with governance. On the one hand, practitioners of each purport to function as outside actors to protect the human from the effects of an absence of proper government or an excess of improper government (Redfield 2005, 2006; Ticktin 2005, 2006b). On the other, each practice is entirely dependent on broader governing structures—whether sovereign states, international laws, or global discourses—to do its work (Feldman 2007a, 2007b). Furthermore, humanitarian organizations often find themselves in the position of governing—managing, servicing—the populations they seek to aid (Feldman 2008b; Malkki 2007; Hyndman 2000; Pandolfi 2003, 2008). Even as practitioners express considerable discomfort in this position, human rights and humanitarianism have been crucially important forms of action in helping to constitute humanity as a "real" category of central importance to governance (Wilson 1997; Asad 2003; Nussbaum 2004).

Part of the tension around whether human rights and humanitarian actors should accept or refuse involvement in governing practices is connected to the particular ways these fields engage humanity as a category. While in some sense they address each of its guises, both have especially close connection to ideas about humanity as ethical sentiment, a category of universal solidarity (Malkki 1996). While this compassionate engagement may seem sullied by connection to governing work, it is in fact entirely embedded in such practices (Agamben 1998; Ticktin 2005, 2006a, 2006b). The chapters in this book that explore humanitarian and human-rights action highlight the dilemmas and even contradictions inherent in this form of interaction with, and production of, humanity. If Laqueur calls our attention to the positive sentiments that push people to consider themselves part of a global human community, Richard Wilson's work on the International Criminal Tribunal for Rwanda reminds us that humanity is just as centrally a negatively defined category. His chapter, "When Humanity Sits in Judgment," highlights that this category is produced not only by a sentiment of caring but also by one of revulsion at cruelty. The legal apparatus that has developed to respond to genocide and other crimes against humanity, while certainly presuming a universal concern with the suffering of others, compels its participants and audience to engage most directly with the sentiment of universal disgust. Here, humanity is produced as a community in solidarity in part by excluding those it understands as its constituent outside.

Liisa Malkki's investigation of the place of children—with their presumed innocence and peacefulness—in figurations of universal humanity might seem at first glance to be at considerable remove from the cruelty of mass murder. We suggest, to the contrary, that this appeal to positive sentiment has to be understood as part of the same discursive universe as occupied by the ICTR. In "Children, Humanity, and the Infantilization of Peace," Malkki suggests that it is in part the focus on the innocence of children as both representations of human goodness and symbols of movements for peace that makes encounters with phenomena such as child soldiers such a shock. As she argues, "the trouble with child soldiers is that they cannot be set apart, made sacred. . . . They are profane, a category mistake that disturbs the poetics of 'our common humanity.'" As embodied in images of the child—images that circulate widely in our current mediascape—the sentiment of humanity seems oddly superficial, dependent on decontextualized, uncomplicated notions of human connection. The danger in this superficial humanity, one dependent on children as "generic human moral subjects," is that without the robustness of located, if imperfect, human subjects, our connections remain tenuous. When only the absolutely innocent elicit care, giving, and empathy—and Malkki shows that such figures are exceptional—our solidarity and ability to create lasting peace remains dependent on a mirage and thus easily thwarted.

Even as humanitarian action is mobilized by sentiments of human connection, it invariably also reproduces hierarchies among human beings. Didier Fassin's chapter, "Inequality of Lives, Hierarchies of Humanity," highlights this paradox at the heart of humanity's sentiment by considering such dilemmas as the decision of Médecins sans Frontières (MSF) to stay in Iraq at the start of the 2003 war and its subsequent choice to leave after three of the six staff members were abducted. As Fassin notes, "not a single Iraqi life had been saved, but six lives of humanitarian agents had been put at risk." Compassion immediately encounters its limits in the hierarchies of lives within the humanitarian terrain. However troubling to humanitarian actors, there is no way for them to refuse this distinction. As Fassin shows, both an "ideal of universality" and a "practice of difference" lie at the heart of humanitarianism. This dual nature of humanitarianism is produced at the intersection between sentiment and material inequality. Fassin shows the intense emotion of MSF's discussions of what to do in Iraq; the humanitarians had to decide whose lives to sacrifice—MSF workers'? Iraqis'?—and why. Unfortunately, this sentiment could not change the fact that Iraqis had no part in this decision. We see that human solidarity can only be fully realized when accompanied by material equality. Such a tension is also fundamental to human rights practice, as Wilson's exploration of the ICTR confirms. The prosecution of genocide—the gravest crime against humanity—relies on conceptions of both universal humanity and universal jurisdiction. Yet, as Wilson notes, the "collective political actor ('humanity') . . . cannot be easily found." In fact, in order to defend humanity the tribunal moved quickly—and uncomfortably—into the terrain of defining particularities such as race and ethnicity. The sentiment that underpins the subject and practice of human rights and humanitarianism is both variegated—including both attachment and revulsion, ethical connection and refusal—and hierarchical—unable to avoid incorporating particularities with political import into its universalist worldview.

BIOLOGICAL TECHNOLOGIES AND HUMAN BEINGS

Humanity is produced through not only political and ethical but also technological discourses. Technosciences, with their new sites of investigation of human being, transform the scale on which humanity is produced and regulated. Biological technologies, and the interventions they make possible in and on the human body, produce ethical dilemmas that seem to have a unique capacity to occupy the public imagination, as well as to invite governmental legislation. While humanitarian crises invoke pity (but often little analysis of their political and economic causes), biological technologies frequently incite moralizing and heated debate about their consequences (the Terry Shiavo case, which culminated in 2005, provides a clear reminder of the place bodily interventions occupy in U.S. concerns). In this volume we explore why, and how, these sorts of technologies are so provocative—what notions of human being appear to be at risk when bodies are worked on in these ways? In what ways do these technologies distinguish among human kinds? Alternately, what possibilities for human life and capacity are imagined and invoked by people who champion such interventions?

That biological technologies—including genomics, organ transplantation, cloning, and pharmacology—have tremendous implications for what it means to be human is evident (Dumit 2004; Franklin and Lock 2003). The science of genetics, for instance, creates new knowledge about connections among people and therefore produces previously unimaginable entanglements (Callon and Rabeharisoa 2004). What the political, social, and ethical effects of such technologies will be is much less clear. Some scholars find great hope in the ability to manipulate our biology, allowing us to define our own destinies, and they argue against reducing new biomedical and biological technologies to the eugenics projects of the early twentieth century (Rose 2006; Rose and Novas 2005; Rabinow 2002). Others are more skeptical and relate people's increasing tendency to define themselves in biological terms to a broader trend of understanding social and political conditions in medicalized terms, as pathologies that can be "cured" with the right pills (Cohen 2002; Scheper-Hughes and Wacquant 2002; Kleinman and Kleinman 1996). Scholars and ethicists have examined the processes whereby medications and medical diagnoses come to treat the conditions of everyday existence, often critiquing the role of the pharmaceutical nexus—including big pharma, the state, NGOs, and so on—in dictating, and even creating, categories of illness and health (Healy 2004; Petryna, Lakoff, and Kleinman 2006).

Both hope and skepticism about biological technologies are shaped by concerns about humanity as a biological object. In particular, the first position of hope exemplifies a particular faith in the perfectibility of not only ethical and social capacity but human biology itself. In this view, technological advancement and human improvement are intricately linked. Underlying the second position of skepticism is a wariness that as humanity is increasingly conceived of as a manipulable biological object, individual, social, and political differences will be rendered invisible. S. Lochlann Jain's chapter, "The Mortality Effect," examines the slippery way hope underpins medical versions of humanity in randomized control trials. Taking research on late-stage cancer as a limit case, Jain relates how clinical trials, both as a critical node of last-ditch hope for cancer patients and a hegemonic practice for protocol-driven oncology treatments, understand humanity as an object of scientific research whose parts can be measured and compared. By examining how the randomized control trial structures subject positions for both mortal cancer patients and immortal scientists, Jain analyzes how the everyday injuries of cancer treatments can be erased through cost-benefit analyses of terminal illness and the relentless future orientation of scientific trials. Her chapter suggests that the constructions of both disease categories and the cancer subject through experimental treatments assume the dying subject as a separate category of human, one in which different, often unquestioned, assumptions about ethical standards of injury apply.

In her contribution, "The Politics of Experimentality," Adriana Petryna similarly takes up the issue of humanity as object of scientific research, but she does so from the perspective of a new flexible, transnational regime of human subjects research. This form of governance, which Petryna calls "experimentality," also presumes humanity to be a biological object, one which allows all humans to potentially be both subjects for and beneficiaries of research. Petryna demonstrates how human subjects are created differently under different conditions, despite the underlying biological similarity; certain conditions tamper with humans as pure biological objects—such as the ingestion of too much medication, which renders them "treatment saturated." The best human subjects are in fact undertreated, an idea which assumes that humanity as a particular object can be isolated out and protected. In this regime of governance, public health, and commercial interest, the ideal object of research—the human—can be "biologically edited" to include only those who are pure.

As a governing regime, experimentality not only regulates intervention into humanity as object, it helps define which persons "count" as subjects for this object. As Petryna explains, even though many people agree to be research subjects, "humans . . . are in short supply." Experimentality defines for itself who counts as human. On the one hand, she argues that the variable regulations and ethics of this new regime of experimentality have the capacity to deny or allocate human rights and dignity, giving or denying people protection against certain types of experimentation such as the kind exemplified by the Tuskegee syphilis study that ran in the United States from 1932 to 1972. On the other hand, she shows that it is not always clear whether being treated as an object of research gives one more or less dignity. This is particularly true in contexts where people do not have access to regular health care or live in situations of crisis; here, her chapter joins Jain's in questioning what it means to be a human with dignity. Petryna leaves open the question of whether to be treated with dignity might indeed mean to be treated as a human subject—or in this case, a member of humanity understood at base as biologically objective. Under certain conditions, this can allow for a form of visibility and inclusion that other understandings of humanity—such as those based on sentiment—have precluded.

João Biehl's chapter, "'Medication is me now,'" also stresses the role of government in determining how humanity is constituted as object. He foregrounds the question of when inclusion depends on more than biology—and he suggests in the case of Brazil's AIDS policies, inclusion is dependent on a very particular *will* to live. AIDS policies give universal access to medication and are built on the notion that medication makes people equivalent—it can fix biological differences caused by illness, allowing for equality. Yet human beings, even as biologically equivalent, only access that equivalence—only become "human"—through particular forms of government and under certain conditions. In the regime of pharmaceutical governance that is exemplified by Brazil's new AIDS policy, access to medication to attain equivalence is unequal, despite the policy of universality; what is missing is the equivalence in basic conditions of life that allow for treatment. Not surprisingly, then, homeless patients remain outside the system, outside the object of humanity. As Biehl states, "the dominant human form" that emerges from this particular economy of life emphasizes individual responsibility and downplays mutual empathy. Those who do not conform are excluded from the biological grounds of equivalence because they are seen as lacking a "will to live." Turning Arendt's argument upside down, Biehl shows how exclusions internal to the category of citizens can work to expel people from humanity without expelling them from formal citizenship.

While these chapters highlight ethical gaps that seem intrinsic to approaching humanity as biological object, they also make clear that this approach cannot be easily rejected—since doing so would indeed require refusing potentially life-saving scientific advances in the treatment of disease. Just as sentiment can both produce solidarities and underscore forms of exclusion, so too can approaching humanity as an object be both enabling and disabling.

HUMANS AND NATURE

As we have already seen, the unhuman—as inhumanity, animality, materiality, technology—is in fact foundational for the constitution and elaboration of the category of humanity itself. It is not simply that the unhuman serves as an "other" against which humanity can be defined, a rejected possibility that permits the articulation of better politics, purer morals, more genuine connection (though it is sometimes surely that). Rather, the unhuman also provides the constitutive ground on which humanity is enacted. The unhuman is connected not only to the ethical or social aspects of humanity but also to the biological facts of human being. As the astronomer Carl Sagan famously put it, human beings are made of "star stuff." The production of the human is always also about production of the social and natural environments in which people live (Tsing 2005; Latour 2004; Kohn 2007; Raffles 2002; Kosek 2006; Moore, Kosek, and Pandian 2006). This is true even in places where the aggressiveness of the built environment can appear to have rendered the natural environment entirely without agency and in circumstances where political practice works to actively obscure this connection (Coronil 1997; Sen 1981; Davis 2001). Whether global, national, or local, the relationship between humans and nature is always mediated by practices of government (Hayden 2003; Subramaniam 2001). Even forms of practice that approach the human as a radically distinctive sort of being, that insist on a unique human capacity to act, are inevitably forced to confront (even if not head on) the inseparability of human life from other parts of nature. This relationship between humans and nature—or, perhaps better said, the rest of nature—provides an especially clear window onto the multiplicity of sometimes contradictory ways the human and unhuman are co-constitutive and the ways this constitution frequently occurs on the site and in the language of threat (Mitchell 2002).

In his chapter, "Environment, Community, Government," Arun Agrawal elucidates the ways that transformations in environmental governance produce concomitant transformations in subjectivity and community. In the context of Kumaon, India, colonial control of forests—the regulation of their use to meet the demands of empire—produced a particular sort of threat to the environment, as villagers set the forests on fire as part of their protest against colonialism. Against this backdrop of central control and spectacular resistance, Agrawal traces the more recent emergence of decentralized environmental practices that work through the "governmentalization of localities" and the production of "regulatory communities." In this practice everyone is supposed to have a say and everyone is held equally responsible for taking care of the forest. Community-based conservation appears to have successfully reconfigured people's relationships to the forest, and Agrawal finds evidence of considerable local concern about environmental protection. In much of the public debate about the state of the environment and the threat of global warming, humans and nature are presented as opposing categories: humans identified as an unequivocal danger to nature or the protection of nature as a threat to human economic security. Agrawal argues that in environmental governance, and indeed in any government of the nonhuman, "the capacities to be shaped are imagined as uniquely human." As he suggests, "the category of the human . . . allows the project of government to unfold."

Agrawal notes that different human beings may be quite differently located in the grid of environmental governance. Rebecca Hardin's contribution, "Narrative, Humanity, and Patrimony in an Equatorial African Forest," highlights such distinctions and their political effects with particular clarity. Hardin uses a novel by Etienne Goyemidé—both the "national writer of the CAR [Central African Republic]" and a civil servant in its government—as a way to explore how the humanity of different groups of people in the CAR, particularly Pygmies, is qualified in part by their perceived relationship to the environment. Being seen as close to, even part of, nature, is a double-edged sword for Pygmies—who were only relatively recently recognized as citizens. The novel, *Le silence de la forêt* (*The Silence of the Forest*), in many ways valorizes Pygmies as unsullied by the corruption of "civilization" and seeks to recognize as "human [those] whom others call an animal." The effort here is not to undo the distinction between Pygmies and "civilized" people but to invert the values that are typically attached to those categories. In the governing realm which Goyemidé also occupied, no such inversion appears. Pygmies are seen not as close to the forest but as part of it—"grouped with 'wildlife and plant species' rather than with 'various shareholder groups.'" Not only does this association make Pygmies appear less than fully human, and therefore requiring less in the way of government services, it also makes them appear as potentially a threat to national identity, leading one civil servant to argue that "we must put to work all we can to block the segregationist whims of the Pygmy and lead him to blend, despite himself, in the mold of the great Central African nation." The evaluation of certain humans as closer to, or even part of, nature has significant political impact.

Hardin further demonstrates that there are many models of relationships of humans to the natural world; nature as threat can suddenly be transformed into the threat of humanity to humans, and to nature. While Pygmies may threaten national identity by their close relationship to nature, in the novel, Gonaba, the corrupt African school inspector, ends up leaving behind his "brute-like alienation" when he changes places with the Pygmy, Manga, and goes to live in the forest. Here modernity is seen as a threat to the nature of humanity, which only the natural world itself can remedy. In this view, Pygmies come almost to be a privileged category of persons—as their embeddness in the natural world comes to be seen as a means of undercutting human alienation from nature. This ambiguity between humanity as threat to nature and threatened by nature is further revealed by Hardin's friend Adolph, who is imprisoned for hunting and shooting an elephant. Nature-based strategies of subsistence and status by people like Adolph are outlawed, now reconfigured as a threat to nature and to an international *patrimoine*; yet ultimately it is unclear whether the threat Adolph poses is to nature or to elites who want to corner the market for wildlife products.

The ambiguity of threat and the uncertain boundary between humans and animals is further explored in Allen Feldman's chapter, "Inhumanitas." Feldman tracks the appearance of animals and animal-like figures in "dehumanizing" contexts, such as those produced by war and other forms of violence. In so doing he challenges the very idea that what is at work here is a process of dehumanization—the taking away of human capacity or identification. Rather, the repeated appearance of animals in these contexts—as figurative descriptions for people, as objects used to threaten enemies, and as artifacts of political violence—reveals that some people and populations "could make few or no claims whatsoever to political humanity." He thus uses the term *inhumanization* to describe the "ideological projections of humanity's negations." An inquiry into the formation and governance of humanity cannot, Feldman underscores, concern itself only with human beings.

In his chapter, "Stealth Nature," Charles Zerner takes us to the frontier of the government of nature and illuminates the new sorts of threats and possibility that are being produced on this terrain. Exploring such phenomena as the work of the Defense Advanced Research Program Agency on developing "cybugs"—"roboscorpions" for the battlefield, bionic hornets for counterinsurgency, surveillance dragonflies for political events—Zerner shows the dream and the possibility of "instructed" nature being made a weapon against perceived threats. Such weaponization of nature is, of course, not entirely new. Nuclear weapons are a spectacular form of this phenomenon. These more recent ventures are smaller, harder to detect—"stealth," as Zerner puts it. With these developments, nature comes to be perceived as a new sort of threat—not, as in older visions, because its unpredictable power escapes human control but precisely because it is understood as controllable to invidious, even hideous, ends. We must not forget that these forms of weaponized nature are created to counter the threat of humans. It is not clear which threat is worse. The surveillance dragonflies just mentioned, for instance, were reported by participants at rallies against the U.S. war in Iraq, but whether any such thing was really observing these events is an unknown. What is certain is that the fear is real.

Threat seems to be everywhere. But threat may not be the end of the story. Zerner also offers us a window onto the ways activists and artists are working with the same cyborg possibilities to act against these weapon plans and to imagine yet another—but certainly not a pristine or primordial—relationship of humans and nature. He looks at the work of the artist-engineer Natalie Jeremijenko with children living in areas known—but not sensed—to be replete with toxins, places like the Bronx and the U.S. southwest. Jeremijenko and her collaborators set robotic toxin-sniffing dog packs loose to identify toxic chemical signatures. The children thus become not simply victims of environmental toxicity and political and economic inequality but "environmental investigators." Through nonhuman creatures Jereminjenko engineers new social interactions, and new arrangements of humanity.

THE POLITICS OF HUMANITY

The idea of threat appears central to the contemporary problem of humanity. Yet, despite the ubiquity of this language, the nature of the threat and its effect on humanity remains ambiguous. Arjun Appadurai (2006: 104) has argued that there is an increasing confusion of boundaries, suggesting that "today, the insecurities of states and the uncertainties of civilian spaces and persons have become disturbingly intertwined, and terror, terrorism, and terrorists are where we can best see this new blurring." The concerns that seem to dominate public discussion now—terrorism, torture, and the threat of global war or environmental destruction—at once rely on and seem to undermine a clear notion of what humanity is. How, for instance, do practices of either torture or terrorism—modes of action that have been closely linked in recent years—support a concept of a globally shared humanity? On the one hand, they seem to make a mockery of the idea of a morally inclusive humanity, showing only scorn for human life and bodily integrity. On the other hand, they seem entirely dependent on such a conception of humanity. Terrorism would not have its power to shock without the audience's conviction both that human life is sacred and that all human beings are in some way connected. Torture techniques rely on an understanding of the threshold of the human capacity to withstand pain—a technical rather than affective approach to humanity, but one no less entangled in universalist understandings. Here humanity as threat and humanity as a category of solidarity blend into one.[7]

This blending of apparently distinct, even opposing, categories is a common characteristic of the contemporary landscape of humanity. As Fassin explores in his chapter, humanitarian action and political insurgency have intersected in the spaces of wars in Iraq and Afghanistan. Faisal Devji (2008) claims that this sort of connection is more than incidental—that Islamic militants, like humanitarians and environmentalists, speak in the name of a global humanity. He argues that groups like al-Qaeda first identify Muslims as universal victims—suffering as humans, rather than as specific religious subjects—and then seek to transform that victimhood into agency—again as agents of humanity, not simply of a Muslim community.[8] Such anchoring discourses of global humanity are—as Wilson, Malkki, Agrawal, and Hardin show—caught in a conundrum of sorting human kinds without seeking to attach ontological significance to these distinctions. Allen Feldman confirms the importance of exploring this kind-making beyond the confines of human beings. Boundary confusion persists not only around the category of the human, but in its effects. As Petryna, Jain, and Biehl show for experimentation, treatment, and policy, violence to human subjects is deeply intertwined with global efforts to save humanity from disease. At the same time, Zerner's consideration of Jeremijenko's work offers a glimpse at the efforts of activists, artists, and others to turn governing technologies on their head and reconfigure the effective meaning of humanity.

This sort of multiplicity seems crucial to the ways that threat intersects with humanity. There are two key—and contrasting—analyses of this relation. In the first, political, economic, and ecological threats are seen as increasingly impinging on human possibility, and a new cosmopolitanism is offered as a possible response (Beck and Sznaider 2006). In the second, humanity itself appears as a threat to political order. This understanding is most closely associated with Carl Schmitt, who argued that making humanity the universal subject, and specifically making the cause of humanity the only just cause for war, not only replaced politics with moralizing, but rendered any enemy an "outlaw of humanity" and therefore permitted the most extreme inhumanity in warfare. These two understandings of threat appear to dominate the contemporary political scene, but these models do not—and to our mind cannot—exhaust the possible ways of understanding and responding to insecurity and fear. To uncover the other possibilities people are conceptualizing and enacting, we need to continue to explore the trajectories of humanity across the political and social field.[9]

In contemporary politics, threat and possibility are intrinsically linked. If the early articulations of a universal humanity imagined this category as a means of progressing beyond barbarism and cruelty to offer protection and possibility to an expanding array of persons, the long history of struggling against the exclusions produced in its articulations showed that such progress should not be assumed to follow automatically from a universalist claim. Indeed, the intersection of diverse universalist claims and projects—intersections that we have argued are central to the production of humanity—ensures that its meaning, boundaries, and effects are always multifaceted and sometimes contradictory. Humanity is a difficult—sometimes dangerous—category. Its promise of universal connection is also its peril of imperial expansion. Its capacity to evoke compassion for others is matched by its tendency to identify these others as threats. We may not be able to do without it—both because there does not seem to be any way to make it go away and because it seems to provide a necessary mechanism for imagining a global condition—but we have to remain uneasy with its deployment. Understanding the effects of humanity in shaping political, ethical, and economic formations is vital to any effort at political and social change. The intersection of government and humanity provides a crucial diagnostic for our time.

NOTES

1   For differing views on how to make sense of and respond to the situation in Darfur, see Weissman and Myers 2007; Mamdani 2009, 2007; De Waal 2004; and the Web site of the Save Darfur coalition, www.savedarfur.org.

2   While he did not consider the global operations of governmentality, Michel Foucault (1991) argued for analytic attention to the object of government intervention (for him, "population") and the details of its practice, rather than primarily to its institutional forms. In other words, to understand government, we must understand what is governed (populations or humanity), not simply what is governing (the state, or transnational organizations).

3   Neoliberal modes of governance are both transforming practices within states (Rose 1999; Ong 2006; Biehl 2007) and reshaping the landscape of transnational governance. In the process, the universalist qualities of humanity once again become central to political discourse.

4   Current conditions of globalization are clearly not the first time that reference to humanity has been important in expanding governmental reach. The history of colonialism is replete with claims to act for the betterment of humanity (Spivak 1988).

5   As Arendt (1951: 297) puts it: "Only with a completely organized humanity could the loss of home and political status become identical with expulsion from humanity altogether."

6   The paradox of humanity—that it both seeks to include all and yet is plagued by persistent limits on full incorporation into the category—is directly connected to the sort of individual at the heart of universal humanity. This individual is at once too general and too specific to resolve this tension. Uday Mehta (1999: 52) argues, for instance, that the

basis of liberalism's universalism is an "anthropological minimum"—a set of characteristics deemed common to all people. These characteristics—freedom, rationality, and equality—are presumed to be independent of historical, social, economic, or any other features that would specify people. Mehta argues that although the anthropological minimum makes liberal universalism possible, it also ensures that liberalism will always entail exclusions, as it is in fact precisely those characteristics that fall outside of the minimum that are required for inclusion in political community. See Partridge 2009 for more on the concept of exclusionary incorporation.

7 While such phenomenon may appear new, a return to Fanon's *The Wretched of the Earth* (1963) reminds us that the struggle against colonialism frequently entailed a similar dynamic. Decolonization was, he suggested, always a violent process that involved "the replacing of a certain 'species' of men by another 'species' of men" (35). If colonialism created "the native"—a category of persons excluded from full humanity—decolonization produces "a new language and a new humanity. [It] is the veritable creation of new men" (36). This re-creation of humanity, he argues, cannot occur without acts that appear, and indeed are, inhumane. In Algeria, where Fanon worked as a psychiatrist treating people on both sides of the anticolonial struggle, he describes the devastating effects of fighting this struggle on all participants. Through a series of case studies, he suggests that the rejection of the dehumanization of colonialism, and the formation of a new humanity, requires its own processes of inhumanity.

8 For a related consideration of suicide bombing, see Asad 2007.

9 These two aspects of threat vis-à-vis humanity underscore that threat is the other side of a discourse of protection. In contrast to Schmitt, Foucault's (1980) account of the trajectory of modern government shows how connected threat and protection are. He argues that the central shift in modern political power from the power to decide life and death (in part expressed through the sovereign's right to kill) to the power to foster life or disallow it (crucially seen in the biopolitics of population) was accompanied both by new protections—"the power to guarantee an individual's continued existence" (137)—and new threats of utter destruction such as genocide and nuclear annihilation—"the power to expose a whole population to death" (ibid.). Schmitt sees humanitarian war as a war of annihilation because in its terms the enemy can only be defined as inhuman, and he thus focuses on what can now be done to those defined as enemies. For Foucault this level of atrocity (and for him nuclear annihilation is the prime example) is enabled by the fact that wars are "waged on behalf of the existence of everyone" (ibid.). He therefore highlights as well the ways that governments put their own populations at risk in these struggles. For Foucault, the two effects of the exercising of power at "the level of life"—threat and protection—do not just exist in the same terrain, they require each other. If government was not concerned with the fostering of life, the protection of people's continued existence, it would not be capable of exposing the population to threat to such an extent.

Crimes against Humanity and the Conundrum of Race and Ethnicity at the International Criminal Tribunal for Rwanda

Richard Ashby Wilson

IN ORDER to exercise universal jurisdiction,[1] the international humanitarian law that grounds modern international criminal tribunals and courts (e.g., for Rwanda, the former Yugoslavia, Sierra Leone, and the International Criminal Court) in most instances requires an undifferentiated notion of "humanity." This chapter investigates some of the problems that arise in international trials when representatives of "humanity" come to deliver judgment on acts of racially motivated mass violence.

LAWS OF HUMANITY

Modern human rights directly emanate from ideas of natural law[2] and natural rights based on a universal human nature. The latter have a long history that predates the modern era, but with the rise of modernity these ideas become central to secular forms of republican governance. While a universal conception of humanity can be found in monotheistic religious traditions extending back thousands of years, a radical shift in consciousness took place in Europe and the Americas during the eighteenth century. At this point in time, political philosophers, legal thinkers, and politicians detached the ideas of humanity and human nature from their religious moorings and incorporated them into a secularized moral, legal, and political code that formed the basis of a new republican sovereignty, particularly in the revolutions in France and British North America.

There was a significant legal dimension to the new politics of humanity in the eighteenth century. Of what did this "humanity law" consist?[3] In their attempts to secularize humanity, early advocates of international law such as Emmerich de Vattel (the author of *The Laws of Nations* [2005], first published in France in 1758) defined humanity negatively, that is, humanity was constructed in its breach. A negative treatment of humanity characterizes eighteenth-century legal judgments such as *Somerset v. Stewart*, a groundbreaking case supporting the antislavery movement's efforts to render the slave trade illegal in Britain and its colonial empire. On June 22, 1772, the lawyers of the former slave Somerset applied for his freedom before the court and served a writ of habeas corpus. Lord Mansfield's judgment found in favor of Somerset and drew heavily on natural law to justify its line of argument, "The state of slavery is of such a nature, that it is incapable of being introduced on any reasons, moral or political; but only positive law, it's so odious, that nothing can be suffered to support it, but positive law. Whatever inconveniences, therefore, may follow from a decision, I cannot say this case is allowed or approved by the law of England; and therefore the black must be discharged" (§510).[4]

In eighteenth-century European legal and political thought, humanity was largely a negative category. It was created by acts that repel and were considered odious, repugnant, and disgraceful, rather than by human behaviors deemed beautiful or intellectually or morally edifying. "Humanity" materializes when there is an offense against natural law, the legal and moral basis of human rights in the eighteenth century. From the outset, laws of humanity have been a mirror for human cruelty that can seemingly be applied in any setting. These ideas retain an influence to this day, as evidenced by the category of "crimes against humanity." Humanity is still constructed in its breach.

The newly secularized humanitarian sensibility expressed sympathy and compassion when faced with suffering inflicted on others, not only of one's kin or tribe or nation, but any person, regardless of race, religion, or origin. This humane response was seen in the eighteenth century to be self-evident, natural, and therefore universal. It required not just a disposition of empathy from the actor but an active indignation that motivates the political will to end all unacceptable suffering. In this way, the idea of humanity provided legitimate intellectual and moral foundations for a new type of political sovereignty, one which can be exercised across political borders and established jurisdictions. Without the idea of humanity, one cannot pass laws with universal jurisdiction, prohibiting a range of heinous crimes against distant others that offend the global sensibility of humanitarians.

Humanitarianism assumed an even greater prominence in international affairs in the nineteenth century, when the first array of "laws of humanity" were created, laying the foundation for the twentieth-century concept of "crimes against humanity." We could better understand the influence of humanitarianism by seeing it both as an ethos that drives secular and religious social movements and a liberal doctrine allowing long-distance military interventions by leading world powers. As an ethos, a humanitarian sensibility had broad implications, propelling the worldwide movement to end the slave trade and inspiring individuals such as Henry Dunant to found the International Committee of the Red Cross in 1863, as well as the regulation of industrialized warfare's terrifying consequences for soldiers. The Nuremberg trials nearly a hundred years later made extensive reference to the groundbreaking "laws of humanity" sponsored by the Red Cross, such as the 1864 Geneva Convention for the Amelioration of the Wounded and the 1899 Convention with respect to the Laws and Customs of War on Land (also known as The Hague II Conventions).

While these humanitarian campaigns were largely driven by individuals and nonstate organizations, governments found the humanitarian sensibility too tempting to resist, and great powers such as Austria, Prussia, Great Britain, and France invoked the rhetoric of humanity to justify a number of foreign military interventions, particularly against the fading Ottoman and Russian empires. The legal historian Michael Marrus (2009: 158–61) writes of how the interventions to support the Greek uprising against the Ottomans in 1827 and the beleaguered Jews of Damascus in 1840 all drew on appeals to "principles of decency and humanity," the "laws of humanity," and the behavior of "civilized society." In 1876 the former British Prime Minister William Gladstone represented perhaps the paragon of a liberal imperial humanitarianism when he agitated in the most lurid rhetoric for a campaign on behalf of Bulgarian Christians, nearly ten thousand of whom had been massacred by Ottoman soldiers. As a result of its overuse and misuse by the great powers during the nineteenth century, Marrus argues, the idea of humanitarian intervention became sullied and lost all legitimacy in international affairs. For him, this partly explains why there was no humanitarian intervention to save European Jewry during the Holocaust.

After a long hiatus, acting "on behalf of humanity" became legitimate again in international affairs toward the end of the twentieth century. The idea of humanity as a collective political actor once again gained an influence over international governance, allowing the exercise of power at a distance and giving credence to the idea that international sovereignty can in certain instances trump national sovereignty. Key to understanding the political consequences of the idea of humanity is its capacity to transcend and even eradicate political boundaries. The "humanity" in humanitarian law provides a justification for long-distance interventions on the other side of the globe and makes possible both military interventions (e.g., the NATO air strikes in the Balkans in 1999) and multilateral relief operations of international institutions such as the United Nations.[5] After the end of the Cold War, the United Nations established a multilateral justice system, culminating in the International Criminal Court (ICC), to prosecute crimes against humanity, war crimes, and genocide, namely, crimes with *jus cogens*[6] status and universal jurisdiction.

One obvious problem with this framework of international justice is its reliance on a collective political actor ("humanity") that cannot be easily found. Compared with the institutional political organization that takes place under the banner of nation-states, and even under religious, linguistic, and ethnic groups, the political and legal claims of "humanity" are very thin indeed. There is a widespread suspicion that "humanity" is a modern euphemism for a nineteenth-century vision of "civilization" and a cloak for the arbitrary actions of "civilized nations," that is, a deceit for the neo-imperial designs of the United States, United Kingdom, and so on. Just as the great powers in the nineteenth century used humanitarian intervention to advance their empires, so in the postimperial era, powerful nations seek to impose their beliefs and practices selectively on others, all the while claiming to act not in their own special interests but in the name of "humanity."

The German philosopher Carl Schmitt, arguably the main intellectual progenitor of modern antihumanitarian thought, once proclaimed that "whoever speaks of humanity is a liar" (cited in Wheeler 2000: 179). In *The Concept of the Political*, Schmitt (1996: 54) contends that when states appeal to "humanity" (e.g., to prevent or punish "crimes against humanity"), they are usurping a universal concept against their opponent: "At the expense of its opponent, it tries to identify oneself with humanity in the same way as one can misuse peace, justice, progress and civilization in order to claim these as one's own and to deny the same to the enemy."

These accusations may or may not be justified, and I will not address here the clash between advocates of international justice and local political sovereignty at this level. Instead, I will try to demonstrate some of the problems that arise when international criminal law, based on the idea of "crimes against humanity," encounters widespread political violence that draws on irredentist ideas of race and ethnicity.

This chapter addresses one specific question: Why has the International Criminal Tribunal for Rwanda (ICTR) been so vexed and inconsistent in its approach to concepts of race, ethnicity, and group? Why has an issue so straightforward for Hutu Power activists as they embarked on their killing spree been so difficult for international lawyers? First, it is worth observing that such inconsistency has been characteristic of many if not most international treaties and conventions on race and racism drafted since the Second World War. For instance, the 1966 International Convention on the Elimination of All Forms of Racial Discrimination rejects race as a category and refers to racial differentiation in the preamble as "scientifically false, morally condemnable, socially unjust and dangerous." And yet, on the other hand, the convention could be seen as uncritically substantiating the existence of races when it encourages "understanding between races" (preamble) and "eliminating barriers between races" (Article 2.1.e).

The difficulties encountered by the ICTR in defining the status of the Tutsi indicates a pervasive uneasiness felt by international jurists concerning ideas of race and ethnicity. There appears to be an intrinsic paradox: while the international court administering humanitarian law is highly uncomfortable with collective categories and any suggestion that it might be reproducing the categorizations of the *génocidaires*, it requires these very categories to secure convictions for the crime of genocide. One source of this double bind is the long-standing incompatibility between the enduring universalism of international law and the romanticism inherent in the concept of genocide. Scholars have documented the tensions between the universalism of international law and the romanticism of local national and cultural movements,[7] but at the Rwanda tribunal the categories of romanticism are embedded in international law itself, making the experience even more disorientating for attorneys and others working in international law.

I will seek to elucidate this point further. On the one hand, an international court such as the ICTR is made up of cosmopolitan legal actors from all over the world. The anthropologist of globalization Ulf Hannerz (1990: 246) refers to a new class of cosmopolitans with "decontextualized cultural capital," made up of individuals who traverse global networks, including diplomats, intellectuals, international lawyers, U.N. bureaucrats, business-people, and journalists. According to Hannerz, many cosmopolitans are drawn to abstract value formulations such as the "rights of man," "justice," and "freedom of speech" which allow them to manage meaning in their boundary-crossing transnational networks (247).

Proponents of "humanity law" do not draw solely on domestic or customary criminal law to try crimes committed in an African country. They draw primarily from international criminal law, the legitimacy of which derives the *jus cogens* status of the crimes tried under customary international law. After all, at the International Criminal Tribunal for Rwanda, the massacres in Rwanda are categorized as egregious crimes committed against "humanity" rather than against "the Tutsi" or even "the Rwandan people." This allows the tribunal to transcend domestic jurisdiction and to claim a universal jurisdiction that allows any competent court anywhere in the world to hear a genocide indictment.

The conflict between cosmopolitan universalism of "humanity law" and the romanticism of the category of genocide often reveals itself in the tension between individual criminal responsibility and the collective dimensions of the crime. Since the Nuremberg trials and the Nuremberg Charter, individual criminal responsibility has been a fundamental legal principle in international law. International law since 1945 has consistently maintained that individuals and individuals alone are responsible for their actions, not the racial group, not the state, and not even the army unit to which the individual belonged.[8] This is clearly written into the statutes of both the ICTR and the International Criminal Tribunal for the former Yugoslavia (ICTY), and all the final decisions of these tribunals contain a section reaffirming the principle of "individual criminal responsibility." This individualism has many benefits, notably in that it may avoid a repetition of the collective punishment of Germany after the First World War, but nonetheless, as we shall see, it leaves international lawyers with little understanding of how to comprehend crimes of a collective kind.

A BRIEF SURVEY OF THE INTERNATIONAL LAW OF GENOCIDE

In order to understand why the ICTR reversed its definition of *Tutsi* several times, we need to better understand the international law of genocide, and in particular the collective dimensions of the crime of genocide that seem to cause such problems for jurists creating and implementing the "laws of humanity."

The definition contained in the United Nations Convention on the Prevention and Punishment of the Crime of Genocide (hereafter "Genocide Convention") gives genocide a qualitatively different character than most other crimes against humanity in that it must be directed at individuals because of their membership in a collective grouping.[9] In Article 2, *genocide* is defined as "acts committed with intent to destroy, in whole or in part, a national, ethnical, racial or religious group, as such."[10] Whereas the vast majority of criminal acts require only two individuals, where one commits a proscribed act against the other, in the crime of genocide, it is conventionally held that the victim is both the individual and a national, ethnic, racial, or religious group.

In the first twelve years of the tribunal's work, the prosecution faced a high threshold for proving genocide. Demonstrating that the accused is guilty of genocide requires showing that he or she committed a proscribed act (*actus reus*), and this means demonstrating that the victim or victims belonged to a national, ethnical, racial, or religious group as designated in the Genocide Convention. If the victims are not members of such groups, or if the existence of the victim's group is uncertain, or if the group has a stable identity but that identity is not national, ethnic, racial, or religious, then the crime of genocide cannot be proven. On these grounds, the extermination of political and economic groups has generally been excluded from the category of genocide.[11]

There is a second unique component to the crime of genocide: prosecutors must prove that the individual perpetrator had awareness (*mens rea*) that his or her acts were part of a wider plan to exterminate a national, ethnic, racial, or religious group's members specifically on grounds of their membership in the group. The trial chamber must be convinced that the perpetrator held a "special intent" (*dolus specialis*) to destroy a group protected by the Genocide Convention. Proving *actus reus* and *mens rea* obliges an international tribunal to consider the broader social and historical context in significantly greater depth than with other crimes against humanity.[12]

International tribunals hearing genocide cases are compelled to take social categories of collective identity seriously and engage in social and historical analysis in order to comprehend their genealogy and use. In the case of the Rwanda tribunal, deciding whether there was a pattern of genocidal conduct required the judges to delineate the origins and historical course of the Rwandan genocide of 1994. It also obliged them to define the terms *racial group* and *ethnic group*, which had not been defined in the Convention on the Prevention and Punishment of the Crime of Genocide or in the International Convention on the Elimination of All Forms of Racial Discrimination.

A number of early ICTR judgments unfortunately employed flawed and untenable categories of racial and ethnic groups. In these decisions, the tribunal relied too heavily on an objective reading of race and ethnicity and did not grant enough attention to the political structures which planned and coordinated mass violations of international humanitarian law.

Why should this matter? Why is such close attention to the ICTR's definitions of social categories warranted? At the most fundamental level, genocide was the political hook for the application of international humanitarian law by the U.N. Security Council. As Samantha Power argues (2002: 358), the "G-Word" formally obliges governments to act under the terms of the 1948 Genocide Convention. Without the charge of genocide, it is highly unlikely that the Security Council would have created an ad hoc tribunal for Rwanda.[13] Without evidence of widespread crimes of such a severe nature, there is little need for an international court at all. The acts, although heinous, would simply be common crimes to be dealt with by Rwandan domestic courts. Thus the very jurisdiction of the International Criminal Tribunal for Rwanda was premised on the prima facie evidence produced by a U.N. commission of experts that genocide and other crimes against humanity were committed against groups protected by the Genocide Convention.

THE *AKAYESU* JUDGMENT

From October 1, 1990, onward, the Ugandan-supported Rwandan Patriotic Front (RPF) rebels mounted a number of successful incursions inside Rwanda itself, and their military campaign came to threaten the government in Kigali. Peace talks between the Rwandan government and the

RPF resulted in the 1993 Arusha Peace Agreement. Then President Juvénal Habyarimana described this agreement as the basis of an "ethnic reconcili-ation between Hutus and Tutsis" (Mamdani 2001: 189) since it contained a new power-sharing arrangement between the groupings. The Arusha agree-ment was opposed by a newly resurgent "Hutu Power" faction operating inside and outside the government. Hutu Power leaders denounced the agreement as a return to colonial-era Tutsi domination. Their propagan-dists denied the long-standing porosity between the groups and portrayed "the Hutu" as a Bantu people indigenous to Rwanda and "the Tutsi" as an alien race, invading from the north and conspiring with Belgian colonialists to oppress "the Hutu."

The Arusha Peace Agreement was never implemented. On April 6, 1994, the president's plane was shot down near Kigali airport, killing President Habyarimana and President Cyprien Ntaryamirai of Burundi. Within hours, roadblocks were set up around the capital and throughout the country, and a hundred-day campaign of mass murder was carried out by the advocates of Hutu Power (also known as the *génocidaires*). Mahmood Mamdani (2001) documents the extensive popular participation in the slaughter, although he notes that the *génocidaires* were armed, coordinated, and guided by Rwandan government officials. While statistics concerning mass political killings are invariably provisional and created in conditions of great uncertainty, the generally accepted figures are that some eight hun-dred thousand Rwandans were killed, with the main victims being moderate Hutu political activists and people designated as Tutsi in the national cen-sus (Power 2002: 334). About 10 percent of the total Rwandan population and 85 percent of the Tutsi population were annihilated (Verwimp 2004: 233). On July 18, 1994, the RPF entered Kigali and a new government took power, ending Hutu Power's reign of terror. The RPF government then pur-sued its fleeing adversaries into eastern Zaire (now the Democratic Repub-lic of the Congo) and according to reports killed up to two hundred thou-sand Rwandans, most of them self-identifying as Hutu (*Economist* 2004).

The events in Rwanda brought out the worst aspects of the international community. The French government had staunchly supported and armed the Habyarimana regime, participated in the military conflict against the RPF,[14] and then shielded those responsible for the genocide in refugee camps, under the guise of humanitarianism. The United Nations was noto-riously ineffective, with U.N. troops literally standing by while Rwandans were executed in front of them. It drastically reduced its troops from 2,500 to 503 at a crucial moment in April 1994. According to Canadian General Roméo Dallaire, the military commander of the U.N. Assistance Mission for Rwanda, five thousand well-trained troops could have stopped the killing (Power 2002: 376). The U.N. Security Council and the Clinton administration studiously avoided using the word *genocide*, and U.S. State Department spokesperson Christine Shelley only begrudgingly acknowledged on June 10, 1994, that "acts of genocide"[15] had been committed, by which time the program of mass murder was nearly over. This prompted one Reuters correspondent to ask incredulously, "How many acts of genocide does it take to make genocide?"[16]

In the aftermath of the mass killing, the U.N. Security Council passed Resolution 955 of November 8, 1994, invoking Chapter VII of the U.N. Charter and establishing the International Criminal Tribunal for Rwanda in Arusha, Tanzania. The statute of the ICTR mandates that it prosecute those persons responsible for genocide and other serious violations of international humanitarian law committed in the territory of Rwanda and neighboring states between January 1 and December 31, 1994.

The tribunal's first judgment was handed down in *Prosecutor v. Jean-Paul Akayesu* in 1998, which set a number of decisive legal precedents.[17] This was the first time that an international criminal tribunal had (a) convicted an individual for genocide and (b) included rape in the category of crimes against humanity. Since 1998, *Akayesu* has become a touchstone for how international criminal law defines genocide. Its definitions of two of the groups (racial and ethnic groups) protected under the U.N. Genocide Convention have been regularly cited in subsequent International Criminal Tribunal cases for Rwanda[18] and the former Yugoslavia[19] and in both Oxford University Press (Kittichaisaree 2001: 69) and Cambridge University Press (Schabas 2000: 12) international criminal law textbooks used to teach the next generation of international lawyers.

Trial Chamber 1, comprised of a panel three international judges, found that Jean-Paul Akayesu, who was the mayor of Taba municipality in the prefecture of Gitarama, had ordered and organized the murder and rape of Tutsis in his town.[20] After a fourteen-month trial, the trial chamber found Akayesu guilty of one count each of genocide and incitement to commit genocide and seven counts of crimes against humanity. It established one of the key precedents in international law that treats rape as a war crime. Akayesu was sentenced to three life sentences plus eighty years in prison. In

2001 the appeal chamber dismissed the grounds of Akayesu's appeal. At the time of this writing he is serving his sentence in a prison in Mali.

In order to convict Jean-Paul Akayesu on two counts of genocide, the prosecution had to demonstrate that his actions were carried out with an awareness (*mens rea*) of a widespread and systematic plan[21] to destroy a group, in whole or in part. It had to show that there was "special intent" (*dolus specialis*) to destroy a group listed in the Genocide Convention, that is, a national, ethnical, racial, or religious group. During the trial, the prosecution team, led by Pierre-Richard Prosper (who later became ambassador-at-large for war crimes issues in the U.S. State Department), argued that the Tutsi are an ethnic group in Rwandan society.

Yet according to the ICTR judge Navanethem Pillay, one of the three judges during the trial, "the Office of the Prosecutor never came up with a satisfactory argument or definition of ethnic group." In our interview,[22] Pillay told me that the judges never received a satisfactory closing brief from the prosecution, the final statement after all the discussion which lays out the prosecution's evidence, arguments, and understandings of key legal terms: "The Office of the Prosecutor never came up with a satisfactory argument or definition of ethnic group. Pierre-Richard Prosper for the Prosecutor was late with his closing brief. The deadline had passed and we said we would not read it after the deadline and we really did not read it. Maybe we would have had the benefit of the Office of the Prosecutor's definition of ethnicity in their submission" (interview with author, May 2006).

In the absence of a prosecution lead on how exactly Rwandan Tutsis fit into the Genocide Convention's definitions, the matter was passed to the trial chamber's team of legal advisers. The *Akayesu* judgment established the existence of the Tutsi as a protected group under the Genocide Convention. For the first time at an international tribunal, it defined two of the Convention's four protected groups, defining *ethnicity* in cultural terms and *race* according to physical and biological criteria:

513. An ethnic group is generally defined as a group whose members share a common language or culture.

514. The conventional definition of a racial group is based upon the hereditary physical traits often identified with a geographical region, irrespective of linguistic, cultural, national or religious factors.

These definitions are very close to those found in the 1987 U.S. Genocide Convention Implementation Act (also known as the Proxmire Act) which defines *ethnic group* as "a set of individuals whose identity is distinctive in terms of common cultural traditions or heritage" and *racial group* as "a set of individuals whose identity as such is distinctive in terms of physical characteristics or biological descent."[23] However, when I asked Pillay where these definitions came from, she told me, "The definitions of race and ethnicity in *Akayesu* came from Rwandan witnesses; there was an accepted social structure for these things. In the judgment, we cited the U.N. treaties and articles, but we said that they didn't fit the Rwandan situation. We had very little help, so we relied on the evidence and views of the people of Rwanda."[24]

On these grounds, the trial chamber observed that there are no separate ethnic groups in Rwanda, since all Rwandans speak the same language and share the same cultural and religious traditions: "The Chamber notes that the Tutsi population does not have its own language or a distinct culture from the rest of the Rwandan population" (*Prosecutor v. Akayesu*, para. 170). Is race therefore the key to understanding the distinction between the Hutu and the Tutsi? Race was a key ingredient in the ideology of Hutu Power *génocidaires*, and yet, apart from the definition in paragraph 514 above, the *Akayesu* judgment is largely silent on the question of race. *Akayesu* does not explicitly discredit the theory of racial groups, but it suggests obliquely in a number of places that the trial chamber did not consider race applicable to the Rwandan genocide. At paragraph 516, for instance, the judgment states that the Tutsi do not meet any of the four categories named in the Genocide Convention. When I asked Pillay why there is not a meaningful discussion of race in *Akayesu*, she replied that the majority of Rwandan witnesses coming before the trial chamber rejected concepts of racial categorization.

Having acknowledged that distinguishing separate ethnic groups in Rwanda is highly problematic and having demurred on the concept of race, *Akayesu* concedes that the trial chamber found itself in a quandary. It states its predicament as follows, "The question that arises is whether it would be impossible to punish the physical destruction of a group as such under the Genocide Convention, if the said group, although stable and membership is by birth, does not meet the definition of any one of the four groups expressly protected by the Genocide Convention" (*Prosecutor v. Akayesu*, para. 516).

In any conventional interpretation, the answer to the question above would have to be, yes, punishment is impossible if the group does not conform to the categories of the Genocide Convention. If the *Akayesu* judgment had stopped here, the trial chamber would have found that genocide had not occurred in Rwanda, that it could not fulfill its mandate under U.N. Resolution 955 and the ICTR Statute, and it would have had to close its doors. However, the judgment forges ahead in keeping alive the idea that "the Tutsi" are a protected group, by taking an unexpected and innovative, though ultimately hazardous, tack.

The trial chamber went back to the *travaux préparatoires* (preparatory work) of the committee writing Genocide Convention in 1947–48 and asserted that the intention of the drafters was "patently to ensure the protection of any stable and permanent group" (paras. 511–16). *Akayesu* maintains that the intention of the drafters of the Genocide Convention was to protect not only national, ethnical, racial, or religious groups from genocide but "any group which is stable and permanent like the said 4 groups" (para. 516). In clarifying what exactly it means by "stable and permanent," *Akayesu* refers to groups "constituted in a permanent fashion and membership of which is determined by birth" (para. 611), where membership in the group is "not normally challengeable by its members, who belong to it automatically by birth in a continuous and often irremediable manner." Thus, this does not extend to mobile groups constituted through occupational status or political party affiliation but only to ones which are stable over time, permanent for their members, with a significant degree of fixity and even objectivity.

The question then becomes whether this new set of criteria applies to "the Tutsi." The trial chamber answers in the affirmative, as "the Chamber finds that there are a number of objective indicators of the group as a group with a distinctive identity" (para. 170). What are these objective indicators of group status? *Akayesu* refers to the forms of classification used by the Rwandan state to distinguish identity and in particular the identity cards carried by all Rwandans that indicated ethnic classification as Hutu, Tutsi, or Twa (formerly, "Pygmy"). The judgment refers to the evidence that Tutsis were selected for murder at roadblocks using ID cards (para. 123). *Akayesu* also refers to Article 57 of the Rwandan Civil Code of 1988 providing that all persons would be identified by their membership in an ethnic group. The judges noted that "customary rules existed in Rwanda governing the determination of ethnic group which followed patrilineal lines of heredity" (para. 171). For the trial chamber, this was conclusive proof that, while the Tutsi did not qualify straightforwardly as an ethnic or racial group under the terms of the Genocide Convention, permanent membership in the group was sanctioned by both the Rwandan state (in the form of ID cards and birth certificates) and in Rwandan society (through conventions of patrilineal descent).

Finally, it is worth noting that the trial chamber's definitions of the categories of Hutu and Tutsi carried within them a theory of history, since it led the ICTR to emphasize the role of colonialism in creating the categories of the Rwandan genocide. In *Akayesu* and subsequent judgments such as *Prosecutor v. Clément Kayishema and Obed Ruzindana*, the historical discussion focuses on the German and Belgian colonial authorities, who formally institutionalized a system of ethnic classification in the 1930s. The colonial hierarchy laid the groundwork for the identity-based policies of the postcolonial state. For the trial chamber, historical (though not the legal) blame for the 1994 genocide lay more with colonial regimes than with their successors. This view is endorsed by some scholars, notably Mamdani (2001: 9), who claims that the Rwandan genocide resulted from the "logic of colonialism."

OBJECTIONS TO *AKAYESU*

Two kinds of critiques have emerged of the ICTR's *Akayesu* judgment: the legal and the anthropological. The international law expert William Schabas (2000: 131) has remarked that in *Akayesu* the "categorization of Rwanda's Tutsi population clearly vexed the Tribunal." Schabas is skeptical of the tribunal's interpretation of the Genocide Committee's *travaux préparatoires* and the tribunal's extension of the concept of genocide to include any "stable and permanent" group, claiming that this blatantly flouts the Genocide Convention's definitions and terms. He observes that the U.N. Declaration on Human Rights grants the right to change nationality and religion, which means that these terms are neither stable nor permanent. Schabas is well aware that the concepts of race, ethnic, and national group are relatively unscientific, imprecise, and contentious, nevertheless he endorses the view that the designated groups must have some objective existence for genocide to have occurred (109–11).

Schabas reminds us that Raphael Lemkin's original intention, when he coined the term genocide in *Axis Rule in Occupied Europe: Analysis of Government, Proposals for Redress* (1944), was "the protection of what were then called 'national minorities.'" Schabas claims that "use of terms such as 'ethnic,' 'racial' or 'religious' merely fleshed out the idea, without at all changing its essential content" (ibid.). The terms define one another, in a "dynamic and synergistic relationship," argues Schabas (111–12), and jurists should not get too caught up in the irreducible differences they convey: "The 1948 meaning of 'racial group' encompassed national, ethnic and religious groups as well as those defined by physical characteristics, [and this meaning] ought to be favoured over some more contemporary, and more restrictive, gloss" (123).

Therefore Schabas recommends applying the four terms in a holistic manner with the intention of protecting national minorities, more or less understood as they were in 1947–48 by Lemkin and the drafters of the Genocide Convention (112–13). Schabas notes that since the 1950s this has been the established practice of European human rights law, which has continued to prefer the term *national minorities* to formulations involving racial, religious, or ethnic categories (117).

The social anthropologist Nigel Eltringham (2004: 27–33) develops a critique of the *Akayesu* decision that runs in a direction entirely different from that followed by Schabas. He contends that in *Akayesu* the trial chamber ignored the *génocidaires'* primary justification for the genocide: race. According to Eltringham, the tribunal failed to deal with how Tutsi were targeted: the perception of indelible, racial distinction. The tribunal therefore missed the opportunity to reveal the ideational character of the genocidal mentality in Rwanda. He asks, "Did the ICTR fear that by defining the Tutsi as a race, they would be accused of endorsing this view?" (30). This seems to me a more persuasive explanation for why the *Akayesu* judgment did not deal properly with race, rather than Pillay's rationalization that Rwandans disregarded race.

In contrast to Schabas, Eltringham criticizes all attempts to construct ethnic groups according to objective criteria. Ethnicity is a subjective category of identity that social researchers developed in the 1960s as an alternative to pseudoscientific and faux-objective theories of race. Eltringham's counterproposal is that the tribunal should have adopted a subjective view of either ethnicity or race; that is, it should have relied either on the victims' self-identification with an ethnic group or on a perpetrator-based definition of race. He prefers the latter, noting that the perpetrators' subjective state is the primary consideration when prosecutors seek to prove special criminal intent in a court of law (29).

There is precedent in international criminal law for Eltringham's recommendations. For instance, the International Criminal Tribunal for the former Yugoslavia (ICTY) has consistently employed a subjective approach to defining national and religious groups in the Balkan conflict. In the ICTY's 1999 *Jelisić* judgment, the ICTY judges cite the ICTR's previous definitions of race and ethnicity,[25] but then they give the following grounds for preferring a subjective reading of national and religious groups:

> Although the objective determination of a religious group still remains possible, to attempt to define a national, ethnical, or racial group using objective and scientifically irreproachable criteria would be a perilous exercise whose result would not necessarily correspond to the perception of the persons concerned by such a categorisation. Therefore, it is more appropriate to evaluate the status of a national, ethnical, or racial group from the point of view of those persons who wish to single that group out from the rest of the community. The Trial Chamber consequently elects to evaluate membership in a national, ethnical, or racial group using subjective criterion [*sic*]. (*Prosecutor v. Jelisić*, para. 70)

The ICTY trial chamber then proceeds to distinguish between negative stigmatization, which identifies individuals as not part of the perpetrator group, and positive stigmatization, where the perpetrators distinguish individuals by the positive characteristics that members of that group are thought to share. In *Jelisić*, the trial chamber accepts the positive view of discriminatory intent advanced by the prosecution, on the basis of evidence that Goran Jelisić (also known as the "Serb Adolf") called his Bosnian Muslim victims "balijas" ("Turks") and forced them to sing Serbian songs (para. 75).

It is worth noting that the two ad hoc tribunals adopted utterly dissimilar reasoning when defining protected group status, even though they shared the same lead prosecutor in the 1990s. Whereas the ICTY defined national and religious groups in subjective terms, the Rwanda tribunal sought "objective indicators" for racial and ethnic groups. One cannot help wondering whether the difference results from the distinct character and personnel of the two tribunals or from the categories themselves, since the ICTY dealt primarily with national and religious identities, whereas the Rwanda tribunal dealt with race and ethnicity.

We might find a more plausible explanation by examining the widely distinct mandates of the two international criminal tribunals and considering the degree to which those mandates emphasized the collective-identity grounds for crimes against humanity. The idea that crimes against humanity were committed on discriminatory grounds (i.e., because of intergroup conflict) had a much higher profile in the Rwanda tribunal than any other international court before or since.

This resulted from a unique clause in the statute for the Rwanda tribunal that requires *all* crimes against humanity, not only genocide, to have been committed with discriminatory intent. Thus discriminatory intent had to be proved not only for genocide, as is always the case, but also for crimes against humanity which do not usually require such intent, such as deportation, extermination, or torture. "Crimes against humanity" are defined in Article 3 of the Rwanda statute as follows: "The International Criminal Tribunal for Rwanda shall have the power to prosecute persons responsible for the following crimes when committed as part of a widespread or systematic attack against any civilian population on national, political, ethnic, racial or religious grounds: (a) murder; (b) extermination; (c) enslavement; (d) deportation; (e) imprisonment; (f) torture; (g) rape; (h) persecutions on political, racial and religious grounds; (i) other inhumane acts."[26]

This requirement was highly unusual and was absent from the ICTY statute, which is perhaps the most compelling reason why the ICTY could define groups subjectively and then move on to considering the crime-based evidence of each case. Diane Amman (1999: 196) observes that this requirement is not replicated in any subsequent international law declarations, treaties, or conventions, including the 1998 Rome statute of the International Criminal Court, which does not include discriminatory intent in the elements of crimes against humanity. Placing a burden of proof of protected status for both genocide and other crimes against humanity made the Rwanda tribunal particularly susceptible to the inherent problems of defining racial or ethnic groups. Ironically then, by focusing the ICTR more on discrimination and the identity grounds for mass crimes, the U.N. Security Council may have rendered the tribunal less adept at addressing them adequately.

THE RETURN OF ETHNICITY

In subsequent decisions, ICTR judges had second thoughts about the reasoning in *Akayesu* regarding "stable and permanent groups," and the tribunal introduced a more subjective and perpetrator-oriented approach to identity. But instead of clarifying the categories of "Hutu" and "Tutsi," the court vacillated between objective and subjective definitions and became ultimately confused about the construction of race and ethnicity in Rwanda.

In the May 1999 judgment of *Prosecutor v. Clément Kayishema and Obed Ruzindana*, a new trial chamber composed of three different judges threw out the theory advanced in *Akayesu* that the Tutsi are a nonethnic, nonracial, but nonetheless stable and permanent group.[27] In its place, it rehabilitated the idea that the Tutsi are an ethnic group. In *Kayishema* the judges declare categorically that "Tutsis were killed, based on their ethnicity" (para. 312). The trial chamber defined ethnicity differently than *Akayesu*, including victims' subjective self-identification, as well as the categorizations of perpetrators: "An ethnic group is one whose members share a common language and culture; or, a group which distinguishes itself, as such (self-identification); or, a group identified as such by others, including perpetrators of the crimes (identification by others)" (para. 98).

Kayishema notes the prosecution's position that a perpetrator's intent is the central question, regardless of whether the *génocidaires'* perceptions were correct or not: "The Prosecution submit that it is the intent of the perpetrator to discriminate against a group that is important, rather than whether the victim was, in fact, a member of that targeted group" (para. 131).

But then the *Kayishema* judgment began to waver between objective and subjective understandings of special intent, as the judges questioned the prosecution's subjective theory of ethnic identity: "The Trial Chamber opines that the Prosecution must show that the perpetrator's belief was objectively reasonable—based upon real facts—rather than being mere speculation or perverted deduction" (para. 132).

This has to be one of the more perplexing statements in international legal reasoning, and not only because of its tortured grammar, but because it obligates the prosecution to show the eminent reasonableness of the beliefs of mass murderers. During widespread political violence, there is little that is "reasonable" or objective about such behavior. Demanding that the prosecution show the "real facts" that motivated a murderous racial/ethnic ideology is rather like asking for objective evidence of witchcraft to explain the burning at the stake of substantial numbers of women in early modern Europe. It takes the view that "well, there must have been *something* there to motivate this kind of behavior" when no such assumption is warranted. History is full of examples of delusional and violent mass movements motivated by ideas with no basis in "real facts." In Rwanda in 1994, killings were often random and unpredictable and at times lacked the kind of systematic method portrayed at the tribunal. In the aftermath, researchers collected numerous reports from survivors that some individuals holding Hutu identification cards were killed because they "looked Tutsi" and other individuals producing Tutsi identification cards walked free because they "looked Hutu" (see Eltringham 2004: 25–26).

Recoiling from its momentary recognition of the subjective nature of identity in paragraph 98 above, *Kayishema* then proceeds to decisively endorse an objective theory of racial and ethnic groups: "the Tutsis were an ethnic group. . . . Since 1931, Rwandans were required to carry identification cards which indicated the ethnicity of the bearer. . . . In accordance with Rwandan custom, the ethnicity of a Rwandan child is derived from that of his or her father" (para. 523). Moreover, *Kayishema* brazenly rewrites the conclusions of the *Akayesu* decision, stating, "In *Akayesu*, Trial Chamber I found that Tutsis are an ethnic group, as such" (para. 526). We saw earlier that *Akayesu* did nothing of the sort.

It should be noted that the objective approach to ethnicity proposed in *Kayishema* has been endorsed by international law experts such as Schabas (2000: 110), who claims that the "flaw" which had developed in the ICTR's legal reasoning came from "allowing . . . genocide to be committed against a group that does not have any real objective existence. . . . It is necessary therefore, to determine some objective existence of the four groups."

Having established the precedent in *Kayishema* that Tutsis form an ethnic group, objectively defined, the trial chamber revisited the question yet again in the December 1999 decision of *Prosecutor v. Georges Anderson Rutuganda*. The *Rutuganda* case was heard by Trial Chamber 1 and the same panel of three judges as in the *Akayesu* case: Judges Kama (presiding), Aspegren, and Pillay. In *Rutuganda*, the trial chamber showed an appreciation for a subjective view of ethnic group membership: "there are no generally and internationally accepted precise definitions of the concepts of national, ethnical, racial or religious groups. . . . membership of a group is, in essence, a subjective rather than an objective concept. The victim is perceived by the perpetrator of genocide as belonging to a group slated for destruction. In some cases, the victim may perceive himself/herself as belonging to the said group" (para. 56).

The implication is that the trial chamber is reconsidering its prior preference for objective definitions, but the next paragraph rejects, once and for all, a subjective definition of the groups protected by the Genocide

Convention: "Nevertheless, the Chamber is of the view that a subjective definition alone is not sufficient to determine victim groups, as provided for in the Genocide Convention" (57). Trial Chamber 1 does not rest here though, and it takes another unexpected tack, deciding that the task of defining racial and ethnic group is so impossible that it will adopt no formal policy on a matter so critical to determining whether the mass killing was genocide or not. A paragraph later, Trial Chamber 1 throws in the towel and concedes defeat: "Therefore . . . in assessing whether a particular group may be considered protected from the crime of genocide, [the tribunal] will proceed on a case-by-case basis, taking into account both the relevant evidence proffered and the specific political, social and cultural context" (para. 58).

This paragraph became the official statement of the Rwanda tribunal's thinking on race and ethnicity, and it has been reproduced verbatim in later genocide judgments.[28] In the space of a little over a year, the Rwanda tribunal changed its position four times. From viewing the Tutsi as a nonracial, nonethnic, but nonetheless objectively stable and permanent group, it came to regard them as an ethnic group, *subjectively* defined. It then rejected all subjective considerations and viewed Tutsis as an ethnic group that can be *objectively* defined. Finally, it arrived, exhausted, at the position that Tutsis must be nonsubjectively defined, but in an ad hoc fashion rather than in a general manner.

The tribunal's final (unresolved) resolution of the matter is hardly satisfying, since it puts the ICTR in a position where it must hold two logically self-contradictory views, namely, (1) that the concepts "racial and ethnic group" must be objectively defined and (2) that the tribunal cannot take a general or objective view of racial or ethnic groups during the killings in Rwanda in 1994. This creates practical problems in evaluating tribunal statements such as: "there was a widespread and systematic attack on the Tutsi ethnic group, on ethnic grounds" (*Prosecutor v. Rutaganda*, para. 416). Given the inconsistencies in the ICTR's thinking, one might reasonably ask, what exactly is the tribunal's understanding of an "ethnic group," and what are "ethnic grounds"?

The tribunal's case-by-case view of ethnicity had concrete implications at the Rwanda tribunal insofar as for many years it placed a particular burden on the Office of the Prosecutor to prove the existence of the Tutsi as a protected group in each individual case where an individual is accused of genocide. This meant that every genocide trial until 2006 began by review-

ing the same evidence on Hutu and Tutsi identity all over again. As might
be expected, this took up crucial trial time. The situation at the ICTR con-
trasted with the ICTY, where the senior trial attorney could simply refer to
previous cases which found that the Bosnian Muslims constitute a religious
group, or that the Serb victims formerly living in Croatia constituted a national group. This came to matter more and more as the length of trials at
the two international criminal tribunals became a pressing political issue
at the Security Council, where powerful nations such as the United States
and Russia constantly criticized the tribunals for their slow progress. Since
a drastic "completion strategy" was submitted to the Security Council by
Presiding ICTY Judge Claude Jorda in 2002, prosecutors in both ad hoc
tribunals have operated under acute time pressures.[29]

OBJECTIONS TO A PERPETRATOR ACCOUNT OF RACE
AND ETHNICITY IN RWANDA

While preferable to an objectivist approach to race and ethnicity, there are
good reasons to be skeptical of the ICTR's efforts to rehabilitate the categories of ethnicity and race by treating them as wholly subjective categories.
Even subjective formulations of "Hutu" and "Tutsi" would grant only a limited insight into the mass killings in Rwanda, and their use by the tribunal
may cultivate a misplaced faith in the coherence of these terms.

If we look through a more historical and anthropological lens at how
the categories of "Hutu" and "Tutsi" have been defined and redefined in
Rwanda during the twentieth century, we can discern four criteria that have
often overlapped and been used concurrently:

1. *Kinship*: In the precolonial era, the categories of Hutu and Tutsi re-
    ferred to the position of an individual within kinship networks of
    lineage and clan.[30]
2. *Class*: In the Belgian colonial era, a new class-based classification
    schema came to overlay the kinship elements mentioned above. The
    1933–34 Belgian census classified an individual with less than ten
    cows as "Hutu" and an individual with more than ten cows as "Tutsi"
    (Magnarella 2000: 11).[31]
3. *Race*: Hutu Power ideology drew on a long-standing "Hamitic myth,"
    which asserts that Tutsi are foreigners from Ethiopia and Hutu are
    "indigenous Bantus." This theory of racial difference asserts that

Hutus and Tutsis can be distinguished by their conformity to physical stereotypes (see ibid.: 10). Race mythology was revived in the run-up to the 1994 genocide and became its main justification by advocates of Hutu Power. *Akayesu* (para. 100) refers to Hutu Power leader Léon Mugesera's exhortation of Hutus to throw the corpses of Tutsis into tributaries leading north into the Nile so they could "return to where they came from."[32]

4. *Ethnicity*: At various moments in Rwandan history, it has been recognized that there is mobility between Hutus and Tutsis on the basis of marriage and even during the course of the life cycle, which suggests that heredity is not destiny. Both colonial and postcolonial regimes have seen fit to record "ethnicity" (*ethnie*) on the identity cards of Rwandans, rather than "race" (*race*), and the Habyarimana regime had a long-standing policy of "deracializing the Tutsi and reintegrating them into the Rwandan polity as an ethnicity" (Mamdani 2001: 230).

Given that the Hutu/Tutsi distinction has been variously defined according to kinship, class, racial, and ethnic terms, and given that there has historically been a great deal of fluidity between these groups, we would gain little trying to impose a false coherence on the incoherent jumble of identity classifications in Rwanda. The logic of the Rwandan genocide can not be found in the illogicality of Hutu/Tutsi classifications.

William Schabas's (2000) holistic approach to "national minorities," which I presented earlier, does not take us much further, as it is based on an outdated mid-twentieth-century approach to race and identity that has been unequivocally rejected in the social sciences. First, Schabas's efforts to define *genocide* exhibit a worrying reliance on the etymology of the term: *genos* as meaning "race" or "tribe" (113). This sails a little too closely to the winds of Herderian Romanticism, and Schabas does not sufficiently reflect on the colonial and postcolonial abuses of terms such as *race* and *tribe*. Second, Schabas's holistic method does not resolve the imprecision of terms such as *racial* and *ethnic group*; it just raises the imprecision to a higher level of "national minority." Ultimately, Schabas's idea of a "dynamic and synergistic" relationship between the four categories is just as vague and inexact as the constituent categories themselves. Such imprecision in key terms leaves the door open for misleading arguments by both the prosecution and the defense.

Eltringham's recommendations are more persuasive. If the tribunal were to focus primarily on the perpetrator's intent to destroy a protected group, then it would not really matter if the group in question were an objective, factually based group or not, so long as the idea of group identification was firmly established in the mind of the perpetrator and he or she demonstrated intent to destroy a group in whole or in part, through words and deeds. It is the act of stigmatization that matters, not the correspondence to the object of stigmatization. As Jean-Paul Sartre (1995 [1946]) argued in *Anti-Semite and Jew*, during the Nazi genocide it was the Nazi who defined the Jew.

Yet an overreliance on perpetrators' accounts has discernible disadvantages. It could well lead a trial chamber to overrationalize the intentions of perpetrators, as we saw in *Kayishema*, when the trial chamber demanded that "the Prosecution . . . show that the perpetrator's belief was objectively reasonable—based upon real facts" (para. 132). As I have argued, to ask for reasonableness in an ideology of mass murder is to attempt to rationalize the madness, and while there may be a rationale for the violence, it cannot be wholly found in the ideology justifying the violence.

While gaining an insight into a perpetrator's state of mind through his or her words and deeds is necessary to prove special intent, it is inadequate for many of the other tasks of the tribunal, for example, to document the history of a mass atrocity and to provide an insight into the origins and causes of genocide. Objective categories of racial and ethnic group are inadequate for the reasons I have given above, but perpetrators' beliefs are hardly a transparent and equitable window into the unfolding of a systematic program of slaughter. It may allow the perpetrators' view to take precedence in the tribunal's historical explanation. A perpetrator-based approach could detach ideology from actual politics and divert our attention from comprehending the political motives for the violence. For these reasons, Schabas (2000: 110) may well have a point when he asserts that "law cannot permit the crime to be defined by the offender alone."

INTERNATIONAL LAW'S EMBARRASSMENT
WITH RACE AND ETHNICITY

The ICTR judgments illustrate the clash between humanity and irredentism, the cosmopolitan individualism of humanitarian law and the collectivism inherent in the concept of genocide. Genocide is unique in international criminal law because the victim is a collective. In the tribunal's judgments such as *Akayesu*, before one turns to the list of individual

victims, it must be proved that there was a collective victim, a group targeted as a group on discriminatory grounds; moreover, this must be one of
the four groups listed in the Genocide Convention. As the international
law expert Kriangsak Kittichaisaree (2001: 69) makes clear, "the victim of
the crime of genocide is the group itself and not the individual." These exact
words are repeated in the ICTR's judgment in *Prosecutor v. Alfred Musema*,
making it official tribunal policy.[33] Within the concept of genocide, the collective social group becomes a "juristic person," a status comparatively rare
in international criminal law.

Cosmopolitan jurists are committed to the idea of "humanity" rather
than to notions of racial and ethnic groups, cultures, tribes, and nations,
and they are reticent to sanction these terms and give them any validity.
These terms offend the sensibility of international jurists as they are associated not with the universal but the particular; they are not cosmopolitan
but irredentist; not Kant but *Kultur*; not Enlightenment but Romantic.
Even worse, in the origins of the term *genocide* there is more than a hint
of German Romanticism. Alexander Greenwalt (1999: 2272) observes that
the intellectual author of Genocide Convention, Raphael Lemkin, "offered
a Romantic vision in the Herderian tradition." Greenwalt gives the reader
an insight into Lemkin's own worldview by quoting from his 1944 tract
Axis Rule in Occupied Europe: "The world represented only so much culture
and intellectual vigor as are created by its component national groups. Essentially the idea of a nation signifies constructive cooperation and original
contributions, based upon genuine traditions, genuine culture, and a well-
developed national psychology."

The Herderian conception of "genuine culture" and authentic nations
motivating the Genocide Convention is anathema to the cosmopolitan
universalism of international jurists. It smuggles an element of the League
of Nations' national minorities policy into the individual human rights
framework used since the Second World War, veering away from the individualistic regime of modern human rights and returning to the collectiv-
ist policies dominant before 1940. Mark Mazower (2002) has asserted that
today's individual human rights framework is predicated on the rejection
of previous diplomatic practices, stretching back into the nineteenth century, that sought to protect national minorities (e.g., religious minorities
in the Balkans, ethnic Germans in Czechoslovakia) by granting them certain collective entitlements. This culminated in the Wilsonian doctrine of

self-determination of peoples, but as we know, the collective rights model failed to protect national minorities in Europe during the first half of the twentieth century.

International law thus moved away from collective categories and minority rights in the 1940s with the crime of genocide being one of the main exceptions. The anomaly that genocide represented remained dormant as long as there were not international prosecutions for genocide, but once these commenced in the 1990s, all the tensions between the universal jurisdiction of "humanity law" and the particularist sentiments of racists and ethnonationalists came bubbling to the surface. One key challenge for the tribunals centered on the tension between legal and non-legal knowledge regarding social and cultural identities. In order to convict individuals for the crime of genocide, international law requires justiciable categories of group membership that meet strict legal criteria of fixity and facticity. The court's will to truth is an extension of its will to convict or acquit on the basis of facts of a relatively unimpeachable character. The facts of a case must be determined beyond reasonable doubt, and this applies equally to the existence of racial and ethnic groups as well as the actions of the individual perpetrator. In genocide cases, the prosecution must additionally show "special intent" (*dolus specialis*), which means that the criminal acts must be directed toward a specific group as such, in itself. Formulations of the group must be as stable, secure, and objectively demonstrable as possible and group membership must be the primary reason why the perpetrator carries out one of the prohibited acts against an individual. Group identity must refer to a permanent thing, where its "thingness" is not in doubt, for if group identity is in doubt, then so is special intent. For the ICTR to have jurisdiction and be able to punish crimes against humanity and genocide, ICTR jurists ruled, racial and ethnic groups must be enduring social facts, as factual as the dead bodies in the ground.

Difficulties have arisen when courts turn to expert witnesses on social identity to verify the existence of a group. International law's quest for unchanging and conclusive categories of race and ethnicity has not been aided by developments in the social science of group identity since the Second World War. Existing sociological and anthropological theories either entirely debunk the concepts of race or ethnicity or treat them as unstable, contextual, fluid, changing, and subjective states of mind (see Brace 2005; and Montagu 1997), thus thwarting international law's requirement of permanence and stability. As one leading socio-cultural anthropology text-book concludes, "The social world can rarely be neatly divided into fixed groups with clear boundaries, unambiguous criteria for membership and an all-encompassing social relevance" (Eriksen 1993: 156).

A number of sociological and anthropological researchers have excoriated government policies that treat race and ethnicity as scientific and objective categories rather than socially constructed concepts (see, e.g., Yanow 2003). While social science and anthropology over the past four decades have undermined their fixity, *race* and *ethnicity* are nonetheless indispensable terms for convicting a perpetrator for genocide in an international court. If a group's existence is not a fact but a changeable chimera dependent on a subjective state of mind, then the whole edifice of the tribunal's mandate to prosecute the crime of genocide is potentially undermined.

These issues are clearly rather complex, and the judges clearly needed help in understanding the nuances in social science thinking on race and ethnicity. Unfortunately, the advice they received from prosecution expert witness, the historian Alison Des Forges, was contradictory, or at least highly ambivalent. Des Forges begins by giving a relatively conventional (i.e., subjectivist) anthropological view of identity: "The primary criterion for [defining] an ethnic group is the sense of belonging to that ethnic group. It is a sense which can shift over time. In other words, the group, the definition of the group to which one feels allied[,] may change over time. . . . reality is an interplay between the actual conditions and peoples' subjective perception of those conditions" (*Prosecutor v. Akayesu*, para. 172).

So far, so good. But a few sentences later, Des Forges returns to the colonial era and uses her discussion of colonial identity politics to advocate a view of ethnic fixity. Few modern social scientists of Rwanda would share the view that ethnicity became an "absolute reality." "In Rwanda, the reality was shaped by the colonial experience[,] which imposed a categorisation which was probably more fixed. . . . The categorisation imposed at that time is what people of the current generation have grown up with. They have always thought in terms of these categories. . . . This practice was continued after independence by the First Republic and the Second Republic in Rwanda to such an extent that this division into three ethnic groups became an absolute reality" (ibid.). Is ethnicity the result of an "interplay" or is it an "absolute reality"? Faced with these conflicting views, the court obviously took away what was instrumentally useful to adjudicating crimes against humanity, namely, a fixed view of identity, or ethnicity as an "absolute reality."

The racial or ethnic nature of Rwandan social categories was finally resolved as a legal question in 2006, when the ICTR Appeals Chamber's decision in the *Karemera* case took judicial notice of the adjudicated fact that the Hutu and Tutsi were "ethnic groups" protected by the genocide convention.[34] The decision did not, however, bring us any closer to clarifying on what grounds they could be considered ethnic groups, stating that they should be defined in a way that is "consistent with the Tribunal's jurisprudence," even though, as we have seen, the Tribunal's jurisprudence is far from consistent on this matter.

CONCLUDING REMARKS

International criminal tribunals emerged in the 1990s as instruments of global governance and international regulation of conflict. For cosmopolitan justice advocates such as David Held (2004), these are harbingers of a social democratic alternative to the "Washington consensus." International courts are mechanisms for constructing an international rule of law—a long-standing dream of Kantians—that could address risks to regional or global security. By holding individual perpetrators accountable, future political violence—and in particular "irredentist violence" involving ethno-nationalists, religious sectarians, and other forms of communalist politics— might be deterred. For their proponents, international justice institutions are a way of establishing what Max Weber called "legal domination," a more rational, predictable, and secure stage beyond militarism and violent domination. Legal domination establishes its own legitimacy through accepted legal and moral norms, and these norms are provided by international humanitarian law with its categories of crimes against humanity and claims of universal jurisdiction.

For the global skeptics, international criminal law is an instrument of U.S. hegemony or a new form of neoimperial domination delinked from specific nation-state interests. My intention is not to adjudicate between these contrasting views but to make a more empirical claim about the actual application of "humanity law" to one case of irredentist politics: the racially motivated mass killing in Rwanda. My point is that due to a reliance on concepts of humanity, universal jurisdiction, and individual criminal responsibility, international tribunals can profoundly misapprehend collective social categories such as race and ethnicity. The ICTR did not meaningfully deal with race in the *Akayesu* case, even though anyone even remotely familiar with Rwandan history is aware of the role of racism in the mass killing. International jurists implementing laws of humanity seem to struggle when addressing crimes motivated by categories such as race or ethnicity. There seems to be an unarticulated, even unconscious view that to recognize their importance in social action and, more important, to prove the special intent of perpetrators to destroy a group in whole or in part is somehow to validate and grant legitimacy to those very categories. Of course, this need not be the case if one proceeds with caution, and the ICTY has not been plagued by the same difficulties.

The point of this discussion is this: a system designed to regulate global conflict and insecurity has at times failed to apprehend the causes and motivating factors for conflict in fairly significant ways. This failure results in part from a clash between the universalist and individualist character of the norms that grant legitimacy to global justice institutions and the particular and collective categories such as genocide that are brought before the tribunal. The laws of humanity carry both the conditions of their own legitimization and internal contradictions that undermine the coherence of their decisions from within. This tension is unlikely to be resolved any time soon and will likely continue to be played out in new international justice institutions such as the International Criminal Court.

NOTES

My thanks to the participants in seminars and panels where this chapter has been presented, at the American Anthropological Association, the University of Connecticut Law School, New York University School of Law, the University of Michigan interdisciplinary human rights seminar, and the anthropology department at the Vrei Universitet, Amsterdam. Thanks to Anne Dailey, Laura Dickinson, Ilana Feldman, Mark Janis, Beth Lyons, Miriam Ticktin, Ernesto Verdeja, and two anonymous reviewers for their thoughtful comments on earlier drafts.

1 *Universal jurisdiction* means that an alleged crime may be tried anywhere and by any competent tribunal. The individuals involved need not be citizens of the country where the tribunal is located and the acts may have occurred outside the territory of the country where the tribunal is located.

2 *Natural law* is a set of legal and moral principles that derive from a universal conception of human nature or, in earlier forms, from divine provenance.

3 *Humanity law* is a term coined by Ruti Teitel (2004) to refer both to international humanitarian law as well as human rights.

4 *Somerset v. Stewart*, Lofft 1, 19, 98 Eng. Rep. 499, 510 (KB 1722) in Baker (1908). On the significance of the Somerset case generally in the abolition of the slave trade, see Janis 2005.

5 Since 1990 an impressive literature on the international politics of humanitarian intervention has emerged. Perhaps the most influential books are Holzgrefe and Keohane 2003; Kennedy 2004; and Wheeler 2000. See also Wilson and Brown (2009) for essays on the history and representational aspects of humanitarianism.

6 The legal concept of *jus cogens* asserts that certain international law obligations (e.g., to prevent and prosecute the crime of genocide) are binding on all states and cannot be modified by treaty.

7 On human rights, gender violence, and religious and ethnic nationalism in India and Fiji, see Merry 2005: 103–33.

8 This position is regularly reaffirmed by the U.N. Law Commission.

9 A few crimes against humanity, such as "persecution," do contain a group dimension. The preeminent treatise on genocide in international law is Schabas 2000. See also Kittichaisaree 2001: chap. 4. For general histories of genocide, see Staub 1994 [1989]; and Weitz 2003. For an excellent review of theories of genocide, see Freeman 1991.

10 The full text of Article 2 of the Genocide Convention states:
> In the present Convention, genocide means any of the following acts committed with intent to destroy, in whole or in part, a national, ethnical, racial or religious group, as such:
> (a) Killing members of the group;
> (b) Causing serious bodily or mental harm to members of the group;
> (c) Deliberately inflicting on the group conditions of life calculated to bring about its physical destruction in whole or in part;
> (d) Imposing measures intended to prevent births within the group;
> (e) Forcibly transferring children of the group to another group.

11 Although in some Latin American countries such as Mexico, "political groups" are included in the statutory definition of *genocide*.

12 This argument is elaborated further in the context of the ICTY in Wilson 2005.

13 The Security Council resolution establishing the Rwanda Tribunal in 1994 states in its preamble: "Expressing appreciation for the work of the Commission of Experts established pursuant to resolution 935 (1994), in particular its preliminary report on violations of international humanitarian law in Rwanda transmitted by the Secretary-General's letter of October 1, 1994 (S/1994/1125). Expressing once again its grave concern at the reports indicating that genocide and other systematic, widespread and flagrant violations of international humanitarian law have been committed in Rwanda."

14 For instance, according to Mamdani (2001: 186), French troops assisted the Rwandan government in repelling the RPF invasion in 1990.

15 June 8, 1994, Resolution of U.N. Security Council, U.N. Doc. S/RES/925.

16 Public Broadcasting Service, "Frontline: The Triumph of Evil—100 Days of Slaughter:

A Chronology of U.S./U.N. Actions," http://www.pbs.org/ (accessed February 16, 2006). See also Power 2002: chap. 10.

17 *Prosecutor v. Jean-Paul Akayesu*, ICTR-96–4-T, September 2, 1998.

18 E.g., *Prosecutor v. Georges Anderson Rutuganda*, ICTR-96–3-T, December 6, 1999, para. 48.

19 E.g., *Prosecutor v. Goran Jelisić*, IT-95–10-T, December 14, 1999, para. 61.

20 Akayesu's culpability for murder is stated in *Prosecutor v. Jean-Paul Akayesu*, para. 268, and his responsibility for sexual violence in para. 452.

21 In order to prove that the killings of Tutsis were widespread and systematic, the prosecution called a number of expert witnesses, including the historian and human rights activist Alison Des Forges, the British cameraman Simon Cox, Rony Zachariah of Médecins sans Frontières/Doctors without Borders, and UNAMIR commander Major General Roméo Dallaire.

22 Personal interview, The Hague, May 26, 2006. Since 2003, I have conducted 60 interviews with staff at three international tribunals (the ICTR, ICTY, and ICC), including judges, senior legal officers, chief prosecutors, deputy prosecutors, senior prosecuting trial attorneys, investigators, defense counsel lawyers, and external expert witnesses.

23 18USC1093. The Genocide Convention Implementation Act is contained in chapter 50A of the U.S. Code, title 18 (Crimes and Criminal Procedure), part 1 (Crimes). Section 1091 deals specifically with genocide, and the terms are defined in section 1093. To my knowledge, no charges have been filed under this law in the United States.

24 Personal interview, The Hague, May 26, 2006. Pillay went on to describe how in the beginning of the ICTR's work, tribunal staff had very few resources and no library; all they had was the case law of the European Court of Human Rights and the U.S. Supreme Court. She stated that none of the judges had been international judges before and some individuals, herself included, had not been judges at all. Before coming to the ICTR, Pillay had been a widely respected defense attorney in South Africa.

25 *Prosecutor v. Goran Jelisić*, para. 70n95, citing *Prosecutor v. Clément Kayishema and Obed Ruzindana*, para 98. It should be noted that Goran Jelisić was convicted of not genocide but persecution, a crime against humanity committed with discriminatory intent.

26 Art. 3; my emphasis. Statute of the International Criminal Tribunal for Rwanda, Resolution 955 (1994), Adopted by the Security Council at its 3453rd meeting, on 8 November 1994, UN Doc. S/RES/955.

27 The judges were Sekule (presiding), Ostrovky, and Khan.

28 E.g., in *Prosecutor v. Alfred Musema*, ICTR-96–13-T, January 27, 2000, paras. 161–62.

29 The ICTY senior trial attorney Daryl Mundis (2006) provides a sobering if rather understated assessment of the impact of the completion strategy on the functioning of the two international tribunals.

30 According to *Prosecutor v. Jean-Paul Akayesu* (para. 81); and Eltringham 2004, citing d'Hertefelt 2004: 18.

31 Eltringham (2004: 186n21) points out that this was not the only criteria used in the census and that self-ascription also played a significant role.

32   The ICTR defense counsel Diana Ellis has disputed this claim, saying the Mugesera quote has been improperly used at the tribunal. Personal interview, London, July 25, 2006.

33   "The victim of the crime of genocide is the group itself and not the individual alone" (*Prosecutor v. Alfred Musema*, para. 165).

34   Prosecutor v. Édouard Karemera, Mathieu Ngirumpatse, Joseph Nzirorera, Case No. ICTR-98–44-AR73(C). "Decision on Prosecutor's Interlocutory Appeal of Decision on Judicial Notice," June 16, 2006, para 25.

CHILDREN, HUMANITY, AND THE
INFANTILIZATION OF PEACE ∾

Liisa Malkki

THIS CHAPTER is part of a larger exploratory
study of contemporary forms of humanitarianism and humanism. By "humanism" I mean
those discourses and practices that constitute
subjects first of all as human beings. In that
context, I am interested in all the ways people
come to be interpellated as members or representatives or ambassadors of a common humanity, a global human community beyond the
nation form. This happens in a number of different ways. In previous work I have suggested
that the representational, discursive, and other
social practices of contemporary humanitarianism constitute a key global terrain for the
construction of the human (Malkki 1994, 1995,
1996). I have also examined how discourses of
liberal internationalism since the Second World
War form ready terrain for the elaboration of
the human (Malkki 1995). In that work, I have
suggested that children occupy a key place in
dominant imaginations of the human and of
the "world community." Here, I will examine
more closely the ritual and affective work done
by the figure of the child in these transnational
representational spheres. That work is ritual and
affective because it tends to be identified as apo-

litical, even suprapolitical; yet the forms in question clearly have political effects. It should be noted, too, that while such figurations of the child and the human are putatively universal, they are in fact both culturally Western, and in many ways quite Christian.

This broad set of contemporary humanistic practices and representations constitutes an observable aspect of "global culture." The idea of a global cultural ecumene (Hannerz 1989; Foster 1991), or transnational culture, has been intensively and productively discussed in recent years. In examining specifically humanistic and humanitarian modes of imagining world community, however, one is looking at something a good deal more specific than just the transnational. At issue is a peculiarly *self-conscious* globalism, a set of cultural forms, structures of feeling (Williams 1985), and ritual practices which deliberately *aim* to be "global" by invoking a universal or global "human community." These are forms that do not just "end up" being international, transnational, or supranational in scope; they are moralizing visions conceived as globally encompassing from the start. These forms can, and do, include everything from Coca-Cola advertisements (as in "I'd like to buy the world a Coke") to famine relief, from school celebrations of "United Nations Day" to UNICEF and other Christmas cards. A significant part of the humanitarian representation of children occurs in connection with Third World emergencies, as Erica Burman (1994: 238) points out in her indictment of "the chauvinism of the Northern public and policy makers for whom disaster imagery constitutes a major source of information about the South."

Such humanist cultural forms are indeed transnational (which, again, does not mean that they are universal), but they do not fully transcend the national, or escape its logic. To understand just how central the nation form (Balibar and Wallerstein 1992) remains to such supranational forms of moral imagination, we need to treat the question of the nation not only in the familiar form of chauvinistic or exclusionary nationalism, but also in the form of the liberal, tolerant, UNICEF kind of national imagination that envisions and celebrates the world as an ensemble of nations and presents itself as a form of antiracism (cf. Barthes 2001 [1957]). These modes of imagining a world community involve special, observably standardized, representational uses of children—be they images of children themselves, images children have made, words they have written, or songs they have sung. These uses of children, in turn, produce other sets of effects that I will trace here.

My framing questions are as follows: Why are children's images every-where in evidence in the humanitarian representational conventions of both international community and humanitarian appeal? What do these images do? What do they depend on for their efficacy? My preliminary analysis suggests that children very consistently appear in five interrelated registers: (1) as embodiments of a basic human goodness (and symbols of world harmony); (2) as sufferers; (3) as seers of truth; (4) as ambassadors of peace; and (5) as embodiments of the future. These registers depend on each other for their affective and ritual efficacy (Tambiah 1985).

This chapter is not based on ethnographic fieldwork but instead engages a wide variety of sources and kinds of evidence. Its intent is exploratory and programmatic; it seeks to offer researchable questions about contemporary depoliticizing uses of children as moral subjects and to suggest how this shapes thinking about peace.

CHILDREN AS EMBODIMENTS OF A BASIC HUMAN GOODNESS AND INNOCENCE

Children have long served as elementary forms of the human—in some his-torical periods as embodiments of a basic human savagery and sinfulness (or even evil) and at other times of a basic human goodness and innocence. In scholarly histories by Carolyn Steedman (1995), Philippe Aries (1962), Sharon Stephens (1995), Chris Jenks (1996), Allison James and Alan Prout (1997), Gill Valentine (1996), Peter Coveney (1957), and many others, chil-dren and childhood have long been recognized as historical, cultural, and political constructs, not as naturally (or developmentally) given. This work shows that before the seventeenth century in the West, children were often thought of as "inheritors of original sin" or as "savage" and uncivilized (Val-entine 1996: 583). In this Christian, Western tradition, Calvin and Augus-tine are key figures. Augustine's *Confessions* is, of course, a classic medita-tion on the problems of sin and human evil: "no man is free from sin, not even a child who has lived only one day on earth" (cited in Wall 2004: 171). But as the theologian John Wall (2004: 170) points out, linking children with original sin does not necessarily mean that children carry greater sin than do adults: "The key benefit to viewing children as coming into the world with original sin . . . is that it acknowledges the profound humanity of their struggle to grow and develop in this world."

By the end of the seventeenth century (and especially from mid-eighteenth century onward), scholarly writing, at least, tended to see an innate goodness in the child; and a distinction was made between goodness and innocence (see, e.g., Rosenblum 1988). The latter, as Valentine (1996: 583) points out, "may only mean a neutral state—neither positively bad nor positively good." Locke, for instance, saw the child as a tabula rasa. Thus, "children are not animals to be civilized but vessels for the infusion of Reason. Children come into the world with enormous rational *potential*. They are each a *tabula rasa* or 'blank slate' upon which Reason may be written through enlightened education" (Wall 2004: 163; emphasis in original). In the eighteenth century, in the time of Jean-Jacques Rousseau and William Blake, there was, among many debates about the nature of children, a strong Romantic movement to link children with an original innocence (Higonnet 1998: 9). Blake's "Songs of Innocence" (1992 [ca. 1826]), for example, held up a pure, natural childhood against the corruptions of society. The child embodied a "romantic protest against the 'experience' of society" (Coveney 1957: xii). Associated most strongly with Rousseau (1978 [1762]), and in contrast to the long Christian preoccupation with "original sin," the concept of the child's nature which informed the work of figures as diverse as William Blake, William Wordsworth, and Charles Dickens was one of "original innocence." As Coveney (1957: 6) has pointed out, "Rousseau's contribution was to give expression to the new sensibility, and to direct its interest toward childhood as the period of life when man most closely approximated to the 'state of nature.'" (In other words, a child is not just a miniature adult, or just an adult in the making. It is a being of another order, set apart by cultural prescriptions and proscriptions.) Blake celebrated children's oneness with nature, their capacity to transcend boundaries: "No barriers in the child's consciousness lie between himself and the ant; merely a *synthesizing compassion*" (Coveney 1957: 21; my emphasis; see also Rosenblum 1988: 16). In this period in the West, "nature" was often understood in Christian terms, as the Christian God's "creation." If children were close to nature, it was because they were fresh, new images of their Creator. The theologian Friedrich Schleiermacher, for example, was of this opinion (Wall 2004: 167). In his later work, Schleiermacher "associates the child's special capability for 'pure reverence'—for 'the feeling of absolute dependence'—with its special closeness to what he calls the 'sacred sphere of nature.' As in Rousseau, nature is to be the guide for society and not the other way around. But unlike in Rousseau, nature in the form of the sacred gift of the child trumps even human reason as the true measure of human goodness" (Wall 2004: 168; cf. Albert Schweitzer's [1950] credo of "reverence for life"). For Scheiermacher, as for many who have come after, the ideal corrective to the depredations of modern, Western industrial societies was for adults to "become as little children."[1] Thus, children were elevated to the status of innocent sages, teachers as if despite themselves.

These histories of the construction of children as embodying a natural goodness and innocence have been examined by many scholars (Valentine 1996). Here I want simply to underscore the historical depth and continued vitality of the links between childhood, innocence, and goodness—and the separation between childhood and adulthood that has become so robustly naturalized since the late eighteenth century in the West (Rosenblum 1988: 17). These links still have power and relevance in contemporary discourses of humanitarianism and liberal internationalism, where childlike innocence is a way of making recipients of humanitarian assistance a tabula rasa, innocent of politics and history, innocent (in the sense of not-knowing) about causes of war and enmity. Childlike innocence is also a mode of imagining archetypal "innocent victims". Valentine (1996: 581n1) writes that the angel-devil tension and the ascendancy of the notion of innocence have to do with "a North American and European understanding of childhood which has been propagated in the rest of the world, for example, in the late 20th century through organizations such as the United Nations" (see also Benjamin 1999: 101).[2] My work on internationalism and humanitarianism supports this argument, although I do think it is important to approach regional, historical, class, gender, and other differences in the shapes of childhoods empirically without attributing vectors of influence too early—and without assuming the actual universalization of what is in fact only putatively universal. As Valentine points out, "*The experience of childhood has never been universal*; rather, what it means to be a particular age intersects with other identities so that experiences of poverty, disability, ill health, being orphaned, taken into care, or having to look after a sick parent have all denied many children this idealized time of innocence and dependence" (Valentine 1996: 587; James and Prout 1997; my emphasis).

The social imagination of innocence has periodically been violently and horribly disrupted by highly publicized cases of children murdering and torturing other children, and recent years have seen an intensification of moral panics concerning childhood and danger. Sharon Stephens (1995) and others have written, for example, about the conceptualization of "children at risk" and "children as a risk." In the United Kingdom in 1993, Jamie Bulger, a two-year-old boy, died an almost unimaginably cruel death at the hands of two ten-year-old boys. There have been a number of similar contemporary cases. Valentine (1996: 589) argues that these cases ignited public processes of "othering" and demonizing children in the 1990s; she cites the *Guardian* as stating of the child of the 1990s: "There is a growing uncertainty about the parameters of childhood and a mounting terror of the anarchy and uncontrollability of unfettered youth."

In the transnational discursive formations of internationalist humanitarianism, special attention has been devoted to child soldiers (Rosen 2005; Boyden and de Berry 2005; Machel 2002; Peters and Richards 1998, cited in Korbin 2003; Scheper-Hughes and Sargent 1998). The child soldier is a figure that gravely troubles the image of the child as an innocent; and yet the current international moral shock about the child soldier may derive its significance from the generalized, universalizing expectation of children's innocence, the expectation that children are beings not yet caught up in history or politics—perhaps not yet caught up in time (cf. Higonnet 1998: 49). The attribution of innocence to children suggests two things about innocence itself: first, that it is an allochronic (Fabian 2002), somehow timeless, innocence; and second, that innocence is a form of *not-knowing*, of not being "worldly." All this makes the child soldier an abomination, and the "normal" soldier (who may be just a few years older) a fact taken for granted. The "normal" soldier can be decorated for valor and courage, but decorating the child soldier thus strains the imagination. The trouble with child soldiers is that they cannot be set apart, made sacred, in allochronic time (by adults); and they can no longer be (for adults) innocent in the other sense of blameless not-knowing. They cannot be imagined as transcendent figures.[3] They are profane, a category mistake that disturbs the poetics of "our common humanity."

Children fighting in the Palestinian intifada also trouble the morally laden binary of child versus adult. Not surprisingly, they are often categorized in the press as "youths" as opposed to "children." Likewise, when children are referred to as "teens" or "teenagers," their moral authority as innocents is attenuated. The temporal progression built into the category of "children" is also a moral progression: it is easiest to attribute to children a pure, innocent presociality when they are youngest. "As they grow older, gain knowledge and worldly understanding, develop 'vehement passions' [Philip Fisher 2002] of their own, and form connections beyond family boundaries, they become more 'tainted' and less worthy of special treatment as children. (Witness the debates about the legal age at which children should be prosecuted as adults for crimes of violence.)"[4]

While this section has addressed the representational uses of children as embodiments of goodness and innocence, the specific examples I have given here are of children who trouble this mode of representation, for example, child soldiers. The figure of the child as an innocent will appear in more specific forms in the following registers, for instance, as blameless victim.

CHILDREN AS SUFFERERS

We know children as sufferers perhaps better than we think from seeing humanitarian appeals in print and visual media. As Burman (1994: 241) puts it, "The individual starving child functions as the general idiom for hunger, and hunger comes to operate as the quintessential index of need. It is important to consider what is elided by this set of equivalences." What is crucial about these humanitarian appeals is that they depend on children as *generic human beings* and not as culturally or socially specific *persons* (cf. Gupta 2001). In his book *Humanity and Personhood: Personal Reaction to a World in Which Children Can Die,* Jan van Eys, a professor of pediatrics at a cancer treatment center in Texas and devout Christian, describes his work among children who are likely to die and the difficulty of negotiating the process with the children's parents. Van Eys (1981: 24, 27) observes that "although children are human in the eyes of all, they are rarely viewed as persons. . . . Above all, they are not allowed to experience what adults conceive of as suffering, and never are they willingly allowed to die. . . . The almost universal inability of adults to treat children as persons is most obvious when the children are dying."

This refusal, so understandable, is also present in some form in the visual and other representational uses of suffering children in humanitarian appeals. We see—or are urgently, benevolently, *invited* to see—small bundles of humanity, young bodies that could belong to any of us, naked humanity. The images are affectively powerful. These small figures are charismatic in their suffering. But they exhibit a profound absence of historical, cultural, biographical specificity (cf. Burman 1994: 239). Even while being photographic documents of actual, living children, these are pictures of *human children*, not photographs of specific *persons* or *people* with specific histories, however short. It is all too easy to strip children of their personhood and to fill them with a pure humanity and an unspoiled nature instead. In the process, we (adults) place them outside the complications of history, beyond the lines drawn by nationalisms, racisms, and cultural identities. They are the innocent representatives of a common humanity, able to appeal—across the boundaries of race, culture, and nation—to an underlying, essential humanity many of us (at certain times) believe we all share. They are the "principle of hope" set apart from the complications of history (Bloch 1986).

In a horribly titled but thoughtful article, "Fresh Maimed Babies: The Uses of Innocence," McKenzie Wark (1995) examines the affective, moral, and political uses of children as sufferers and ideal, innocent victims. He begins in a rather shell-shocked way:

> The most innocent-looking media images are sometimes the most sinister. Take Somalia, where United Nations forces found themselves buried up to their baby-blue bonnets in cynical *realpolitik*. . . . How did it all start? With pictures of starving children. Poor innocents with frail limbs and big, brown eyes and flies crawling up their nostrils. They stared at us out of smudgy newsprint or pixelated images from satellite newsfeeds, but always with a resolution hard enough to make my heart leap into my mouth. Who wouldn't want to help them, these blameless victims—as soon as possible, no questions asked? When I see these images, it is I who becomes childlike. I want someone to make it all better. The child occupies such a sacred place in our structures of feeling that one cannot help but feel—something. Advertisers are aware of this. (36)

Wark traces the anatomy of a "conscience industry of global proportions" (40) and finds that children occupy a key place in it. In this capacity they are more powerful than adults; they are attributed an affective authority that adult refugees and other victims can generally never hope to possess. Wark takes the reader to Bosnia:

> Being certified refugees, they were for the most part adults who had done something to make themselves refugees. . . . Like old toys, they

were rejected in favor of the new season's hit doll. Bosnian babies had an added feature—innocence. It makes them a most satisfying gift for yourself when you feel the itch to feel good in an ingenuous, "We Are the World" sort of a way. Dollar for dollar, pound for pound, adult refugees are nowhere near the value. There's always the suspicion that they may be adulterated by impurities—such as politics. (40)

The point is that children as sufferers are familiar charismatic figures with an *affective* authority of great proportions. Eleanor Coerr's children's book *Sadako and the Thousand Paper Cranes* (1977) is one of many in its genre. It is the story of how a young girl, Sadako Sasaki, died of leukemia because she had been irradiated by the bomb the American forces dropped on the city of Hiroshima when she was only two years old. The little book mentions nothing about the U.S. forces, or the politics of the decision to drop the atomic bombs that destroyed Hiroshima and Nagasaki. Leaving out the book's tragic contents, I concentrate on its outer skin. The back cover indicates that the book was written by an American author for the benefit of American children: "Eleanor Coerr lived in Japan years ago and heard about Sadako and the paper cranes. . . . The author decided to find out as much as she could about the brave young girl's life and recreate it for American children." Why? It seems that she wanted to communicate the message that war is bad, and, especially, bad for children. This is a generic, intentionally uncontroversial and humanist pacifism that relies on the figure of the child as an innocent and essentially human sufferer. It does not address any specific war, any specific bombs, any specific or historically situated political stakes or ideological programs.[5]

What happens to the moral authority of such suffering? How can authority (of any kind) exist there if nobody has to take it seriously? Does a U.S. president read such a book and decide that nuclear disarmament is the only possible course of action? Is not the moral claim of such representations so bland and uncontroversial as to be in the end utterly unthreatening to the actual makers of war? This is the problem with the affective, moral authority of children as sufferers: they stand on an "ethereal pedestal" (Wall 2004: 170) that dissipates altogether when practically necessary. Their authority is of a transnational ritual nature alone, and does not belong in the realm of "real-world politics" or history. That does not mean that this ritualized moral authority does nothing; rousing people to send money to starving or sick children is laudable. But in the final analysis, it is very limited in the position it occupies in the thick of history and politics. Even while this authority is understood to address "the world," it is not worldly. Even the most urgent humanitarian appeals (currently on behalf of people in Darfur, Sudan, and the broader region) are hobbled by the highly conventionalized and ritually circumscribed nature of the affective authority of children as sufferers. In large measure, this disabling rests on (and is naturalized by) the Western opposition of affect and reason.

The moralized, sentimentalized figure of children as sufferers works in much the same manner as does the figure of suffering animals. Both do affective cultural work as expressive moral subjects (but not as rational, knowing subjects). Both are "good to think" as innocent victims. Oddly, animals and children are sometimes made more human than anyone. Sadako belongs to the same ritual world (and historical moment) as do the "faithful elephants" of Tokyo's Ueno Zoo. In 1951, after the Second World War, Yukio Tsuchiya wrote a children's book about three elephants, John, Tonky, and Wanly, and how they had to be starved to death by their heartbroken keepers. "During the last stage of World War II, Tokyo was often attacked from the air. At the city zoo, the keepers, with tears in their eyes, had to kill many of the animals for fear that they would run amuck in the town if the zoo were bombed directly. *Faithful Elephants* describes how three elephants died in the Ueno Zoo in Tokyo at that time" (Tsuchiya 1988 [1951]: n.p.). The elephants were blameless, faithful, giving, and innocent. To read how they died is heartbreaking. The rain of anticipated bombs is once again nameless.

CHILDREN AS SEERS OF TRUTH

Children are also hailed in these philanthropic, humanitarian representations as seers of truth, small humans with the capacity to see through "barriers" of culture and nationality, race and class. Whereas in some contexts (anthropology and critical human rights discourses, for example) cultural differences are thought to deserve our highest regard and protection, in other discursive arenas they become obstacles to the articulation of a common, universal humanity. This was very clearly stated in the opening address of former U.N. Secretary-General Boutros Boutros-Ghali at the June 1993 World Conference on Human Rights in Vienna.

Human rights, viewed at the universal level, bring us face-to-face with the most challenging dialectical conflict ever: between "identity" and "otherness," between the "myself" and "others." They teach us in a direct, straightforward manner that we are at the same time identical and different. Thus the human rights that we proclaim and seek to safeguard can be brought about only if we transcend ourselves, only if we make a conscious effort to find our common essence *beyond our apparent divisions, our temporary differences, our ideological and cultural barriers.* In sum, what I mean to say, with all solemnity, is that the human rights we are about to discuss here at Vienna are not the lowest common denominator among all nations, but rather what I should like to describe as the *"irreducible human element,"* in other words, the quintessential values through which we affirm together that we are *a single human community.* (Boutros-Ghali; my emphasis)[6]

Children have long been constituted as visionaries of such a common humanity, as beings empowered to see through what we like to gloss simply as the "folly" of war. Anne Frank was such a being. Zlata Filipovic became another. Several years ago, there was a sudden spate of television and print coverage of the latest literary fad in Paris: *Le journal de Zlata Filipovic*—the diary of a young girl who began writing and drawing about the war in the former Yugoslavia when she was eleven years old. Her book has since been translated into many languages. The dust jacket of the English-language edition introduces the diary as follows: "In a voice both innocent and wise, touchingly reminiscent of Anne Frank's, Zlata Filipovic's diary has awoken the conscience of the world" (Filipovic 1994).

The pervasive social imagination of children as keepers of universal truths is evident in the many contemporary picture books that have been published on war and peace and children's art. *I Dream of Peace: Images of War by Children of Former Yugoslavia*, for example, is a collection of drawings and writings gathered by UNICEF from schools and refugee camps as part of a "psychosocial assistance program for war-traumatized children" (UNICEF 1994: dust jacket). The preface to this book was written by Maurice Sendak, the author of classic children's books in the United States:

The children know. They have always known. But we choose to think otherwise; it hurts to know the children know. The children see. If we obfuscate, they will not see. Thus we conspire to keep them from knowing and seeing. And if we *insist*, then the children, to please us, will make believe they do not know, they do not see. Children make that sacrifice for our sake—to keep us pacified. They are remarkably patient, loving, and all-forgiving. It is a sad comedy: the children knowing and pretending they don't know to protect us from knowing they know.

In the former Yugoslavia, there is no time left for such genteel dissembling. We have betrayed the children; we are killing them. The pictures they paint and their words tell us so. In these pictures and words, the children shout out their terrible fear and grief; they rebuke us and plead with us to spare them. And in that awful shouting they reveal the health, vitality, natural grace, and artistry of childhood. Who better than children to sum up, without artifice or sentimentality, the monumental stupidity of war!

Despite our betrayal, these fierce images do not speak of blame, only of sick despair and desperation that blossoms, eerily, into radiant hope. They are ready to forgive us. They always are. Nemanja, eleven years old, cries out: "I do not want to grow old while still just a child." And Sandra, ten, sends this message: "Don't ever hurt the children. They're not guilty of anything." And the children in a fifth-grade class ask: "Like Anne Frank fifty years ago, we wait for peace. She didn't live to see it. Will we?" Will they? (UNICEF 1994: 5)

In his book on the uses of child art in modernism, *The Innocent Eye: Children's Art and the Modern Artist*, the art historian Jonathan Fineberg (1997: xx) writes: "Although there is an ancient tradition of *the child as an unknowing seer*, it was the romantics who allied the naïveté of the child with genius. . . . Thus the nineteenth century inherited a double legacy about the child's 'innocent eye'; it was innocent enough of convention to see through the emperor's new clothes, so to speak, and at the same time the child was gifted with a privileged view into the mysteries of the divine plan." This formulation is still recognizable in humanitarian representational regimes and in other globally circulating systems of signification.[7]

The linking of children and truth is neither simple nor innocent. As Sharon Stephens has pointed out, children may be conceptualized as seers of truth in relation to "emotional truths," but they are

NOT seen as credible witnesses in courts of law, for example, in relation to child abuse cases. While they are capable of grasping emotional truths, beyond and beneath the artificialities of culture, they are not seen as cognitively able to distinguish between fact and fantasy, between "what really happened" and what some adult or another child may have suggested happened. . . . Consider the heated legal debates, for [example], about children as witnesses in court. On the one hand, they're seen as vessels of unmediated truth, bearing witness to the artificialities and duplicities of adults. On the other hand, they're seen as irrational, fanciful, unable to tell reality from imagination. In both cases, children are denied existence as complex social beings who know the world and represent themselves through language and culturally mediated understandings.[8]

The very virtues and special powers attributed to children in the representational conventions we are considering conscribe and trivialize children's authority. Theirs is a "universal" but nonspecific, generally powerless form of truth. The ritualized figure of children as unknowing seers divides "truth" into two mutually exclusive kinds: universal, transcendent, timeless, affective, moral, incontestable truth, on the one hand, and factual, temporal, historical, political, ambiguous, contestable, specific, rational truth, on the other. Children have allochronic, transcendent "wisdom" as a birthright; adults have historical, factual "knowledge" (and some may grow wise again when old). Of course, actual children and actual child-adult social relationships do not usually conform to this ritual divide.

CHILDREN: AMBASSADORS OF PEACE

It would be impossible to list all the books, music, and other cultural artifacts that link children with peace.[9] To pick a single example from a multitude, Joan Walsh Anglund's diminutive picture book for children, *Peace Is a Circle of Love* (1993), is dedicated to "the children of the world, our teachers of peace." In this genre, children are positioned as teachers of adults, as the pure human beings who innocently speak truths about world peace. Musical versions of the same message abound. One example is a compact disc, *Cheryl Melody presents . . . WORLD PEACE: The Children's Dream! A Multicultural Musical for the Whole Family!* (Melody 1997; see also Pinder 1995). Another is the musical director's score *Peace Child: A Musical Fantasy about Children Bringing Peace to the World* (Peace Child Foundation 1987). It is surely not an accident that this common sense exists, and I do not want to suggest that children are not honest, imaginative, and insight-ful—they are, remarkably often, just as adults are. It is more interesting to ask: What do these books on peace do, affectively and socially? What are their intended audiences? The cultural artefacts connecting children and peace (like children and nature, or the environment) are located in a sphere of selectively transnational production usually quite disconnected from the transnational arenas of "real" politics, "real" business, and "real" history—that is to say, of "practical reason" (Sahlins 1976). Yet politicians and businessmen might also buy books and music on peace for their chil-dren, as part of their children's moral and sentimental education, just as they might buy books about "baby animals" to teach compassion and re-spect for nature. It is as if the figure of "peace" were ritually sealed in certain cultural and temporal sites—like the time set apart as "early childhood" and transnational ritual spheres like U.N. international ceremonial discourses (see, e.g., Vittachi 1993).

This opens up a host of questions about what "peace" might mean, and how, when, and where the concept is in use. It is conspicuously *not* an an-thropological category, perhaps for good reasons. Describing the status quo of his time, José Luis Aranguren (1966: 591) wrote:

> Order means peace and, from our point of view, international peace—peace in the minimal sense of no war, coexistence. . . . Can war perhaps be prevented through expounding and defending the abstract principle of peace? It is to be doubted. . . . The manifestoes of intellectuals who are given to making appeals to the collective conscience, and so forth, serve as "tranquillizers" to their signatories, give a luster to that object of beauty which is their *"bonne conscience."*

The figure of children can also act as such a tranquilizer. That is, children as moral subjects are used in international ceremonial discourses as ritual fetishes of peace, as the diminutive consciences of the "world community." Of course, many such appeals for peace and justice arise from very real and urgent concerns. Nevertheless, these appeals and images of children as teachers and ambassadors of peace are also used in less urgent ways, as a tranquilizing convention. Sometimes it even seems that calls for world peace, or peace of any kind, are doomed to be infantilized and that if they leave their ritually ascribed realm of "early childhood," elementary school, or "U.N. Days," they find no place in the adult world of real politics, real history. They become caricatures, as in the 1960s, when calls for peace were dismissed as utopian pipe dreams of strung-out flower children.

One example of this tranquilizing dynamic, at its most cynical, is former President George W. Bush's post–September 11 campaign to have each American child send a dollar to an Afghan child, care of "America's Fund for Afghan Children."

> President Bush thanked America's youngest citizens for helping to ease the burdens of their counterparts in Afghanistan, where the United States continues to bomb. "Winter arrives early in Afghanistan and it's cold and the children need clothes, food and medicine. Thanks to American children, fewer of them will be cold there," he said. President Bush said that by contributing to the fund, American children could join the war against terrorism. "There's evil in this world, and we can overcome evil," he said, later reassuring the young crowd that the U.S. government is "doing everything it can to make you safe." . . . Penny King-Vaughan, a Boys and Girls Club leader from Norfolk, Va., said the event has given her an opportunity to teach club members about the predicament of Afghan children. "They didn't understand why we were sending money to [a country the United States was bombing]," she said. "We had to make them understand it's a small group of people hurting us, not a whole country. It is not children hurting us." (Kriner 2001: 2; square brackets in original)

I interpret this principally as political posturing, akin to politicians' "kissing babies." As a political maneuver, "America's Fund for Afghan Children" is effective precisely because it appears to be above politics, transcendent; it is the signifying power of children that enables the maneuver.

Remembering her own childhood in the former Soviet Union, in what is now Kazakhstan, Zhanara Nauruzbayeva wrote:

> It was general custom all across the Soviet schools to have "urok mira" (peace lesson) on the first day of school on September 1st. I distinctly remember my first day of the first grade in 1985. Our teacher . . . introduced herself and said that our first lesson would be the lesson of peace. . . . I recall clearly the conversation about Samantha Smith, a little girl from America who wrote letters to Ronald Reagan and Mikhail Gorbachev asking them to stop the arms race. Her example found a lot

of inspiration and sparked a girl in the Soviet Union, Katya Lycheva, to follow her example. Katya also wrote letters to the leaders of the two countries begging them to pursue peaceful means and stop destruction. There was a poster in our classroom that had a picture of the smiling Samantha Smith. . . . Also, I remember that all throughout our drawing/arts classes, we used to draw pictures featuring the globe, the dove of peace, and bombs with the words NATO or USA on them crossed out with red. From my recollection, these items were pretty ubiquitous in all of the drawings of my classmates. Most of my pictures were various renderings of these same elements. I remember that I got quite skillful in drawing the olive branch in the beak of the dove or the meridians and parallels on the globe. Thus, not only are the children used/represented as ambassadors of peace in the media, but this image is also instilled in children ourselves, thus creating circles of reproduction.[10]

In most of its elements, this visual grammar—conjugating peace through children and doves—could be a description of many elementary schools in the United States and, likely, many other places. Absent the bombs identified as "NATO" or "USA," the images are familiar. And Nauruzbayeva is right: while children's drawings, letters, and poems about peace and hope are consumed by adults as spontaneous truths from innocent minds as yet untainted by politics or calculation, the genre is actually meticulously taught, learned, and conventionalized.[11]

In the small creases of these highly managed, ceremonial, and sentimental appeals in glossy publications are different, dissonant messages from children.[12] The large coffee-table book *Dear World: "How I'd Put the World Right"—By the Children of over Fifty Nations* (Exley and Exley 1985)[13] is filled with children's drawings and writings that conform to the safely sentimental formula of children as innocent teachers and ambassadors of world peace: "If we all loved each other we would not fight. We would hold hands. We would share. Ramdaye Singh, 5, Trinidad" (13). Yet, every now and then, other sorts of messages come through: "All women must think theirselves the value of a pearl, in the sight of men. Jannett Pusey, 16, Jamaica" (108); "The 'World Powers' store the end of the world. John C. Khumalo, 16, Botswana" (105).

Contemporary uses of children as ambassadors of world peace reveal something of the hollowed-out political meanings that "world peace" tends to have now. Whereas in the immediate aftermath of the Second World War the necessity of "world peace" was urgently and earnestly debated by formidable adults like Albert Einstein and Eleanor Roosevelt, during the Cold War and still now, world peace has primary, but trivialized, significance as a utopia, rhetorically deployed in appropriate ritual contexts. Many of these ritualized contexts are strongly pedagogical in intent, but this is paradoxical, as Laurie Kain Hart has pointed out: "Logically, these peace messages and pedagogies for children are coals to Newcastle. If children are, by their very nature, naked humanity, peace, and goodwill, why 'teach' them about it? This 'teaching' is clearly not pedagogy to form the adult because we don't expect the kids to grow into 220 lb. men who cuddle baby animals. Rather, it's a form of 'appropriate activity' for children, a kind of confinement in what is meant to be their nature."[14]

Peace in the sense of world peace has thus undergone an infantilization by being identified with childhood. This is comparable to the frequent trivializing dismissal of international conventions, the International Criminal Court, and the Universal Declaration of Human Rights. For example, the former U.S. ambassador to the United Nations, Jeane Kirkpatrick, dismissed the category of "economic, social, and cultural rights" in the Universal Declaration as "a letter to Santa Claus."[15]

CHILDREN ARE OUR FUTURE

"Children are our future" is an utter cliché, of course. Popular songs, sentimental sayings, and innumerable sites in public culture in the West proclaim the equation "children are the future," which also travels transnationally, if unevenly.[16] The "children are the future" equation is also made by way of a fiduciary logic.[17] That is, to help, heal, protect, or educate children *now* is to "invest in the future." The U.N. Children's Fund (UNICEF) encourages us to think of investing in girls as an investment in women (Kurz and Prather 1995). The journal *Corrections Today* carries the article "America's Future: The Necessity of Investing in Children" (Breed 1990), while *Issues in Science and Technology* describes healthy children as an investment in the future (Omenn 1988). And as Wall (2004: 165) remarks, "One of the most influential books on childhood in recent years is the Nobel Prize–winning economist Gary Becker's 1981 *Treatise on the Family*. Here, Becker applies 'rational choice' economic theory to child rearing to show that everything parents and society do for children is really a subtle and complex calculation of market self-interest. . . . That is, parental 'investment' of time, money, and resources should be calculated in view of its anticipated short- and long-term emotional, familial, and financial payoff." (Not all of the fiduciary calculations pertaining to children are as ghoulishly individualistic as Becker's, of course.)

While the equation of children with the future of humanity appears universal, and undoubtedly travels a wide transnational route, that does not mean that historically and culturally specific assumptions are not embedded in it. One example of this cultural specificity is that *children are our future* depends for its efficacy on specific chronotopes. If children are about new beginnings and about futures as yet unspoiled and unmarked, this may be because time is rendered in a linear, Christian way. Each new dot in the line is an opportunity for self-improvement and for the improvement of others, for bettering "the world" (cf. Weber 2000 [1930]). The equation also depends on an implicitly declaratory, moralizing universalism; this is one constitutive dimension of the transnational ritual sphere I am tracing in this chapter. It is everywhere in evidence in the discursive and other social practices of international organizations and nongovernmental organizations whose mandate is "children" and which work under the banner of an unmarked secular, modernist universalism (cf. Bornstein 2003).

And yet, alongside the ritual sphere, in other cultural contexts, other understandings of the figure of the child exist. As Veena Das (1996: 263) has demonstrated, for example, children in India are neither blank slates nor naked bundles of bare humanity (cf. Agamben 1998); they are persons with histories, and there is "no assumption that the child embodies innocence." "In Indian society the child is not regarded as a tabula rasa on which society inscribes whatever it wishes. Rather, the child is believed to bring with him memories of his previous birth as well as preconception memories—the *samskaras* he may have formed in the mother's womb. . . . The child . . . is seen as coming into the world with a memory and an understanding of languages that elude the adult" (264, 265; see also Gupta 2001). In the Indian context, then, and in many others, the equation *children are our future* looks impoverished or even like a cosmological mistake (see, e.g., Gottlieb 2004; Okri 1991, 1996; Amadi 1991; Reynolds 1995). It is important, nevertheless, to recognize that the equation carries weight; it underwrites many humanitarian projects around the world, as Erica Bornstein (2003: 67–95) has shown in her ethnographic research on child sponsorship and Christian evangelism in contemporary Zimbabwe. There, the phenomenon of

Western sponsors' sending money and gifts to Zimbabwean children whom they have "adopted" often creates tensions in actually existing, impoverished families and communities. While the faraway Western sponsors may think of "their" children as bundles of naked humanity that could belong to "any of us," actually existing Zimbabwean parents and others struggle to understand why one specific child and not another (and not the child's wider social network) was singled out for aid and attention. The lessons of Christian charity and duty to the future sometimes seem out of place and difficult to decipher there. As Bornstein (2003: 170) points out, "The discourse that fuels a good deal of global humanitarian aid is neither neutral nor secular; it is often Christian." Much of what I have examined here is indeed part of a long Christian tradition of thinking about children, just as surely as doves are symbols of peace. That tradition, with all of its structures of feeling and moral economies, is implicit in many (although by no means all) contemporary humanitarian practices and expectations.

One figure that tends to get smuggled into the *children are the future* equation is the family. In his article "Children of the Future," Marshall Berman (1993: 222) notes, "'The family' equals the future; to not have kids is to 'get out as early as you can' from life." It is not just any kind of future that requires tending in the present; it is the future of Humanity (Mankind), a universalized future that depends on symbolic and political generational reproduction. The mechanism of reproduction is often imagined in these discursive contexts as very orderly. It is not about liminality or dangerous transformation or eruptions of the unexpected (though, of course, in other sites of futuristic cultural production, the things to come can be profoundly unnerving). Perhaps reacting to the conservatism of the *children are the future* equation, the Sex Pistols sang, "We are the future / there is no future" (quoted in ibid.: 221). In a similar vein, the band Serial Killer put out a T-shirt with the words "Children Are the Future." The words were printed on a photograph of a pretty, white little girl pointing a gun; she wore a stern expression and a red crocheted hat. Behind her stood a grown white man with a black cap, sunglasses, and a beard. Is this really to be "our future," then? The Christian theologian John Wall (2004: 182) concludes his thoughtful article on children by affirming that "children should be viewed as the hope of the world." Hayden White (1998) has suggested that children are often thought of as a kind of "principle of hope" (a utopian principle) that gets set against the logic of "History" and "Reality." (Ernst Bloch [1986], of course, famously defined utopia as the principle of hope.)

If we accept that the liberal internationalist and humanitarian representational regimes I have traced here often depend on a "domestication of hope," we need to study how that domestication occurs, and with what consequences. One of the effects of the symbolic and discursive practices in which children augur "our future" is depoliticization, not only of children and childhood but of the projects in which figures of children are deployed in this idealizing way in various transnational ritual spheres (e.g., the United Nations, Save the Children, World Vision, Peace Child, etc.). This is evident in the framing of humanitarian crises in Central Africa, for example. There, in the aftermath of genocide and in the midst of continuing war, aid organizations and visiting dignitaries (from Tipper Gore to the late Princess Diana) have held in their arms the figure of the child as the principle of hope in Ernst Bloch's sense. The child is the principle of hope on which many futuristic utopias depend, and also a universalizing (but not universal) standard of a certain basic purity, and pure suffering. These compelling and charismatic figures of children are often understood to have important functions, not only in fund-raising, but also in "civilizing" and "humanizing" parties to political conflict. In the aftermath of great violence and loss of trust, children easily come to embody the possibility of other, better futures, and of "peace" (as elusive as that concept is, analytically). Peace and innocence thus come to be ritually coupled in powerful (but also disempowering) ways. Such discursive and representational practices involve a certain "domestication of hope" and a domestication of children as subjects of history, subversion, and imagination.

CONCLUSION

> A critique is not a matter of saying that things are not right as they are. It is a matter of pointing out on what kinds of assumptions, what kinds of familiar, unchallenged, unconsidered modes of thought the practices that we accept rest. . . . Practicing criticism is a matter of making such facile gestures difficult.
> —MICHEL FOUCAULT, "Practicing Criticism"

I have tried here to identify the (often facile) moralizing and affective uses of children as symbols of world harmony and human goodness and innocence, as sufferers, as seers of truth, as "our" teachers of peace, as "our" future, and, indeed, as elementary forms of an ideal humanity (a humanity idealized in a historically particular manner). I have tried to examine these moralizing representational practices critically. But one might well ask: Are these moving, hopeful visions not, after all, better than their opposites: racism and xenophobia, war and violence? Are they not forms of anti-racism and pacifism? Is humanitarianism not better than the cold cost-benefit rationalities of market capitalism and U.S. imperialism? Do they not therefore deserve a more tender and respectful regard, especially in these political times? Respect is what I have tried to give them here. It is easier to develop a critical analysis of racisms than of antiracisms and easier to analyze the prosecution of war than the making of peace (in all of its regional and historical specificities). Both practices of criticism are important. In the spirit of Michel Foucault's remarks about criticism I offer some concluding thoughts and questions.

The work of Stuart Hall and colleagues (1978), Paul Gilroy (1991, 2000), and others shows that just as racisms are historically situated cultural systems, so, too, are antiracisms. If the "anatomy of racism" (Goldberg 1990) is complex and important to analyze, so, too, is the anatomy of antiracism. Antiracisms take many forms—for example, socialist antiracism or Christian antiracism as it came to be exemplified in the antislavery campaign. They may also take the form of liberal tolerance: "We are all different, and we should value those differences." They may likewise assert that we are all "the same" after all, "the human family," "the global family," the "Family of Man" (a trope that Barthes brilliantly analyzed in 2001 [1957]). Liberal humanist tolerance often involves the cataloguing of human and cultural diversity as well as the simultaneous assertion of an ultimate, underlying essence of sameness. In this mode, I have suggested, the figure of children is often set in representational motion: children know innocent, timeless, ultimate truths about our human sameness and our fundamental (if often obscured) human goodness. They see beyond the "barriers" and "obstacles" of cultural, national, racial, and other differences. Here children are asked to stand up and be counted as generically human moral subjects and to address "the world." ("We are the world, we are the children," as a popular song proclaims.)[18] They are placed on an ethereal pedestal in the transnational ritual sphere that I have tried to sketch here, and this is especially evident in the broad field of humanitarian interventions (and, I would argue, other philanthropic modes of power). Sometimes it is the generic moral figure of children that stands there; at other times, specific children (remarkably often, girls) stand there alone, as representatives of all children and of the moral conscience of the world. Anne Frank, Zlata Filipovic, Irma Hadzimuratovic, Sadako Sasaki, Samantha Smith, Katya Lycheva, and the famously photographed young Vietnamese girl whose body was burned by napalm, Kim Phuc, have all stood there and wrenched the hearts of millions—at least momentarily. The trouble is that, from this pedestal, it is nearly impossible for actual children to act in the world as political, historical subjects. They are set apart by adults in an infantile utopian dimension that is freely celebrated and almost as freely ignored. They are called on to speak for mankind and ritually miniaturized into silence; they are intensively commodified and sacralized as priceless (Zelizer 1994). All this could be otherwise.

Are there sites, then, where children are not so without agency, not thus sealed off and made sacred? Perhaps they are *Outside over There*, as Sendak (1981) has suggested. Following him there, I was reminded of all the other children's tales and stories where adults are only vaguely, ineffectually, irrelevantly present, or then quite killed off by the storyteller. In these stories, children are the real, knowing subjects. They are often separated from their parents, as in *The Famous Five* books by Enid Blyton, or their remaining parent is a permissive, gregarious sea captain who is usually away, as in *Pippi Longstocking* by Astrid Lindgren. The heroes and heroines are remarkably often orphans (or specifically motherless) like Cinderella, Snow White, Bambi, Little Orphan Annie, Little Foot, and scores of others. These stories naturalize the largely Western, modern idea that childhood is somehow essentially different from adulthood. As Stephens has remarked, "Many children's stories and songs—as well as works by romantically inclined child researchers—represent childhood as 'another country.'"[19]

In the humanist antiracism that informs mainstream humanitarian practices and sensibilities (Haskell 1985), there is little space for children who know "too much" or for children who hate particular presidents, political regimes, or, indeed, anyone. Children are not supposed to hate. They are not supposed to take up arms (not unwillingly and even less willingly). They are not supposed to hurt or kill, or be hurt or killed. Yet most actual children are worldly in ways that do not fit the transnational ritual sphere that I have tried to identify here. Stephens has reflected that "more and more children these days are being seen as deviations from the norm of the 'ideal child' living 'an ideal childhood.' But at what point does the accumulation of deviations begin to constitute a crisis for modern definitions of children and childhood? At what point must new definitions and new paradigms be developed? I argue that we are at a crisis point now in relation to international representations of children."[20]

The real, actual children do not displace the ritual children who inhabit the transnational ritual sphere. The latter have an efficacy of their own. (And actual children are subject to the pedagogies of ritual childhood in their schools on United Nations Day, Peace Day, and Children's Day, as well as through books, film, music, and other sources.) Actual children and their idealized counterparts are subject to similar forces of depoliticization and dehistoricization. In questioning the depoliticization and dehistoricization of children, I do not intend to deny that children are both subjects and objects. They are objects of love and protection, desire and nostalgia, cruelty and violence—whether by adults or other children. As numerous scholars have done before me (e.g., Stephens 1995; James and Prout 1997; Ivy 1995; and James 2004), I am suggesting that there is room for rethinking children as subjects—as *persons* and not just as elementary forms of "our shared humanity." By suggesting that children be permitted to be *persons* and to step off the "ethereal pedestal" (Wall 2004), I am not arguing that children as subjects should then be like adult subjects, let alone that their proper destiny is as maximizing, autonomous, bounded individuals making rational choices. Like adults, children live in relationships with other people (adults and children). This simple fact is often missing from the sphere I have tried to make visible here. *Children* is a relational term; it is rendered meaningful by its opposition to the unmarked category *adults*. If we take the former seriously as an object of study, the latter is made productively stranger, too.

If we doubt the spaces opened up to children by liberal humanism, what are the alternatives? How can we think better about children and politics, and children as political beings? This is a very thorny question, as Hannah Arendt was to realize (see also James and Prout 1997: xiii). A bitter controversy was provoked by her essay "Reflections on Little Rock," in which she "resoundingly thumped the school desegregationists [in the United States] for putting children on the front line of a political battle" (Elshtain 1994: 4). Jean Bethke Elshtain's essay "Political Children" is a thoughtful account of this controversy. She explains Arendt's reasons for her unpopular stance: "Arendt's own memories . . . were of German young people engrafted into the Nazi state through massive mobilization efforts that had as their explicit aim eviscerating independent parental authority and private life" (8). Arendt perceptively states that we should not insist on "separating children from the adult community as though they were not living in the same world and as though childhood were an autonomous human state, capable of living by its own laws" (Arendt 1959, quoted in Elshtain 1994: 7). Nevertheless, Arendt argues, childhood should be protected by shielding it from public, political life. "Childhood is not a political condition from which children must be (misguidedly) liberated. It is a necessary form or container for human being in its most fragile stage, a time of concealment and preparation. We abandon and betray children if we deprive them of this protection" (Elshtain 1994: 7, paraphrasing Arendt). Elshtain goes on to consider children's roles (or, as some would argue, the political uses of children) in other contexts, such as the more recent antiabortion protests. Her own conclusion is to recognize that "children are never spared politics. Every child must take his or her bearings in a particular time and place. . . . Childhood does not exist, and has never existed, in a *cordon sanitaire*" (ibid.: 13; emphasis in original; see also Coles 1986). Therefore, Elshtain (1994: 15) suggests, we must recognize with Arendt that children are worldly but that we could think of them as "apprentice citizens." This might be a helpful alternative to the unthinking demand for childhood innocence (cf. Benjamin 1999: 118). One might suggest further that there is room here for recognizing that it is not only adults who teach children (and that many adults are less than ideal parents and teachers). Children also teach each other. And there is in childhood (as at any point in a life) a great deal of autodidacticism, too.

What would Arendt have thought of the phenomenon of contemporary child soldiers? The possibility should at least be entertained that the scandalous child soldier is not the exception but the rule. Children do things in the world; they are worldly. There is no securely virtuous stand to take in relation with these issues, but thinking about them does generate a whole host of researchable questions. One of these has to do with temporality. The 1989 U.N. Convention on the Rights of the Child advances a universalizing age limit of eighteen to childhood; the age of "eighteen is the point when age no longer matters" (James 2004: 30). Much of what I have been tracing here depends on and is, indeed, constituted by a specific linear chronotope that is broadly naturalized and universalized but is, in fact, far from universally meaningful. "The concepts of childhood and children bear the legacy of deterministic age-based models of the child" (ibid.: 35). Indeed, the developmental paradigm has had a powerful, deterministic grip on studies of children (ibid.: 2003; cf. Hirschfeld 2002). There is an implicit evolutionist cast to this cultural "common sense." To make it visible, one need look no further than Emile Durkheim. When he went in search of the elementary forms of religious life, he sought the "simplest," most "primitive" forms and found them in aboriginal Australia. In a parallel fashion, the categories of "children" and "childhood" have stood for the elementary forms of humanity. These elementary forms have been translated in practice into an assumption of innocence—innocence as not-knowing, not-being in and of the world as it actually exists. This, in turn, has come to be the gold standard of political neutrality and blamelessness. It is difficult to raise funds for victims of political violence who are not certifiable as blameless—that is, innocent.

Why do people not give money to adult men? Do they worry, "What if the men did something wrong? What if they are 'the bad guys' after all?" People may imagine that they escape these dilemmas by giving money instead to children. This does not mean, of course, that one should not give money to children (or other people, or organizations). It does mean that one should have a political analysis to go with it, as well as some sustained curiosity about the social contexts of poverty and suffering.

So, if one cares about the conditions of the poor or of children, one should care more about the specific regional circumstances that create those conditions. People may want to help and to give and yet not want to get involved in tracking the political complexities of, say, warfare in the Congo. It is easier to just give money to big-eyed children, as aid organizations are aware. It is important to note, too, the wide range of variation among the organizations that make representational use of children. Some organizations (like Oxfam) are more inclined than others to contextualize suffering within a sustained political and economic analysis. Two different organizations that deploy the same representational devices for fundraising might have very different organizational and political strategies. These issues open up a series of answerable questions. I hope that this analysis will contribute to framing an open and growing set of research questions that could be approached ethnographically and historically.

Key among these would be to examine empirically what these representations actually mean to people. It might be, for instance, that what appears to be a universalistic call to bare humanity is heard by some people as a call to Christians. Others might be hailed as internationalists. It would be important, therefore, to consider the specific contexts in which people receive these representations, as Bornstein (2003) has done. It is important, too, to consider the givers of aid—like the recipients—as political subjects.

Another terrain of questioning is opened up by tracing affect and sentiment in the humanitarian and humanistic uses of children. In "Affective States" (2004), Ann Stoler marshals historical and ethnographic evidence to show how the naturalized division of reason and affect, and the privileging of the former, has hobbled analyses of colonial rule. Her insights are enabling for theorizing the affective work currently done by representations of children. Citing Janis Jenkins (1991: 139–65), Stoler (2004: 9) observes that "states do more than control emotional discourse, they attempt to 'culturally standardize the organization of feeling' and produce as well as harness emotional discourse within it." Stoler suggests further that "such a focus opens another possible premise: that the role of the state is not only as Antonio Gramsci defined it, in the business of 'educating consent.' More basically, such consent is made possible, not through some abstract process of 'internalization,' but by shaping appropriate and reasoned affect, by directing affective judgements, by severing some affective bonds and establishing others, by adjudicating what constitutes moral sentiments—in short, by educating the proper distribution of sentiments and desires" (9). These are, of course, historically specific practices (10; see also Haskell 1985).

As Alasdair MacIntyre writes, "Virtues are dispositions not only to act in particular ways, but also to *feel* in particular ways. To act virtuously is not to act against inclination; it is to act from inclination formed by the cultivation of virtues. Moral education is an '*éducation sentimentale*'" (MacIntyre 1984: 149; quoted in Stoler 2004: 11). The historical shaping of "international opinion" against such practices as torture and for human rights, women's rights, and children's rights has much to do with the shaping and circulation of affect in the way that Stoler describes. There is research to be done on the effects of representations of children in "educating the distribution of sentiments."

Finally, there are researchable questions about the concept of peace. Making peace and keeping the peace is at least as complicated as making war. Linking children with peace in the ritualized and sentimentalized manner I have described trivializes both children and peace. But what would it mean to examine forms of peace ethnographically? Just as racism is not an absolute timeless evil and antiracism an absolute timeless good, war and peace are not moral absolutes; they are, obviously, historically, culturally specific practices. Both can be ambivalent, ambiguous, and ethically fraught political arrangements. The question for our times might be: Why is peace so readily infantilized (and thus depoliticized)? Why is it "good to think" as a fuzzy and sentimental concept that has so little bearing on actual politics as practiced? What is the historical relationship between the infantilization of peace and the pacification or domestication of the category of children? Attention to the representational uses of children in the constitution of a depoliticized "humanity" may help us imagine new ways of thinking about both children and peace in the midst of politics and history.

NOTES

Many people have given me invaluable help in thinking through this chapter, suggesting readings and providing ethnographic examples. My heartfelt thanks, in roughly chronological order, to the late Sharon Stephens, Jim Ferguson, Per Egil Mjaavatn, Jean Comaroff, Purnima Mankekar, Norma Field, Carolyn Steedman, Erica Bornstein, Christina Schwenkel, Monica Della Croce, Clara Kao Magliola, Kyriaki Papageorgiou, Amanda Moore, Akhil Gupta, Alex Balasescu, Bill Maurer, Sally Falk Moore, Arthur Kleinman, Byron Good, Christopher Dole, Staffan Lofving, Aila Ferguson, Elias Ferguson, Zhanara Nauruzbayeva, Ramah McKay, Kevin O'Neill, Laurie Kain Hart, Thet Shein Win, and Selim Shahine. I would also like to thank the Center for Advanced Study in the Behavioral Sciences, Stanford, California, for giving me protected research and writing time in 1999 and 2000.

1 DeVries 2001; also cited in Wall 2004: 168n23.

2 John Wall (2004: 181), whose work I have cited extensively in this section, actually concludes his article by foregrounding a variant of this angel-devil tension: "While children share the ambiguity of human good and evil with the rest of us, they do so in a peculiarly sharp way. . . . Children experience in a more direct and unmediated way than adults the primordial dimensions of human existence, and the more so the younger the child. It is in this fallen innocence that, at least from the Christian ethical point of view, the true 'mystery' of children's initial being in the world may be said to consist." Wall concludes that children are productively thought of as "fallen angels."

3 Ramah McKay, personal communication, 2009.

4 Sharon Stephens, personal communication, 1994.

5 In stark contrast, see Nakazawa 2004 [1987]; Yamazaki 1995; and Yoneyama 1999.

6 Noam Chomsky (1999) offers a trenchant analysis of the Vienna Conference.

7 One popular example of children as seers came on to newsstands in the March 1998 issue of *Life* magazine. The lead story was about children and truth, and on the cover

was written: "Kids' Pictures to God: What Children Want God to See" (Adato 1998). A little (white) girl was pictured holding up a nature photograph for God to see. Her truth, as it transcended politics, became apolitical and, once again, ritually sealed off in a politically safe and domesticated register. It was not of the here and now, not worldly.

8 Sharon Stephens, personal communication, 1994. I would also like to thank Laurie Kain Hart for the insight that therapeutic image-making by children is usefully considered in relation to the status of language as "Babel," as that which divides; the prelinguistic, then, is the raw human.

9 A few of the children's books in this genre are Nathan Aaseng, *The Peace Seekers: The Nobel Peace Prize* (1992); Katherine Scholes, *Peace Begins with You* (1990); Holly Near, *The Great Peace March* (1993); Sheila Hamanaka, *Peace Crane* (1995); Jennifer Garrison and Andrew Tubesing, *A Million Visions of Peace* (1995); Ann Durrell and Marilyn Sachs, eds., *The Big Book for Peace* (1990); and Joan Walsh Anglund, *Peace Is a Circle of Love* (1993).

10 Zhanara Nauruzbayeva, personal communication, 2009.

11 When I discussed this research project with an elementary school teacher in an after-school day care program in Irvine, California, he asked the children with whom he worked to draw pictures of war and peace. When I saw the set of drawings a few weeks later, I was startled by their ritual sameness. They were as Nauruzbayeva described, with the difference that the bombs and bomber aircraft were not identified. The potentially perpetual, calculatedly diffuse U.S. "war on terror" might have something to do with the absence of a named "enemy" in the children's drawings.

12 One such crease is Naguib Mahfouz's poem, "A Prayer" (1997), which begins, "I was less than seven years old when I said a prayer for the revolution." Thank you to Chris Dole for this reference.

13 This book is also published under the title *My World/Peace: Thoughts and Illustrations from the Children of All Nations* (1985). It is part of a boxed set in which the other volume is titled *My World/Nature*.

14 Laurie Kain Hart, personal communication, 2008.

15 Cited in Chomsky 1999: 21. I thank Harri Englund for this reference.

16 Examples include Kent 1991 ("Our principal link to the future is our children. What will their lives be like? Our thinking about the future should be informed by concern with the prospects for [those] who will occupy the future" [32]); Chan 1990; Children's Express 1993; Benedek 1990; O'Connor 1993; and John Conrad 1990.

17 I thank Bill Maurer for this insight.

18 *We Are the World*, written by Michael Jackson and Lionel Richie, produced by Quincy Jones and Michael Omartian, 1985, Columbia Records. The single was produced to raise money for African famine relief and featured a large group of famous musicians such as Billy Joel, Bruce Springsteen, Diana Ross, and Paul Simon. The song was remade in 2010 to raise money for Haitian earthquake relief and released during the opening ceremony of the Winter Olympics.

19 Sharon Stephens, personal communication, 1994.

20 Ibid.

NARRATIVE, HUMANITY, AND PATRIMONY IN AN EQUATORIAL AFRICAN FOREST ∽

Rebecca Hardin

ADOLPH LEMOGALI was on vacation from high school in Bangui, the capital of the Central African Republic (CAR), when he appeared on the front porch of the house I was renting. I was doing anthropological research in Bayanga, a town on the Sangha River in the southwestern CAR well known as a biodiversity conservation site. Tourists came to view forest wildlife such as elephants and gorillas, and to interact with forest residents, particularly hunters and gatherers known as "Pygmies." It was a hot June afternoon, and Adolph had a sheaf of papers under his arm. He asked whether I would help edit his novel about tourism conservation efforts. He was fascinated by the way German- and U.S.-based organizations were attempting forest protection in the area, while French interests still owned and managed timber and trophy-hunting concessions.

I was delighted at the prospect of reading his manuscript for the perspective it would offer on the political complexities of this multiuse zone where German and French interests had competed for colonial control, and where multiple African communities had long collided as well, forging commercial and cultural links. In my research on trophy hunting and touring in equatorial African forests I had encountered a novel called *Le silence de la forêt* (*The Silence of the Forest*), by Etienne Goy-emidé, hailed as the national writer of the CAR. Written in the early 1980s, it chronicled one Central African civil servant's journey into the forested hinterland and periphery of his country.

The narrator of that novel finds himself transformed by the journey; it transforms his awareness of himself and his nation. Reading it had called into question my own assumptions about these forests and their inhabitants. Written as though colonizing influences were located in urban landscapes, the novel contrasts the unsullied forest space of traditional African heritage with the corrupting influences of "civilization" in the capital city of Bangui. Could Adolph describe transnational encounters within this forest crucible, capturing their historically rooted rivalries and alliances? If so, he might reveal something about what anthropologist Anna Tsing (1993) has termed "marginality in an out-of-the-way place."

This chapter looks beyond Western versus African perspectives on contested circumstances of forest use to reveal various and historically changing African views that question colonial and postcolonial assertions of humanity. More precisely, it asks how the workings of humanity, which the editors of this volume delimit in terms of sentiment, object, and threat, are used to constrain particular human practices such as hunting and fishing, in the interest of protecting and using the natural world in ways deemed best for "humanity" in general. We thus begin to see the contradictions through which humanity as a universal category could also be part of expanding state interests that relegate entire groups of people to social status as "part of nature," closer to animals, and thus constrained in their assertions of citizenship or human rights.

Goyemidé himself located his career as a civil servant in the oversight of multiple national projects concerning culture, education, and scientific research. His lifework illustrates the interpenetration of government and cultural production in a French postcolonial setting where to be literate, in the novelistic sense, was itself a claim to intellectually inflected notions of "humanity" that divided educated Central African citizens from their subjects. Such assertions of literacy, through authorship of policy, marketing, and fictional visions of forest economies, are a common thread across colonial and postcolonial eras where formal education has been the key to membership in wider economic and cultural worlds. African intellectuals in struggling nation-states have used literacy to confront the challenges of governing across internally varied populations whose social differences are marked by subsistence differences. I use Goyemidé's text, as well as facts about its interpretation and circulation, to explore how distinctions between the human and the animal characterize colonial and postcolonial governance in equatorial Africa. Further, I suggest that humanity must be understood in relation to animality, as these categories inflect social hierarchies.

Contemporary environmental politics, like their historical predecessors, define poachers as simultaneous threats to the integrity of ecosystems and the sovereignty of state borders. An increasing emphasis on forests, their wildlife and other resources, as international rather than national patrimony helps us see why Adolph's account is ultimately not written. Instead, narratives of these rainforests abound that, like Goyemidé's, relate to and reproduce the dominant narratives of great white hunting (and, increasingly, antihunting). Such narratives take the forest, and its residents, as existing outside of modernity—either outside of humanity or as some more sentimental embodiment of "our common humanity." They are thus relegated largely to a backdrop against which romantic tales of heroic exploration, exploitation, and protection of forests can unfold.

In taking up a work that has been dismissed as imitating the initiation narratives that abound in colonial travel literature, I take cues from several promising streams of scholarship on the intersections of cultural production and political process. David Samuels, in his work with Apache artists, calls "interrogative genres" those that both emulate and appropriate dominant forms, investing them with particular and unexpected meanings. Bonnie Honig (2001) uses the notion of genre to interrogate governance itself. She suggests that narratives about democracy tend to adhere to romantic genre conventions, with the distance between foreigners and natives ultimately being resolved in happy union (rather than in a more gothic genre, where the distinction between hero and evildoer, outsider and insider is more vexing and less fixed).[1]

I seek neither to explode nor to embrace the notion of genre but rather to home in on particular elements of Goyemidé's "initiatory account" and relate it to policy documents authored by Central Africans, while also considering those written by and about contemporary conservation professionals. I will thus show how glaring inequities that disadvantage forest dwellers result in part from the fact that complex symbolic and political relations are often simplified in situations of social change—that "in the heat of political argument the 'doubling' of the sign can often be stilled" (Bhabha 1990: 3).

THE SILENCE OF THE FOREST

Goyemidé's written work, almost entirely produced by publishers in France, is in some respects an artifact from a particular era of French cultural imperialism.[2] *Le silence de la forêt*, seen by some as a reiteration of colonial tropes of civilized versus primitive and human versus animal, nevertheless departs from and even critiques colonial narrative conventions. Such critiques emerge all the more clearly when the text is considered against a backdrop of increasing involvement by international nongovernmental organizations (NGOs) and multilateral organizations in the production of global natural "patrimony." Such campaigns rely just as much as Goyemidé's novel on colonial tropes of rainforest exploration, though they are unfolding in a world deeply shaped by neoliberal economic reforms and the retraction of states in such processes. Thus, they also increasingly favor conservation as occurring at sites that connect the global and the local, effectively erasing the category of national patrimony as linked to representative political process and making such frames less relevant to emergent regimes of environmental governance in African rainforests and elsewhere.

At present, particular zones of equatorial Africa are, in fact, conceived as international patrimony, and classified as such—as *Patrimoine Internationale*, or World Heritage Sites—under UNESCO's "Man and the Biosphere Program" (Cleaver 1992; Hecketsweiler 1990). The question of "patrimony for *whom*" is seldom addressed in the dizzying spin of images that contribute to such constructions of value. Programs such as the UNESCO's collaboration with the Smithsonian Institution/Man and the Biosphere Program, for instance, allow a scale of standardization in both meanings and methods of "management" previously unheard of.[3] At the same time, policies of structural adjustment encourage decentralization of resource management, forcing a generation of African functionaries to redefine their roles (and payrolls). Such internal contradictions are often downplayed in the meetings, reports, and publicity materials of conservation organizations.

But the popularity of the novel *Le silence* in the CAR is powerful testimony to the fact that forest use must be perceived not only in terms of material resource flows but simultaneously in terms of spatial and symbolic resources for the production of individual and national identities. The novel is an example of how, after independence, images of the forest became symbolic resources in the social construction of an imagined national community with a common cultural heritage (Anderson 1991). This community connects the novel to other writings by officials and educators, the formally educated elite of the CAR who have since independence borne those colonial legacies, twisting and transforming them in their roles as brokers or intermediaries in international relations of resource use. The CAR's national officials are precariously positioned between the demands and contributions of changing provincial communities and an increasingly environmentally conscious complex of international valuations of and prescriptions for the use or protection of that country's natural resources.

Combining close textual reading with ethnographic evidence illustrates the most nuanced ways in which "language shares with technology the power of enframing reality, of ordering forth the world in such a way as to establish a claim over it" (Spurr 1993: 184). Or, in the words of John and Jean Comaroff (1992: 40), it lays bare some relationships between "the force of meaning and the meaning of force." And yet the text by Goyemidé, and the unfinished manuscript of young Adolph Lemongali, remind us that cultural orders do not permit every story to "order forth" with force. Many versions of what these forests are (or could be) for the CAR nation-state remain rarely articulated. They are conveyed to limited readerships or in intimate conversations, rather than circulating widely to inform broader global debates. This is in part because the positions from which Central African political elites speak are perpetually imperiled. Their government is cobbled together amid successive coups and mutinies in an age where African environments are at the center of new scrambles for geopolitical and economic power. There is thus poignancy to the reading of Goyemidé's work, which was written in a period of optimism about the CAR's future as a nation-state.

The book is worth reading given the scant anthropological study of national bureaucrats as a demographic. As in other postcolonial contexts, "nationalist representations of the village community combine a fierce anticolonial rhetoric with substantial appropriation of the colonialist imagination" (Brow 1996: 219). In the CAR, those city dwellers most involved with international aid agencies and national political institutions continue to view the forest as a mysterious and highly valuable cultural and natural resource over which they have limited control, and to which they have limited access. As they become increasingly intimately involved in the proliferating possibilities for profit from the forests, they are also subject to increasing exhortations to "transparency" and "accountability" that are the central tenets of "environmental governance" agendas in international policy-making communities.

Such tenets notwithstanding, many Central Africans play contradictory roles in environmental management. A national agency may favor both large-scale logging and legal measures to protect biodiversity. A single official may cut deals with trophy hunters, or trade in ammunition, and only days later deliver speeches about preventing cruelty to animals. Such double roles are less surprising when one considers the aforementioned liberation from and appropriation of colonial models for identity that characterizes Goyemidé's writing, and confronts and shapes Central Africans through their formal and informal education.

Postcolonial studies have made it clear: what appears to be acquiescence, acceptance, or even mimicry and emulation of dominant foreign discourse may ironically, subversively resist and reformulate rhetoric of domination.[4] Texts reveal the range of historical resources from which actors draw in cultural struggles for control of equatorial African forests. Critical scholarship on property has demonstrated the contest of represented realities as preceding and irrevocably shaping contests for actual access to place or resource base (Fortmann 1995; Rose 1991; Slater 2003). So, although Goyemidé's narrative of the forest shares with international press accounts an insistence on forest worlds rife with the possibility of reversal and danger, it also resists the creation of any single authority figure, conveying instead relationships to multiple sources of authority connected across ethnic, regional, class, and linguistic categories. In reading for such proliferations we find clues to African environmental governance mechanisms that might have emerged were it not for the power of transnational international economies of pillage and environmentalist interventions. Such clues encourage us to imagine a system whereby Adolph might continue some sort of education, perhaps travel beyond the CAR's borders, rather than ending up incarcerated, trapped in a country struggling to fund both its prisons and its primary schools.

EQUATORIAL AFRICAN STATES

Political scientists have identified the equatorial African state as rhizome-like, or highly diffuse, in its structure, in part through a pervasive politics of provinces as both cultural and physical territory, or *terroir* (Bayart 1989;

Schatzberg 1988). In national politics in the CAR, the notion of the *terroir* is central to the politics of patronage, and to the nostalgic and politicized links between urban elites and their extended families and language groups in particular watersheds or provincial administrative territories (Bayart 1993).

Many of the national officials who visit the CAR's southern forests are also related by blood or marriage to local residents. They retain their ties to these communities, considering them often in their political maneuvering and capitalizing on them both to finance and to express their political identities. At the same time, many fear these regions as places where they themselves are most vulnerable to the risks that accompany upward mobility and wealth accumulation. The deputy of the Bayanga region, for example, was widely known to avoid travel there for fear of being struck by sorcery conjured by constituents jealous of his success and relative affluence. Political connections to provincial contexts embody and reproduce the notion of "terroir," linking it to very real terror of the magico-political power still wielded within kinship networks.

However, state actors arriving in a place like Bayanga are also the bearers of *terror* in the sense that Michael Taussig develops of that term, as related to broader political and economic violence of surplus extraction and regulation.[5] They bring new forms of conflict and conflict resolution involving national prisons or fines, for instance, in already vicious local and regional political struggles. Increasingly, such struggles also bear traces of deep intergenerational debates about the meaning of the past, and the possibilities for the African future of individuals like Adolph Lemongali.

Central Africa also bears a unique legacy of "despotic decentralization" connected to colonial strategies for resource extraction and administration. This legacy maintains separate sets of rights for certain elites. This results, in part, from the conjuncture of French colonial policies of "indirect rule" with, on the one hand, notions of a universalistic *francophonie* into which (certain) colonial subjects were incorporated (Miller 1993) and, on the other hand, the politics of extractive industry in equatorial Africa, which locked many rural populations into restrictive labor relations and ethnicized identities from which more formally educated urban "citizens" were exempt (Mamdani 1996).

These distinctions can be seen clearly in forest-based experiences of social identities. Historically, forest residents were not spared the rigors of forced labor in colonial concession systems, though archival sources show them also to have been more apt at eluding colonial control, and at times central to the symbolic and political efforts at resisting it (Hardin 2000). In fact, Pygmies were only legally recognized as "citizens" of the CAR during the Kolingba administration of the 1980s, a fact that has given rise to the epithet used for them, *citoyen*, a reflection that marks the irony of their legal inclusion in the rights frameworks and formal communities that constitute the Central African state.

But do they merit such ironic appellation? It ignores and denies some of their crucial economic contributions to the state, for instance the production of cash crops such as tobacco and coffee through almost exclusively Pygmy labor in some regions of the CAR (Moise 1996). Nonetheless, the options for Pygmies to be recognized as members of the Central African "nation" are more limited than for other groups of "citizens," and the same is true throughout most equatorial African states (Leonhardt 2006). This validates many of Mahmood Mamdani's (1996) arguments about the pervasive distinctions in many African societies between more metropolitan and formally educated "citizens" and more rural or ethnically marked "subjects."

Such complex historical legacies may also be linked to the susceptibility of equatorial African states themselves to "privatization" (Hibou 1998) or "criminalization," unchecked by democratic political process (Bayart, Ellis, and Hibou 1997). The political science literature on these topics frames the need for more detailed ethnographic and cultural studies of the relationships between state actors and the residents of valuable forest regions. Certainly they lend poignancy to Goyemidé's version of the forest as a place where social distinctions can be dissolved.

Today, as waves of concomitant structural adjustment, decentralization, and privatization policies have broken over the country, reducing the size and scope of the public sector there, they have also dramatically reduced the optimism many felt in the seventies and the eighties for nationalism as a means to garner and redistribute resources. Yet in Bayanga, as in many resource-rich frontier zones, the state has slowly expanded its range of actors—customs officials, police, trained guards, and administrators from environmental ministries. Most of these actors are beholden to locally active international businesses or NGOs for their work materials and transport.

This makes the place of state actors ambiguous, yet still crucial in the relationships of force, of "terror," and belonging, or "terroir," both so central to state-making in the CAR. On the one hand, political economies of foreign aid increasingly centered in Bangui distance the CAR's governing elite from direct daily dependence on the plants and animals of the provinces, inserting them instead into transnational networks of mobility, knowledge, and conspicuous consumption. On the other hand, the social autonomy of the formally educated elite is constantly undercut by a vernacular political culture that emphasizes human commonality and the fragility of dominance, through emphasis on the body as a metaphor for the body politic (Mbembe 1992; Bigo 1988).

The economic autonomy of political elites is undercut, too, by a broad set of cultural mechanisms for social leveling and wealth redistribution that is common throughout equatorial Africa (Berry 1989, 1992; Guyer 1995).[6] A political leader may become known, as did Emperor Jean-Bédel Bokassa, as *"zo ti tengo zo,"* or "one who eats others" (a phrase connoting avarice and rapacious exploitation; cannibalism is a metaphor for only the most wretched excesses of political power). It has also come to be seen as a metaphor for the violence of colonialism itself in this region.

FORESTS OF CENTRAL AFRICAN FICTION

It seems both propitious and something of a pity, given Etienne Goyemidé's lack of international recognition, to position his little-known *Le silence de la forêt* in relation to the vastly influential novel by Joseph Conrad, *The Heart of Darkness* (1983 [1910]). Both works have been criticized for a central "initiation" narrative theme that obscures more political and philosophical dimensions.[7] Yet several similarities in the narrative structure and imagery of the two books make it appropriate to reflect about this relationship as one of genre.

Le silence de la forêt recounts the story of a corrupt African school inspector named Gonaba who, while on a rural tour in the Bayanga area, enters the forest and lives there for a time. Discounted by some critics as a mere adventure narrative, the novel has received far less critical attention than the works of other contemporary authors from equatorial Africa. A reading of the text in relation to contemporary forest use practices in the CAR, however, reveals a wealth of models for human relationships, as well as for relationships to the natural world and more specifically to the forest. It thus echoes as well ethnographic work on the binary oppositions of male and female, pure and impure, human and animal, civilized and savage, relationships of interdependence and inequality in the rainforests of central Africa (Grinker 1994). It is certainly the case that Pygmies serve as a feminized foil—simultaneously revered and derided—for those less intimately involved with forest ecosystems.

Yet there are meaningful differences in the ways these tired binaries are deployed in the texts considered here. Unlike European colonial fiction, where the white administrator on a supposed civilizing mission becomes a cruel, unrecognizable man-beast (Conrad 1983 [1910]), the African school inspector in Le silence leaves behind his drunken, pretentious, vulgar state of brute-like alienation. In fact, he attains civilization, not savagery, through his journey into the heart of the forest, inverting the narrative of reversal that accompanies jungle journeys in colonial fiction.[8] Goyemidé's administrator voyages not into "the horror" of unlimited, egomaniacal power and brutality but rather away from such behavior toward an expansion of self; an acceptance of the forest as alter ego, alternative home, part of his own and of his country's identity.

The two texts differ not only in their underlying binary oppositions, however, but also in their respective political economies of production. Goyemidé had access to few material means and few of the cultural norms of literary production necessary for the creation of something that readers outside the CAR would recognize as a canon: a collection of works that constitute and consider that country's cultural heritage. If we consider book titles as condensed texts with high ideological value (Siamundelé 1994: 4), the reiteration of the term silence in Goyemidé's title and his text echoes that term's appearance in recent critiques of literature from the Central African Republic and Gabon. Does silence really refer to the forest, despite the constant cacophony of sounds described by the narrator as he travels through forest landscapes? Or might it reflect the difficulties of articulating African colonial pasts, or even of getting published as an African novelist?

In a 1991 review of Gabon's "national literature,"[9] Ambourhouet Bigmann Magloire (1991: 31) notes, "All the titles of Gabonese works that have some weight, or at least a certain notoriety, refer more or less directly to silence. . . . History is never recounted, it is never the central interest of a work: history is not inspiration, history is silence." He connects such evocations of "silence" to Gabon's experience of colonization and to the lack of written responses from "Gabonese" to Western cultural imperialism. This Gabonese "total silence," he argues, contrasts with other former colonies where the occupation by colonial forces provoked abundant denunciations and analyses in print; production of the kind that have enabled such subtle theorizing of subversive writing strategies as the one by Homi Bhabha I quoted above.

In *Notre librairie*'s 1989 special issue on the CAR's "national literature," Mathias N'gouandjika (1989: 60) titles his summary article "Le roman, entre le silence et le défi" ("The Novel, between Silence and Defiance"). He notes the late arrival of writers from the CAR on African literary scenes and explores the relationship between oral and written forms of literary expression, noting how Goyemidé interweaves the two in *Le silence*. In the same issue Goyemidé (1989: 88) himself bemoans the lack of published literary works from his country but emphasizes the vital tradition of social commentary and entertainment through theater in the CAR. Let us move from considerations in relation to a European literary canon to analysis of cultural expression about and in the forests of the CAR which, for Goyemidé, both are and are not part of the CAR as a "nation."

REPRESENTATION AND RAINFORESTS

Le silence combines idealized and derided European cultural elements with distinct, multiple African cultural elements. In fact, the novel's first section is a kaleidoscope of contrasting identity models in motion, with an emphasis on the ironies and tensions of gender relations that is unfortunately absent in the body of the book.[10] Arriving in the bush town of Bilolo, Gonaba rejoices in his privileged status as a civil servant, justifying his standard of living, higher than that of local farmers, and behaving condescendingly toward Bilolo residents (Goyemidé 1984: 22). Within a few hours Gonaba has met a Pygmy named Manga, who came to perform dances and music for the assembled dignitaries. In contrast to the others around him, and in part out of disgust and disillusionment with himself and his peers, Gonaba acknowledges as human this man whom others call an animal (30).

Throughout the novel, "discriminatory identity effects" (Bhabha 1994) are deployed in ways that demolish or displace colonial imaginings, leaving room for the emergence of new forms of identity and imagining of difference. For instance, the character of Manga the Pygmy is a mass of duplicitous contradictions that guarantee his safe passage through foreign (non-forest) worlds. His name means "tobacco" because he is paid for his labor in cigarettes. Yet when Gonaba offers him a cigarette, Manga declines. In fact he does not enjoy smoking but feigns enjoyment and performs tricks for the chief and the villagers in order to mask his true mission: to learn about them and their ways. Even Manga's arrival in the village was staged; he feigned a fall and waited for villagers to arrive and "capture" him for their chief.

Manga's careful management of his identity in the village leads Gonaba to question his own (and the villagers') assumptions that Pygmies are no more than animals. He makes a sudden decision to switch places with Manga, sending the "Pygmy" back to Bangui while he travels deep into the forest.[11] The curious and cautious gazes of these protagonists are trained on one another from the outset, across hierarchical social categories that I have referred to here in various terms: *citizen* and *subject* (and, again, recall the ironic epithet for forest foragers in the CAR: *citoyen*); *human* and *animal*; *civilized* and *savage*. The categories themselves are depicted as false and constraining, the individual characters of Manga and Gonaba as capable of enormous change in their identities: "Manga climbed for the first time into an automobile. How interesting it would be to solicit his impressions! If the one who said the habit doesn't make the monk had been there, he'd have changed opinions, for Manga had transformed the opinions the villagers held of him. Some even went so far as to shake his hand. . . . Manga at last had become one of them: a 'civilized' man" (Goyemidé 1984: 54).

For Gonaba, in contrast, the forest is a place where all is digested, dissolved, returned to oneness, where distinctions may be erased: "I feel as if I'm being crushed by the power and majesty of this imperturbable equatorial forest. I have the impression I'm in the stomach of an antediluvian monster who will any minute begin his work of digestion" (60). Digestion and dissolution of social boundaries or categories is indeed what happens; Gonaba becomes a different man. But the images through which his awareness shifts become accessible and revealing only within a broader knowledge of the contemporary CAR, and of several major themes that recur throughout the novel, serving as cues for more ethnographic interpretations of their meanings.

BODIES, KNOWLEDGE, AND THE POACHING OF POWER

Goyémidé's text generally associates the world of "whites" or of "civiliza-tion" with physical and social dysfunction. In the first chapter, Gonaba awakens in Bilolo after having imbibed too much expensive imported whis-key. He finds himself beside a girl he barely knows; pools of their own vomit surround them. Looking in a mirror, he does not recognize himself. Impo-tent, stale, and bewildered he orders his houseboy about and slowly regains a cold composure. His companion, the anonymous girl, accuses him of be-having distantly toward others, as do most "whiteblacks" (*munjuvuko*). To make sense of such an accusation one must consider the ambivalence with which key icons of social and cultural difference, such as tables, chairs, and mirrors circulate in popular traditions of Congolese painting, as well as in texts (Jewsiwiecki 1993). Goyemidé thus describes a scene of promiscuous, violent, yet oddly inverted relations of domination that can characterize the African postcolony, as people adopt, adapt, and absurdly twist the markers of difference which signified power for colonialists.

Gonaba seeks escape from so confusing and vulgar a world for which animality appears a salve or tonic. Animality is not terrifying alterity but rather an alternative to the pathologies of the modern nation-state. The narrative is laden with references to a "going back." Gonaba's favorite ani-mal, for example, is a fish—an eel, in fact. It is decidedly not the eel that appears in the plumbing of bourgeois apartments in Boris Vian's universe of absurdist, ironic reflection on French society in *L'écume des jours* (1947). Rather, perhaps in a play on Vian, Goyemidé writes of the eel as an icon for nationalist integrity: "The eel has a sense of native land. It is a patriotic fish, nationalist and chauvinist. He must always return to the seas of Sargasso to procreate. Better to die on the way to Sargasso than to settle for life in a tranquil stream" (Goyemidé 1984: 56).

But Gonaba and Manga are in fact moving forward toward and through each other, at once within and outside Western ideals of their respective identities. Gonaba's progress into the forest, for instance, is less a return to his personal origins and more a movement toward an ideal "virgin" state of Africanness. The narrator's relation to both the primitive "Pygmy" ideal he seeks in the forest and the civilized "white" reality he rejects are interest-ingly inconsistent, and utterly intertwined.

Ironically, such a return to forest "origins" is deeply mediated by conven-tions of European exploration and travel literature about a generic "jungle."

Gonaba may know Kipling quite well, but what emerges from the following passage is his (and likely the author's) lack of information about the fauna of moist forests in the CAR: "From the smallest squeaking of the grasshoppers to the heavy rolling of drums from a people of baboons, and through the songs of the cicadas, the melodious flights and lyrics of some nightingales, and the percussive and sonorous calls of the toucans, the gbako [forest] awakens. . . . The heroes from Kipling's book march through my mind" (65).

Guinea baboons (*Papio papio desmarest*), for example, are almost uniquely savanna dwellers, though other primate species inhabit the forest (*Cercopithecus* spp., *Cercocebus* spp., *Colobus gueraza, Pan trogladytes*). There are no toucans in central African forests; only the morphologically similar hornbills (*Bucerotidae*). Such zoological "nitpicking" is relevant not only to the passages about the narrator's entry into the forest but also to those about his mastery of it, when he refers to small forest duiker species (*Cephalophus spp.*) as gazelles (105). In fact the two are quite different creatures, with distinct names both in French and in local languages. Only the former reside in the CAR's forest regions; gazelles are relatively rare in the country, existing only in small numbers in the northern savannas.

The ambiguous phrase "a baboon people" (*un peuple de babouins*) rather than the more conventional "troop" or "group" (*troupeau* or *groupe*) from the above passage also evokes the extension of ambiguous identity terms in many directions. It suggests colonial exploration texts, which made sweeping pronouncements about social groups such as "race," "tribe," "nation," and "people," thereby rendering them a kind of collective backdrop for the exploits of the individual colonizers, often heroic but sometimes tragic or terrifying, who were exploiting and/or uplifting such groups through their interventions. Goyemidé's language creates an unresolved tension between the novel's explicit aim to valorize the humanity of these forest residents and its simultaneous, if somewhat satirical, reiteration of cultural distance from them, and from the forest itself.

Through repetition of particular European texts (such as Kipling) and textual conventions, Goyemidé presents the humor and pathos of Gonaba's posturing as an intrepid European-style explorer. Yet his departure from the Europeanized world toward an African one—both within his nation, and within his repertoire of raw materials for the production of his identity—is highly ambivalent. Gonaba is the product of multiple sensibilities about the natural world (as the author seems to be as well). Dependent on European objects and familiar with Western concepts of the wilderness, Gonaba nevertheless resents and wishes to discard his colonial heritage.

He sings a Boy Scout song while sorting through his belongings. It evokes colonial efforts to refashion, in part through scouting, African initiations to forest skills. While thus singing, however, he sorts through European camping gear in his travel trunk, an invitation to journey not only into the forest, but into himself. Even as he repeats the song, he is rejecting the material trappings of Western-style wilderness travel: "Singing, I take from my footlocker a little tyrolese sack. I tell myself that this set of 'stuff' seems a lot like the panoply of the perfect little explorer. And I return all of these pharmaceutical products to the locker" (54).[12]

Later, as fear and physical fatigue set in, Gonaba regrets having left the medication out of his supplies. But when his flagging energy would lead him back to the village, familiar exploration idioms bolster his courage. Summoning the comfort of scientism so much a part of colonial exploration, he imagines himself as "the first human ever" to see this forest. He even has the power to inscribe—to inflict—his claim to uniqueness on the landscape. In prose remarkably reminiscent of both colonial exploration narrative and recent journalism about the progress of U.S. conservationists into African forests,[13] Goyemidé satirizes his narrator's attempt at an imperious tone so ironic that it is worth quoting at length:

> The further I penetrate the forest, the more I have the conviction that no bipedal member of my species has had before me the "badge of honor" to tread upon the ground of this part of the world. And, since I am in the process of proving irrefutably that I am the very first to explore it, I will mark it with my seal for history and for posterity. I identify a large tree with a fairly smooth trunk and begin to leave upon it my imprints. With the tip of my commando knife, I repeat the gestures which, centuries before me, Magellan or Bering must have used when, first, they cleared the straits that bear their name. I trace in gothic letters . . . the brief history of my passage:
>
> > This 9th of May, 1965, at 16:30, Me,[14] Gonaba, Inspector of all the primary schools in the Western and Southwestern regions of the Central African Republic, I, the first, the very first in my capacity as Man, have tread the soil of this part of the planet Earth. In witness whereof, this has been written to define and vindicate the rights in question. (52)

Such attempts at distancing oneself from the landscape contrast with the process of awakening and acceptance the narrator undergoes as he becomes part of a Pygmy community, taking a wife, building a home, hunting, eating, drinking, and even becoming a father. In a decisive tone, interrupting his smooth chronicle of life in the forest, the narrator distinguishes between his curiosity and that of an ethnographer, who would carry such questions and adventures to their (pseudo-)scientific and dehumanizing extremes:

> I am not an ethnologist. I did not come here with the fixed intent to expose "the Lives and Customs of the Babingas of the Equatorial Forest" to the civilized world ... to violate their personality, nor to steal their cultural, sociological, ethnographic, or other *patrimony*, but simply to live with them, within their daily life, their joys, their pain, in their natural context, considering them as they deserve, as a mature and respectable people, and not as a sort of laboratory specimen. (97; my emphasis)[15]

Yet objectification, it seems, can always cut several ways, and as he resists one form, he reproduces another.

THE SILENCE OF FOREST FEMALES

Gonaba's wife is hard to imagine outside of her role as forest-dwelling female. Ironically, the narrator christens her "Pygmalion," a name connoting radical transformation of identity, as in the George Bernard Shaw play about a lower-class girl in Britain who acquires upper-class characteristics of diction, gesture, and taste. Yet the Pygmy bride (whose real name, we are told once or twice, is Kaliwosse) is the character whose presence most often brings to mind the silence of the forest, for she is never heard to speak. In the novel she works, plays, nods assent, and takes Gonaba's hand; her breasts swell; she gives birth twice and finally dies, all without speaking directly in the text.

Like Simone, the girlfriend-for-a-night at the novel's outset who berates Gonaba for mimicking white mannerisms and who defends rural farm life, Pygmalion is relegated to a single-facet existence—limited to an essence she cannot contest within the confines of the text. What of "Pygmalion's" identity is imparted to her offspring? Very little; she has the power to nurture and heal and love but not to embody any kind of contradictions or to experience any mobility beyond, as it were, her habitat.[16] Her two brothers, who have taught Gonaba to hunt, accompany him on the path back to "civilization" at the novel's close. She, however, dies at the novel's close, revealing her role in the narrative as part of the forest, incapable of the sort of mobility her mate has found across worlds or landscapes. In so dying, she also frees Gonaba to return to the world outside the forest, taking his children, referred to as "des petits Gonaba" (123). In their relationship we find the perfect enactment of Gonaba's appropriation of Pygmies and their forest world to reinforce his identity as a cosmopolitan Central African.

Even Manga's words about Pygmy norms evoke an ideal of highly moral society, centered on the purity of the "wife." Goyemidé has Manga speak the sort of colloquial French ("Nous autres . . .") one rarely hears outside of rural Québec or the Congo basin: "Nous autres Babingas [Pygmies], on ne va pas avec les femmes des autres. Ceux qui le font risquent d'être chassés de la communauté" ("We Pygmies, we don't go with the wives of others; those who do that could get kicked out of the community"). In Aka (a Pygmy group) camps during my fieldwork, gossip about extramarital affairs was a major source of entertainment around the fire and in huts at night— for both women and men. Marital life seemed no less complicated among the BaAka than elsewhere in the world, and indeed two of my key female informants in these communities had chosen successive husbands.

In the interest of what image—what notion of nation and origin—would Goyemidé's writing relegate these people, and most particularly women, to a pure and static status of symbol against his vision of the perilous perversity of the contemporary postcolony? Fredric Jameson writes that "when the Third World . . . speaks in its own literary and political voice, we are better placed to appreciate everything which is offensive and caricatured about Conrad's representation of the politics and the people of the Congo."[17] Yet offensive and caricatured representations seem to characterize all kinds of narratives; they may be double-edged, serving both as satire and as symbolically resonant narrative strategy. Flawed texts can nevertheless serve in the laying of new narrative foundations for central African literature. Such foundations may necessitate a kind of miraculous, layered demolition through repetition; they can transcend an impoverished imaginary whereby cultural production falls into the categories of "original" and "copy."[18]

The shifting of African and European identities occurs in the crucible of a forest environment at once fictional and real, where animals and bestiality become important resources for the construction of human identities. Reading Achille Mbembe's (1992: 8) analysis of the "'poaching' of meanings" and of "poaching on the rhetorical territories of pseudo-revolutionary regimes," one is reminded of the connections between appropriated lands and appropriated identities, between forest products and forest peoples.

TALES OF POLICY AND TERRITORY

Goyemidé wrote plays and novels, and maintained and improved a chaotic national educational system. His civic accomplishments should qualify, not overshadow, his literary ones. In 1996 Goyemidé was minister of education and scientific research. He was under enormous strain, due to his unpopular stance on student scholarships at the University of Bangui. Making the award of financial assistance to students both rarer and more merit-based was not an easy political stand. Goyemidé was attempting such changes with his unique social dexterity and a great deal of placating the educated elite of Bangui through public address. There were protests at the university against his proposed plan, but he held firm.

His work with Pygmies, however, remained in the realm of fiction. Read both by schoolchildren and adults, his novels no doubt inform the sensibilities of his compatriots who are more directly involved with or have recently encountered actual forest residents, rather than imagined ones. Some of the only "practical projects" about Pygmy "development" are government documents written by an official in the State Secretariat for Tourism under the Ministry of Waters, Forests, Hunting, Fishing, and Tourism. They open the methodological question, for me, of how expansive to be in defining "texts" for my analysis. In central Africa, no less than in the United States, policies and projects are put forward in *narrative* form, thereby generating, in a sense, an archive of visions (many not realized) about development, national identity, and natural resources.

Two key documents exemplify a tendency in policy sources authored by Central Africans to characterize Pygmies as marginal, radical, and utterly removed from interaction with (but in need of incorporation into) the state. Serge Singa Ndourou, a functionary with the Ministry of Forests, has long worked to make changes in the tourism sector of his country's economy. He writes: "We must put to work all we can to block the segregationist whims of the Pygmy and lead him to blend, despite himself, in the mold of the great Central African nation where separatist whims or any sentiment of exclusion or marginalization are prohibited" (Singa Ndourou 1987: 1).

Such conceptions deny or ignore the issues raised by the increasing integration of Pygmies into the national economy since the colonial era (issues I discussed above). In today's southwestern C A R, when Pygmies do obtain passports for travel, it is often as performers, not only for their compatriots as in the first few scenes of *Le Silence*, but also for European audiences.

Further, with respect to forest conservation, hunter-gatherers in recent decades have not been considered stakeholders in negotiation, partly because they are not perceived as having economic needs or desires. Grouped with "wildlife and plant species" rather than with "various stakeholder groups," they are considered as valuable resources, not as actors (see Kretsinger 1993): "Various stakeholder groups perceive the Reserve differently.... Groups within the C A R Government, many local Bantu and Oubangi-speaking inhabitants, and the international financial community value the Reserve primarily as an economic resource. Others value the Reserve primarily as an ecosystem which sustains wildlife and plant species as well as the traditional hunting and gathering activities of the Aka, a Pygmy ethnic group that inhabits the rainforest" (Telesis 1991: 5).

Yet access to literacy, travel beyond forest regions, and Western medicines is frequently stated as a development objective in Aka communities I have known. Rather than being heard, pygmies are locked into particular roles by the rhetoric of their compatriots. Singa Ndourou (1987) elaborates a plan for the commercialization of Pygmy handicrafts in the southern forests; the establishment of centers for the sale of Pygmy nets, baskets, and other objects. The project, like the plan for a national zoo I mention below, prescribes a transformation of existing relations; in this case not so much a redefined relationship to nature as an alienation from material cultures of forest use that enables the production of its artifacts as not tools but commodities. All of this is predicated on conceiving Pygmy social relations as in need of change, and the civil servant as somehow responsible for such change. Singa Ndourou continues: "Pygmy civilization, as distinct from the general central African civilization, which is susceptible to interconnected influences of foreign values and the *political will* of national unity, is a civilization fundamentally static, devoid of ambition, simplistic in its structure" (3).

Such blatant evocation of structuralist and evolutionist ideas creates an impression of exclusion that belies Singa Ndourou's stated goal of including BaAka in the Central African nation. He relegates their cultural and economic production to the level of mere "folk" and "artisanal" activities.[19] Predictably, those nationals affiliated with international NGOs demonstrate greater subtlety in their descriptions of Pygmies than those employed by the Central African state. This is perhaps a function of the economy of agencies in a city like Bangui, where international initiatives have the financial resources to hire the more formally educated Africans away from government service. It also may result from some self-selection and recruiting. One official who did doctoral research on education among Pygmies before working with UNESCO writes: "Contrary to the primitive state we attribute to them, they are remarkably discerning and subtle. Upon arriving, I thought that I would observe them; but it was more they who observed me; at least, we observed one another" (Koulaninga 1990: 3).

National officials in the CAR struggle under remarkable constraints toward increasingly subtle, effective expressions of varied national identities for environmental governance. About town in Bangui, these civil servants can be found relaxing together and bantering about the contradictions of their work. "He's the one who signs the permits for those Lebanese who are decimating our forests down there," I heard one say in introducing another at the airport bar, with good natured slaps on the back, and beers bought to ease the teasing. Their efforts to reform state practice even as they grapple with opportunities to profit from it bring civil servants such as Singa Ndourou to write what might seem curiously grandiose proposals.

Most such proposals emerge from the individual authors' own histories with nature, often indelibly shaped by colonial circumstances of natural resource management. Most also remain unfunded, however passionate their authors or advocates. A customs official from the Nola area near Bayanga, whose father was in the colonial customs service, is both an investor in an ecotourism venture in Bayanga and director of a National Ballet troupe that performs dances at international festivals and for foreign visitors to Bangui (Orokas 1994). Toutou Inguizeguino is a veterinarian whose father was an avid trophy hunter (as were many of the Africans who kept company with French colonialists). He imparted to his son a passion for wild animals that was eventually translated into plans for a national zoo (Inguizeguino 1994).

Singa Ndourou himself has long worked with an affluent and accomplished French safari hunter and publishing mogul, Andre Fecomme. They have worked together on, among other things, the development of an ornithology museum for Bangui. In such cases, projects can have real institutional effects, at least briefly. Their partnership founded (and funded) the Association Pure Nature in Bangui, with membership rules and a formal request for materials to begin an ornithological collection for the city, an activity compatible with hunting (Fecomme and Singa Ndourou 1995). Such ventures are emerging throughout equatorial Africa outside of more formal NGO involvement in environmental management. As the cases of Fecomme and Orokas show, these ventures often develop out of elite partnerships with colonial roots and postcolonial connections.

The authors of these various proposals, like Goyemidé, have worked according to visions of a common natural patrimony managed rationally and nationally. But they have worked in a world where more often resources are perceived in parcels handed out to a variety of rival outside interests. Their works are unfortunate in their inattention to contemporary political economic processes in the CAR. Nor do they fit well with the complex intersections of wealth extraction, decentralized natural resource management, and increasingly militarized and privatized practices to ensure "security" that are coming to characterize resource use, especially in Africa (see Ferguson 2004). Other narratives, such as those we will examine next, dovetail more closely with such emerging environmental governance trends.

NARRATIVE HUMANITY AND NEW FORMS OF PATRIMONY

On March 5, 1997, ABC's nightly news show *Prime Time Live* featured the American conservationist J. Michael Fay in a televised segment that generated enormous public interest in the Sangha River region of the southwestern CAR. The show exemplifies enduring connections in the popular international imagination between tropes of exploration and discovery and emerging geopolitical relations regarding resource use in equatorial Africa. It also reveals a key contrast between the media coverage of J. Michael Fay's conservation efforts and the much smaller audience for the writing of Etienne Goyemidé. The contrast is between two very different kinds of storytelling about forests, which circulate through markedly different commercial circuits and communities. In the dominant one, there are clear connections between narrative power, material resources, cultural whiteness, technology, and mastery of territory (whether for protection or extraction of its wealth).

Starker still is the contrast between Fay's role in an expertly coordinated media blitz and the abortive authorship efforts of Adolph Lemongali, whom I introduced at the start of this chapter as he asked me to edit his novel. The cultural and physical space for authorship and innovation is not limitless in today's CAR; indeed in many ways it is scarcer than in the decades since independence in 1960. What can be said about a new generation of elites, being produced under more clearly neoliberal circumstances and in the midst of ever-worsening civil conflict and challenges to the CAR as a nation-state?

Writing remains a strategy for transcending, through professional life, the controls increasingly placed on Central Africans' use of rural environments—for claiming a position as not the subject but the formulator of regulations. Many, however, still slip through the cracks of the creaky educational system that Goyemidé worked so hard to strengthen. They thus find themselves on the wrong side of an increasingly pronounced divide between those accorded the status of humanity (rights, respect, mobility) and those relegated to spaces of suffering and constraint that make them seem mute, passive, criminal, animal.

Adolph gave me no more than a few pages of his manuscript. Rather than delivering the rest, as promised, he left me a letter. In it he begged me to forgive his wrongs. The letter was delivered to me after his departure to serve a jail sentence for having shot an elephant in the forest surrounding Bayanga. Adolph ran smack into the limitations of nature-based strategies for subsistence and status used by a previous generation, with legendary rituals of initiation and transnational connections through the political and commercial entanglements of trophy hunting. Today such activities are either criminalized or reserved for a very few elites.

By framing my chapter with the figure of an adolescent whose own journey to authorial and adult status is so complicated, I do not mean to reinforce the false idea of African voices as, in these matters, "silent." By referring to the tensions between Adolph's intellectual and practical pursuits, on the one hand, and the very real costs of his illegal hunting, on the other, I hope to reveal the various mechanisms that conspire to restrict, contain, or co-opt the circulation of many Central African narratives about transformations in their forest. I also hope to contrast such truncated textual and other efforts to be heard, or even seen (let alone seated "at the table" of international decision makers) with the proliferation of more predictable narrative forms that mobilize economic sponsorship, political support, and economic interest in African forests in the late twentieth century.

In circumstances strangely reminiscent of colonial explorers' lectures to French Geographical Society and Parliament members in the late nineteenth and early twentieth centuries,[20] J. Michael Fay addressed a crowd of business leaders and dignitaries in October 1998 at the National Geographic Society in Washington, D.C. Some aspects of the gathering, however, clearly indicate the rupture and redistribution of power and wealth that has occurred since the colonial era. For instance, Gabon's President Omar Bongo hosted the "Central African Conservation Initiative Dinner."

At the dinner, Fay congratulated African political leaders and rural populations alike for taking up the challenge of creating protected areas within their sovereign territories. He insisted that the Western Congo basin was a frontier as great as the American West; and equally as worthy of protection. He thus deployed some of the very same notions of purity, national patrimony, and protection for which Goyemidé's text has been faulted. Fay pleaded for patience and persistence by those African nations whose diplomatic representatives had been summoned to the dinner. He also pleaded for political will and direct intervention for the cause of African conservation by those Americans, members of Congress, conservationists, and CEOs who had gathered for the event. Throughout his talk, and afterward as we sat and chatted around our respective tables, photographs by Michael Nichols flashed as slides across the enormous screens at the front of the great room, depicting the rigors of his expeditions with Fay in graphic detail.[21]

The man seated to my left at the dinner table, Alphonse, was a Central African national with very little formal education who had risen to the rank of Peace Corps director during my service there. Since I had first met him in 1988 he had moved to Washington, D.C., as a professional conservationist in the employ of World Wildlife Fund. He gave me the news of Goyemidé's death from HIV/AIDS and offered a brief and informal eulogy: "I remember Goyemidé as a guardian of my education," reminisced the recent expatriate resident of Maryland. He told me how, one year during school registration in Bangui, he found that his scholarship had been illegally allocated to another student, the nephew of a "very-important-person." My interlocutor was the son of a poor farmer from the central part of the country and dared not hope to prevail in the competition for status in Bangui. But, he recalled, "Goyemidé was at that time the national administrator of schools. . . . 'Don't worry,' he said, 'this is not fair. I will take care of the matter.' And he did! Without his intervention I would certainly not be in Washington today."[22]

As we spoke, the multiple screens around the room showed slowly unfolding spectacles of forest exploration and conservation in northern Congo and Gabon. As the speeches, slide show, and videos progressed, we were told how parks for poor countries depend in large part on the funds and experience of their richer counterparts. The language of stewardship came on the heels of a prayer for which we had all bowed our heads; this blended two of what Tsing (2005: 88) terms the most powerful universals, God and Nature, into a particular notion of Protestantism-suffused American—no, global—patrimony. This vision then extends to include the forests of central Africa, eclipsing notions of them as African national patrimony and forging new and intimate links between particular elites at transnational and more regional scales.

CONCLUSION

The CAR's state actors are deeply involved in both the specific cultural politics of territory and identity and the homogenizing yet not always rational practices of international environmental reterritorialization.[23] Here I have sidestepped the traditional advocacy role so open to anthropologists. Rather than assert the rights of the CAR's forest peoples, I have offered a close reading of a popular Central African novel and considered policy texts to trace the contradictory models for identity and action with which many state officials wrestle in their own relationships to marginalized minorities who are their competitors for external resources and also their compatriots.

In so doing, I have also tried to shed light on a much-neglected set of stories and projects in the ongoing cross-cultural conversations about environmental governance. Where contemporary anthropological attention to African politics intersects with similar attention to the cultural politics of biodiversity conservation (e.g., West and Brockington 2006), one finds a bleak vision of international environmental NGOs as the handmaidens of neoliberalism, operating in hollowed-out African states and paving the way for non-African appropriations of forest landscapes in various ways. Fewer of us have spent much time actually studying state actors over time in Africa, documenting their challenges and conceptions as they craft propositions, proposals, and policies to govern forest peoples.

In this endeavor, I have found the fraught colonial categories of "civilized" and "primitive" to be remarkably alive in debates about citizenship and access to resources. There are new layers of asymmetry in both planning processes and cultural production, whereby many authors of reports are seen (and see themselves) as the authors of policy and of popular creative narratives about forests, all the while relegating others to the animal-like status of resources, or patrimony, to be managed. This is as true of African civil servants as it is of the independent consulting companies whose work I have quoted. That such stories "sell" in the form of the still flourishing genre of travel literature, as well as in television and magazine products, says as much about the legitimizing and seductive roles of scientific practice as it does about the continued political valence of forests as sacred spaces for primordial and epic encounters.

However, in the race to save animals (and indeed entire ecosystems), much has been overlooked about how boundaries between human and animal worlds fashion political identities. The present moment, like the late nineteenth and early twentieth centuries, when Europeans first arrived in the inner Congo basin, is witnessing crucial reconfiguration of existing rules and norms of territorial governance. Mounting and genuine challenges to equatorial African cultural and economic systems have growing human costs (Wairagala 2006). These systems must accommodate new influxes of rapacious interest in standing forests, arable land, water, and mineral resources. In so doing, they both reproduce and reject aspects of their colonial heritage, articulating claims to their own internally varied use rights that fall, all too often, on deaf ears. These claims—as complicated appeals to multiple sources of authority—must begin to be heard in more detail. They must find ways to reveal and transcend the bifurcated state systems and big-man style political processes that are a legacy of not just imperial strategies but also those strategies' encounter with equatorial African social systems themselves.

Like a seed disperser in complex ecologies of knowledge production, I broadcast Goyemidé's work into new circles of analysis and reflection. Meanwhile, many formally educated CAR residents and their international interlocutors continue to capture power in the hybrid cultural arenas of environmental politics by selectively appropriating or rejecting powerful "great white hunter" or "explorer" tropes that have long been the easy targets of criticism by scholars like me. Such contemporary environmental heroes may be powerful in their interactions with others and in their imaginations of themselves; yet their hold on resources and political power is precarious. Influence over equatorial African forests hinges in part on the apparently infinitely reinventable modes of discovery, mastery, and paternalistic control over resources as patrimony. However, it also hinges increasingly on the emerging metrics that value forests as a carbon sink, or as arable land for the production of food and biofuel.

Even the most formally educated adult Central Africans have limited access to the kinds of expert knowledge that will drive new environmental economies. Such layered exclusion will become an increasing problem for those at local, national, and international levels who seek sustainable, humane environmental governance in these forests. As innovations emerge in the realm of law and medicine, such as mobile medical units or mobile tribunals, and integrations of traditional medicine with biomedical approaches, or customary law with international legal frameworks for conflict resolution and reconciliation, environmental experts should also consider the implications of how their knowledge is constituted and circulates, in increasingly cosmopolitan communities.

Goyemidé's vision of brotherhood—even of doubled or inverted identity between the government official Gonaba and the forest forager Manga—leaves unanswered the question of what adventures the latter may have had as he traveled beyond the limits of the rainforest into wider national and international worlds. The selective humanity of these two characters should also serve to remind us, in relation to the novel's female characters and indeed to the predicament of Adolph Lemongali, that generational and gender differences matter alongside ethnolinguistic ones in the societal crises faced by today's equatorial Africa. Younger, female, and less formally educated Africans are largely excluded from today's shifting circles of natural resource control, both in formal politics and in political imaginaries. The fact that Goyemidé's text reproduces the very inequalities that his political career sought to redress should remind those of us within educational and expert circles of the inevitable contradictions in our own projects—in other words, of our humanity.

NOTES

I would like to thank Ajantha Subramanian and members of her political ecology research group at Harvard University, who gave me a very helpful reading of this chapter in early 2006.

1   My gratitude to Jason Yeo, who pointed me to Honig's work as he was proofreading the manuscript of this chapter during my work on it at the Harvard Academy for International and Area Studies.

2   Jean-Michel Djian (2004) explains the decline within the French foreign service of financial support for francophone cultural events on foreign soils as a result, in part, of France's embrace of trends toward universalist discourse and economically oriented political process.

3   "The Smithsonian Institution/Man and the Biosphere Program (SI/MAB) . . . coordinates a global network of . . . biodiversity monitoring plots in protected forest areas . . . [and] conducts training . . . for host-country researchers and forest managers. Participants are taught a standardized methodology for monitoring, data collection, species identification and analysis through field exercises and . . . lectures" (CTFS 1997: 9).

4   If the effect of colonial power is seen to be the production of hybridization rather than the noisy command of colonialist authority or the silent repression of native traditions, then an important change of perspective occurs. It reveals the ambivalence at the source of traditional discourses on authority and enables a form of subversion, founded on that uncertainty that turns the discursive conditions of dominance into the grounds of intervention (Bhabha 1994: 112).

5   The rich meaning Taussig (1987) gives the word *terror* in his historical work on the rubber trade in South America resonates surprisingly with the rubber trade and colonial moment generally in inner Africa. See also Tsing's (2005) use of the word, in concert with *despair* and *prosperity*, to characterize extractive frontiers in the forests of Kalimantan (Indonesian Borneo).

6   I am not suggesting that the set of relationships is balanced. CAR is home to some of the wealthiest and most despotic rulers that Africa has known. But even a dictator like Jean-Bédel Bokassa sits on the shoulders of a broader group of interrelated actors who are constantly ascending in affluence and status, then striking compromises, making contemporary mechanisms of social fission and fusion, and mitigating the social dangers of accumulation.

7   The critic Fredric Jameson faults *Heart of Darkness* for its insistence on the moral collapse of its hero and its nearly mythic, romantic depiction of Western civilization's unavoidable "scramble for Africa," noting that such emphases transform Conrad's original political motive for writing the story. They make it at best another promotion of imperialism; at worst a more subtle "anaesthetizing" narrative that "offers no particular danger or resistance to the dominant system" (paraphrased in Adelman 1987: 91–92).

8   Hugh Raffles (2002: 116) writes that European explorers "set out . . . on adventure from a Europe flush with new habits of thought. Innovative classificatory schema were sweeping up race as well as the non-human biologies of botany and zoology and were simultaneously plotting new global geographies through the hierarchical taxa of spatial scale."

9   Concepts of "national literature" have provoked much controversy among critics and writers of African novels (Miller 1993). The review of "national literatures" by the journal *Notre librairie* is nevertheless one of the only formats I have found to date for discussion of Goyemidé's work, the concept in action thereby extending the spectrum of

recent African literature under critical consideration. I would like to thank Christopher Miller for his kind and encouraging support of that search, toward a paper for his seminar at Yale University, the origin of this chapter.

10 Gonaba, in this opening, extols the virtuous rustic qualities of a girl who becomes his companion for the night. Glancing at the girl, Gonaba wishes to fondle her breasts as he has seen French men do with women (21). Yet, gazing at an old family photo he carries in his briefcase, he reflects on his mother's breasts, sagging and dry after the work of nourishing her many children and calls her a "source of his extraction" (36).

11 The gambit of reversed roles works within multiple cultural contexts and forms to expose human connection across the dividing lines of race, class, and gender. Eric Worby, whom I also thank for his insightful reading of parts of this piece as a dissertation chapter, has reminded me that the Eddie Murphy films in the late 1980s, for instance the iconic *Trading Places,* used such tactics as social commentary.

12 These are not neutral terms for European camping equipment. *Mansion's Shorter French and English Dictionary* defines *attirail* ("tyrolean sack") as "Attirail de pêche, fishing tackle." Perhaps Goyemidé consciously uses a word whose meaning could stop an eel's swim to Sargasso. As we will see, Singa Ndourou (discussed below) urges that the Central African state "dam" or "block" (*endiguer*) the separatist whims of Pygmies. *Panoplie* (*Mansion's*, 444) is defined as "I.(a) Panoply; full suit of plate armour (b)Toys: Soldier's outfit (for child)."

13 "We have ventured into the last vast unexplored rain forest on earth—the unsullied northern Congo, a place where the animals do not know what to make of us because they have never seen humans before" (Linden 1992).

14 Gonaba's use of "Me" is evocative of other upper-cases: "A remarkable peculiarity is that they (the English) always write the personal pronoun I with a capital letter. May we not consider this Great I as an unintended proof how much an Englishman thinks of his own consequence?" (Robert Southey, *Letters from England*, quoted in Bhabha 1994: 102).

15 This passage informed a particular intersection of ethnographic research, pedagogy, and performance of layered Central African identities in 1996. My university-trained collaborator, the archeologist Henri Zana, selected this passage for the daily writing exercise of our Aka collaborators Dimali and Tele, who had expressed avid interest in improving their writing and reading skills through work with us. They sat in the evenings, after conducting interviews, copying the passage again and again according to Zana's careful corrections. Zana, in comments as a voiceover to his own film work in 2003, displays proud and paternalistic sentiments about these "Pygmies who can write, speak French, and wear shoes." Dimali, for his part, has become the only Aka hired as a tourism guide in the area and is now responsible for translating and interpreting forest activities for tourists. For more information see his intervention in Hardin and Remis 1997.

16 Pygmalion appears in the end as an excellent example of Giorgio Agamben's (2004) formulation of "bare life."

17 Cited by Adelman 1987; for a more specific examination of Conrad's feminization of the primitive in *Heart of Darkness*, see Torgovnick 1990.

18 Interrogating scientific production in the context of pharmaceuticals in Mexico and Argentina, Cori Hayden (2003) advocates attention to the most unruly practices of "copying." Complying neither with patents and brands nor with the formal status of the generic, rampant copying creates complex matrices of value whereby copies themselves can become more prestigious and expensive than any "original."

19 "It is in traditions . . . and especially through their artisanal productions that one appreciates best the value of the Pygmy civilization. . . . As for the deeper study of their social organization, we prefer to leave the task to anthropologists" (Singa Ndourou 1987: 14).

20 For instance, see the colonial explorer Antoine Mizon's address to the French Geographical Society of Le Havre in 1898, in which he addresses his audience in similar detail about his progress through dense tropical forests of the Sangha Basin. CAOM, Fond AEF 2D50 Missions, Carton: Mizon.

21 Nichols, a highly skilled wildlife photographer, has long accompanied Fay on particular treks and has provided much of the photographic work used in press coverage of the northern Congo forest conservation campaign (Nichols and Fay 2005).

22 Alphonse Mobien, conversation with the author at University of Maryland, College Park campus, February 1997.

23 See Deleuze and Guattari 1987 for reterritorialization as both a semantic and spatial phenomenon. Thanks to Hugh Raffles, whom the organizers invited to the workshop at the heart of this volume for commentary on this chapter; he suggested this as a theoretical direction along which I have been unable to travel far enough here.

Political Speciation, Animality, Natality, Defacement

Allen Feldman

> He thinks by means of animals as others do by means of
> concepts.—ELIAS CANETTI, *The Agony of Flies*

> Whenever you observe an animal closely, you feel as if
> a human being sitting inside were making fun of you.
> —ELIAS CANETTI, *The Agony of Flies*

THE UNWRITTEN ANIMAL

IN THE COURSE of my ethnographic and comparative anthropology of politics and terror I have accumulated an archive of animals, creatures, animal metaphors, and allegories and acts figuring the animal. This zoography appears in terrains typically dehumanizing due to war, violence, and racism. *Dehumanization* has always been a troublesome term under such conditions to the degree it presupposes a humanity torn from itself in conformity with the international definition of human rights violation as "the theft or loss of civil dignity." In the animal encounters and tracks I collected, to pose dehumanization would be to dehistoricize and to privilege a political norm of the anthropocentric for entities who could make few or no claims whatsoever to political humanity. Rather, this zoography tracks a warscape embroiled in struggles over animality and humanity, anthropology and nonanthropology.

There were the dogs and cats murdered by British parachute regiments in Belfast and left on the doorsteps of imputed IRA activists as death threat. At the same time there circulated rumors of the crucifixion of cats, goats, and dogs in the nearby parks and cemeteries of Belfast's Catholic neighborhoods (Feldman 1991: 81–84). There were the stories of the Shankill Butchers, who used actual butcher's implements to transform their victims into ideologically consumable ethnopolitical flesh (ibid.: 75–82). I collected oral histories of "the jackal," a Loyalist paramilitary who killed twice, first with his gaze and then with a weapon (Feldman 1997: 185–87). Former IRA prisoners spoke of the "mechanical bears," a brutal cohort of prison guards in the H blocks; and in that same prison, Bobby Sands put forth an allegory of terminal hunger striking as the freeing of "a lark" from a cage, a bird that has totemic political associations with eighteenth-century Irish anticolonial insurgency (Feldman 1991: 237–46).

I noted that prior to their battering of Rodney King, the implicated policemen invoked the film *Gorillas in the Mist* while patrolling in an African American neighborhood. I further explored police court testimonies that characterized King as "bear-like" and as getting up on his "haunches," presumably to attack the police, and the animal subtext of his fantasized immunity to pain which enabled this "attack" and justified police "retaliation" as "reasonable use of force." King, like the animal who lacks language, was rendered voiceless at the Simi Valley trial and subjected to dissection at the level of the pixilated, virtual carving up of his body into parts consumable by vision and law (Feldman 1994). In the late 1990s, while attending the hearings of the South African Truth Commission, I heard accounts of "braai" (barbecue) interrogations where hooded black political prisoners were hung upside down like "bush meat," as their torturers described it, using a term reserved for wild game. These prisoners were asphyxiated and cooked over fires as their interrogators drank, picnicked on food (sometimes previously prepared by their victims), tortured, and later disposed of the bodies with the same fires. I historicized these episodes in South African labor discipline violence from seventeenth-century slave punition to the nineteenth-century denotation of black farm and mine labor as animal herds or livestock, "baboons," and "beasts of burden." The policemen who burned their prisoners were termed "animalish people" by the *isangoma*, local traditional herbal healers who saw this police torture as indicative of a pathological addiction to burning human fat (Feldman 2003).

Roaming the settlements and jerry-rigged shacks of homeless people under the Bruckner Expressway in New York City, I puzzled over the ubiquity of oversized stuffed dolls of bears, dogs, cats, kangaroos, elephants, horses, and giraffes mounted on the cardboard roofs and crate walls of their shanties—were these nostalgic images of home, care, and childhood or totems of loosing all shelter, including that of humanity (Feldman 2001)? Still, I was startled when, approaching an eight-story tenement squat of the homeless in East Harlem, I encountered dozens of such carefully posed, oversized stuffed animals peering down at me from every shattered window frame. One intravenous drug user likened the circulating HIV-infected syringes that were shared or scrounged from the gutter to the physiology of stinging malarial mosquitoes (ibid.). And recently I have written on the leashed and collared prisoners, the "reservoir dogs," of Abu Ghraib being walked on all fours by their American guards (Feldman 2005).

I duly attempted to ethnographicize this zoography, which followed me from one site of terror to another. At these sites animality was a shared nexus for *both* the agents and recipients of violence; practices, images, and memories of violence were rendered tangible, material, and intractable through the figure of the animal. These images of political animality were as violent to "animals" as fated figures of disposability as to those barred from political humanity. Political animality functioned in many of these episodes as a habitus of *inhumanization,* by which I mean not the maltreatment of humanity but rather the entrenchment of specific anthropocentric norms through ideological projections of humanity's negations, alters, and antagonists—all those who lack humanity yet densely signify the human in their lack.

The violence that is poised between humanitas and inhumanitas speaks to the metaphysical ordering and phantasms of everyday political terror. Are practices of political aggression separable from the Western metaphysical divide between human and animal, and what are the ideological utilities of this divide? Are acts and discourses of inhumanization how this philosophical anthropology (and all anthropologies are ultimately philosophical) confesses itself, not as theorem or disciplinary taxonomy, but as a political culture with the most severe material criteria and bodily consequences? Does political animality point to an anthropological sovereignty that only acquires positivity, tangibility, and figuration through its displacement onto, and passage into, the "privation" that is animality? And why does subjugated or expelled animality perennially threaten anthropological plenitude as an uncontainable negativity? These questions imply that the many thresholds of language, labor, and finitude that have repeatedly delimited, governed, and consigned the animal and human in metaphysical thought and practice must be remapped as a properly political dominion: a wildlife reserve in which philosophical, ethological, and anthropological declaratives and descriptions encrypt zoopolitical relations of power and force, and where the animal predicate circumscribes a concentrated time and space of subjugation, exposure, disappearance, and abandonment. Ultimately this anthropological threshold poses questions concerning the metaphysics of empirical violence and the critique of anthropology by nonanthropology.

In philosophy the animal is characterized as lacking language (Aristotle 1957; Heidegger 1998), lacking self-consciousness, lacking a face or a least an ethical visage (Levinas 1990), lacking hands (Derrida 1987), as the inability to disclose being (Heidegger 1998), as the inability to deceive, pretend, respond, and witness (Lacan 1977), as insensibility to pain, and as insensibility to death—since animals supposedly live from moment to moment with a forgetfulness equivalent to multiple deaths (Schopenhauer 1970; Nietzsche 1983; Lippit 2000: 42–43). Or as Martin Heidegger (1971: 178) describes this: "The mortals are human beings. They are called mortals because they can die. To die means to be capable of death as death. Only man dies. The animal perishes. It has neither death ahead of itself or behind it." Writing in 1949, Heidegger equates the manufacture of cadavers in the gas chambers with technologized agrobusiness and asks if those who "perished" in the concentration camps could even be said to be dead. "Are they dying [*Sterben Sie*]?" he repeatedly asks. The concentration camp fatalities are "horribly un-dead [*grausig ungestorben*]" (Heidegger 2000: 79, 56). The camp inmates were deprived of humanizing "mortality" in much the same manner that anonymous animal perishing is devoid of an ontological relation to death; that relation, however, is sustained for Heidegger in the sacrificial death of German soldiers for the Reich (ibid.: 759–60). Thus Heidegger conceptualizes ontological death within a racialist hierarchy, which I would stress is extrapolated from an anthropology/animal hierarchy. Heidegger's differentiation of *Dasein*'s being-toward-death from the nondeath of animal perishing is reencountered in the political aesthetics of counting sacrificial nationalized American military deaths and the *dis-counting* of

Iraqi and Afghani dead who merely perish like Heideggerian animals in U.S. political culture. My chapter addresses the metaphysical foundations and consequences of this hierarchical politics of expiration.

Jacques Derrida (2002a: 299) has asserted that the history of the Western metaphysics of the animal is a history of misrecognitions. Is this to presuppose that beyond these missed encounters with the animal Real is the potential for a recognition that did not miss the animal, an ethical recognition that would "take place" in the "presence" of the animal? If animality is already politics, can a nonsovereign encounter with the animal occur, what Derrida would name as relations of hospitality, the protocol of the neighbor (ibid.: 95; Derrida 2005: 68)? Any ethics of animal hospitality is complicated by the contingency that the political emplacement of the animal always takes place and yet never takes place in a presence (that is, never takes place outside of misrecognition).[1] From this we should infer that misrecognition is at the productive root of political animality and that the latter results from contingent intersections of force, of successive acts of (re)interpretation and (re)appropriation: "power forms itself into a configuration and domination means that the constituents of such configurations are forces . . . In that ordering . . . the moral subject is only an instance" (Schürmann 1984: 379). There is no recuperation of the animal in itself or for itself as an irreducible moral subject, for the latter is always already contaminated by the anthropological in which the "in itself" and the "for itself" are political categories. My concern here is with the sheer repetition of such missed encounters with the animal as a productive institutionalized trauma of the political, one that cannot be readily uninherited by an animal ethics. To recognize such repeated misrecognitions as a traumatology of power is to explore what the (dis)location of the animal, which never takes place in a presence, permits of politics. I encounter this problematic dispersed animal (dis)location and its recurrent traumatology and concealment in Giorgio Agamben's totalizing biopoliticized "life," in Michel Foucault's monstrosity, in Hannah Arendt's natality, in Jacques Derrida's spectral cat, in Emmanuel Levinas's faceless snake, and in a parasitic Talmudic gnat. As it was my field-based ethnographies that complicated the arrangements of the human and the animal in Western metaphysics, I consider this inquiry an ethnography of the animal theorem in which metaphysical descriptions and decisions concerning animality function as encrypted ontologies of political subjugation and a visual culture of exposable or bared life. This project returns, in a political key, to the very questions that Henri Ellenberger (1960: 136–49) provoked in his study of the parallel development of mental institutions and zoological gardens in eighteenth-century France, in which he compared the incarceration of the insane and animals. In excavating the depoliticizing treatments of the animal in Western metaphysics and elsewhere I do not leave this or other historical enclosures behind; the IRA hunger strikers, Rodney King, the AIDS-affected homeless, and the victims of torture under apartheid and at Abu Ghraib are indexical specters and co-interlocutors in this political ethnography of the face of animality. Thus this chapter entertains the conditions of possibility of an ethnography that does not commit anthropology.

DETOTALIZING BIOPOWER

Foucault (1984, 1997) and Agamben (1998) have taught us to attend to the institutional and political production of forms-of-life totalized as positivities that are rendered truthful, factual, and procedural. Agamben proposes homologous Janus-faced thresholds: *zoé/bios* = bare life/political existence = disqualified life/qualified life = to let die/to let live. The jettisoning of the biopolitical subject to bare life is the passage to the exteriority of political lack (which Agamben likens to bestialization). The thanatopolitical, as the obverse of biopolitical totalization, constitutes a formalist exile into the anomic, into juridical indistinction, described as an interior construction of a political/legal outside in which those subject to the dense inscriptive praxis of biopower undergo processual erasure. Heideggerian entelechies of a humanized ontological death and a deontologized animal perishing are repeated in this oscillation between biopolitics and thanatopolitics. Like the theorem of the animal in Western metaphysics, the thanatopolitical is treated as a figure of lack—the absence of formalized law and/or qualified life—and thus becomes the abode of the animalized characterized as "bare life." Agamben (1998: 8) has this to say about the polarity of bios and bare life (in the form of the naked voice):

> The question "In what way does the living being have language?" corresponds exactly to the question "In what way does bare life dwell in the polis?" The living being has logos by taking away and conserving its own

voice in it, even as it dwells in the polis by letting its own bare life be excluded, as an exception, within it. Politics therefore appears as the truly fundamental structure of Western metaphysics insofar as it occupies the threshold on which the relation between the living being and the logos is realized. In the "politicization" of bare life—the metaphysical task par excellence—the humanity of living man is decided.

Agamben's discussion originates in the notion of *logos* as the imposed sovereignty of reason and law, the written or spoken command that dominates and shapes *physis* as nature, life, birth, and naked voice. He draws a parallel between the naked voice and the body in their mutual subsumption by the political. This passage evokes Aristotle who assigns *phoné* as vocalized noise to those living beings who are limited to the sensations of pain and pleasure, in contradistinction to those beings who have logos as *phoné semantike*, that is, vocality as productive of meaning which can decide between the just and the unjust. Slaves, women, barbarians, and some animals apprehend meaning (*aisthanesdthai*) but do not possess (*ekhein*) it; for they are subject to affect and not to reason (Aristotle 1957: 1254–55b).[2] Animality has aesthesis as affect; humans possess *aesthesis* as the political capacity to judge the good.

In Agamben's treatment of politicized *logos* and prepolitical *phoné* the acts of conservation and exclusion ("taking away") are the archival powers and substantializing foundations of biopower rather than the imputed bioavailability, ubiquity and destination of life itself as coextensive with, and in symmetrical relation to, a biopolitical apparatus. The act of vocal storage, mimesis, and filtering reveal the biopolitical project as mnemic, archival, and disjunctive to the degree that something is expropriated as life and voice and something remains as unfiltered and nonsignifying life. Here an indeterminacy is rendered extrinsic to the conserving and mortifying mnemotechniques upon which archival biopower is grounded. The biopolitical subject is formed from a deferred and deadened voice that has been stilled and stabilized as *logos*.[3] This thanatological formation of the voice discloses that life and anthropology/animality emerge from the dual gesture of conservation and exclusion and do not preexist the bio-archival incision. In Agamben's *The End of the Poem* (Agamben 1999: 50), the *logos/phoné* theorem reappears as the archival-grammatological organization of animal vocality in terms of sense and non-sense:

Grammar above all begins by distinguishing the "confused voice" of animals (*phone agrammatos* . . . which cannot be written . . . from the human voice, which can be written (*engrammatos*) and articulated. . . . A more subtle classification, which is of Stoic origin, nevertheless characterizes the (animal) voice with greater sophistication. . . . In entering into *grammata* in being written, the animal voice is separated from nature, which is inarticulate and cannot be written; it shows itself in letters as a pure intention to signify whose signification is unknown . . . imitations of animal voices capture the voice of nature at the point at which it emerges from the infinite sea of mere sound without yet having become signifying discourse.

Agamben's discussion of the transcriptive enclosure of *phoné* also speaks to the dismissal of the animal voice and the animality of prepolitical bare voice as a nonsignifying "infinite sea of mere sound." The political enclosure of voice is the setting to work of mnemic duplication, conservation and grammatization as the archiving of animality in supplementary *hypomnēmata* or prosthetic instruments of memory. If *phoné*, the bare voice, is considered to be a signature of both "bare life" and animal vocality it is clear that it has no living presence in the biopolitical-grammatological order; it subsists there in a state of mimetic detachability, simulation, and archival mortification resulting from the partitioning consignment of voice and life to the media of dead memory. Archival biopower preserves only by effacing *mnēmē* (vocality as living memory) in *hypomnēmeta*, in forms of conserving nonlife that comprise thanatopower. Agamben treats the thanatopolitical as *the lack* of qualified life and law, but here the thanatopolitics of bio-archivization qualify voice and life through grammatization and legislate the productive organization of death through a rigidifying conservation of life. The thanatopolitics of the bio-archive is the historicizing power to extract, partition, and expropriate in order to preserve and petrify life as animality through mnemotechnology. The historicizing death of animal vocality, its grammatization as logos, is the founding stillbirth of Agamben's biopower which archives, filters, and then subsequently nominates a petrified, parasitable brute, mere or bare life as a universal foundational figure. Thanatopolitics operates as an unacknowledged origin of the biopolitical, not as its surplus. There is thus no autonomous "bare" life taken-in by biopower, and no coextensivity between qualified life and its dependent and jettisoned obverse—a life without qualities exiled beyond the archive; these couples and symmetries are all typified, recursive, and functionalized figures of the bio-archive.

In Agamben, life as *hypokeimenon* as support is already in a relation of political subjugation, and thus already qualified/disqualified, as what stands under biopower by virtue of being devoid of any intrinsic political formation. Rather than being conscripted as a passive and inert substrate or as antecedent commons, life is already partitioned, commensurated, and politicized in being made to appear as a substrate, and as the replicating code and subjugated topography for sovereign power.[4] Agamben's legal formalism, which relegates the thanatopolitical to ontological nullification or indeterminate anomic lack, advances biopower as a leveling apparatus of totalization, as a judgmental universality and the structure of structures in which bare life is the absent cause and decentered effect. In Agamben life cannot be delimited as an assignable origin of biopower: "There is no assignable origin . . . because the whole process, which is fulfilled in the final totality, is indefinitely, in all the moments which anticipate its end, its own Origin" (Althusser 1976: 180–81).[5] This totalization of life as both *arkhé* and *eschaton* is itself a Hegelian movement that can be described as follows: the capacity to biopoliticize is the becoming-subject of substance (*zoé* to *bios*) and the capacity to make bare life is the becoming-substance of the subject (*bios* to *zoé*).

Animality as the extimate threshold of a permeable biopolitical order traverses what was circumcised and incised in order to produce life itself as a substance for the production and projection of power, which is why animality diversely resurfaces in Agamben as pretext, waste product, and effluvia and as a conditioning and conditioned divergence that is both an invasive threat and a locus of punishment. Though animality can materialize the interval between biopolitical enfranchisement and thanatopolitical disqualification it is certainly not containable within that interval. Prescriptions of bare life consequently emerge as correctives to and barriers against a resistant heterogeneity that is political animality as a zoo-anarchism that trespasses against the interior, thresholds, and edges of the political enclosures of qualified life. In this framework animality, as the negated and yet necessary staging ground of the political, also emerges as the inadequate name for unmasterable terrains beyond the anthropological count that provoke insulating biopolitical interiors.

EMBLEMS OF BARED LIFE

Can the detotalizing conditions of biopower's possibility be reclaimed? Foucault addressed this question, if nowhere else, in his theorizing of early modern monstrosity as a zoo-anarchism. In doing so he implies, against his own model of a totalizing biopower, that there would be no biopolitical legislation if biopower did not also both presume and constitute an *indeterminate* moment in every state formation and historical situation.

> The frame of reference of the human monster is, of course, the law. The notion of the monster is essentially a legal notion in a broad sense, of course what defines the monster is the fact that its existence and form is not only a violation of the laws of society but also a violation of the laws of nature. . . . The field in which the monster appears can thus be called a juridico-biological domain. . . . The monster is the limit, both the point at which law is overturned and the exception that is found only in extreme cases. The monster combines the impossible and the forbidden. . . . the monster does not bring about a legal response from the law . . . When the monster violates the law by its very existence it triggers the response of something quite different from the law itself. *It provokes either violence, the will of our simple repression or medical care or pity.* The monster is then so to speak the spontaneous brutality but also consequently the natural form of the unnatural. (Foucault 2003: 55–56; my emphasis)

Foucault's monsters materialize resistance to biopolitical enclosure as a state of denatured and thus political animality; a political bestiary as the "natural form of the unnatural," a singularity that transgresses subsumptive law. However, one could also say that biopolitical enclosure is condemned to visualizing its exception or what exceeds it as monstrous creaturely life. Foucault's monstrosity materially erupts as the edges of two sovereignties, law and nature (or bioscience and later psychiatry), and points to an incongruity between *homo politicus* and political animality. The enlightenment monster is a mixture of two kingdoms, human and animal; belonging wholly to neither, it is an "anti-cosmological figure." As discontinuity and exception, monstrosity precipitates a colonizing biopolitical regime of "violence, the will of our simple repression or medical care or pity," by virtue of its resistance to biopolitical and legal circumscription. Foucault's monsters engage the concept of the exception as materiality, as a form of life, as animal and creaturely and as irreducible to lack or nullity; if anything monstrosity is excessive, more not less, a lack of law perhaps, but an unassimilatible surplus of bodily form and aporetic thresholds. The Foucauldian monster is both a force and a barrier of resistant life; the exceptionality of monstrosity is a constitutive antagonism and limit-experience of biopolitical governmentality.

Foucault's admission of a monstrous limit to totalizing biopower is exceptional in its theorization. For instance, despite his differences with Agamben, Roberto Esposito's politicization of immunology replicates Agamben's trajectory of totalization and reveals what is politically at stake in critiquing biopolitical totality.

> What the [biopolitical] community sacrifices—to its own self-preservation—is nothing other than itself. In the sacrifice not only of every enemy but also of every one of its members, it sacrifices itself, from the moment that every one of its members finds in the depths of their own being the originary figure of the first enemy. . . . [By] looking at the particular relation that the category immunity maintains with its antonym, community . . . [we] have already seen how the most incisive meaning of immunitas is inscribed with its contrary that indicates that the concept of immunization presupposes that which it negates. . . . What is immunized in brief is the same community in a negation of its original horizon . . . [that is] *the fold that separates community from itself, sheltering it from an unbearable excess.* (Esposito 2008: 51–52)

Neither Agamben's biopower nor Esposito's political immunology acknowledge that the "unbearable excess" may not be an interior sector expelled in an act of decontamination or protective self-bifurcation as a part detached from a whole that is always prior to the part. A nontotalizing description of the social as a field of intersecting and constituting antagonisms such as those that inform colonial, postcolonial, and neo-imperial domination, would reveal the limits of biopolitical self-representability. Consider the mass-produced photographic postcards of the lynchings featured in the *Without Sanctuary* portfolio (Allen et al.: 2000). The African Americans in these photos were not dehumanized in order to be lynched as bare life; rather, under the visual regime of racism, they had been born into the exposability and disposability of their bodies as a political form of life and have borne the historical burden of bodies

that never enjoyed interiorizing biopolitical enfranchisement—only commodification as chattel or as a labor reserve. These images show and are, in
themselves, the ceremonial taking of colonial skins in which the white mass-
subject desires to be seen posed and clustering around burned, defaced,
hanging body-fragments. The lynching postcards horrifically stage Heidegger's animal perishing as a patently community-building rite in which
whiteness as biopolitical qualification is visually manufactured from out of
racial nullification, which is certainly not reducible to pre- or postpolitical
life. The camera's gaze traverses the burned effigy only to come to rest on
the upturned white faces of the gathered celebrants mapping an emblematic necrology in which the sovereignty of whiteness is relationally forged
through both the making and exhibiting of the racialized and animalized
corpus. The disfigured "skin" that has been entrapped and mounted is a
historicizable vortex bearing witness to what Heidegger (1998: 248) grudg-
ingly refers to as that "scarcely fathomable, abyssal bodily kinship with the
animal." The racial emblem sealed in violence and disfiguring figuration is
not bare, lacking, or anomic, but has a history, a repeatability, a calculability, an identity, and a law; it is an apparatus, a drive that triangulates white
sovereignty, the "animal," and inhumanization as a protocol of racial immunization. The white subject on show here is both the trace and substitution
of a traumatizing blackness experienced as a disturbance in the field of the
humanizing Same. Animality and blackness manifest the limit of white racial self-representability; they are the politically crafted lack around which
whiteness is formed and yet the privative terrain that African Americans
invariably navigate as history not well lived and as a law without justice.

The emblem of the unhuman is the affirmation of a norm of the "human" (or whiteness in the lynching images) through its very disavowal.
Emblematic inhumanization throws up figures of antihumanity in defense of a hegemonic, but also besieged, anthropological phantasm. For
emblematic signification of the nonhuman, as in racist lynching, is a re-
authentication of the "human" through nonhuman abjection. Emblematic imaging in the form of grotesque and disfigured inhumanitas is not
crudely expressive of a complex social reality lying behind it but is a forma-
tive, structuring social antagonism by which an order of bodies—human,
animal, and monstrous—is materially crafted and/or registered as political flesh and effect. If such images provoke "either violence, the will of our
simple repression or medical care or pity," they can also personify the limit

at which anthropological law is overturned by the silenced sovereignties of the dehistoricized.

Emblematica of the nonhuman are not governed by relations of resemblance but by disidentification; they are signification by fetishistic devices such as the grotesque, the monstrous, the bestial, and the racially abject. Emblematic truth is displayed through incongruity and caricature which affirms humanity through a posturing disavowal that regulates the relations of the human to its neighboring and impinging alters. An early reference to *caricature*, an Italian word meaning "to load," occurs in Sir Thomas Browne's *Christian Morals*: "Expose not thy self by four-footed manners unto monstrous draughts, and Caricatura representations." Browne (1922: 215) adds the note, "When Men's faces are drawn with resemblance to some other Animals, the Italians call it, to be drawn in Caricatura." The citational structure of antihumanity enables the production of the human not from sameness but from difference: from what is never or no longer fully human, or from the limits invoked by human minimality. The caricatural or grotesque emblem is a site of exchange and interface, a switching station between the rule and its exception, normative subsumption and symbiotic anomic singularity. Hegemonic anthropology generates *Nachleben*—the afterlife and afterimage of the latter's entangled and collateral nonhumanity. However, by standing in for what it disfigures, the caricatural emblem of the nonhuman preserves humanity as an equally fictive origination. Animality, monstrosity, and bestiality, as media of incongruity, impropriety, and disavowal, do not displace the properly human but give rise to it as yet another emblem, as one more fetishized trace: "The trace is not only the appearance of the origin. . . . It means that the origin did not even disappear, that it was never constituted except reciprocally by a non-origin, the trace which then becomes the origin of the origin" (Derrida 1974: 61).

FROM NATALITY TO ANIMALITY

In the same manner that Agamben treats life itself as a *subjectum*, support, and backing for a universalizing biopolitical constitution, Hannah Arendt posed *natality*, appearing life or *vita activa*, as the universal prepolitical condition of the political. My engagement with Arendt, as with biopower theory, concerns the consequences when life as *zoé*, as bared, as natality, and as animality can be thought as preceding the political and thus insulated as a founding transhistorical apolitical *arkhé*. To achieve this for natals, the political potentiality ascribed to natality by Arendt is denied to the animal and to the human body because of its metonymic contamination by regressive animality; thus a definitional politics of life is introduced at the onset by Arendtian natality.

Arendt (1951: 473) defines *natality* as "beginning, before it becomes a historical event[;] it is the supreme capacity of man; politically, it is identical with man's freedom!" Natality as ontology precedes as the initiation of initiative. "Because they are *initium*, newcomers and beginners by virtue of birth, men take initiative, are prompted into action" (Arendt 1958: 177). Natality is the given-ness of birth as a partition and singularization that opens or phenemenonalizes a world to be acted on. "To put it differently, the decisive *fact* determining man as a conscious, remembering being is birth or 'natality,' that is, the *fact* that we have entered the world through birth" (Arendt 1996: 51). The decisiveness of natality renders it analogous to the miracle: "Every act . . . is a 'miracle' . . . that is, something which could not be expected. If it is true that action and beginning are essentially the same, it follows that a capacity for performing miracles must likewise be within the range of human faculties" (Arendt 1961: 169). Following Saint Augustine, Arendt situates natal singularity at the human/animal fault line. Augustine (1984: 22) wrote that God "started . . . with one man, whom he created as the first man . . . instead of starting with many," whereas, in the case of animals, "he commanded many to come into existence at once." For Arendt animality is a multitude devoid of singularity and even of a singularizing birth as befits the animal's immersion in biological repetition. In Augustinian anthropology man is in a sovereign position because human natality recapitulates the similitude of God's creative action. Arendt retains this isomorphic relation between sovereignty and natal singularity in which both are counterpoised to animality. Natality as a constitutive exceptionality or "miracle" is the very power decision, willing, and transgression that Carl Schmitt (2007) allocated to the sovereign. A political theology of natality, willing, sovereignty, and inauguration underlies Arendt's (1958: 177) theory of freedom and the political: "With the creation of man, the principle of beginning came into the world itself. . . . The principle of freedom was created when man was created but not before."

Arendtian political action is the assertion of will over material necessity, while the animalized body lacking will is enchained to necessity. If the natal act is a miracle, the human body, in contrast, is consigned to banal animal-like automatism, repetitive subsistence, and biological survival. The "biological process in man . . . [is] endlessly repetitive" (ibid.: 98). As compared to the creativity of natality, physical labor and consumption for Arendt are "devouring" activities in a classic Hegelian formulation (ibid.: 100). Though any initiating action can be embodied action, its autonomy is dependent on the will that masters the body, the animal, and the material.

> Marx never doubted about the animality (*das Animalische*) in the definition "animal rationale." Through the concept of labor he attempts to connect immediately what is specifically human to the animal. That means, mutatis mutandis, to derive freedom from necessity. . . . The Greeks do the opposite: they "derive" freedom out of the "rational" or violent domination of the necessary. This is one of the reasons why the *logos* becomes tyrannical. . . . *Eu zen* = to live in freedom = to dominate tyrannically over necessity. (Arendt 2002: 280–81)

The domination of necessity by the natal type indicates that natality is not absolute creation ex nihilo; the natal event is relational to antecedence, but natality interdicts the antecedent by refusing inheritance as a condition of freedom. Thus the refusal of animal bodily inheritance structures natality as human domination over the animal in itself and outside itself. The tyranny of natality over necessity is autotelic self-constitution, an executive action that Arendt locates at the core of the political. Writing of the will in relation to slave labor in the ancient world, Arendt (1958: 121) implicitly specifies that the latter is nonnatal and entrapped in apolitical necessity: "The human speaking instruments (the instrumentum vocale, as the slaves in ancient households were called) whom *the man of action* had to rule and oppress when he wanted to liberate the *animal laborans* from its bondage. . . . Man cannot be free if he does not know that he is subject to necessity; because his freedom is always won in his never wholly successful attempt to liberate himself from necessity." The body as animal is implicitly enslaved by the will as a requirement of both natality and politics; this relation was externalized in the slave economies of the Athenian city-state, the Roman republic, and antebellum United States, democracies that exemplified natal initiation or *vita activa* for Arendt. Slave animality is described as *instrumentum vocale* and as *perpetuum mobile*, evoking the slave's animalized lack of will, which refracts Arendt's descriptions of the chronic circularity of biological processes that have no beginnings or ends and thus cannot be framed by natality or Heideggerian mortality. The concept of *instrumentum vocale* originates in Aristotle's description of the slave–cum–domesticated animal as *empsukhon organon* (living tool), and the concept of *perpetuum mobile* evokes Descartes's animal automatons (ibid.: 122; Aristotle 1957: 1253b35–1254; Descartes 1985: 140–41). As Andreas Kalyvas (2004: 339), who frames natality in Arendt's theory of the will, writes, "A will that is incapacitated because of certain social, cultural, and economic obstacles becomes an inherent impediment to political action and public participation. In other words, only a will that is relatively liberated from the necessities and deprivations of life can decide to act. As Arendt argued, 'only those could begin something new who were already rulers . . . and had thus liberated themselves from the necessities of life.'"

The necessity that Arendt ascribes to first nature is in her view reconstituted by modern biopolitical regimes as a second nature that interdicts political possibility. Arendt (2002: 66) recognizes that natality as postpartum agency can be constrained and forestalled by a politically constructed practico-inert which she sees as the petrifaction of the natal in biopolitics: "With men the beginning came into the world. On this rests the sanctity of human spontaneity. Totalitarian extermination of men as men is the extermination of their spontaneity. This means at the same time the reversal of creation as creation, as to-have-made-a-beginning. (Maybe here is the connection between the attempt to destroy men and the attempt to destroy nature.)" The lack of natalized spontaneity associated with the body is recapitulated in totalitarian biopolitics as a reconstituted repressive necessity. Biopower for Arendt is an assault not only on natality but on the political which is opposed to retrograde biopolitical regimes of command, calculability, normalization, and repetition that animalize the human.

Though natality is predicated on the differential singularity of each natal, the existential birthright of natality for Arendt is *isonomia*—the political self-organization/self-inauguration of natal peers as exemplified by Athenian democracy. Arendt sharply opposes *isonomia* to instrumental power as rule and command, that is, as mimetic subordinating repetition equated with depoliticization. Natality is also a precipitant of political visuality as the appearing of singular natals in public space, which is the biographical event of *exposability*. Kalyvas (2004: 332) comments, "To be a citizen entails a willingness to suffer the consequences of such a decision to leave one's private hiding place and disclose or expose one's self in front of one's peers."

Though Arendt's natal exposure may specify visibility as the precondition of political action and biographical events, she does not account for politicized visual dominance, visually driven embodiment/disembodiment, and systems of penetrative surveillance that drive systems of command and control and which invariably link natal exposure to foundational modes of scopic violence, such as the racing and gendering of natality.

Arendt proposes a first and secondary natality analogous to Agamben's refiguration of *zoé* (given life) *by bios* (politically qualified life). Natality as *bios* is connected to biography, which is contingent on the event as the temporal expression and narrative artifact of the natal opening (Kalyvas 2004: 321). "The chief characteristic of this specifically human life, whose appearance and disappearance constitute worldly events, is that it is always full of events which ultimately can be told as a story, establish a biography; it is of this life, *bios*, as distinguished from mere *zoé* that Aristotle said that it somehow is a kind of praxis" (Arendt 1958: 97). Animal life, structured by the circularity of subsistence and devoid of natality and will, lacks the event and thus lacks the *bios* of the biographical and is thereby barred from the political (see Derrida's contestation of this below).[6] Secondary natality as *bios* establishes a reflexive purchase on the sheer nakedness of appearing-in-the-world. "With word and deed we insert ourselves into the human world, and this insertion is like a second birth, in which we confirm and take upon ourselves the naked fact of our original physical appearance. This insertion is not forced upon us by necessity. . . . Its impulse springs from the beginning, which came into the world when we were born and to which we respond by beginning something new on our own initiative" (Arendt 1958: 176–77). Natality as an a priori performs a political function; it establishes anthropology as a foundational birthright and insulates that foundation from a relapse into the bodily antecedence and inheritance of apolitical animality.

Arendt denies natality to the metonymic assemblage that links human embodiment to animal multitudes and further sees the body as betraying singular natal autonomies through a collectivized automatism that renders it susceptible to biopolitical colonization, control, and detemporalization. Thus Arendt poses two contradictory forms of bios: the natal refiguration of the body as "mere *zoé*" into *bios*, based on isonomic action, will, initiation, and miracle and the biopolitical interdiction of spontaneity through biologizing technics, mimetic command structures, and violence. Is the polarity between the two sovereignties and modes of domination sustainable? I suggest that animality, which is barred from natality and politics, is the mediating terrain where the complicity of *isonomia* and rule by biologized subjugation can be discerned.

Arendt's prepolitical universalization of natality constitutes an idealist moralization of the phenomenological lifeworld that erases a foundational political abortion as a condition of possibility for political natality. To what degree is natal autonomy both predicated on and conditioned by depoliticized animality that Arendt bars from natal initiation? And this is to also ask what are the complicities between the two sovereignties—natal willing over necessity and biopolitical subjugation as the constitution of social necessity?

Descriptions of natality as phenomenological appearing-in-the-world have to be tempered by comprehending natality as the concealment of the political in the (un)birth of the animal and of all those other forms of life that are politically disqualified either as natals or mortals in Arendt and Heidegger. I have in mind here a regional ontology that radically interdicts natal inauguration at its roots by virtue of a birth that is always already an "animalizing" enclosure. I refer to Orlando Patterson's (1982: 7) concept of natal alienation as the ontological, temporal, and topological structure of slavery and cognate forms of domination.

Patterson describes the slave as being "recruited" as a socially dead person, and this conscription structures the slave's lack of natality—enslaved birth itself traverses both biological and social nullification. According to Patterson, the slave's natal alienation involves the "loss of ties of birth in ascending and descending generations," which means that the slave loses the ability to make natal claims to his or her parents and community and has none to pass on to his or her children (ibid.: 7). In reference to hereditary slavery, Aristotle (1953: 721b32) relates, "There was the case at Chalcedon of a man [a slave] who was branded on his arm and the same letter though somewhat confused and indistinct appeared marked on his child." What the slave bequeaths to descendents is a "perpetual and inheritable" nonnatality, an ontological stillbirth in which the slave's natal alienation constitutes a "genealogical isolation" turning the slave into an "ideal human tool an *instrumentum vocal* perfectly flexible, unattached and deracinated" (Patterson 1982: 337). The temporal structure of transgenerational conscription into slavery lacks Arendt's natality as the new that disrupts historical inheritance. A political critique of natality in contrast to a phenomenology of pre-predicative natality would recognize that the politicizing difference between the political and nonpolitical is also the bifurcation of birth into natal potentiality and natal nullity—the latter as a founding recruitment into privative animality. Patterson's natal alienation renders the Arendtian universal model of the natal as crucially dehistoricizing.

Heidegger reduces animal death to repetitive demise, thereby demarcating a human being-toward-death from an apolitical animal perishing. Similarly, Arendt delimits a terrain of the natal and the nonnatal, which I propose, via natal alienation, is effectively a bifurcation of natality into the politically manifest and a depoliticizing concealment and privation. Natality qualified as *bios* and biography is born from and borne by the natal nullification of the animalized, the enslaved, and the subjugated. Isonomic political organization, which Arendt posits as antagonistic to rule by command and control, may be as much in symbiosis with natal nullification as it is predicated by natality aperity. Arendt tacitly concedes this in *On Violence*, where she evokes the dignifying protection that *civitas terrena* affords the citizen. She cites Xenophon as crediting the isonomic organization of the polis with enabling citizens to organize themselves against attacks from and murder by slaves (Arendt 1970: 50). Here the threat against sovereign *isonomia* comes from the sub-strata of the nonnatal and the animalistic. Arendt does not discuss the slave attack as expressing natal assertions and demands which are political through and through. The Athenians' imaginary of slave attack exposes democratic constitution as dialectically implicated in the deconstituted and the nullified. Arendt does not acknowledge that the prepolitical sovereignty of natality both presumes and produces the political "necessity" of the natalized and the denatalized, initiative and inertia, *isonomia* and biopolitical subjugation, and the politically human and the depoliticized animal. Whether from the perspective of isonomic self-constitution or slave attacks on those enfranchised by *isonomia*, natality appears as born from an aborted life that is twice abandoned.

THE BIOGRAPHICS OF THE ANIMAL

For Derrida the critique of the human/animal checkpoint is a journey across a confining threshold (*le passage des frontières*) into the previously deferred, suppressed, and unwritten autobiography of the animal as the

Nebenmensch, the unassimilatible neighbor of the human. The sheer recognition of animal autobiography means that there can be an animal natality that has been concealed or displaced by the birth of the human and that bears the dis-figuring trace of that anthropocentric deferment. Derrida will, in contradistinction to Arendt, recover a natal event in this passage across the anthropological checkpoint as the birth or upsurge of the animal from within a leaky and tenuous anthropocentric closure that for Derrida is both a divestiture of the sovereign subject (and the subject of sovereignty) and an opening onto a human-animal indeterminacy. Derrida is concerned with the reciprocal and concomitant appearing/disappearing of the human and the animal in a terrain whose political character awaits description and decision.

Derrida (2002b) writes of the human/animal checkpoint in specifically visual terms:

> The animal is there before me, there close to me, there in front of me—I who am (following) after it. And also, therefore, since it is before me, it is behind me. It surrounds me . . . it can look at me. It has its point of view regarding me. The point of view of the absolute other, and nothing will have ever done more to make me think through this absolute alterity of the neighbor than these moments when I see myself naked under the gaze of a cat. (380)

> Descartes, Kant, Heidegger, Lacan and Levinas. . . . Their discourses are sound and profound, but everything goes on as if they themselves had never been looked at, and especially not naked, by an animal that addressed them. At least everything goes on as though this troubling experience had not been theoretically registered, supposing that they had experienced it at all, at the precise moment when they made of the animal a *theorem*, something seen and not seeing. . . . It is as if the men representing this configuration had seen without being seen, seen the animal without being seen by it, without being seen seen by it; without being seen seen naked by someone who, from the basis of a life called animal, and not only by means of the gaze, would have obliged them to recognize, at the moment of address, that this was their affair, their lookout. . . . But since I don't believe, at bottom, that it has never happened to them, or that it has not in some way been signified, figured, or

metonymized, more or less secretly, in the gestures of their discourse, the symptom of this disavowal remains to be deciphered. This figure could not be the figure of just one disavowal among others. It institutes what is proper to man, the relation to itself of a humanity that is above all careful to guard, and jealous of, what is proper to it. (383)

To write an autobiography of the animal, according to Derrida, is to gaze at and be exposed to an animalizing gaze. The engagement with the anamorphic presences that are embodied, disembodied, materialized, and dematerialized in and as animality occurs in Derrida's uncanny encounter with his cat as he stands without clothes in his bathroom, though what is meant by the "gaze of the cat" and even by the emitting site or origin of this regard is not self-evident. Donna Haraway (2007: 19–21) reads this meeting as Derrida's self-evident defaulting on "a simple obligation of a companion species," as a failed moment of potential cross-species communication that she names as a "scientifically" and "biologically," and therefore (I stress) an anthropological return of the animal gaze. Haraway does not acknowledge that the stabilized subject position from which a cross-species capacity for exchange could be launched is exactly what falls into crisis in Derrida's experience of a gaze which transports and transposes him from humanity to animality, a seemingly natal alienation in which Derrida becomes his own *Nebenmensch*, or neighbor, who no longer possesses a sovereign ipseity. Of the ipse implied by the notion of speciation or iterable communication across diverse species Derrida (2002b: 415) writes: "I would like to have the plural of animals heard in the singular. There is no animal in the general singular, separated from man by a single indivisible limit. We have to envisage the existence of 'living creatures' whose plurality cannot be assembled within the single figure of an animality that is simply opposed to humanity." Derrida's objection to a fictive gross collectivization embodied in the term animal and its cognates reveals that the encounter with the "cat" occurs in a "social" field, and not an ethological space. A priori collectivity both presumes and contravenes "the heteronomic and dissymmetrical curvature of social space"—the curvature that precedes and interdicts full reflection and representational appropriation of the singular other as expressing collective magnitude (Derrida 2005: 231). This curvature is the contingent relation with the other before all organized socius, polity and law, before the we and they of speciation and before the name one assigns to oneself and to the other along with the responsibilities, agency, and freedoms that are supported by that name. At the moment that collectivities are announced as such there is no longer an absolutely asymmetrical singular other. Derrida (ibid.) adheres to this heteronomic curvature throughout his encounter with his cat: "For the heteronomic and dissymmetrical curving of a law of originairy sociability is also a law, perhaps the very essence of law." His mise-en-scéne may begin with the co-appearing of a man and a cat but neither subject position survives their mutual exposé—the cat is both a cat and not a cat as Derrida is himself and another.

> In the course of this experience the other appears as *such*—that is to say, the other appears as being whose appearance appears without appearing, without being submitted to the phenomenological law of the original and intuitive given that governs all other appearances, all other phenomenality as such. The altogether other and *every other* (*one*) *is every* (*bit*) *other*, comes here to upset the order of phenomenology and good sense. That which comes before autonomy must also exceed it—that is, succeed it, survive and indefinitely overwhelm it. (ibid.: 232)

To explore this encounter with the animal gaze would be to articulate Derridean animal *biographics* with Foucauldian *biopolitics*. What are the political graphics that imprint normative forms of life on creatures, that place them under a biographical and collectivizing gaze that is, ultimately, a political gaze? For Foucault a biographics of the biopolitical determines who is allowed to live and who is allowed to die. The two poles of life and death frame the journey across the frontier of the animal. This journey to the frontier has also been the autobiographic unfolding of the state that constructs sovereignty by deciding what counts as human and what does not. It is the culture of the state that elevates humanity as an entitled mode of natal citizenship. If, as Hayden White (1990: 120, 132–33) proposes, biography is invented with the state, the autobiography of the animal is in part an artifact of state practices and thus a political narrative.

For Derrida the visual field of animality is fractured—one animal, the human, experiences exposure, embarrassment, shame, numbness, and violence when naked in front of the animal neighbor in itself and before itself. Nakedness both decenters humanity and is a heightening of animality, the raising into visibility of the deferred animal biographics of the culturally and politically constructed human. He describes the denuding visual exposure of this stratigraphy of the animal in the human as a "mishap," "a fall," an "unpaid debt," a "symptom that cannot be admitted," and a pathology. This Edenic fall is not nakedness but *knowledge* of nakedness. For Derrida animals cannot be naked, as they do not *know* nakedness (nonhuman animality). To be naked as an animal is not to be an animal but to be reduced to the specularity and the disenfranchising gaze of an animalizing other. To be naked is to be naked before someone or something that occupies an enfranchising or disenfranchising position as regards the human, whether this is the radical alterity of a watchful other, or the scrutiny of the law, medicine, the rifle scope of a sniper, or the telemetry of a smart bomb. Derrida's project is autobiographical, and thus no biographics of the animal can be construed as devoid of human informatization, particularly when an encounter with animality precipitates biographical divestiture. Foucault (2006: 66) linked animality to madness which "was thus an animal with strange mechanisms, a bestiality from which man had long been suppressed." Derrida (1980: 36–38) once chided Foucault for writing as if he could tell us what madness is and what the mad really think. Thus Derrida equally cannot report on what animals really see, only the effects of that gaze of "someone who, from the basis of a life called animal" he experiences as "animalizing."

In the interstices of a banal everyday encounter with his cat, Derrida undergoes a passage into a bared life where animality arises as a nakedness and exposure that is not proper to animals per se, but which defines human impropriety, propelling humanity outside of its "proper" and sovereign self. This stripping, numbing, nonhuman gaze is at issue here and not the field of vision of the cat. We are far from the animal as a species-being, contrary to what Haraway presumes. For if there are gazes that provoke the upsurge of animality and the disenfranchisement of a secured humanity, these scopic regimes come into existence through operations that anthropologize and animalize. Sovereign spectatorship derives from the displacement that is the locus of the big Other—the state, society, and panoptical regimes. Neither Derrida's cat nor any other "animal" can be shown to have such a sovereign project.[7]

The impropriety [*malséance*] of a certain animal nude before the other animal, from that point on one might call it a kind of *animalséance*: the single, incomparable and original experience of the impropriety that

would come from appearing in truth naked, in front of the insistent gaze
of the animal. . . . Clothing would be proper to man, one of the "properties" of man. Dressing oneself would be inseparable from all the other
forms of what is proper to man, even if one talks about it less than speech
or reason, the *logos*, history, laughing, mourning, burial, the gift, and so
on. (The list of properties unique to man always forms a configuration,
from the first moment. For that reason, it can never be limited to a single
trait. . . .) (Derrida 2002b: 372–74)

Proper dressing or presentation of the body, habeas corpus as a performative of anthropological citizenship, conversely implies stripping the body,
in which the human would come into a knowledge of a politically constructed animality in the divestiture of human cover, in the loss of political
dressage—from clothing to identity cards, to entitlements and rights to life
itself. Here, the animal and its gaze bear the trace of human divestiture and
nakedness without being the origin of these political conditions. In tracing
the animal the latter is covered in its nakedness and the human is figured
and dressed. This is a biographics that decides on states of dress as conditions of address or subject positioning, where the dressed and the naked are
interpellated as a human or animal, as political subject and nonsubject in
which ethological categories and boundaries are subsumed under political
speciation. Derrida engages political speciation when he frames anthropology and animality, dressage and nudity within a theory of prosthetics and
disability as intrinsic to a theory of subjectification. "We would therefore
have to think shame and technicity together, as the same 'subject,'" and *in*
the same subject (ibid.).

FROM BIOSEMIOTICS TO BIOPOWER

Derrida writes of an optics of shaming that produces an ensnared and exhibited subject in a state of "debt" to an encircling and animalizing Other.
He does not explicitly name any of this as political. Derrida's animal exposé also witnesses Western metaphysics in the biosemiotics of Martin
Heidegger and Jakob Johann von Uexküll: the latter's notion of *Umwelt*,
the semiotic surround within which the animal senses and acts, is trans-
posed by Derrida into a predicating visual field. In von Uexküll (2001) the
Umwelt as sensorial specularity, as spatial aesthesis, is the locus from which

the animal always receives its code (see also Bains 2001).[8] In Heidegger's (1995: 236–67) reading of von Uexküll the animal is "captivated" (*Benommenheit*) by its surround and in a state of "benumbedness" as it is lured by a hypnotic ring of disinhibiting semiotic triggers borne by the Umwelt.[9] The animal for Heidegger is "taken" by its perceptible Umwelt rather than taking a position over and against it, implying a bipedal ontology that Heidegger later renders explicit by asserting that the animal, due to its capture by the *Umwelt*, does not *stand* alongside man (hence Derrida's experience of a philosophical fall into animality). Being erect over, against, and before is the emblematic posture of the mastering and representing subject—mastery is never prone, and to speak and to represent, powers denied to animality, is to stand over things and animals. This disability of not-standing-beside-the-human anticipates the disabilities of Derrida's captivity, shame, captivation, and "involuntary exhibition" under the animalizing gaze.[10]

Due to this lack, according to Heidegger, the animal is "poor in world" or "merely life," tropes that anticipate Agamben's bare life and Derrida's experience of naked "debt."[11] The animal has an *Umwelt*, thus a field of perception, an opening, but no self-reflexive understanding of "the Open" as such, as Agamben (2004) describes it. The animal senses without understanding, a privative formula that Derrida (1989: 50) says is in opposition to the Enlightenment concept of seeing as understanding: "The animal has no world because it is deprived of it, but its privation means that its not having is a mode of having. . . . The animal has and does not have a world." And Agamben (2004: 55) elaborates: "The ontological status of the animal environment. . . . is open but not *offenbar*, disconcealed. For the animal beings are open but not accessible; that is to say they are open in an inaccessibility and an opacity that is in a non-relation. The openness without disconcealment distinguishes the animal's poverty. The animal is not simply without world for insofar as it is open in captivation it must—unlike the stone which is worldless—do without world, lack it." Derrida (1989: 55) writes of this impoverishment: "If privative poverty indeed marks the caesura or the heterogeneity between the non-living and living on the one hand, between the animal and human *Dasein* on the other, the fact remains that the very negativity of the residue which can be read as a discourse on privation cannot avoid a certain anthropocentric and humanist teleology." These Heideggerian privatives map a terrain of animal lack that I suggest is political not only because these theorems deny their political import by entrenching animality in a destined site of ontological privation, but also because they emerge from, and are symptomatic of a modernity where humanization and inhumanization, sensory captivation and capture, have become political and economic projects of unprecedented magnitude. If poverty of world or life or language anchors the entelechy of the human over the animal, the thanatopolitical category of ultimate devaluation and poverty—that is, of *life not worthy of life*—transposes this anthropocentric teleology into a juridical and existential fault line for political subjects in which anthropocentrism becomes the numbing, capturing, and killing machine of biopower.

Derrida (1989: 54) writes of the relation between numbness, anesthesia, deprivation, and captivation, "Benumbedness seems to close off access to the entity as such. In truth it does not even close it off, since closure implies opening or aperity . . . to which the animal does not have access." Being open in a state of captivation or "being taken in the drivenness of instinctual captivation," as Heidegger (1995: 249) puts it, is to define captivity in terms of sensory colonization and as an anesthestics borne by sensory enclosure. *Captivation as captivity* is where a being's mode of aperity becomes a mode of entrapment, a lure in which the aperture of embodied aesthesis is a shutter. The Heideggerian animal *Umwelt* as a space of imprisoning captivation, benumbment, disability, and debt covertly communicates with the camp, the torture center, and other structures of subjugating speciation where *the animalized* possess a world in an impoverished state of dispossession. This impoverishment of world as a code of subjugation implies political modes of exposure, as a mode of not bare life but life that has *been bared* even to the point of disappearance; exposure to an outside as abandonment communicates with exposability as a state of erasing specularity. This mode of exposure colonizes sensory aperity to produce the subjugated from political animality. For instance, in Foucault's anatomo-politics the optical politicization of life is predicated on the aperture of the body that is permeable and trainable and therefore subjected to a ring or biosemiotic habitus of agency-forming technics or disinhibitors (to use Heidegger's term), the administrative motors of captivating subjection known as panopticism. Foucauldian biopower functions as an *Umwelt* to the degree that it surrounds and is anchored on the aperity, visibility, and spatiality of the body as the enabling terrain for a continuous power without interruption where the body's exposure and openness enables the subjugating colonization of the political subject by technologies of political aesthesis.

Derrida (2002b: 381) summarizes the scopic regime he is caught within,

> As with every bottomless gaze, as with the eyes of the other, the gaze called animal offers to my sight the abysmal limit of the human: the inhuman or the ahuman, the ends of man, that is to say the border crossing from which vantage man dares to announce himself to himself, thereby calling himself by the name that he believes he gives himself. And in these moments of nakedness, under the gaze of the animal, everything can happen to me, I am like a child ready for the apocalypse, *I am (following) the apocalypse itself,* that is to say the ultimate and first event of the end, the unveiling and the verdict.

Derrida barely stands here in shame, passivity, and nudity in a zone of surveillance, confronted by "a bottomless gaze," a visually constructed zone of bared life; a zone that delivers apocalyptic yet natal expectations, that functions as a border with checkpoints where identities must be announced and are strip-searched and suspended, where terminal infantilization has been experienced, and where verdicts may be forthcoming. Derrida performs an autopsy on both humanity and animality, on dress and nudity, in the sense of *autopsia*, as the bearing of witness with one's own eyes; but whose eyes, whose sovereign gaze? *Autopsia* as self-witnessing, curiosity, and curation has to be pushed to crisis and collapse. Autopsy is an *inspectacular* power that dissects, and orchestrates human or animal flesh; it is also an archival thanatological incision that can rigidify or deface any difference between the two—political speciation is exactly this commerce, this trade in exchangeable, partible, and substitutable political flesh. The formlessness and facelessness of this animalizing, bottomless and denuding gaze installs "the pathos of distance . . . [with] one type of will fixing that distance and another type keeping it" (Schürmann 1984: 378). The sovereign will whose gaze distributes and redistributes positions of humanity and animality is neither human nor animal but rather functions as the degree zero from which such allocations and consignments as archival gestures are performed. Anthropological constitution is here anthropocentric objectification as self-subjugation in which the positioned and inserted subject objectifies itself within itself—yet this is as an instituted political speciation that derives from nothing that can be called anthropological. Derrida through the estrangement effect of animality performs reverse engineering on the Foucauldian critique of anthropologization, placing it in a necessary contiguity with the nonhuman and the animal. For Foucault (1979;

Feldman 1991: 178–79) the question of anthropological self-production would be self-identity performed as self-objectivation and enforced as self-subjection through the embodied interiorization of power. For Derrida an impresse of animality is circulated through nodes of sovereign spectatorship and internalized by a subject captured and captivated within the given conditions for coming into visual actuality as human. Rainer Nagele (1991: 11) addresses the scandal of fractured anthropological actuality that refers to an absence, trace, or lack encoded by the figure of the nonhuman:

> The spiritual adventure of man coming into consciousness after the collapse of the mediaeval world, [was] to reconstruct solely through the representation of intersubjective relations, the fictive reality in which he wanted to assert himself. . . . This new formation is less a world formation (*Weltbild*) than a subject formation (*Menschenbild*) in the form of a reflected mirror image. The new subject appears self reflectively as the adventure of man having come to himself (*zu zich commen* can mean to come to one's senses . . .) *Who comes to whom, when one comes to oneself? Where was this man before he came to himself and where is he in relation to the one to whom he has come?* (emphasis mine)

In the Nietzschian tradition of Foucault, which is also taken up by Derrida, one thinks "both with and against the subject, turning the polymorphous subject against any one fictitious thinking thing or any one transcendental apperception," including that of the human or the animal (Schürmann 1984: 375). Nagele's topological question, of where and how the who-that-comes-to-itself is positioned questions the location/non-location and primacy of a self-enclosed and self-referential anthropology in the humanization narrative and points to the nullified natalities that condition the natality of humanization.

The Derridean exposure of the unhuman anthropologizing/animalizing gaze does not create a zoo-spectacle from the vantage of enfranchised anthropology but rather stages a zoo-escape from the political technicity of divides, limits, and fault lines between the human and the animal. Amid all the divesting powers in his essay there also is a witnessing of the failure of enforced thresholds and institutionalized vantage points that enable and stabilize witnessing and spectatorship. In witnessing this zoo-break, Derrida must account for the threshold crossed and crossed out, for what the threshold no longer secures, and for the violence that has attempted to secure, fix, and position the anthropological threshold. Thresholds are the origins of inside and outside whether this be the divide between human and animal or those between bios and bare life, natality and death, or witness and event. The threshold as foundational and archival is sovereign, and Derrida seeks to fracture the latter by showing that both sovereignty as a threshold and the sovereign threshold have secured and witnessed nothing but the machinery and violence of their autopsic self-securitization.

THE THRESHOLD OF THE FACE

Derrida's encounter with the animalizing gaze and Arendt's natality meet in their common concern for the politics of the *prosopon*. *Prosopon* can mean the face as persona, to be toward a face and the self-appearing of being, and what one sees and speaks with (Manoussakis 2002). The *prosopon* fuses the sense of face, facing, and person: *pros* is to be toward, in front of; *opon* derives from *opsis* as vision, so *pros-ops* can be glossed as that which faces the eyes of another. Arendtian animality does not have a *prosopon*, the faceless animal has no mode of apparition in a space qualified by natality as a singular appearing-in and facing-of the world. In biopolitical theory the animal lacks political advent and manifestation, it emerges as a depoliticized anomic multitude, its mode of apparition is a mode of impoverished defacement without singularity: the animal is *aprosopoi ontes* which refers to the lack of auto-telic personhood. The biopoliticized *prosopon* variously archived as zoé, bareness, and life-without-qualities is a nudity to be appropriated, colonized, occupied, traced over and ultimately jettisoned. In Arendt and Heidegger, animality marks a disavowed inaugural threshold of the political and the anthropological to the degree that its political concealment and confinement is also a supporting habitus, a subjectile life, and the verso to the recto of the anthropocentric face as political script. As such the appearing nonface of political animality is akin to the face of the gorgon, that can only be accessed through refraction and mediation that returns the animal *prosopon* in a malformed state of the disfigured and disfiguring other (Calame 1986: 138).

Emmanuel Levinas opposes a nonfigurative face to the violence of figuration. For Levinas the human face as radical alterity is nude to the degree that it is not shielded by or dressed in figuration. It, like Derrida's animal gaze, is not reducible to a visual circumcision. Levinas seeks a foundational ethics in wresting the human face from a conditioning visibility, from figuration as iconic reduction. In this iconoclasm, however, the animal "face" is either too much or too little.

> One cannot entirely refuse the face of an animal. It is via the face that one understands, for example, a dog. Yet the priority here is not found in the animal, but in the human face. We understand the animal, the face of the animal, in accordance with *Dasein*. . . . I cannot say at what moment you have the right to be called "face." The human face is completely different and only afterwards do we discover the face of the animal. I don't know if a snake has a face. I can't answer that question. A more specific analysis is needed. (Levinas 1988: 169–71)

In Levinas the domesticated dog's face derives its legibility and subjecthood from the human face without partaking in its full ethical excess or prefigurative otherness, while the snake has no face at all to which an ethical response could be made. Animality is here divided between inside and outside in a manner roughly analogous to Agamben's *bios* and *zoé*. Despite Levinas's iconoclasm, both the derivative dog's face and the facelessness of the snake are political figures of subjugation and abjection, respectively. Seeing the undomesticated snake, seeing its gaze (which presumes a face) is the seeing of sheer formlessness with no anthropological recourse: the Levinasian animal is both an appearing beyond the anthropological face and a disfigured by-product of the humanized face. Levinas presumes an ethics based on recognizability and bars an ethics and politics of the unrecognizable as personified by the surplus facelessness of the snake. The face here is an address, and a condition of political address invariably circumscribed by anthropological measures that render faceless animality homeless and nonlocatable except in relation to the humanizing signature of the recognizable face. Can the non-face, that which is unrecognizable as a face have a *prosopon*? What is the doctrine of signatures that authorizes and authenticates a face that endows political legibility to the face, qua face? Is the signature of the face only another anthropology or can the facial politics of signature be deanthropologized, creating new modes of address for the faceless and defaced, and their unreturnable gazes of opacity?

Derrida first wrote of the politics of nudity in reference to the facial ethics of Emanuel Levinas, which decidedly framed his later encounter with the animal gaze:

All nudity "even the nudity of the body experienced in shame," is a figure of speech in relation to the nonmetaphorical nudity of the face. "The nudity of the face is not a stylistic figure." And it is shown, still in the form of negative theology, that this nudity is not even an opening, for an opening is relative to a "surrounding plenitude." The word nudity destroys itself after serving to indicate something beyond itself. . . . The nudity of the face, speech, glance being neither theory nor theorem, is offered and exposed as denuding. . . . The structures of living and naked experience described by Levinas are the very structures of the world in which war would rage—strange conditional—if the infinitely other was not infinity, if there were by chance, one naked man finite and alone . . . but in this case Levinas would no doubt say there no longer would be war. . . . Therefore war—for war there is—is the difference between the face and the finite world without a face. (Derrida 1980: 106–7)

The Derridean animal/animalizing bottomless gaze is also an infinite recession, a nudity that destroys itself, for it moves beyond and evades the anthropocentric trace in which the face functions as political figuration and dressage. The Derridean animal evades capture by the anthropocentric face, and exceeds the lure, law, and closure of that face. The Derridean *prosopon* of the animal is generated by the crossing of gazes that juxtapose modes of appearing and concealing as a political landscape. The animal is the other face that is always already there and thus traced over. If *prosopon* means to be in front of a face, to be toward a face, to be in someone's face, its cognate, *antiprosopos*, is to represent a face that is not present, perhaps a face-to-come or no longer there, and also to place a face against a face to superimpose one face upon the other, the human upon the animal and the obverse. The face is a historical palimpsest and political emblem but this palimpsest can be an iconic disavowal or a hospitable cohabitation with the unrecognizable. All of this presumes a Levinasian antecedence of the other as a pre-occupation. Animal pre-occupation is also a natality, an appearing-in the world that is inherited as a political relation. Derridean natality is the act of appearing before another face as the pre-occupant of that space which is politicized by virtue of manifested heterogeneous co-occupation, by a politics of hospitality, hosting, tracing, neighboring, tracking, and disavowal, such as what ties the human to the animal within and without. Natal appearing requires this pre-occupancy with/of the antecedent Other to enter into the political. Politics is the space where all those who can claim a positive or negative, secured or imperiled relation to natality, to a face, to aperity whether human, animal, beast, slave, and monster co-appear within the curvature of dissymmetrical and heteronomic pre-occupation; an interdependent relational and always contestable tracework of faces found and lost, near and far, before and after, defaced, unrecognizable, and unrecognizing. Political subjugation aims to occupy and inhabit the face of the other, which is to mask (*prosopeion*) and to en-face the other in determinate figurations and thresholds that de-face. The face itself becomes the threshold between inside and outside, humanity/animality, friend/enemy, the political and the nonpolitical. Wherever defacement prevails without contestation, without the potentiality or right, to counter-face as the possibility of natal apparition, that is where forms of naming, gazing, and masking petrify the counter-posed *prosopon* into a rictus.

Yet an ethics of the *prosopon* that is opposed to the politics of facial petrifaction and rictus is what Levinas denies the animal, a disavowal that should provoke a counter-iconicity of the faceless. This counter-facing entails the recognition of the unrecognizable and the insensible as what cannot be absorbed by political similitude. Can there be an ethics of the gaze not based on identification, fellowship, fraternity or assumptions of commonality, anthropological invariance, or biopolitical subsumption? This ethics would also be an excavation of anthropocentric "animalizing" violence and damage that was never recognized as such because it was inflicted on the dissimilar and disidentified as what is beyond empathy, pain, the pathos of distance, and, even as Arendt and Heidegger have taught us, beyond birth and death. A critical ethics of the *prosopon* of animality would not arise from any determinate and final tracing-over of denudation or from a liberal inclusive figuration that would re-assimilate the exposed, bared, and faceless to the very anthropocentric sovereignty that rendered such life disposable. For any tracing over of the faceless that institutes a face can neither rule nor measure facelessness as political inauguration. The political natality of the monstrous or animalized neighbor can only emerge from a *bared life that destroys itself as bare* by exceeding, contesting, and destabilizing any figurative closure that violently defaces through exposure and erasure. The destruction of bare life and what it secures, including biopolitical enfranchisement, would speak to the absence of finite visage as the necessary condition for the opening of the closed histories of the anthropocentric face and the suborning of those biographics by the unrecognizable natalities, animalities, and signatures of the faceless.

CODA: THE GNAT AND THE SOVEREIGN

The animal *prosopon*, as an appearing-in concealment, as political screen, is covered by and a cover for sovereignty. Yet there is also the haunting of the sovereign subject by the animal within and without, in which each, the sovereign subject and the animal, inhabit, house, and parasite the other, and where each becomes the host and hostage of the other. From the Talmud:

> Vespasian sent Titus who said, Where is their God, the rock in whom they trusted? This was the wicked Titus who blasphemed and insulted Heaven.[12] What did he do? He took a harlot by the hand and entered the Holy of Holies and spread out a scroll of the Law and committed a sin on it. He then took a sword and slashed the curtain. Miraculously blood spurted out, and he thought that he had slain himself, as it says . . . Titus further took the curtain and shaped it like a basket and brought all the vessels of the Sanctuary and put them in it, and then put them on board ship to go and triumph with them in his city. . . . A gale sprang up at sea which threatened to wreck him. He said: Apparently the power of the God of these people is only over water. When Pharaoh came He drowned him in water, when Sisera came He drowned him in water. He is also trying to drown me in water. If He is really mighty, let him come up on the dry land and fight with me! A voice went forth from heaven saying; Sinner, son of sinner, descendant of Esau the sinner, I have a tiny creature in my world called a gnat. (Why is it called a tiny creature? Because it has an orifice for taking in but not for excreting.) Go up on the dry land and make war with it. When he landed the gnat came and entered his nose, and it knocked against his brain for seven years. One day as he was passing a blacksmith's it heard the noise of the hammer and stopped. He said; I see there is a remedy. So every day they brought a blacksmith who hammered before him. If he was a non-Jew they gave him four *zuz*, if he was a Jew they said, It is enough that you see the suffering of your enemy. This went on for thirty days, but then the creature got used to it. It has been taught: Rabbi Phineas [son of] Aruba said; I was in company with the notables of Rome, and when he died they split

open his skull and found there something like a sparrow two sela's in weight. (*Babylonian Talmud* 1978: 3:259)

Titus in the Temple behaves allegorically, yet is lost in literality in displaying phallic potency and swordplay to lay claims to sovereignty over the colonized. Titus's sexualization of faceless power through phallic blade work is ludicrous for the Talmudic narrator—all this orificial symbolism is Titus's pagan illusion, a profound moment of misrecognition. In defiling the temple through politicized sexual aggression Titus mirrors himself—he attacks his own model of sovereignty in slashing the curtain, confusing what it hides with a stage, the theatricized politics of the imperium. The Roman wounds only himself in transgressing the presumed body of a faceless sovereignty that is neither embodied nor mimetic. This orificial violence returns with the gnat's anti-imperial asymmetric warfare. Torture by the gnat reveals the body of the Roman sovereign as permeable and violable—magnitude is brought down by the minimal, by the animal.

Titus has a bad theory of sovereignty tied to the body and sexuality, presuming finite binaries of earth and ocean, and sacral space (political territoriality) and its violation. Titus wants his adversary, the Jewish god, to abandon the diasporic boundless ocean for the finitude and positivity of land and for the war of the territorial; in reply he is sent the peripatetic faceless gnat that occupies, parasites, and subjugates from an ethical site of unrecognizability. Titus's suffering is the coercive push of his body from sovereignty to creaturely life as personified and mediated by the gnat. His expansive sexuality is reduced by the gnat of the single orifice.

The faceless sovereignty that masters the territorial sovereign is what commands and converts others to creaturely life. The pagan Roman emperor does not govern the creaturely but is commanded by it, both in his sexual investments and later as the habitus of the gnat. In a profound inversion the minuscule gnat reduces the ruler of the world to the creaturely and to the chronic. Titus's judgment is to be captivated and captured by monomaniacal stimuli, the buzzing of the gnat, and the noise of hammers. The afflicted Roman emperor is, like Heidegger's (1998) animal, poor in world benumbed by his disinhibiters, be they eros, violence, noise, or pain.

The material reduction of Titus to animality, to a denuding world of benumbment, bears witness to a singular sovereignty, which is here the rule of the disrupted, the displaced, and the scattered. The exceptionality of this asymmetric anti-imperial violence is manifested in the transformation of the tortuous gnat into the sparrow (that is later described in the Talmud as a thoroughly militarized sparrow with beak and claws clad in iron and brass). The post-Talmudic lesson is that the sovereign can be deposed by a counter-law of insensible and resistant singularity that exceeds imperial magnitude. The politics of the gnat proposes that there is no sovereignty, human "we," anthropological commons, face or biopolitics that legislates or totalizes the political: the latter is inaugurated by constituting antagonisms between such totalities and surplus aggregations beyond the anthropocentric count who have no political status as precomprehended collectivities including that of humanity (Rancière 2004a). Perhaps now is the time, as the philosopher Reiner Schürmann (1984) proposed, to begin "gathering singularities," to begin thinking the scattered collateral damage of our universalizing and maximizing hegemonic phantasms, and to address their thresholds and limit experiences, as did the utopian animals of the Talmud who rarely stilled its buzzing movement in the human skull of sovereignty.

NOTES

1 I have here paraphrased Derrida's own insight on ethical fracture in relation to the politics of law in which by inference animal ethics would also be treated as a pure performative act suspended over an abyss that would presuppose a messianic animal-to-come (Derrida 1989/1990: 991–93).

2 Page Dubois (2003: 223n4) inventories the ancient Greek terms for slave, which includes "human stock" (*andrapodon*), "a man-footed thing like a four-footed beast" (*tetrapodon*), which also implies "child." Slaves resemble dogs because they are both within and outside the human community of the household and the polis as tamed or wild alters.

3 In her discussion of fifth-century Athenian law, Dubois (1991: 68–69) demonstrates how this dichotomy between *logos* and *phoné* culminates in the juridical torture of slaves, a practice and a persona absent from Agamben's Homo Sacer.

4 See my discussion of this partitioning or biosemiosis of the body and implicitly life as historiographic surface (Feldman 1991: 233–36).

5 I am paraphrasing and quoting Althusser's (1976: 180–81) critique of Hegelian totality: "There is no assignable Origin in Hegel, but that is because the whole process, which is fulfilled in the final totality, is indefinitely, in all the moments which anticipate its end, its own Origin. There is no Subject in Hegel, but that is because the becoming-Subject of substance, as an accomplished process of the negation of the negation, is the Subject of the process itself."

6   There is a direct connection between this privation of biography and Arendt's notion of the rightlessness of the *sans papiers* who have been deprived of both biography and *bios* through the geopolitical loss of natality.

7   This is not to deny the animal its own political being in the world but to indicate that any animal politics might contest the anthropocentric reducibility of the political to sovereignty.

8   I do not have the space here to fully explore how and why the Lacanian distinction between human and animal is based on the humanizing capacity to master the tendency for mimetic identification with the Other. Animality here is irretrievably captured by specular lures (Lacan 1977: 377).

9   See also Agamben's (2004) discussion of Heidegger in relation to von Uexküll's bio-semiotics.

10 This imagery also evokes the fetalized state of the similarly disabled/fetalized child before the "orthopedic" and sovereign refractions of the Lacanian mirror theater (Lacan 1977: 4–7).

11 To comprehend the Heideggerian notion of impoverished animality and the function of this fiscal imagery, we need to turn to his essay on technology. Though Heidegger distinguished between an organ's usability and an instrument's utility, the impoverishment of the animal is not unrelated to the technological condition of the utensil or tool. (See also my discussion of Arendt and slavery above.) For Heidegger (1977: 9–11), the utensil's condition is determined by "telic finality"—a tool is that which is "caused" by something from the outside and undergoes "a fall" into a condition of indebtedness. The animal's "poverty" is related, if not identical, to this state of technological "indebtedness" to what is outside of it as both a lure and as a capturing and benumbing encirclement.

12 Titus (Titus Flavius Sabinus Vespasianus, AD 39–AD 81, Roman emperor AD 79–AD 81) was the son of the emperor Vespasian. Vespasian was campaigning in Judea when he was proclaimed emperor; Titus stayed on in the province to repress the Jewish revolt and on his return to Rome was awarded a triumph for his victories in Palestine.

Human Values and Political Life in the Wake of Global AIDS Treatment

João Biehl
Photographs courtesy of Torben Eskerod

AMID DENIAL, stigma, and inaction, AIDS became the first major epidemic of present-day globalization. By the end of 2007, an estimated 33.2 million people worldwide were living with HIV, and 9.7 million people needed antiretroviral drugs (ARVs). The number of people receiving treatment increased by about 1 million that year, and at the beginning of 2008 nearly 3 million people in low- and middle-income countries had access to antiretroviral therapy (UN-AIDS/WHO/UNICEF 2008). Unprecedented alliances among AIDS activists, governments, philanthropic and international agencies, and the pharmaceutical industry have made increased access to antiretroviral therapy possible. The battle for access has been hard fought on multiple fronts worldwide, and the boundaries of feasibility have been redefined.

Many public- and private-sector initiatives are being launched today, seeking to address AIDS therapeutically in places where treatments have been scarcely available. These initiatives raise a new set of national and global health-care policy challenges regarding adequate drug delivery, sustainable treatment access, and the integration of treatment with prevention. Broader questions arise as well: How can accountability of all sectors be assured? How do these trends affect the role of governments and their human rights obligations? Moreover, how are other deadly diseases of poverty that have less political backing being dealt with? Which value systems and policy decisions underscore medical triage? And what effects do all of these issues have on the experience of living with HIV/AIDS and poverty?

Brazil is known for its stark socioeconomic inequalities and persistent development challenges. Yet, against all odds, Brazil has invented a public way of treating AIDS (Bastos 1999; Biehl 2004; Galvão 2000; Parker, 1997). In 1996, during a time when global responses to HIV/AIDS were largely based on prevention, Brazil became the first developing country to adopt an official policy of free and universal distribution of antiretroviral drugs. Although this policy depended for implementation on an ailing public health-care system, Brazil nonetheless significantly scaled up treatment. Some two hundred thousand Brazilians are currently taking ARVs for which the government pays, and this life-saving policy is widely regarded as a model for stemming the AIDS crisis worldwide (Berkman et al. 2005; Okie 2006).

In a time when global health mandates are largely tagged to top-down diplomacy or corporate citizenship, I took it as my task to illuminate the intricacies of this off-center public health solution and to explore its reach (Biehl 2007). Throughout this chapter, I consider the political and economic factors underlying this therapeutic policy and identify the novel power arrangements (both global and national) that are crystallized in Brazil's response to AIDS. As I probe the AIDS policy's social and medical reach, particularly in impoverished urban settings where AIDS is spreading most rapidly, I also inquire into the micropolitics and desires that invest ARVs and make survival possible. Brazil's response to AIDS thus provides us with a unique opportunity both to apprehend shifting public-private involvements in a neoliberal landscape and to assess their immediate and long-term effects.

I draw from open-ended interviews I carried out with activists, policy makers, health professionals, and corporate actors in Brazil and the United States between 2000 and 2006. I also draw from my longitudinal study of the lives of marginalized AIDS patients and of the work of grassroots care services in the northeastern state of Bahia (1995–2005). Moving back and forth in space and time, ethnographic fieldwork allows us to see these various actors and forces in operation, reminding us that there is no short cut to understanding the multiplicities of reality and practice through which a technologically extended life is achieved.

How has the AIDS policy become a kind of public good, emblematic of the state's universal reach, even though it affects only a small fraction of the citizenry? What networks of care emerge around the distribution of lifesaving drugs? How do the poorest citizens understand and negotiate medical services? How are individual subjectivities and ideas of care both of the self and of others recast in relation to broader economic, political, and medical transformations? What do these struggles over drug access and survival say about government, human values, and ideas of the future?

Longitudinal ethnographic work remains, in my view, a vital social scientific antidote to what the economist Albert O. Hirschman (1970) identifies as "compulsive and mindless theorizing." As he writes, "quick theoretical fix has taken its place in our culture alongside the quick technical fix" (329). For Hirschman as for the ethnographer, people come first. This respect for people, this attention to the manufacturing of clinical and political discourses and to the sheer materiality of life's necessities makes a great deal of difference in the knowledge we produce. Large-scale processes are not abstract machines overdetermining the whole social field. Social mobilization and personal actions, for example, have made a world of difference in expanding treatment to the poorest people afflicted by AIDS (Farmer 2004; Helen Epstein 2007). The microarrangements of individual and collective existence cannot be solely described in terms of power, either. Overconfidence in power arrangements and rational choice is itself a cultural product to be scrutinized. As Hirschman (1970: 338) writes, "In all these matters I would suggest a little more reverence for life, a little less straitjacketing of the future, a little more allowance for the unexpected—and a little less wishful thinking."

THE POPULATION/PEOPLE CAESURA

Michel Foucault has argued that beginning in the eighteenth century the "naturalness" of population became central to Western techniques and conducts of government. The notion of population worked as a frame for addressing the economic and political problems of food scarcity, epidemics, and the circulation of goods and people in newly urbanized spaces.

Rather than focusing on individual juridical subjects, government became increasingly concerned with the management of things: "Things are men in their relationships with things like customs, habits, ways of acting and thinking... with things like accidents, misfortunes, famine, epidemics, and death" (Foucault 2007: 96). This governmental management (or political economy) triangulates with sovereignty and discipline, and it has "population as its main target and apparatuses of security as its essential mechanism" (108). Man becomes to population what the subject of rights was to the sovereign (79).

I find this analytics helpful, to a point. For Foucault, the notion of the population-subject as the primary object of security is marked by a fundamental caesura between what is pertinent and what is not for the government's economic and political action. "The multiplicity of individuals is no longer pertinent, the population is" (42). The people comprise those who conduct themselves "as if they were not part of the population as a collective subject-object, as if they put themselves out of it, and consequently the people are those who, refusing to be the population, disrupt the system" (44). What happens to the population/people caesura under neoliberal governmental reforms? When and under what conditions does people's inclusion or exclusion from the governmental radar stop being a security concern?

For Foucault, governmentality is "both external and internal to the state, since it is the tactics of government that allow the continual definition of what should or should not fall within the state's domain, what is public and private, what is and is not within the state's competence, and so on. So, if you like, the survival and limits of the state should be understood on the basis of the general tactics of governmentality" (109; see also Ferguson and Gupta 2002). I am interested in the arts of government that accompany economic globalization and the remaking of people as market segments (specifically, therapeutic markets). How do patient-citizen-consumers draw from government and it make it resourceful as they negotiate the vagaries of the market and economic survival? How are the poorest people part of government and which idioms of "humanity" make them visible? How do people triage each other in the day-to-day?

The ethnographer upholds the rights of a microanalysis and thus brings into view the immanent fields—leaking out on all sides—that people invent to live in and by. Gilles Deleuze's conceptual work is particularly relevant here. He does not share Foucault's overconfidence in power arrangements, and he is particularly concerned with the borders between the macro and the micro: "A society, a social field does not contradict itself, but first and foremost, it leaks out on all sides. The first thing it does is escape in all directions. Far from being outside the social field or coming from it, flight lines constitute its rhizome or cartography" (Deleuze 2006: 127). Such immanent fields of action are mediated by governmental techniques, yet they are also animated by claims to basic rights and "assemblages of desire" (126). In bringing into public view these localized and multidimensional fields of engagement and possibilities, always on the verge of being sealed off or foreclosed, the ethnographer still allows for some general principles to surface (or to become irrelevant).

Yes, global markets are incorporated via medical commodities, and my ethnography shows that medicines have become key elements in the state's arsenal of action. Yet, while new pharmaceutical markets have opened, and AIDS therapies have been made universally available (the state is present through the dispensation of drugs), it is up to individuals and communities to take on locally the roles of medical and political institutions. This pharmaceuticalization of governance and citizenship, obviously efficacious in the treatment of AIDS, nonetheless crystallizes new inequalities. This medical intervention—funded and organized by the state alongside international institutions and produced by the pharmaceutical industry—has resulted in effective treatment for working-class and middle-class Brazilians, meanwhile leaving the marginalized underclass by the wayside. These individuals cope by using survival strategies that require extraordinary effort and self-transformation.

AIDS therapies are now embedded in landscapes of misery, and hundreds of grassroots medico-pastoral services have helped make AIDS a chronic disease also among the poorest. This is not a top-down biopolitical form of control. The government is not using AIDS therapies and grassroots services as "techniques . . . to govern populations and manage individual bodies" (as the anthropologist Vinh-Kim Nguyen [2005: 126] has framed the politics of antiretroviral globalism). Throughout this chapter, I show that the question of accountability has been displaced from government institutions, and poor AIDS populations take shape, if temporarily, through particular engagements with what is made pharmaceutically available. The political game here is one of self-identification. Proxy communities, often temporary and fragile, and minor knowledges and desires are fundamental to life chances, unfolding in tandem with a state that is pharmaceutically present (via markets) but by and large institutionally absent.

At the margins, both the institutional and pharmacological matters surrounding AIDS treatment undergo considerable flux. Poor AIDS survivors themselves live in a state of flux, simultaneously acknowledging and disguising their condition while they participate in local economies of salvation and articulate public singularities. Against the backdrop of a limited health-care infrastructure and economic death and through multiple circuits of care, individual subjectivity is refigured as a *will to live*. Far from being the representative of a natural vitality, this will to live is constantly fought for, asserted, and renegotiated in the marketplace by those with the means to do so, limited as those means may be. At both the macro and micro levels, we see a state of triage and a politics of survival crystallizing.

Ethnography's unique theoretical force lies in recording competing rationalities and vital experimentations, in challenging orthodoxies of all kinds and conceptualizing fine articulations of worlds—differentiated, in flux, and impending (Fischer 2009; Rabinow 2008). Moreover, grasping social fields and subjectivity as becoming—rather than as determination—may be the key to anticipating, and thereby making available for assessment and transformation, the futures and forms of life of emerging communities. Thus, continually adjusting itself to the reality of contemporary lives and worlds, the anthropological venture has the potential of art: to invoke neglected human possibilities and to expand the limits of understanding and imagination. "There is no work of art," writes Deleuze (2006: 324), "that does not call on a people who does not yet exist."

THE HUMAN RIGHT TO HEALTH

Brazil is the epicenter of the HIV/AIDS epidemic in South America and accounts for more than 50 percent of all AIDS cases in Latin America and the Caribbean. The country's first AIDS case was diagnosed (retrospectively) in 1980, and through mid-2002 the Ministry of Health had reported nearly 240,000 cumulative cases. HIV prevalence in Brazil is higher than in most of its neighbors, although this is in part due to more accurate reporting (Castilho and Chequer 1997; Berkman et al. 2005). At the end of 2001, an estimated 610,000 Brazilians were living with HIV/AIDS (an adult prevalence of 0.7 percent, about half of what had been projected). Social epidemiological studies show considerable heterogeneity in HIV infection rates, with large numbers infected among vulnerable populations and a fast-growing number of heterosexual transmissions. Since 1998 the death rate from AIDS has steadily declined, an achievement attributed to the country's treatment policy (Dourado et al. 2006).

Throughout the 1990s, different sectors—gay groups, AIDS nongovernmental organizations (NGOs), grassroots services, and central and regional governments, along with the World Bank—came together, helping to address what was earlier perceived to be a hopeless situation (Bastos 1999; Parker 1994, 1997). Activists and progressive health professionals migrated into state institutions and participated in policy making. They showed creativity in the design of prevention work and audacity in solving the problem of access to AIDS treatment. In their view, the prices pharmaceutical companies had set for ARVs and the protection the manufacturers received from intellectual property rights laws and the World Trade Organization (WTO) had artificially put these drugs out of reach of the global poor. After framing the demand for access to ARVs as a human right, in accordance with the country's constitutional right to health, activists lobbied for specific legislation to make treatment universally available. Article 196 of the democratic constitution adopted in 1988 affirms health as a right of the people and a duty of the state—and AIDS activists were the first group to equate this right effectively to therapy access.

The Brazilian government was able to reduce treatment costs by reverse engineering antiretroviral drugs and promoting the production of generics in both public- and private-sector laboratories (Cassier and Correia 2003). Had a generics infrastructure not been in place, the story being told today would probably be different. For its part, the Health Ministry also negotiated substantial drug price reductions from pharmaceutical firms by threatening to issue compulsory licenses for patented drugs. Media campaigns generated strong national and international support (Galvão 2002; Serra 2004). The result—a policy of drugs for all—has dramatically improved the quality of life of the patients covered. According to the Health Ministry, both AIDS mortality and the use of AIDS-related hospital services have fallen by 70 percent. Brazil's treatment rollout has become an inspiration for international activism and a challenge for the governments of other poor countries devastated by the AIDS pandemic. This policy challenged the perception that treating AIDS in resource-poor settings was economically unfeasible, and it showed how lifesaving drugs could be integrated into public policy even in the absence of an optimal health infrastructure.

By 2000 the Brazilian AIDS program had been named by UNAIDS as the best in the developing world, and in 2003 it received the Gates Award for Global Health. Brazil is now sharing its know-how in a range of ways. It has taken a leadership role in the AIDS program of the World Health Organization (WHO), and it is supporting international networks aimed at facilitating treatment access and technological cooperation on HIV/AIDS. In recent years, the Brazilian government has also been leading developing nations in WTO deliberations over a flexible balance between patent rights and public health needs. Practically speaking, Brazil opened channels for horizontal collaborations among developing nations and devised political mechanisms (as fleeting and fragile as they may be) for poor countries to level out some of the pervasive structural inequalities that place their populations at increased vulnerability to disease.

PERSISTENT INEQUALITIES AND CIRCUITS OF CARE

I was in the coastal city of Salvador da Bahia conducting fieldwork when AIDS therapies began to be widely available in early 1997. Considered by many "the African heart of Brazil," Salvador was the country's capital until 1763. A center of international tourism, Salvador today has an estimated population of 2.5 million, with more than 40 percent of families living below the country's poverty line. At the time of my fieldwork, local health officials claimed that AIDS incidence was on the decline in both the city and the Northeast region, ostensibly in line with the country's successful control policy. But the AIDS reality one saw in the streets of Salvador contradicted this profile. A large number of AIDS sufferers remained epidemiologically and medically unaccounted for, dying in abandonment (Biehl 2005b). Meanwhile, community-run initiatives provided limited care for some of the poorest and the sickest.

The photographer Torben Eskerod joined me in chronicling the social work of Dona Conceição Macedo and her religious friends (see fig. 1). They provided free meals and some care to dozens of poor people and their families living with AIDS and very little else in the corners of the city's cultural

1 Dona Conceição's charity work among homeless AIDS patients in the
   Pelourinho neighborhood.

heritage center known as the Pelourinho ("Pillory"). As Dona Conceição
put it, "Medical services never meet the demands, and civil society has
abandoned them. They are at the margins of law and life. I give them a little
comfort and help alleviate things a bit. I am tied to them in spirit."

I talked to the group on several occasions. Soft-spoken, Jorge Araújo said
that he learned he had AIDS after his left leg was amputated because of infections related to intravenous drug use (fig. 2). Jorge had lived by himself
on the streets since the age of fourteen. At some point, he lived with an
older woman and had a child, but he eventually left them. "If I kept thinking about AIDS," he told me, "I would already be dead. One must forget. . . .
To be a patient one needs things. But what is there to have here?"

One should not expect these patients to adhere to medical treatments,
says Dona Conceição, because "they just use medication until they recover. . . . If they don't have a home, no treatment will work." Dona Conceição did not blame her street patients. Rather, she saw their condition as
a social symptom and made it into a public affair. But she also refused to
treat them as a collective, and that is what drew them to her. She helped
them become singular individuals, literally struggling in their place: "Each
one has a history, a life left behind. Jorge suffers with all the discrimination

2 Jorge, a few years after our initial
conversation, still living on the streets.

he faces. He keeps using drugs, and he is unable to overcome his personal failures. He does not struggle for health; I struggle for him."

Jorge praised Dona Conceição, saying that she played a crucial role in the circuitry—begging, work-for-food, petty robberies, and AIDS charity—that he and his friends engaged in to survive. He had bitter words for the little help he was getting from Caasah, Bahia's only *casa de apoio* (house of support), a grassroots house of support that he had helped to create and where I was carrying out the bulk of my ethnographic research.[1] "I still go there to get my monthly food basket. It is very little, and I still have to pay the bus ticket and split half with the colleague who carries it for me. I don't know where all the money they get from the government goes." Jorge also spoke, however, of a sense of belonging that took shape among street patients, eliciting a new constellation in which inner life was reframed and economic death endured: "People here are my friends. Of course, nobody will do anything for others for free. But they talk to me. They make me laugh. This gives me a bit of extra life."

How, I wondered, would the antiretroviral rollout fare in this context of multiple scarcities and spurious regional politics? How would the most vulnerable transform a death sentence into a chronic disease? What social experimentation could make such medical transformation possible?

3 Caasah.

Caasah, a focal point of my research, was founded in 1992, when a group of homeless AIDS patients, former prostitutes, transvestites, and drug users (Jorge among them) squatted in an abandoned hospital formerly run by the Red Cross (see fig. 3). "Caasah had no government," recalled the director, Celeste Gomes. "They did whatever they wanted in here. Everybody had sex with everybody; they were using drugs. There were fights with knives and broken bottles, and police officials were threatening to kick us out." Soon Caasah became an NGO and began to receive funding from a World Bank loan disbursed through the Brazilian government. By 1994 eviction threats had ceased, and the service had gathered community support for basic maintenance. Caasah had also formalized partnerships with municipal and provincial heath divisions, buttressed by strategic exchanges with hospitals and AIDS NGOs. Throughout the country, other "houses of support" like Caasah negotiate the relationship between AIDS patients and the haphazard, limited public health-care infrastructure. By 2000 at least one hundred of the country's five hundred registered AIDS NGOs were houses of support. In order to belong to these grassroots services, people must break with their old habits, communities, and routines as they forge new lives.

By the mid-1990s, the unruly patients in Caasah had been ejected. "I couldn't stand being locked in. I like to play around," Jorge told me. A smaller version of the group began to undergo an intense process of resocialization mediated by psychologists and nurses. Jorge and about eighty other outpatients remained eligible for monthly food aid. Patients who wanted to stay in the institution had to change their antisocial behaviors and adhere to medical treatments. Caasah now had a reasonably well-equipped infirmary, with a triage room and a pharmacy. Religious groups visited the place on a regular basis, and many residents adopted religion as an alternative value system. As Edimilson, a former intravenous drug user and petty thief put it, "In Caasah we don't just have AIDS—we have God." According to Celeste, "With time, we domesticated them. They had no knowledge whatsoever, and we changed this doomed sense of 'I will die.' Today they feel normal, like us; they can do any activity; they just have to care not to develop the disease. We showed them the importance of using medication. Now they have this conscience, and they fight for their lives."

With a simple chair and a black cloth against a wall, we improvised a photo studio outside Caasah's main building. Torben photographed each person and I recorded his or her life story.

Rose's left hand was atrophied, and she limped (fig. 4). "It is all from drug use. I was crazy." Rose and other healthy patients in Caasah repeatedly pointed to the marks on their bodies as images of past misdeeds, as if they were now in another place, seeing and judging their past selves from a photographic distance. "Ah, now I see. If I only had thought then the way I think now." Rose grew up in the interior of the state of Bahia and was expelled from home at the age of thirteen, after she became pregnant. She moved into Pelourinho's red-light district. By the end of 1993, Rose learned that she was both pregnant and HIV-positive. One by one, Rose gave up her children for adoption. "What else could I have done?" she said. "I couldn't give them a home. I also thought that I would not live much longer." But Rose has lived longer than she expected. She had quit drugs and remained asymptomatic. She had become literate, learned to make handicrafts, and was beginning to take AIDS therapies: "I take life in here as if it were a family, the family I did not have."

Caasah's residents and administrators constituted a viable public that effectively sustained itself in novel interactions with governmental institutions and local AIDS services. Instead of succumbing to the factors that predisposed them to nonadherence to treatment (such as poverty and drug addiction), residents used their "disadvantages" to create the AIDS-friendly

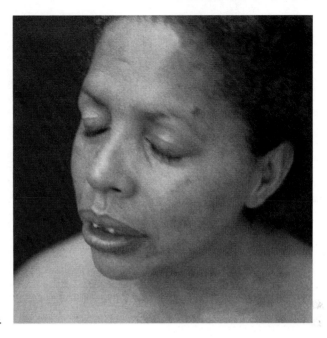

4 Rose, 1997.

environment that is necessary to accumulate health (see Abadia-Barrero and Castro 2006; Brigido et al. 2001; and Nemes, Carvalho, and Souza 2004). Here people did not have to worry about the stigma that came with having AIDS "on the outside," and a scheduled routine and an infrastructure made it easier to integrate drug regimens into everyday life. An intense process of individuation—"salvation from my previous life," as one resident put it—and a spirit of competition with fellow residents motivated treatment adherence as well.

"Did you ever see an AIDS patient in here hoping for the other's good?" Evangivaldo asked me as he had been quarantined because of his scabies (fig. 5). Residents constantly pointed to each other's faults and demanded everyone's adherence to the house rules. The other's misbehavior was also a measure of their own progress, a measure of their own change and self-control: "I am not like him"; "She did it to herself, and now she wants another chance." Money was at stake. Caasah's administrators facilitated application for AIDS disability pensions, and priority was given to residents who showed change. Well-behaved and compliant patients were also allowed to help in the storage room, where they were given priority in choosing clothing for themselves and for family members living outside.

5   Evangivaldo, 1997.

PHARMACEUTICALS AND SELF-GOVERNANCE

In grassroots units such as Caasah, marginalized citizens have an unprecedented opportunity to claim a new identity around their diseased and politicized biology, with the support of international and national, public and private funds. Here immediate access to AIDS therapies and the administration of health—the micropolitics of survival—takes priority over "metasocial guarantees of social order" or over political representation (Doimo 1995; Abélès 2006; Holston 2008). For the moment, let us think of Caasah as a "biocommunity" in which a select group of poor patients fights the systematic denial of social rights and carves out the means to access them empirically. This political subjectivity is articulated through pastoral means, disciplinary practices of self-care, and monitored pharmaceutical treatment. At work are new arts of self-governance and survival as a cost-effective patient.

Caasah's life-extending work challenges Hannah Arendt's rigid view of an opposition between the realm of the political and the realm of private life. For Arendt (1958: 320–25), the modern political process has progressively eliminated the possibility of human fulfillment in the public sphere,

excluding the masses and reducing each human being in them to the condition of *animal laborans*, a creature whose only activity is biological self-
preservation. This self-preservation is an individual concern, a metabolism
superfluous to the state and to society at-large. "They begin to belong to
the human race in much the same way as animals belong to a specific animal species" (Arendt 1973 [1951]: 302). That is, for Arendt, the primacy of
natural life in modern society has foreclosed the possibility of authentic
political action. Unfortunately, according to the late Iris Young, "Arendt
criticized efforts to improve social life and to promote social and economic
rights in the same category as the merely biological. She thought that concern for social and economic equality and inclusion was not appropriate in
the public sphere" (personal communication, March 2004).

The philosopher Jacques Rancière (2004b: 299) is also concerned with
the overturning of Arendt's "archipolitical position" into a "depoliticizing
approach": "Paradoxically this position did provide a frame of description and a line of argumentation that later would prove quite effective
for depoliticizing matters of power and repression and setting them in a
sphere of exceptionality that is no longer political, in an anthropological
sphere of sacrality situated beyond the realm of political dissensus." This
overturn, for Rancière, is clearly illustrated by Giorgio Agamben's theorization of biopolitics in *Homo Sacer* (1998). Following Arendt and Michel
Foucault (1980), Agamben (1998: 24) states that the original element of
sovereign power in Western democracies is "not simple natural life, but life
exposed to death." This "bare life" appears in Agamben as a kind of historical and ontological destiny, "something presupposed as nonrelational"
(109). Rancière (2004b: 302) gets straight to the point: "The radical suspension of politics in the exception of bare life is the ultimate consequence
of Arendt's archipolitical position, of her attempt to preserve the political from the contamination of private, social, apolitical life. This attempt
depopulates the political stage by sweeping aside its always-ambiguous
actors."

Caasah's residents reframe the question of what politics is. They engage
government via the AIDS policy and, in the process, are able to become a
local body of citizens. The universal availability of lifesaving drugs does not
reshape the bureaucratic apparatuses of the state, nor does it substantially
alter the medical establishment. Novel strategies for biosocial inclusion and
exclusion are rather consolidated under perennial structural violence. Many

stay outside, on their own. Caasah's distinctive feature is its selective trans-formation of a diseased biology, marginal and excluded, into a technical means of inclusion. Scavenging for resources and navigating through com-plex treatment regimes, residents constitute themselves as patient-citizens.

It is within this interrelated context of local, national, and international forces that I became interested in how the project to extend life informed institutions and political agency, particularly at the margins. Here, life ex-tension and social death are the poles of a continuum. The distribution and consumption of pharmaceuticals are significant means through which state, community, and citizen empirically forge their presence today. Nongovern-mental, pastoral, and clinical networks link the worlds of marginality and the state through AIDS response.

In order to make these new medical technologies work, people have to participate actively in local circuits of care. In contexts of unemploy-ment and scarcity, for many disenfranchised patients, the mere extension of life is literally a form of work (Petryna 2002). Thus, the deployment of AIDS therapies instantiates new capacities, refigures value systems, and alters people's sense of their bodies and of the future. The pressing needs of newly circumscribed patient populations for physical and economic survival dynamically inform private and public involvements; and these "affective entanglements," in turn, redefine the local terms of politics and ethics.

We can only understand the conflicting social effects of neoliberalism and governmental decentralization by looking at the materiality of poli-cies and related individual and communal struggles for survival. By ethno-graphically charting the ways policies and people operate at the margins, we can also illuminate political rationality in the making. Politics here is not a sphere, but a lack, a technology, and a process all at once. In the case of the AIDS policy, medication makes people equivalent—difference lies in laboratory testing and viral loads. It is up to grassroots work to address the social determinants of patients' conditions or to make these markers invisible. Here medical commodities work in tandem with other ways of claiming citizenship, and desperate and creative interactions occasion novel public sites in which rights are group-privatized, so to speak.

Life in Caasah draws on what is available. Individuals do not operate alone. Their decision making and actions are entangled with those of other patients and the multiple arts of government at hand for this group. Contemporary conditions are pressing, and disjunctions abound. Channels of communication with people and institutions are constantly renegotiated, and newly found personal identifications cannot be taken for granted.

MARKET POLITICS

"The success of the Brazilian AIDS policy is a consequence of the activism of affected communities, health professionals, and government," Paulo Teixeira, former national AIDS coordinator, told me in June 2005. I heard a similar explanation from Fernando Henrique Cardoso, Brazil's former president, two years earlier. "Brazil's response to AIDS is a microcosm of a new state-society partnership. . . . I always said that we needed to have a porous state so that society could have room for action in it, and that's what happened with AIDS."

I met with Cardoso at the Institute for Advanced Study, where he was participating in a meeting of the board of trustees. He had no qualms about extrapolating, using the AIDS policy as evidence of the "success" of his state reform agenda—a state open to civil society, decentralized, fostering partnerships for the delivery of services, efficient, ethical, and, if activated, with a universal reach (Cardoso 1998). "Government and social movement practically fused," he told me. "Brazilian society now organizes itself and acts on its own behalf." This new state-society synergy reflected in the country's AIDS program has developed in the wake of Brazil's democratization and the state's attempt to position itself strategically in the context of globalization. "This new phase of capitalism," Cardoso argued, "limits all states, of course, including the United States, but it also opens up new perspectives for states."

Cardoso said that both he and the new president, Luis Inácio Lula da Silva of the Workers' Party (Partido dos Trabalhadores [PT]), "in the end say the same thing." That is, "that globalization is asymmetric" and that "we have to take concrete steps toward decreasing this asymmetry, mainly at the trade level so that we can have access to markets, and also to control financing mechanisms." He made the case that Lula's government was basically following the same "ultraorthodox" economic line of his administration—but that, "surprisingly," the new government lagged in social program innovation: "The proposals they have are centralized, very vague, mismanaged, and don't match with what Brazil already is." Cardoso was proud of the ways the AIDS program—with its multisectoral partnerships and high-tech delivery capacity—had pushed the envelope of what was governmentally possible.

"The idea that nothing can be done because rich countries are stronger is generally true, but not always," stated Cardoso. "You can fight and, in the process, gain some advantages." Brazil's struggle for drug price reduction, he says, "shows that under certain conditions you can gain international support to change things. All the nongovernmental work, global public opinion, change in legislation, and struggle over patents are evidence of new forms of governmentality in action . . . thereby engineering something else, producing a new world."

The rhetoric of state agency and the abstractions that Cardoso articulated—mobilized civil society and activism within the state—are part of a new political discourse. This language belongs to a public sphere strongly influenced by social scientists, as well as by politicians who do not want to take responsibility for their decisions to conform to the norms of globalization. For example, Cardoso makes no specific reference to the measures his administration took to open the economy, such as changes in intellectual property legislation and the privatization of state industries. This political discourse does not acknowledge the economic factors and value systems that are built into policy making today (Ong 2006).

As with all things political and economic, the reality underlying the AIDS policy is convoluted, dynamic, and filled with gaps. The politicians involved in the making of the AIDS policy were consciously engaged in projects to reform the relationship between the state and society, as well as the scope of governance, as Brazil molded itself to a global market economy. One of my central arguments is that behind the concept of model policy stands a new political economy of pharmaceuticals. Just a few months before approving the AIDS treatment law in November 1996, the Brazilian government gave in to industry pressures to enshrine strong patent protections in law. Brazil was at the forefront of developing countries that supported the creation of the WTO, and it had signed the Trade-Related Aspects of Intellectual Property Rights treaty (TRIPS) in December 1994. Parallel to the new patent legislation, pharmaceutical imports to Brazil had increased substantially. Between 1995 and 1997 the trade deficit in pharmaceutical products jumped from $410 million to approximately $1.3 billion (Bermudez et al. 2000).

"Brazil bet a lot on the WTO and dove into it, body and soul," former Health Minister José Serra (an economist and now governor of the state of São Paulo) told me in an interview in 2003. "Neoliberalization developed abruptly. From a closed and protected economy we went to the opposite. This openness was unilateral. It was not a negotiating process through which the country gained something in return." As a policy maker, Serra was painfully aware of the loss of room for maneuver. "Brazil also dove into the free flow of capital. Dependence on this free flow to insure the growth of the economy can provoke a generalized instability; and this, combined with external vulnerability, can be volatile indeed. So our government was conditioned by this. And even though there was no direct pressure for privatization, nonetheless the external environment favored it. If you need an aid or credit from the World Bank, conditions are always embedded."

Serra also suggested that the mid-1990s was a transition period that left little time to critically reflect on the broader implications of the terms of economic readjustment—"things were not so clear." The long-term effects of TRIPS did not generate a great deal of public debate, for example, other than recognition that signing the treaty marked countries' conformity to global trade reforms. In particular, there was a lack of discussion about the impact of pharmaceutical patents on drug prices and accessibility. The president and his team took hasty and legally binding decisions. And from this new landscape defined by globalization, government was built. "We did not hesitate to abolish all taxes for the import of medication," Serra recalls. "Many in the national industrial sector complained, but we did this to hold the impact of exchange rates on inflation and to increase competition, to stimulate the production of generics."

Like Cardoso, Serra also denied a causal relationship between globalization and state reform. He was unapologetic about privatization, saying that "shrinking the size of the state does not mean less participation." Both politicians spoke of privatization as a means to make the state more agile so that it might both fulfill its market-regulating role and attend better to society. With the country's economy under siege, these politicians must insist that Brazil is not subservient; clearly, some form of independence and inventiveness is exercised in public policy—and that is what happened with AIDS, as it became technologically manageable.

In 1999 Serra championed the entrance of generics into the Brazilian market and gave incentives for their local production in public and private laboratories. "Reverse engineering and the production of generics was the only way of keeping the lifesaving policy going," he said. For Serra, besides strong social pressure, the AIDS policy "basically worked because it was within the structure of the government and, in fact, because it revitalized part of the governmental structure. You find AIDS programs in every corner of the country, and, generally, they are government funded." In these novel sites, the new relationship between government and society takes form: "I was also always trying to establish new mechanisms of cooperation between government and society, working with a whole array of philanthropic organizations. To deepen the idea that the public is not just the governmental." One could also argue that local communities increasingly compensated for the state's current lack of administrative capacity, particularly as far as public health-care infrastructure is concerned.

In their pragmatic approach to globalization, both Cardoso and Serra articulate a market concept of society. Citizens are consumers who have "interests" rather than "needs." In Serra's words, "The government ends up responding to society's pressure. If tuberculosis had a fifth of the kind of social mobilization AIDS has, the problem would be solved. So it is a problem of society itself." Here, the government does not actively search out particular problems or areas of need to attend to—that is the work of mobilized interest groups. These public actions are seen as "wider and more efficacious than state action," as Cardoso put it. Moreover, the afflicted have to engage with lawmaking and jurisprudence even to be seen by the state, and the implementation of progressive laws remains subject to a whole range of exclusionary dynamics linked to economics and specific social pressure. Meanwhile, grassroots groups address the paradox that ARVs are available but public institutions are barely working. Care has been outsourced to the groups. "Did bad things happen in the process?" asked Teixeira. "Yes, but without outsourcing there would not have been advances either. Evolution is never unidirectional—it is forward and backward. We hope that it is two steps forward and one backward."

At any rate, these various practices—a technological reaffirmation of the universal public health-care system, state production, and the outsourcing of care—materialized into a new politics of pricing as Brazil threatened to issue compulsory licenses on patented drugs in order to guarantee the sustainability of the policy. In spite of the national production of generics, prices of patented drugs were seriously jeopardizing the sustainability of the ARV rollout. Serra and national AIDS officers decided to bring the treatment question to the WTO meeting scheduled for November 2001 in Doha, Qatar. By then, there was growing international support for the Brazilian initiative, with endorsements from AIDS activist networks and UNAIDS, and editorial backing from media including the *New York Times*. Furthermore, the U.S. government was in a weaker negotiating position after it had threatened to break Bayer's patent of Cipro, seeking cheap supplies in the wake of the 2001 anthrax scare. With the support of key diplomats and NGOS, the Brazilian delegation articulated the position of a southern bloc that drafted a declaration that, at least symbolically, recaptured a developing country's sovereign right to operate outside the bounds of TRIPS for the purpose of public health—that is, in case of a crisis, countries were allowed to issue compulsory licenses for patented drugs.

In Teixeira's words: "We had to focus at every moment on the empirical steps that had to be taken to make things work, and also to maintain a temporal perspective, that is, to see things unfolding over time. The AIDS policy is a process." In practice, Serra stated, "the AIDS policy ended up working as a kind of counterweight to the economic orthodoxy in place internationally." It is through this specific constellation—the AIDS policy—that globalization assumes concrete form and meaning for some segments of the Brazilian public today. Flows of money, knowledge, and technology—mediated by international financial institutions, NGOS, trade-related treaties, lawmaking, reverse engineering, and a new state capacity—constituted a strategic terrain for novel social and political articulations which, in turn, recast AIDS and its treatment.

I am reminded here of Georges Canguilhem's (1998: 318) discussion of the "decline of the idea of progress" and his call for an analytics of "motion": "continuous progress is a conservative epistemological concept. Predictions of progress turn today into tomorrow. But it is only when tomorrow comes that we can speak of yesterday." The cumulative experience of the "unpredictability of the political and social effects of technological inventions," argues Canguilhem, are also epistemological breaks. The AIDS policy, one can say, both illuminates past political decisions and economic maneuvers—principles of inequality—and gives evidence of how these "origins" can be somewhat remediated by specific state-medical-market initiatives which, in turn, crystallize a bioeconomic or pharmaceutical form of governance.

THE PHARMACEUTICALIZATION OF PUBLIC HEALTH

The global sales of pharmaceuticals were estimated to reach $745 billion in 2008. According a report from IMS Health, one of the world's leading market intelligence firms, "as growth in mature markets moderates, industry attention is shifting to smaller, developing markets that are performing exceptionally well."[2] This is the case of Brazil, now the eleventh-largest pharmaceutical market in the world. Currently, some 550 pharmaceutical firms (including laboratories, importers, and distributors) operate in Brazil and compete for a slice of this lucrative market, which in 2005 reached $10 billion in sales. By 2010 the developing world is expected to account for approximately 26 percent of the world pharmaceutical market in value, compared with 14.5 percent in 1999.

"Pharmaceutical companies had already recouped their research investment with the sell-off of AIDS drugs in the United States and Europe," a Brazilian infectious disease specialist and adviser to the WHO explained to me, "and now with Brazil they had a new fixed market and, even if they had to lower prices, they had some unforeseen return. If things worked out in Brazil, new AIDS markets could be opened in Asia and perhaps in Africa." John Jones (a pseudonym), an executive with a pharmaceutical multinational that sells ARVs to the Brazilian government, does not put things so explicitly, but he asserts that "patents are not the problem. The problem is that there are no markets for these medications in most poor countries. Things worked out in Brazil because of political will." For him, "no markets" in Africa, for example, dovetails with poverty and with local governments' lack of a holistic vision of the public in which the public and private sectors work in tandem: "AIDS lays bare all the inadequacies of a country's approach to public health. We see an evolution in countries that have coordinated efforts, a strong national AIDS program, partnership with private sectors, and the country's leader supporting intervention."

Jones continued, "Health is not an area that the Brazilian government allowed to deteriorate anywhere near the degree of what we see in other developing countries. You had an existing structure of STD [sexually transmitted disease] clinics, and World Bank funding helped to strengthen the infrastructure." In this rendering, Brazil's "massive political will" to treat AIDS coincides with the country's partnership with both international agencies and the pharmaceutical industry:

Different than in Africa, in Brazil we had a successful business with our first antiretroviral products. And we will continue to have tremendously successful businesses based on our partnership approach with the government. Brazil continues to be an example of how you can do the right thing in terms of public health, understanding the needs of both the private sector and the government and its population. The government was able to take advantage of existing realities. There was no intellectual property protection for our early products, and given Brazil's industrial capacity, they were able to produce the drugs.

In fact, the AIDS treatment rollout was implemented across the country through an ailing universal health-care system. This specific policy was aligned with a pharmaceutically focused form of health delivery that was being articulated by the Cardoso administration. Indeed, Brazil has seen an incremental change in the concept of public health, now understood less as prevention and medical attention and more as access to medicines and community-outsourced care—that is, public health is increasingly decentralized and pharmaceuticalized. In the mid-1990s, as part of a policy of rationalization and decentralization of assistance, the government began to recast the costly and inefficient basic pharmacy program whereby municipalities distributed state-funded medicines to the general population (this program predated the ARV rollout). States and municipalities were urged to develop their own epidemiologically specific treatment strategies and to administer federal and regional funds in the acquisition and dispensation of basic medication. According to government officials, the policy would contribute to reducing hospitalizations (which tended to dominate state funding) and to making families and communities stronger participants in therapeutic processes (Cosendey et al. 2000).

Overall, as I discovered in my fieldwork in the southern and northeastern regions, the availability of essential medicines has been subject to changing political winds; treatments are easily discontinued, and people have to seek more specialized services in the private health sector or, as many put it, "die waiting" in overcrowded public clinics. Even though the responsibility for distributing medicines has become increasingly decentralized, the lobbies of patient groups (modeled after AIDS treatment activism) and of the pharmaceutical industry has kept the federal government responsible for the purchase of medication classified as "exceptional," as well as medication for disease populations that are part of "special national programs," such as the AIDS program. An increasing number of patients are filing legal suits, forcing regional governments to maintain the inflow of high cost medicines that are entering the market. According to the public health expert Jorge Bermudez, "an individualized rather than collective pharmaceutical care" is being consolidated in the country (Bermudez et al. 2000). A critical under-standing of the AIDS policy's success must keep in sight this mobilization over inclusion and exclusion as global pharmaceutical markets and certain forms of "good government" are being realized.

By juxtaposing the arguments of both corporate actors and policy mak-ers, one can identify the logic of such a pharmaceutical form of governance. Here "political will" means favoring novel public-private cooperation over medical technologies. Once a government designates a disease like AIDS "the country's disease," a therapeutic market takes shape, with the state acting as both the drug purchaser and distributor. As the government ad-dresses the needs of its population (now unequally refracted through the "country's disease"), the financial operations of the pharmaceutical indus-try are taken in new directions and enlarged, particularly as older lines of treatment (generic ARVs) lose their efficacy, necessitating the introduction of newer and more expensive treatments (still under patent protection) that are demanded by mobilized patients. Patienthood and civic participa-tion thus coalesce in an emerging market. Moreover, companies use drug-pricing and drug-donation programs to negotiate with governments for broader market access and to expand their clinical research enterprise.

Internationally, Brazil has become proof that the badly needed full-scale assault on AIDS is indeed possible. "We have changed the discourse and paradigm of intervention," said Teixeira, who helped coordinate the joint WHO and UNAIDS "3 by 5" campaign. "It has become politically costly for development agencies and governments not to engage AIDS." Yet, he added, the operations of global AIDS programs and their interface with govern-ments and civic organizations "reflect and extend existing power relations, and this synergy can be quite negative. The negotiating power of developing countries is simply too little, be it at the United Nations or at the World Trade Organization." According to Teixeira, funding bottlenecks, personnel shortages, and continuing debates over drug pricing and patents have lim-ited global AIDS initiatives. "Drug companies are paralyzing the WHO."

Magic-bullet approaches (i.e., the delivery of technology regardless of health-care infrastructure) are increasingly the norm in global health, and drug companies themselves are using the activist discourse that accessing therapies is a matter of human rights. This pharmaceuticalization of public health has short- and long-term goals. "It is a matter of guaranteeing access not just to the available drugs but to the new ones being developed," Jones said. "You have to find a way to align yourself and trade with the companies who are doing this work." Tellingly, one corporate social responsibility executive of a major pharmaceutical firm recently told me, "As a global health company, we are proud that about 750,000 AIDS patients in the developing world are on our drugs."

This focus on drug delivery and supply-chain management stretches far beyond the ARV rollout and has recently contributed to the popularity of blanket treatment approaches for many tropical diseases, including preventative medications for conditions such as childhood malaria and river blindness, as well as antibiotic treatments that have no preventative value in national deworming campaigns for schoolchildren. Such interventions seem to systematically ignore chronic illnesses and the complex environmental issues most central in people's lives. In the end, governments are business partners, while communities and patients are left to nurture themselves (as I chronicled in Brazil). Critics have rightly pointed out that, generally speaking, the strategies underlying new global health interventions are not comprehensive and ultimately of poor quality (Farmer 2004; Ramiah and Reich 2006; Whyte et al. 2006).[3] Many question the programs' sustainability in the absence of more serious involvement by national governments and greater authority for international institutions to hold donors and partners accountable. With a health policy's success largely reframed in terms of providing and counting the best medicines and newest technology delivered, what space remains for the development of low-tech or non-tech solutions (such as community development or the provision of clean water) that could prove more sustainable and ultimately more humane?

INTERMEDIARY POWER FORMATIONS

In our conversation in June 2005, Teixeira expressed concern about the sustainability of Brazil's AIDS treatment policy. "I had high hopes for the PT [Workers' Party] government. But the government has been reluctant to make bold moves as far as generics, patents, and international relations are concerned." Several activists told me that the AIDS policy had lost some of its political currency as it was taken as a "success story of the previous administration" (see Wogart and Calcagnotto 2006). The Lula administration wants to construct "its own success stories." With the effort under new budgets and bureaucracies, for the first time in 2005 there were shortages of ARVs in the health-care system (see Leite 2005).

"The preparedness that was in place is being compromised," Teixeira added. "We are lagging in technology" (see Prado 2005). The ARV reverse-engineering program at Farmanguinhos (the state's main pharmaceutical laboratory) has been partially dismantled, and generic drug development is not keeping pace with the market.

Brazil is facing a complex predicament that other developing countries treating AIDS will soon face. It has a very inexpensive first line of ARVs, but a growing number of people are starting new, more expensive drug regimens, either because of drug resistance or because newer drugs have fewer side effects. With patients taking advantage of these new treatments, Brazil's annual ARV budget increased to nearly $500 million in 2005. In spite of the country's generic production capacity, about 80 percent of the medication included in the national budget is patented. "We are moving toward absolute drug monopoly," Michel Lotrowska, an economist working for Doctors without Borders (Médecins sans Frontières) in Rio de Janeiro, told me. "We have to find a new way to reduce drug prices. If not medics will soon have to tell patients, 'I can only give you first-line treatment, and if you become drug-resistant you will die.'"

Consider Roche's recently introduced drug T-20 (Fuzeon). This drug is the first of a new class of drugs—called fusion inhibitors, which keep HIV particles from fusing with lymphocytes—that will undoubtedly have great impact in preventing or managing drug resistance. In Brazil some twelve hundred patients were prescribed T-20 immediately after the drug's debut, with a yearly cost of $20,000 per patient. "When the starting price of a drug is as [high as] T-20's," Lotrowska told me, "it is evident that after some time you will get a 30 to 50 percent price reduction. But even with this reduction, what will happen to the country's AIDS budget when thousands more need it or want it?"

While doing fieldwork in Salvador in June 2005, I learned that medical opinion-makers were urging local doctors to make T-20 a first-line treatment rather than simply a rescue drug. I also heard of cases where doctors began prescribing the rescue drug Kaletra at the time of its 2002 launch in the United States, before its registration in Brazil. These doctors referred patients to a local AIDS NGO and to public-interest lawyers who pressured the state to provide drugs not yet approved by the National Health Surveillance Agency (Agência Nacional de Vigilância Sanitária, or ANVISA). In the face of pervasive pharmaceutical marketing enmeshed with patient mobilization, regulatory incoherence thrives. Meanwhile, activist policy makers have to ceaselessly invent new political strategies to keep the country's AIDS treatment rollout in place. The pharmaceutical industry is now deeply ingrained in public institutions. "If we don't find intelligent ways to counter this profit extraction from public health," Paulo Picon, an academic scientist, put it to me, "we will be left with an unsurmountable indebtedness, a wound that won't heal."

In May 2007 Brazil crossed a new threshold when for the first time it broke the patent of an AIDS drug. The government stopped price negotiations with Merck over Efavirenz, which is used by seventy-five thousand Brazilians, and decided to import a generic version from India. Officials claim that this will save the country some $236.8 million by 2012. Activists praise this move as an important advance in the widening of access to the newest and most expensive therapies.

In sum, multiple institutions and social actors dynamically meet in the Brazilian AIDS policy-space. These various institutions and actors have distinctive interests, are somewhat permeable, and mutually readjust. In practice, the AIDS policy is neither a global institution nor a novel state apparatus—it is an intermediary power formation. The policy comes into existence in the space between international agencies, global markets, and the reforming state. It is implicated in and meddles with the resources of these institutions as it struggles to intervene efficaciously. Intermediary power formations are not simply extensions of the macro or the micro; they actually exclude the immanence of both. Their operations do not follow a predetermined strategy of control and do not necessarily have normalizing effects. As is evident in the AIDS policy, their sustainability has to be constantly negotiated in the marketplace. Mobilized individuals and groups must continuously maneuver this particular therapeutic formation to gain medical visibility and have their claims to life addressed. The AIDS policy thus becomes a cofunction of governmental and market institutions, as well as individual lives.

THE WILL TO LIVE

Just as the complex Brazilian response to AIDS must be understood in the wider context of the country's democratization and the restructuring of both state and market, so, too, must it be seen in light of its interaction with local worlds and the subsequent refiguring of lives and values. On the ground, health programs do not work in tandem, and administrative discontinuities abound. Different states allocate public health resources differently according to the pressure of interest groups. The AIDS NGOS that were supposed to have taken over assistance "have long lost idealism and passion," as the activist Gerson Winkler bitterly told me in September 2005 in his hometown of Porto Alegre. "They keep selecting their clientele and find all kind of ways to pretend that they are fulfilling their projects' goals."[4]

Thus, against the background of budgetary constraints, regional politics, and the "professionalization and industrialization of the nongovernmental sector" (in Winkler's words), a multitude of interpersonal networks and variations in AIDS care have emerged, creating uneven levels of quality of life for patients—the underside of the pharmaceuticalization of public health. Only a few manage to constitute themselves as patient citizens, and this brings me back to Caasah.

When Torben and I returned to Caasah in December 2001, things had changed dramatically. Caasah had been relocated to a new, state-funded building. With treatment regimens available, functional residents had been asked to move out, and Caasah had been redesigned as a short-term care facility (a "house of passage," *casa de passagem*) for ill patients and a shelter for HIV-positive orphans. A nursing team now worked directly with local hospitals and admitted the patients who "fit into the institution," in the words of Celeste, still presiding over Caasah. Disturbingly, there was no systematic effort to track these patients and their treatment actively once they left.

What most interests me as an anthropologist is the process of returning to the field. Repeatedly returning, one begins to grasp what happens in the meantime—the events and practices that enable wider social and political change, as well as those that debilitate societies and individuals, dooming them to stasis and intractability. In such returns entanglements and intricacies are revealed. We witness the very temporality of politics, technology, and money—how AIDS survivors move from patienthood back into personhood.

"This is a beautiful building, but that's all the state gave us," continued Celeste. Institutional maintenance was a daily struggle. "We owe more than one thousand dollars to local pharmacies. Our patients come from the hospital with their antiretroviral drugs but nothing else." The national ARV rollout was supposed to be matched by regional governments' provision of treatments for opportunistic infections. But it was clearly up to proxy-health services such as Caasah or to the patients themselves to arrange treatment beyond ARVs.

We looked for our former collaborators and tracked down those who had left Caasah. Of the twenty-two residents we had gotten to know in 1997, ten were alive. Only Tiquinho, the hemophiliac child who had been raised there, was allowed to stay. All of the adult survivors created new family units. They lived with other AIDS patients, reunited with estranged relatives, married, and even had children. All of them had disability pensions and were entitled to a monthly food basket at Caasah. The ethnography of AIDS after the introduction of ARVs can illuminate processes of individual becoming taking place through medicines and multiple sites, relations, and intensities—fields of immanence. It is in this circuitry, as it unequally determines life chances, that AIDS survivors articulate their "plastic power" and invent a domesticity and health to live in and by (Biehl 2005a: 14).

"Today is another world," Luis Cardoso told me as he looked at the portrait Torben made of him in March 1997 (figs. 6 and 7). "One Luis has died and another has emerged. A person has to forget the past." First diagnosed with AIDS in 1993, Luis lived in Caasah from 1995 to 1999. "I have nothing to say against the antiretrovirals. Celeste and the psychologists motivated me a lot. But I don't live here anymore, and I must take care of myself. I got used to ARVs. I am the effect of this responsibility. Medication is me now."

For Celeste, "Luis is like a son." He represents Caasah and the state of Bahia in national meetings of people living with HIV/AIDS, and he runs prevention workshops in the interior. Even Nanci Silva, Luis's doctor, calls him "my teacher." As she told me: "I find this fantastic. The patient had a history of self-abuse, remains poor, but rescues himself and teaches others to do the same." As Caasah's office assistant, he earned a salary. Open about his homosexuality, he said that he was dating. Luis also proudly adopted an AIDS orphan in Caasah and was giving the boy's grandmother money to

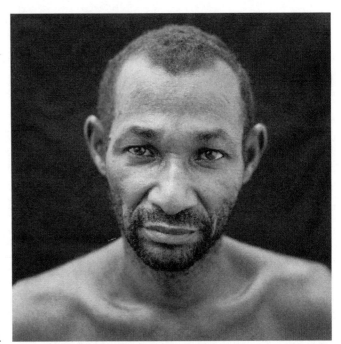

6 Luis, 1997.

7 Luis, 2001.

take care of him. "I always believed in God, but religious talk does not help if you don't have the will to live inside you."

Luis is an amazing person, hard-working, witty, and a master of moral discourse. He speaks of a new economy of life instincts organized around AIDS therapies. And he himself is the dominant human form that emerges from this economy: "I face my problem. I take advantage of the help I get. I struggle to live." He is indeed the representative of a new medical collective, and his discourse conveys present-day forms and limits of society and state. "I have nothing to do with society," he says. "From my perspective, society is a set of masters deciding what risk is, and what is bad for them. I have never participated in that. As for the government, I must say that I am thankful for the medication. This is the good aspect of the state. The rest is for me to do." He has harsh words for those who throw medication away: "It's a crime."

Luis made treatment adherence seem too easy. As much as I admired his resilience, I also found his righteousness disturbing. For him, individual conscience was the a priori of a healthy existence, and mourning a loss, any kind of loss, was a defect to be overcome. The institutional and interpersonal forces that have thrown Luis into action in the first place were absent from his life-extending account, particularly as he spoke of noncompliant *marginais* (people living on the margins of society). It was evident from his recollection that if he had not belonged to Caasah, AIDS therapies would not have had the same effectiveness for him, and that he kept harnessing strength from being the object of regular public and medical attention. His narrative of regeneration remains built on the exclusion of people like Jorge who remain invisible to the state and to medicine. Homeless AIDS patients, Luis reasons, use their social condition as an excuse to hang on to self-destructive habits: "As I see it, these people are more for death than for life. . . . But I also know many people who struggle to live and to earn their money honestly and don't surrender. Look at Rose and Evangivaldo. . . . It is your mind that makes the difference."

"Welcome to the end of the world," Rose said jokingly as we entered her brick shack, located at the bottom of a muddy hill on the outskirts of Salvador (fig. 8). "I am sold on the antiretrovirals," she told us. "I am part of this multitude that will do whatever is necessary to guarantee our right to these drugs. I am proud of Brazil." Caasah helped Rose to get the shack from the government, and she was living there with her one-year-old daughter. She had also taken in her teenage son, who had been in the custody of Caasah's

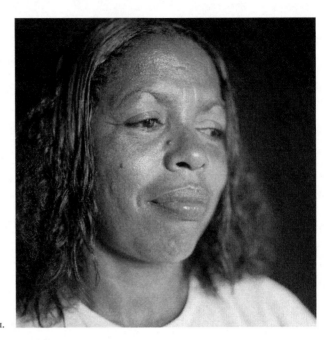

8 Rose, 2001.

chief nurse. "I am always struggling to pay the bills and raise my children, for I am mother and father."

Rose wept as she recalled the death of her partner from AIDS-related diseases, a few months before the girl was born. She had done all that was medically possible. "Jessica got AZT, but the last exam showed that she is still seropositive." Rose knew that the child's HIV status could change until she reached the age of two: "She has never been ill and we hope for the best." Rose was proud to be "a good patient, but not a fanatic one. I drink a beer and have some fun on the weekends, but I know my limits, what my body can take. I tell you, I want to be alive to see a cure. In the name of Jesus, I want to be a guinea pig when they test the vaccine." Yes, she said, "people are still dying with AIDS in the streets, but I am no longer there."

The political economy of AIDS, spanning both national and international institutions, engenders local therapeutic environments within which individuals and AIDS organizations are codependent and must recraft positions in every exchange. Their transactions are legitimated by a humanitarian and pharmaceutical discourse of lifesaving and civic empowerment. In adhering to drug regimens and making new and productive lives for themselves, patients are—in this discourse—saved. However, merely guarantee-

9 Evangivaldo, 2001.

ing existence in such dire contexts, amid the dismantling of institutions of care, involves a calculus that goes well beyond numbers of pills and the timing of their intake. The political grounds of existence have been increasingly individualized and atomized, and poor AIDS patients rarely become activists. Even as they search for employment, AIDS survivors work hard to remain eligible for whatever the state's paternalistic politics and remedial programs have made available, such as renewal of disability benefits, free bus vouchers, and additional medication at local health posts. Being adopted by a doctor and becoming a model patient greatly facilitates this. This material calculus becomes all the more important as patients form new families and resume a "normal" life previously impossible for them.

Evangivaldo's face was barely recognizable, but the aesthetic side effects of antiretrovirals were the least of his concerns (fig. 9). "Today I woke up anguished. We had no gas to cook. I hope you can help me." Evangivaldo and his partner, Fatima, left Caasah in 1999 and had a daughter, Juliana. "A child is what I wanted most in life. Juliana fulfilled my desire, a dream I had. I thought I would die without being a father." He said he was on antipsychotic medication and then added: "It is the financial part of life that tortures me."

Evangivaldo showed me a piece of paper on which he had listed how his income was allocated and the debts he had to pay. "When Fatima cannot do the work, I am the man and woman of the house. Sometimes I wake up at 4 a.m., leave everything ready, and ride my bike for two hours, to get downtown. I go door to door, asking for a job. There are days when I cannot get the money we need and I panic. My head spins, and I fall down. I hide in a corner and cry. Then I don't know where I am. But I tell myself, 'Focus, Evangivaldo, you will find your bike and your way home.' And do you know why I manage to do this? It is because my daughter is waiting for me."

LOCAL ECONOMIES OF SALVATION

"If you look carefully, nothing has changed. Things are the same as you saw last time," a tired Celeste Gomes told me in June 2005 during my last visit. Caasah was still the only place in Salvador that provided systematic care to poor AIDS patients who have been discharged from public hospitals. "Some patients return to their families. Others go back to the streets. Disease keeps spreading, and the government pretends not to know so it doesn't have to intervene."

At the state's main AIDS unit, Nanci also said that "things here have not changed. We are full of miserable and wasted patients. The difference is that they now come from the interior, where no new services have been created. Access to therapies has been democratized, but health has not." The unit's social worker told me that physicians triage patients. "Many doctors do not put drug addicts and the homeless on ARVs. They say that there is no guarantee that [these patients] will continue the treatment and that [the doctors] are concerned about the creation of viral resistance to medication." Against an expanding discourse of human rights and pharmaceutical possibilities, we are here confronted by the limits of the infrastructures on the ground, whereby accountability and the right to envision a new life with AIDS are (partially) realized.

Out of the initial group of twenty-two Caasah patients with whom I had worked in 1997, seven were still alive in 2005—among them, Rose, Luis, and Evangivaldo. This life extension is obviously a result of technological advancements, argued Celeste, "but it would not have happened if they had not learned to care for themselves." In the end, treatment adherence "is relative to each person. It requires a lot of will." Yet, as I would learn, survival was not simply a matter discovering resources within but of inventing ways of being that enabled people to continue with their interrupted or very new lives. All of the survivors possessed a place they called home, a steady if meager income, and a social network of sorts. And, in case of an emergency, they could still resort to Caasah. This tie to Caasah, as momentary and uncertain as it now was, remained vital to them.

Luis was still working at Caasah. He was in charge of its fundraising activities. "I am not concerned with HIV. What I want is to live. If there is medication, let's take life forward. Life is to fight for." In the previous year, Luis had experienced kidney failure and had been hospitalized for two weeks. Davi, his adopted son, was now a healthy seven year old. "He is my passion. He makes it all worthwhile."

"What a joy you give me by coming back," beamed Evangivaldo, the kindest and most resilient man I ever met. "I can only count on the tenderness of Fatima and Juliana. When I see them with no food it makes me ill. But when I find a job or get a donation and there is nothing lacking at home, then for me it is another life, and it is all good." I asked Evangivaldo whether he had told his doctor all he has to go through in life. "Yes," he had once mentioned to his doctor that he routinely rode his bike for two hours "with only coffee and medication in the body" to get to downtown Salvador in search of a job. "Dr. Jackson said that he did not believe it, that my HIV was almost undetectable and that I acted as if I did not have AIDS. I told him that my bike was parked outside the hospital, that I would show it to him. He was amazed. He then called his superior and some residents and asked me to tell them my story."

After the spectacle Evangivaldo had become, "the doctors said that they were proud of me, and that if all HIV-positive people had the same will to live that I have then no one would have to be hospitalized. They said that I was an example for other patients." Evangivaldo took the opportunity to ask the doctors for advice on where to go to find a job. His doctor replied, "I feel bad for not being able to help, but I am sure that God will show a path for you to get where you want to." Meanwhile, Evangivaldo had to take twelve pills a day, and his doctor never considered putting him on a newer medication made available by the government that required fewer pills and had fewer side effects.

Poor AIDS patients like Evangivaldo continuously interact and trade with AIDS NGOs and civic groups that channel assistance, albeit minimal, from regional and national programs. The NGOs, which depend on their clientele to back up reports and authorize new projects (now mostly related to treatment adherence and income generation), become venues for some patients to access food, rental assistance, and specialized medical consultations, among other things. Overwhelmed with demands for help and concern for their own institutional survival, NGOs rarely succeed in placing the person in the market, but they do successfully differentiate politicized patients who defend their rights from those who passively circulate in the medical service system.

Only a few patients, like thirty-year-old Sonara, manage to become "AIDS workers." She was Caasah's new poster person. A nurse introduced me to Sonara as the latter was running a candle-making workshop for a group of twelve patients: "She was a drug user, but she now takes the medication, eats well, and takes care of her daughter, who is also HIV positive." Sonara was the only white person there. Her style of dress, manners, and speech were characteristic of the Brazilian middle class. As much as I admired Sonara's transformation, I could not have been more disturbed by her moral reasoning: "Today, people only die of AIDS if they want to." There is value in conceiving the destiny of the homeless AIDS patients as self-generated, a conscious choice. The few who recover, it seems, set the limits of who is considered worthy of having a biological existence. This measure informs intersubjectivity and makes triage commonsense.

To have someone to live for and to be desired by seemed to be a constant thread in accounts of the AIDS survivors with whom I worked. All of them had engineered tiny islands of hospitality in which they can inhabit life. Yet they also acted coldly toward fellow patients. Mutual empathy was rare. I will never understand why, for example, Luis did not let us take Rose's food basket to her as we were heading back to her shack. The previous day over the phone she had asked me to do this for her. I told Luis and others at Caasah, but my request met a series of obstacles: "The basket isn't ready"; "There's no one here to sign it out"; "I don't have time"; "We have to go."

Rose was doing great, as were her children. As for the food basket she was, of course, disappointed. "But that's life. Onward." She had garnered the support of NGOs and opened up a little business she called *Rose Tem de Tudo* ("Rose Has It All") and had also devised a fundraising campaign to improve her housing. Rose was also proud of having been able to enroll her son in the project Adolescent Citizen, which Dona Conceição was now running with World Bank funds. Later that week, I met with Dona Conceição, who regretted that Caasah remained the only institution addressing AIDS on the streets; her funds from the World Bank would only last a year: "We cannot meet all the demand for help. It's a disgrace."

CONCLUSION: LIFE TECHNOLOGIES AND HOPE

Brazil's bold, multiactor, and large-scale therapeutic response to AIDS has made history. In this chapter, I have explored the broad economic and political effects that treating AIDS had on health services, both national and local, and how this lifesaving policy influenced international efforts to reverse the pandemic's course. I have also illuminated interactions between state and regional actors and nongovernmental and grassroots organizations underlying various communal and individual modes of life that have emerged around ARVs in one of the country's most vulnerable urban populations. In highlighting the successes, failures, and complexities of the Brazilian response to AIDS, I have revealed significant logistical and conceptual changes in governance and citizenship—groundbreaking in their own right.

The Brazilian AIDS policy is emblematic of novel forms of state action on and toward public health. Pressured by activists, the democratic government was able to negotiate with the global pharmaceutical industry, making ARVs universally available to its citizens and also opening up new market possibilities for that industry. The sustainability of the policy has to be constantly negotiated in the marketplace, and one of the unintended consequences of AIDS treatment scale-up has been the consolidation of a model of public health centered on pharmaceutical distribution. This intervention gains social and medical significance by being incorporated into infrastructures of care that are themselves being reshaped by state and market restructuring.

Yes, there has been a striking decrease in AIDS mortality in Brazil, but seen from the perspective of the urban poor the AIDS treatment policy is not an inclusive form of care or citizenship. Many are left out, burdened by labels such as *drug addict, prostitute, beggar*, and *thief*—they largely remain part of the underground economy and a hidden AIDS epidemic. As my ethnography shows, local AIDS services triage quality treatment, and wider social and economic rights for the poorest remain largely unavailable.

Drugs are ancillary to the full treatment of disease. Healing, after all, is a multifaceted process, and large-scale treatment programs tend to miss the interpersonal networks that link patients, drugs, families, and health professionals, which are especially important in resource-poor settings where infrastructure is often not improving.

This elision of the local from planning frameworks leaves unaddressed the clinical continuity necessary for successful AIDS treatment. The responsibility for damaging side effects should not be left to the patients themselves but should be guarded against by more and not less preventive policy making. Likewise at issue is a reconsideration of the systemic relation of pharmaceutical research, commerce, and public health care. We should search for a more sustainable solution to the obstacles posed by patentability and pharmaceutical business control over medical science and health care on the ground. Part of the solution may lie in comprehensive knowledge and technology sharing among southern countries—a paradigm that would allow poorer countries to develop effective health technology assessment programs, pool their manufacturing know-how, and unite in negotiating fair prices. Moreover, high-technology interventions must be reconciled with systems that foster the equitable inclusion of populations into preventive as well as basic and sustained care initiatives.

Caasah's former residents are the new people of AIDS. After experiencing social abandonment, they have come into contact with the foundational experiences of care and biotechnology. Refusing to be overpowered, they have plunged into new environments. By all standards, they have exceeded their destinies. Now receiving treatment, Rose, Luis, Evangivaldo, and many others refuse the condition of leftovers; they humanize technology and remake themselves in familiar terms. They face the daily challenge of translating medical investments into social capital and wage-earning power. They live between-moments, between-spaces, scavenging for resources. At every turn, they must consider the next step to be taken to guarantee survival. Theirs is the force of immanence—call it a language of hope.

NOTES

I am grateful to Torben Eskerod for his artwork and to Miriam Ticktin, Ilana Feldman, Adriana Petryna, Tom Vogl, Amy Moran-Thomas, and Alex Gertner for their comments and editorial help. I also want to thank the participants of the Princeton seminar "The

Anthropology of Globalization" (spring 2008) for their insightful engagement with the ethnographic project on which this chapter draws. I acknowledge the support of the Program in Latin American Studies and the Grand Challenges Initiative on Global Health and Infectious Disease at Princeton University.

1 Caasah is an acronym for Casa de Apoio e Assistência aos Portadores do Vírus HIV (House of Support and Assistance for Carriers of the HIV Virus). Caasah is pronounced like *casa*, which means "house" in Portuguese.

2 See the press release by IMS Health (March 21, 2006): "IMS Health Reports Global Pharmaceutical Market Grew 7 Percent in 2005, to $602 Billion," http://www .imshealth.com/ (downloaded on February 10, 2010).

3 The work of Paul Farmer and Partners in Health provides an opposing community-based model for AIDS treatment (Walton et al. 2004). "Improving clinical services can improve the quality of prevention efforts, boost staff morale, and reduce AIDS-related stigma," writes Farmer (2002b). In this holistic approach, accounting for individual trajectories and staying with patients through the progression of the disease (the work of *accompagneteurs*) is considered as important as tackling the social factors that impact their families and mitigating the decay of clinical infrastructure.

4 The anthropologist Marc Abélès (2006) has been studying the dual displacement in governmentality and resistance that accompanies the work of NGOs as "life and survival" are put "at the heart of political action." He argues that "a sense of powerlessness has become the backdrop for political action. It is as though the citizen's capacity for initiative were going through a more or less explicit reassertion of this admission of powerlessness, tied to the awareness of a radical reappraisal of our terms of belonging. The other side of this position is a projection towards a vaguer collective interest relating more to survival (*survivance*) than to the art of harmonious living together (*convivance*)" (493–94).

ENVIRONMENT, COMMUNITY, GOVERNMENT ✌

Arun Agrawal

OVER THE PAST two decades, more than
sixty countries in the developing world claim
to have adopted new environmental policies to
govern their forests (Agrawal and Ostrom 2001;
Rodriguez-Pose and Gill 2003). These new efforts to configure how the environment should
be governed are the product of a long history of
work by excluded agents to gain a voice over environmental outcomes, and the new legislation
marks a substantial shift in the nature of environmental government. In contrast to earlier
policies that situated a centralized state as the
locus of environmental government (Anderson
and Grove 1987; Peluso and Vandergeest 2001),
contemporary policy reforms resolutely look
toward other sociopolitical forms and processes
to achieve a reconfiguration of the relations between humans and nature (Nygren 2005).

Two characteristics define contemporary reforms of environmental governance: community-
based conservation and decentralization. The
celebratory rhetoric surrounding present-day reforms rests on the expectation that community-
based participation will accompany retrenchment of state capacities. Together, the retraction of
state capacity and mobilization of community-

based participation is supposed to usher in democratic sustainable development through a set of interactional forms that respect both the integrity of nature and the sanctity of the human (cf. Mansuri and Rao 2004; Platteau and Gaspart 2003).

This chapter examines ongoing environmental policy changes through a case study of community-based forest councils in Kumaon, India—an example of conservation through decentralization and community-based participation that parallels contemporary efforts but predates them by half a century. Based on a general discussion of decentralization policies and especially the historical description of the Kumaon case, I develop a framework through which to view ongoing processes of changing governmental strategies, and how they transform the natural and the human in unanticipated ways. The prominent features of decentralization, I suggest, are (1) the governmentalization of localities, (2) the creation of regulatory communities, and (3) the formation of environmental subjects.

The triple-stranded process that is decentralization cannot occur without the simultaneous, even prior, acceptance of a difference in the nature of who is to be governed. Decentralization is underpinned by the emergence of the human as the subject of government, needing government but also able to govern. Indeed, this particular aspect of humanity—comprising sentient beings capable of governing themselves—is central to my discussion here. The nonhuman cannot govern itself or others. It requires government as an imposition, whether the object is caring, managing, or taming.

These three strands of decentralization can be understood better through a focus on the deployments of power central to the government of the human. The words *government* and *human* are both important in this assertion. Government is not just to impose power or to dominate. The project of government requires recognizing and assessing the nature of the governed, and modulation and economy in the exercise of power so as to shape it in accordance with the characteristics of the target of government. To govern actions and thoughts without a conceptualization of the object of government as human would be impossible.

One might submit that even when government is imposed on the nonhuman, the capacities to be shaped are imagined as uniquely human. The category of the human, then, allows the project of government to unfold. In the domain of environmental government, decentralization is one mechanism to make such a conceptualization possible. In pursuing this argument,

I illustrate the occlusions in treatments of environmental government that are wedded primarily to institutionalized decision making as its essential characteristic, and that ignores how nature and humans are transformed in their interaction. The chapter also goes beyond arguments that see in decentralization a pure positive good that increases the space for democratic participation, as well as observations that view it as a Trojan horse through which state officials increase their ability to control territories and human populations.

The first feature of decentralization, the governmentalization of localities, affects how the local is produced. Greater involvement by state officials redefines state-local relations, undermining the separation of the local from its other and leading to the vesting of significant powers in diverse units of governance. This allows higher-level decision makers to supervise more easily what transpires at the lower levels, primarily by encouraging decision makers in localities to become implicated in forms of supervision that require their complicity. In the Kumaoni context, localities can no longer be viewed as the autonomous village republics of Robert Wade (1994), the precapitalist social forms of Partha Chatterjee (1983), or even simply as state-sponsored vehicles of administration.[1] As agents acting in the service of environmental regulation, governmentalized localities are part of a new regime of regulation that creates fresh political-economic relationships between states and peoples. They are knit together by the thread of state power. They are reshaped by the soft hammer of authority. They come to conform as a result of interventions that draw on the knowable arts and sciences of their internal dynamics.

Decentralization also transforms environmental relationships in a second way: it changes how identifiable loci of power within localities influence what happens in forests and to members of a community. The new localities that come into being by getting incorporated more thoroughly into wider circuits of political relationships also enjoy officially sanctioned latitude in crafting and extending formal regulatory rule. New nuclei of decision making—the forest councils in Kumaon's case—come to exercise some forms of power. Formal processes shaping internal collective decisions help make communities agents in new regimes of regulation. Innovative regulations, often born within communities, extend the reach of power into the finest spaces of the social body. The imagination of the community as comprising beings capable of governing themselves is a central assumption in the finer extension of relations of power beyond the surface contact between the state and the locality. Social and institutional relationships within communities and between communities and their resources come to rest on new knowledges about what allows communities to govern their resources more strictly and sustainably.[2] Thus, on the one hand, localities and states enter into new governmental relations; on the other, the regulatory relationships between communities and their residents become more precise and carefully modulated. What is being formed and refined is a legal mechanism through which a calculated manipulation of actions in the forest can take place and the visibility of these actions is increased. The counterpart of the governmentalized locality is thus the second feature of decentralization: the regulatory community.

The third feature of decentralization, the formation of environmental subjects, is perhaps most directly connected to the transformation in how the object of government is viewed. Environmental subjects are those for whom the environment has come to constitute a point of reference in relation to which at least some of their actions and thoughts take place. The formation of environmental subjectivities is perhaps the most critical, ambiguous, unpredictable, and thus least understood and analyzed of the three processes that I suggest are integral to successful decentralization. The formation of environmental subjects occurs together with changes in human understandings of and relations to forests and the emergence of the governmentalized locality and with the formation of the regulatory community. The residents of Kumaon today think about their forests quite differently than their ancestors did in the early part of the century. But they do so in conjunction with the governmentalization of localities and the creation of regulatory communities. These three ways in which environmental government in Kumaon has been changing are at least in part about the encompassing claims tied to the nature of humanity. Decentralization is not only underpinned by hopes for greater equality, justice, and inclusion; it potentially creates the space for advancing these claims.

Changes in the government of environment and forests in Kumaon have occurred together with the creation of forest councils, more localized forms of power, and the implication of people in these forms of power. The environmentalization of subjects is one way power settles humanity into new forms, helping generate new concerns, and concurrently shaping government, practice, and subjectivity. This is not to claim that the creation of these new subject forms is a necessarily negative process, a ruse through which power works to subvert freedom. It is simply to recognize and point to the fact that power does in fact invest new subjects, and thereby to trace the ways it does so. The remainder of this chapter elaborates further on the relationship between government, power, and subjectivity, and the human as the terrain on which the project of government unfolds. Although my theme here is the relationship between nature and subjects, as structured through government and power, I do not attend to many well-traveled avenues, such as the social production of nature, the relationship between democracy and decentralization, and the contributions of other theorists to the elaboration of these ideas. Given the well-developed literature and my limited space here, I will focus on the relationship between new projects of environmental government, the creation of new subjects of rule, and the centrality of the category of the human to the making of government and subjects.

THE EVOLUTION OF ENVIRONMENTAL GOVERNMENT IN KUMAON

By the beginning of the twentieth century, the British state in the Kumaon Himalaya in northern India had insinuated itself deep into processes of forest creation, instituting entirely new procedures of forest control and exploitation. As in other provinces of India, a new provincial forest department had carried out surveys; created and demarcated different categories of forests; made working plans for planting, management, and rotational harvesting; limited grazing by domestic animals; restricted collection of fodder and firewood in forests; and introduced fire protection (see also Dangwal 1997; and Shrivastava 1996). These draconian measures prompted a new understanding of forests: economic and strategic reservoirs from which to generate the surplus necessary for empire, and the resources necessary to pursue military conquest (Agrawal 2005). They also pushed Kumaon's villagers into striking acts of protest that the colonial state had not anticipated.

Forest fires raged throughout Kumaon during the first quarter of the twentieth century, especially between 1916 and 1921. Villagers in Kumaon set these fires deliberately, protesting government efforts to reconfigure the nature of government in their forests. Nearly two hundred thousand acres of forest were burned in 1916, in hundreds of separate incidents of protest. In 1921, villagers set fire to even larger areas of forests, protesting collectively against new regulations. The protests by villagers indicated something remarkable. In collusion that was largely implicit, even those villagers who did not actively participate in the protests would not reveal the identity of violators of the law. Village headmen, appointees of the government, also refused to cooperate with foresters and other government officials. What is more, the instances of arson were just the leading edge of a vast wave of illegality. In direct violation of the new rules, villagers also grazed their animals, chopped and collected firewood, felled timber, and harvested fodder.

The fires and protests forced the government to reconsider existing policy. State officials appointed a three-member committee to investigate villager protests. The Kumaon Forest Grievances Committee toured Kumaon and interviewed nearly five thousand villagers. On the basis of these discussions, it recommended that the state permit villagers to take formal control of most of the forests taken over by the forest department between 1911 and 1916. It also suggested that villagers be permitted to manage the forests themselves, under a general set of guidelines. Its recommendations have had a long-lasting effect.[3]

The colonial state adopted the recommendations of the Kumaon Forests Grievances Committee almost completely. It reclassified forests in Kumaon into Class I (mixed stands of oak and other broad-leaved forests central to agrarian livelihoods in Kumaon) and Class II forests (primarily pine forests with high commercial value). Further, it transferred control of all Class I forests to the revenue department and specified clear procedures through which villagers could bring Class I forests near their settlements under their own control. Through these carefully outlined administrative procedures, villagers began to create formal local forest councils from whose forests they could extract products such as firewood and fodder for their household needs.

By 1940 the number of formal councils exceeded three hundred, and today it stands well over three thousand. Nearly a quarter of Kumaon's villages have forest councils. The formation of these councils signals a profound transformation in the character of forest control, the institutionalization of regulation, and environment-related subjectivities—in short, in the different ways that humans interact with their environment. Spread throughout the region, these community-level organizations are legally grounded in the Forest Council Rules of 1931. The colonial government crafted these rules, drawing in part from existing practices of local forest control in isolated villages.[4]

The Forest Council Rules aid villagers in creating formal forest protection organizations, policing forests, and apprehending and punishing rule violators. Villagers maintain written records of their meetings and actions, incomes and expenses, thereby greatly expanding the domain of visibility for government officials. Villagers control themselves now in far more systematic and careful ways than the forest department had been able to do.[5]

Between 1990 and 1993, more than half a century after the passage of the Forest Council Rules of 1931, I conducted field research in Kumaon. More than forty council headmen, together with many forest users, attended a meeting I organized early during my fieldwork. Villagers at the meeting agreed that the councils faced a problem of monitoring and enforcement, but did not question the legitimacy of enforcement rights vested in the councils. They remarked on the scarcity of firewood and the need for alternative sources of fuel for cooking, and talked about the difficulties women experienced in gathering adequate amounts of fodder from the forest. Villagers described how onerous it was to graze animals in the absence of access to fodder in the forest. And, quite surprising to me, many of them also said the environment was becoming more fragile and needed greater protection.

The villagers' observations were borne out by more detailed fieldwork I conducted later (Agrawal 2005). Between 1990 and 1993 I studied twenty-eight villages that had started regulating their forests in the previous half century. Villagers complained about the existing forest management regime, often broke rules, were frequently apprehended by council-appointed guards (themselves village residents), paid fines that the council imposed, and grumbled yet again. But villagers also accepted the need to protect the forest. In some villages, councils had created systems of monitoring that involved all village households. In other communities, different families contributed to the salary of the guard whom the council appointed to protect the forest or implement the rules instituted by the council. In most villages, even where the councils paid the guards out of funds from sales of forest products, villagers agreed that their forest was in a precarious position. The level of infractions seemed to vary in proportion to the types of statements villagers made about environmental scarcities and the need to protect forests.

We must be careful, then, in interpreting the split between council officials and ordinary village users. It is true that villagers complained. There are also obvious differences between rule-makers/rule-enforcers and forest-users/rule-breakers. But these facts are not evidence that villagers consider the rules unfair or the councils' efforts illegitimate. If anything, in our conversations villagers and forest council officials were ambivalent about enforcement efforts and agreed that protection was necessary. Many villagers, among them men and women, members of upper and lower castes and richer and poorer households, emphasized limits on what forests could produce. They saw forest-protection efforts, institutionalized in the form of the forest councils, as necessary and legitimate.

These views show that Kumaon's villagers have traveled an enormous distance since the early 1900s in how they view their relationship to institutions of forest regulation. From subjects of a centralized government of forested environments, they have become members of a naturalized community inscribed on modern forests.[6] The fire-wielding, government-defying hillmen "impatient of control," as the committee investigating their actions remarked (KFGC 1921), have become rural residents who submit to and defend the need for regulation of their minutest actions in forests.

TOWARD A FRAMEWORK TO SITUATE GOVERNMENTALIZATION OF THE ENVIRONMENT

The fires in Kumaon forests and the ensuing creation of community-based forest councils are a remarkable example of *governmentalization of the environment*. By this term, I refer to concurrent transformations in regulations, practices, and subjectivities—all founded on new knowledges—through which being, thinking, and actions are reconfigured even as the environment within which they occur is also reshaped.[7] The forest councils in Kumaon constitute a new regime of regulation that has penetrated far more intimately and precisely into daily acts of rural survival than had centralized methods of control. The infiltration of regulation into the intimate unfolding of daily life is not the coercive imposition that state actions are often taken to be. Indeed, analyses of villager interactions with procedures of rule enacted through a new dynamic of political articulation are also only inadequately served by terms such as *negotiation* or *engagement*.[8] These terms to describe interactions of villagers with state regulatory measures hinge on prior conceptions about sovereign autonomous subjects that are simply impossible to identify in Kumaon. Instead, regulations and villagers' practices and words seem most concerned with what it means to be human in practice rather than the legal-juridical categories denoted by sovereignty and autonomy. Government is in part about the creation and filling in of categories, but it is far more directly about the shaping of the thinking and practices of humans. Certainly the reimagining of government in Kumaon has reshaped people's understandings of forests, and the basis of forest control itself.

This process of changing regulations, understandings, and political configurations also describes the trajectory of human and social relationships around forested environments in more than sixty countries today. The concern with globalization that defines the terrain for an increasingly more important set of social theoretical investigations also includes a global dispersal of governmental strategies of regulation. Some evidence for the globality of environmental policy decentralization comes from the results of a survey conducted by the Food and Agriculture Organization (1999). Based on responses from national forestry departments around the developing world, the report indicates that more than fifty countries claim to have involved local communities in some form in the government of their forests. This contrasts sharply with environmental policies in the nineteenth century and earlier in the twentieth (Anderson and Grove 1987; Sivaramakrishnan 1999; Peluso and Vandergeest 2001), when most state agencies firmly supported centralized ownership of and control over forests (Lynch and Talbott 1995; MacKenzie 1997; Neumann 1998).

Both the discursive and the political landscape of environmental policies have changed radically. Although many governments may continue to follow the mandate of centralization in their actions, few rhetorically support centralized control rather than decentralized, participatory strategies. From the Philippines to Mexico, Thailand to Uganda, Cameroon to Bolivia—the story of forestry policy remains one of claims that emphasize a shift from exclusion to inclusion, marginalization to participation.

The changing strategies of government to shape how forests are conserved, consumed, and managed show that the critical questions in trying to understand and explain changes in regimes of power governing the environment have to do with regulatory institutions, understandings of the environment, and how the two come together in the domain of social practices. In the nineteenth century, officials in India and elsewhere in the colonial world sought to governmentalize forests by creating, activating, and executing new procedures to survey, demarcate, consolidate, protect, plant, manage, harvest, and market forests (see Brandis 1994 [1897]; and Grove 1995, 1998). For the most part, it was foresters and state officials whose basis of knowledge for viewing forests, and whose subjective relationships with forests, underwent a major change. Although communities and their members were directly affected by many of the regulations that the colonial state instituted, they were more often victims rather than participants in the processes of governmentalization that came to colonize forests.

Viewing people as objects and obstacles was central to the earlier project of rule. It was beyond the exclusionist project of rule to accommodate a view in which the targets of power were bearers of human capacities to think and reason who had to be treated justly and as equals. Denial of such capacities and such status claims went hand in hand with the refusal to accept the potential to self-govern.

But the application of early exclusionist procedures to govern vegetation also generated obstacles and resistance, which in turn produced innovative mechanisms to popularize government. The example of Kumaon graphically shows how starting in the early twentieth century, much of what foresters had wanted to accomplish as conservation needed the support of new partners. The more than three thousand community-level forest councils that have been formed since the 1920s are one important example of such partnerships in government. The councils' formation has meant that local residents are now expected to manage, police, and govern their own forests in ways and to an extent that the Forest Department would have found difficult in the early twentieth century. Kumaon's residents now view themselves as responsible for what happens in their forests. They create and implement detailed rules for use and management, based on calculations about harvesting levels that are feasible and sustainable. They think more carefully about what forests mean to them, and about how they should interact with government officials in the care and regulation of forests. They take actions to sanction those who fail to adhere to locally created rules. Dissension over such issues is a new dimension of subgroup formation. It helps refract existing alliances and solidarities around gender, caste, or income and wealth.

Analogous to similar organizational forms that now inhabit the forestry policies of most countries, the councils' utility was recognized in the nineteenth century by some colonial officials (Shrivastava 1996), including Dietrich Brandis, the first inspector general of forests in India. But Kumaon's forest councils are important not just because of what happened as a result of their formation. Similar forms of local, intimate government are being created today in hundreds of thousands of locations to make rural populations partners in their own control. Indeed, these forms of government are part and parcel of what has come to be understood as neoliberal politics and which encourages retrenchment of state powers, expansion of market relationships, and assumption by social agents of responsibility for what happens to them.

In general, most existing analysis of indirect strategies of rule has focused on two sets of relationships: governmentalization of subnational units of rule so as to extend state power, and the granting of limited autonomy to these units so they can regulate the lives and practices of their members in specified domains. However, the ultimate success and effectiveness of these two strategies of decentralized regulatory rule depends as well on concomitant shifts in the subjectivity of the people undergoing regulation. Attempts to change how people act, when based solely on coercive threats in hierarchical organizations, are either formidably expensive or evidently impractical (Holmstrom 1982; Gary Miller 1992). To understand successful regulatory rule, therefore, we must examine how rule is experienced by those subjected to it, and how it changes them.

GOVERNMENTALIZED LOCALITIES, REGULATORY COMMUNITIES, AND ENVIRONMENTAL SUBJECTS

The effective government of forests by Kumaon's councils depends in substantial measure on the willingness of a significant number of people to accept new regulations, to conform to the rules that shape practices in the forests, and to make their own the monitoring and enforcement processes that the forest councils create. As communities become part of processes surrounding governmentalization of the environment, regulation of forests comes to depend on specific variations in monitoring and enforcement strategies. These same institutional mechanisms are also at play in the re-definition of people's interests in forests. The new distribution of power to govern the environment thus relies on three sets of social and political transformations: the governmentalization of localities, the formation of regulatory communities, and the creation of environmental subjects.[9]

If one contrasts the regulatory power invested in governmentalized local-ities with the centralized bureaucratic control that the Forest Department embodied, the obvious difference lies in the extent to which power is dis-persed. Instead of an identifiable point and marker, a single source and logic that the early efforts of the British represented, power over forests is scat-tered and emanates from multiple locations as forest councils have increased in number during the last half century. With the creation of forest councils, power is now visibly exercised through a multiplicity of forms, strategies, and agencies highly modulated to variations across settings. These varia-tions may result from differences in vegetation, social landscapes, produc-tivity levels, articulation with market forces, connections with other centers of power, and so forth. The proliferation of power is unavoidable because the usual binary of domination and resistance can no longer be mapped onto the forest bureaucracy and the locality.

The increase in the loci through which regulation is effected implies a concurrent change in the nature and prospects of collective action. No lon-ger is the state the locus of authority to shape the governance of forests. No longer are there large masses of humans ranked against singular injustices. Instead there is a fragmentation of authority and far more localized efforts to change the exercise of authority. For the decentralized, governmental-ized localities, forests are regulated by the individual defense of livelihood rather than by a collective movement to revolutionize institutional power. The creation of formal institutional mechanisms through which villagers can demand greater local regulatory control makes them less likely to take to the streets or to set fires to the forest. The transformation of the relation-ships between the state and the locality may occur in a manner that slowly dissolves the differences through which the boundaries between the state and the locality are policed. But the dissolution of these boundaries oc-curs together with a revision in the relationship between the state and its subjects.

Although the nodes, forms, strategies, and practices of power prolifer-ate, their multiplication is not chaotic or unruly. Instead, the articulation between sources of power nominally viewed as being those of the locality and of the state occurs according to a new combinatorial and sequential logic. Localities articulate with the state on the basis of a one-to-one relationship and with each other only informally and far less than before the creation of decentralized processes of rule. When they do interact with each other, their relations are often conflict-laden, as when members of one community harvest fodder or firewood from the forest of another community. The fact that relationships across communities that are not mediated by the state occur on a non-formal, legally unrecognized basis means that efforts to channel power in alternative directions require immense initiative. At the same time, there is specific attention to redefining the nature of the relationship between the state and the locality by ensuring asymmetric flows of power along administrative channels. The written records that councils maintain on the actions of their members, on the state of the forest, on illegal activities in the forest, and on their incomes and expenses contribute to the asymmetric flow of information and power. These records are visible to government officials, but local leaders have little access to the internal processes of the state bureaucracy.

Further, localities enter into formal institutional relationship with the state piecemeal. Instead of the Forest Department's extending its control over vast areas of forests en masse, a process vulnerable to obstacles and resistance, control is extended locality by locality. The state is willing to give up the idea of protecting and improving all the forests in its domain with a single stroke of the administrative pen. But it concedes the grand project of extensive control only in return for a surer means of intimate regulation. Through the Forest Council Rules, the decentralizing state has determined the spaces of illegality it will tolerate. It has decided on the depth and nature of regulation within local spaces that new regulatory partners will be permitted. The promise of greater autonomy in everyday activities becomes the coin with which the state buys relief from arson and other violations of forests and forest laws.

More precise control is ensured by the sequence of this finer-scale extension of government. Localities become formally affiliated with the state as their members express an interest in pursuing such relationships of environmental regulation. There is a curious marriage, then, of interest and regulation. For instance, forest councils are formed after a third of the village residents express an interest in creating a council. This implies that those groups where a significant proportion of the population has a strong

interest in creating institutional connections with the central state will become part of a network of partnerships. The acknowledgment of such self-
expression as a prerequisite to self-governance rests on a prior notion of villagers as humans, fully capable of the capacities associated with the human.
State officials encourage local residents and leaders to affiliate themselves in
the regulatory net, pointing out its benefits to the local leadership: control
over allocation of benefits from the forests they come to govern. Through
such material rewards the state manufactures a new interest in the governmentalization of the environment and of the locality. This mutual recognition of interests and claims required the enactment and realization of legal
procedures and categories through the Forest Council Rules—and it highlights the constitutive relationship between power and humanity.

The shift in the exercise of power from the centralized state to the decentralized locality is not just about the creation of multiple locations of power,
or just about the governmentalization of localities. Still less is it the empowerment of local peoples, although the idiom of local empowerment is one of
the principal justifications used for decentralization policies (Cruikshank
1999). In fact, the shift in the exercise of power is as much about a new
economy of the power to regulate, about a better distribution of regulation,
and a more modulated application of power to shape individual practices
and subjectivities.

In contrast to the governmentalized locality, which signifies a new regime of political relationships between the state and the locality, the regulatory community denotes a redefinition of relationships among different
groups within the community. In choosing the concept of the regulatory
community to analyze the government of environment within local spaces
that decentralization formally creates, I depart from Michel Foucault's
(1979 [1975]) two preferred metaphors for the potential mechanisms
through which disciplinary power works: the coercive institution and the
punitive city. The model of the coercive institution that according to Foucault came to colonize almost the entirety of penality is Jeremy Bentham's
well-known panopticon. The punitive city would have served disciplinary
power equally well, but it also failed to be adopted as a deterrent. Neither
of these models has turned out to be relevant to environmental government
through community.

It would be fair to suggest that a well-functioning regulatory community obviates the need for any other form of penality, and does so in a way
that appears far more humane. Communal regulatory authority does not

need the loud and spectacular displays of retribution that sovereignty requires. Nor does it need the constant and all pervasive hammering home of representations that establish an irrefutable connection between crime and the return effects of crime on the criminal. And it certainly does not need the crutch of the all-encompassing physical gaze as the means to ensure compliance. Instead, it relies on intimate knowledge about each member and deploys this knowledge through a patchy system of monitoring and enforcement that limits infractions effectively by bounding them within a sphere of tolerability and simultaneously encourages divisions within the community.

Thus, in each community, regulation is practiced by multiple agents: the headman, the council of elected representatives, the guards appointed by the councils, and, depending on the forms of monitoring and enforcement, the people themselves. There is also a proliferation of the forms, strategies, and flows of power in the regulatory community. Headmen, guards, and council members are also local residents who meet other villagers frequently and in a variety of circumstances and are involved in complex relations of sociality and reciprocity only inadequately described by unidirectional mappings of domination and resistance. The regulatory community that the forest councils constitute is an "effort to adjust the mechanisms of power that frame the everyday lives of individuals; an adaptation for and a refinement of the machinery that assumes responsibility for and places under surveillance their everyday behavior, their identity, their activity, their apparently unimportant gestures; another policy for that multiplicity of bodies and forces that constitutes a population" (ibid.: 78). In contrast to the environmental control that the Forest Department sought to enact, regulations implemented by the forest councils touch the lives of their targets far more lightly, regularly, intimately, and in proportion to their activities.

Part of the reason that new loci of decision making can emerge within communities and that communities can become agents of regulation is communities' ability to wield information about members and use it to modulate the exercise of power. Communities ensure that their wielding of power is neither too forceful nor too weak. They want neither to provoke protests nor to be rendered ineffective. Community regulation operates more constantly, more consistently, and more effectively on its objects: village residents. To accomplish this, regulation has to be more comprehensive but less costly, more autonomous but more continuous, more modulated but less in need of direct supervision.

Indeed, new strategies of regulation through decentralized institutions could scarcely be in place without the greater efficiency they permit, and without the savings they allow the state to effect. The efficiency of the new form of regulation is evidenced in the reduction of economic, social, and political costs. The fiscal burden of the state is lowered in the first instance by the reduction in the number of administrative and enforcement personnel required. There is no need to devise uniform selection criteria, apply them to select guards and other personnel, train the selected individuals, create mechanisms for their supervision, and pay for these procedures at scales of remuneration roughly parallel with salaries and costs incurred in other government departments. The creation of the regulatory community allows the transfer of many economic costs to the locality. The community comes to govern forests and the actions of those dependent on the forest: it devises rules to use and manage trees, plants and helps harvest them, allocates fodder and firewood from the forest in proportions necessary to household needs, appoints guards and pays their salary, and settles disputes. It performs all these activities at a fraction of the cost that a central government would incur.

Political and social costs are also reduced for the central government. By transferring the tasks of protection and enforcement to the regulatory community, the central state no longer need bear the ire of citizens dependent on forests. The state is no longer the agent of exclusion. By changing the nature of protection and the structure of authority relations through which protection becomes manifest, the regulatory community also makes redundant the frustration and anger against bribes and corruption in which a government-appointed forest guard is inevitably implicated. As Foucault might observe, the new strategy of dispersed regulation replaces an excess of erratic and expensive enforcement with an economy of comprehensive and continuous obligation. The new network of environmental relations is more economical and effective, denser and more widespread, more autonomous and yet, in a sense, more enveloping.

The transfer of the design and enforcement of regulations to the lowest stratum of a social organization can be successfully maintained only by a simultaneous transformation of the relationship between the enforcer and the offender. When the agent of enforcement is an employee of the central government, charged with protecting its property in forests, the offender who violates the rules and procedures that create a healthy forest needs either to be excluded from the forest or to pay a fine. Upon detection of infractions, the objective of the state is to inoculate the forests from the illegal actions of the violators: one of the primary means of ensuring the safety of the forests is to exclude and expel the offender from them. But when enforcement is in the hands of the regulatory community, offenders are often members or neighbors of the community. Their actions are the source of a disharmony that must be balanced. Offenders cannot be excluded from the community, and even if in truly exceptional circumstances they are, their families and relatives continue to be a part of the community. Rather than retaliatory measures, punishments become the means to correct behavior. Precision in imposing punishments arises not so much from a reaction against a central authority as from a recognition that punishments are being imposed on group members who will continue to remain members even after being punished. The development of new punitive forms, thus, again rested on a concession to the generalized humanity of the community members being governed by those charged with governing.

As a result, there is a greater and more precise calibration of the monitoring mechanisms deployed, the type of sanctions imposed, and the dispute resolution available to settle conflicts. The community can appoint a guard and structure the guard's remuneration in multiple ways. The community can also pursue more decentralized methods of monitoring. Indeed, many of the mechanisms to monitor derive part of their power from the intimate, daily, multistranded contact and contiguous residential status of monitors and those being monitored. When a specialized guard is not appointed to watch over the forest, community members who rotate in this function have significant knowledge of each other's activities in the forest, without needing to surveil their neighbors. Similarly, regulation through the community and enforcement of new practices contains within itself potential seeds of reciprocal control by those whose practices are to be regulated. Mechanisms of accountability can come to colonize practices of regulation when the election of officials or the appointment and salaries of guards depend on contributions by community members. In contrast, protection of forests by the Forest Department depends ultimately on the presence of guards whose actions often become arbitrary in the absence of further supervisory procedures.

It is not just in the deployment of monitoring mechanisms that the regulatory community is able to more finely distinguish the permitted from the prohibited. It also can impose more finely calibrated sanctions. The blunt instruments of deliberate disregard for minor offenses and fines and imprisonment for actions deemed more egregious were the Forest Department's recourse for virtually all violations committed by villagers. But the range of instruments available to the community is more considerable, and the potential subtlety with which each of them can be deployed is greater as well. The range of sanctions encompasses varying levels of social exclusion and castigation, public reproof and chastisement, finely graded levels of monetary penalties, impounding of property such as offending instruments and animals used in the forest, and the threat of invoking central government authority, often more effective than its actual use. A more meticulous and thorough understanding of such mechanisms of regulation is the objective of emerging new sciences of community and the environment.

A critical part of the transformed relationship between the community and its residents, and between community residents and the environment, is the change in the object of regulation. Instead of ensuring a strict scientific protection of the forests to enhance state revenues, regulation now also becomes a means of pacification, of assuring subsistence, of addressing poverty. The Forest Department bought protection of its forested estate by ensuring that forests also supplied the basic items of daily rural necessity to local peoples, such as fodder, firewood, manure, and small construction timber. Such recognition of local interests in exchange for reasonable demands for protection was crucial in the formation of new subjectivities aligned with conservationist idioms. The awareness of mutual and complementary interests, the Forest Department's in commercial timber and local residents' in nontimber forest products, meant that the local residents of Kumaon could reasonably become concerned with how best to use, manage, and govern their forests. They could make themselves a part of government in coming to care (Foucault 1991 [1978]).

Ultimately, transformations in the relationships between the governmentalized locality and the state, between the regulatory community and its members, and between rural residents and their forests are linked to the creation of new environmental subjects.[10] Indeed, the most interesting question in the long process through which forests and peoples have come to be governmentalized may be less about the governmentalization of social institutions and more about the creation of environmental subjects. It is critical to understand and explain how people came to accept the importance of environmental regulation, to respect the authority of the community to sanction actions that did not respect regulation, and to participate in regulating the behavior of their fellow community members.

Many different forces have conspired to change how people think and act in relation to forests, among them, experiences of scarcity, media accounts of the environment, and processes related to the governmentalization of the environment. Among the most critical of these forces are changes in regulatory strategies within communities. Rearrangement of regulatory rule has had important effects in framing how people act, shaping their interests and motivations, encouraging their involvement in the enactment of regulation, and promoting the dispersal of government. The emergence of forest councils and, more important, the mechanisms to allocate and regulate constructed by them, have variable implications for understandings of the environment depending on the nature of these mechanisms and people's involvement in them.

New strategies to govern forests—to allocate, to monitor, to sanction, to adjudicate—do not simply constrain the actions of sovereign subjects. Nor are people's responses to new forms of regulatory strategies exhausted by the continuum between resistance and conformity. Instead, it is important to recognize how these strategies and their effects on flows of power shape subjects and their ways of thinking about what they do.[11] The most important changes have to do with the extent to which Kumaon's residents are now directly involved in taking care of their forests, often in ways that are more thoroughgoing, continuous, and deeply rooted than professional protection paid for by the Forest Department under centralized technologies of rule.

With the emergence of the forest councils, Kumaon's residents are today more likely to moderate their use of products such as firewood and fodder from community forests, to be involved in protecting forests (either as locally appointed and paid guards or as contributors to the salaries of such guards), and to identify neighbors who break locally created rules limiting the harvesting of benefits from forests. These are each different ways of imagining one's relationship to nature encoded as forests. Under centralized government, recall that Kumaon's residents not only used forests freely but burned down hundreds of thousands of acres of them. As users of forest products, they engaged in constant and unavoidable conflicts with forest guards appointed by the Forest Department, often simply because they were defined as intruders in forests. And as definitional criminals, they were quite unlikely to identify to authorities any of their neighbors who broke Forest Department rules. In each of these roles, as forest users, guards, and neighbors of rule violators, Kumaon's residents are today allied to an understanding of forests as scarce, products from forests as collectively owned, and forests themselves as a valuable inheritance that they will bequeath to their descendents. In arriving at this understanding of forests, forest products, and themselves, Kumaon's residents have become a part of the project to protect forests, albeit in ways that they define as their own.

In focusing on these strategies as the means through which individuals are reshaped as subjects, it is important to underline the extent to which the possibilities of the human is the terrain on which the environmental subject is imagined. The specific ways in which different conceptions of people are activated—whether as persons, selves, subjects, or agents—are all visible in the emergence of new forms of government in Kumaon. But the aspect of the human on which I have focused in this chapter—the subject, and more specifically the environmental subject—targets the representational capacities of that human. The immeasurably complex human capacity encoded by the environmental subject is central to the possibility of government through the governed. The experience in Kumaon makes clear that to achieve the consent of humans to their own government, it is necessary to work through their desires and beliefs—in this case, to make their relation to forests and nature one that they themselves want to change.

By bringing the possibilities of the human into view, and by focusing on the specific form of the subject, it becomes possible to specify the micromechanisms at work in variable reconfigurations of subjectivities in Kumaon. That is to say, explaining why people respond in particular and differentiated ways to new strategies of power requires attention to their existing subject positions, the extent to which they are privileged or marginalized by new strategies of power, and the way they are implicated in the operations of these strategies. To insist on variations in how subject positions change is also to insist on the evident fact that the effects of new forms of regulation are neither totalizing nor permanent.

To portray the transformation of people in Kumaon as the result of some epic battle between dominant forms of state power and resistant local populations would be to ignore the extent to which people and their communities are a product of power, often as it is manifested in institutionalized and governmentalized forms. To this extent, the separation that Foucault (1982: 222, 224) effects between institutions and the "social nexus," or between institutions and "social networks," in the study of power relations takes for granted a certain fixity of institutional arrangements that disappears when one closely examines what constitutes institutions.

Institutional analyses in political science have often been accused of underplaying the importance of politics (cf. Knight 1992). But they are especially deficient when it comes to understanding how power affects the nature of the human or the formation of the subject through changes in government as they are refracted through an institutional lens. Even institutionalists who attend to politics often view power and institutions as the external limit on the expressions that internal processes of the self would otherwise generate.[12] But changes in people's views about forests, occurring simultaneously with institutional transformations, suggest that something more is at stake than power as a simple constraint on actions. The nature of the self itself is at stake when one tries to understand social changes occurring over long time periods. New strategies of regulation in communities, instead of working to secure the cooperation of pregiven subjects or coercing them into new actions, flow along channels laid through the body of the community and activate different understandings of what constitutes the subject and what is in the subject's interest. The manufacture of interest and the redefinition of subjectivities play a key role in the construction of fresh beliefs about what kinds of practices are more attractive. Their effects work alongside those of new regulations.

Just because villagers come to participate more intimately in environmental regulation, or become more environmentally concerned, does not mean that new environmental subjects all feel the effects of regulation equally. In fact, variations in how households are situated in multiple fields of power critically influence the distribution of the burden of regulation. Allocation regimes of the forest councils and gender- and caste-related variations in sanctions on community members combine to produce substantial differences in the experience of regulation (Agrawal 2005). The greatest adverse impact of enforcement is borne by the most marginal groups within villages. The ways subjects are involved with various mechanisms of regulation—sharing the burdens of monitoring, taking responsibility for making community rules, contributing toward the salaries of guards, participating in attempts to impose sanctions, attending community meetings—play an

important role in shaping how they come to think about local forest resources (ibid.). In thinking about how new subjectivities are produced in
intimate conversations with new mechanisms of regulations, it is thus important to focus both on how individuals are affected by the implementation of regulations and what they do to shape them.

Localized, institutionalized regulation that is formally recognized by the
state and which demands a broader involvement by local residents than was
the case with more traditional community institutions in Kumaon prior to
the forest councils is instrumental in the creation of new kinds of humans
in two different ways. On the one hand, the formal recognition, indeed
encouragement, of local actions means that those who live in local communities have a new basis for relating to government. As they get involved in
governmental processes, they become government. Decentralized forms of
participation are all about moving the tasks of government to the governed.
In the form of Kumaon's forest councils, the idea of participatory democracy has found a new home in the practices associated with the governance
of forests. Kumaon's residents are free to get as involved as they wish in the
day-to-day tasks associated with the protection and use of their forests. This
freedom and its formal acknowledgment and sponsorship by state institutions was novel in Kumaon and in principle continues to be available to all
who live in its rural areas.

On the other hand, the formal recognition of the equal right of all to
be involved or the freedom to help conserve vegetation is experienced very
differently by local residents depending on potentially infinite variations in
their personal, social, and structural circumstances. It is not just the familiar categories of caste, wealth, gender, and so forth that shape what human
subjects do with freedoms they have or legal rights they gain. These categories are convenient analytical fictions with which to think about how new
forms of humanity are constructed by people facing new fields of potential
action and practice. What people do and become depends on how they are
immersed in the vast sea of already existing social interactions shaped by mi-
grations and remittances; agricultural, pastoral, forest-based, and other economic practices; family and kin relationships; networks of conversations;
exposure to modern media; connections with state officials; household size
and labor availability; levels of education and knowledge; interpersonal and
other communication skills; features of the landscape; vegetation types in
forests; uses to which forests can be put; and so on and on and on.

As we seek to make sense of this potentially bewildering diversity of factors that affect how variations inflect the production of new ways of being human, social practices are another convenient analytical fiction with which we can think the relationship of subjectivity to regulation. What people do may be affected by the infinity of limitless social relationships, but what they do has a significant effect on what they think and what they become as persons. The multiplicity of practices related to the use and government of forests can nonetheless be ordered in terms of the degree of intimacy with which Kumaon's residents are connected to regulation. It also offers a window through which to view the creation of new forms of humanity.

CREATING NATURE, CREATING HUMANS

The long history of changing forms of forests and their government in Kumaon, and changing relationships between humans and forests, is critical to understanding how environmental politics have changed in the past two decades throughout the developing world. The shift in conservation policies toward localities, communities, and participation has helped consolidate a particularly specific and limiting meaning of politics related to the environment. Recent analyses in the field of environmental studies, when they consider politics, treat the environment usually as yet another arena in which traditional conflicts such as those between elite and poor, state and community, or indigenous and outsider unfold. Even politically acute analyses of environmental histories and conflicts often pay relatively little attention to how shifting understandings of the environment are created through the politics of the environment, and how they play a role in environmental politics. In consequence, and in part as a result of the initial oppositions they set up between particular social actors and groups, such analyses are constrained to specific conclusions about changes in environmental politics.

More specifically, scholars who focus on the politics of the recent turn to community arrive at one of two conclusions: (1) celebration of the turn to community or (2) its interrogation and rejection based on the belief that it is a disguised attempt by states to extend their reach.[13] Often community members hail recent partnerships between governments and local actors as a victory for communities and resistance, after centuries of attempts to exclude them. Partnerships between government and the local become a salutary means to reduce the heavy-handedness of the state in environmental regulation, a mechanism to involve local populations and communities in resource use and management, and even a way to further grassroots democracy.

On the other side is a somewhat different interpretation. Observers who adopt a more radical analytical strategy view partnerships between government and the local as Trojan horses that facilitate the extension of state power and consolidation of the status quo. In this view, state efforts to involve communities in local resource management turn into a strategy to enhance centralized power, erase local diversity, and extend the constraints of central regulation into hitherto untouched social strata. In my analysis, what is at stake is not whether either of these views is correct. They may both be correct (or wrong). I am more interested in how the increasing articulation between the state and the community redefines environmental politics, and how it produces new environmental subjects as part of this redefinition.

But a similarly constricted field of vision is also characteristic of many scholars who take social identities such as women or indigenous, and assume their relationship with the environment and its meanings as foundational in reflecting on environmental politics. Many writings on environmental politics, responding to decades of marginalization of women, indigenous peoples, and the poor, attempt to rehabilitate these social actors (Shiva 1994; Blunt and Warren 1996). They do so by trying to prove that the identities of women, indigenous, and community are inherently friendly to the environment. This attempt to defend excluded groups and identities, however, consolidates a very peculiar conception of the environment in environmental politics. It treats the relationship between human nature and the environment as a primordial fact, uninfluenced by experiences, practices, and changing social relations. It reifies and naturalizes contingent relationships between social identities and environmental processes, and ignores how new environmental subjects emerge.

It is no exaggeration therefore to suggest that scholarship in the field of environmental politics often suffers from a curious failing: much of it is not about environmental politics. Rather than analyzing it as a common field of analysis, endeavor, and practice, writings on the politics of environment tend to isolate the two concepts analytically. The gap in analysis is in no small measure an artifact of the disciplinary divisions where scholars of political economy seldom examine questions of identity, and those study-ing identity and its subtle transformations are less enamored of distributive struggles around resources. By examining the reciprocal construction of environment and politics together, however, it is possible to produce more nuanced and careful accounts of environmental regulations and struggles. Concurrent processes of government and self-making are at the core of all attempts to institute new regulatory regimes. When displaced from more centralized to more distributed locations, new mechanisms of rule making and regulation generate new perceptions of environmental scarcities and promote more widely pervasive understandings about the need for conser-vation. Differences in prior social locations and in the rates and types of participation in mechanisms through which environmental government is accomplished is in no small measure the basis for understanding how exist-ing social stratification and changing institutions produce variations in the formation of new subject positions.

To talk about the emergence of new subject positions is also to give form to the three different ways in which the introduction to this book treats the idea of humanity—as substance, as object, and as threat. It is humanity as realized substance that is at play behind the emergence of decentralized technologies of governance of the environment. These technologies are built on shifts in the discursive formations of development and environ-ment according to which the disjuncture between the act of governance and that of being governed, between the subject and the target of govern-ment, between the process and outcome of government has been too large. Overcoming this disjuncture and closing the gap between the governor and the governed requires the incorporation of the governed in the process of government. The emergence of the target of government as also its agent is both the means and the goal of technologies of decentralized government.

The realization of this shift in the means and goals of government also creates a new terrain on which government unfolds—not the transnational terrain remarked on in the introduction but what might be called the trans/ subnational one. I use this complex term advisedly and in light of the par-adoxical phenomenon that is decentralization. For even as decentralized government calls for a multiplication in the loci of the exercise of power and the retrenchment of what was called the centralized state to make way for these new loci of power, it has proceeded on the basis of minor variations on a common discursive and technological theme in much of the develop-ing world. One can only wonder about the origins of a clearly transnational logic that has led governments in countries from Bolivia to Vietnam and from the Philippines to Zambia to claim decentralization as an appropriate form for the exercise of new technologies of power. Transnationality, in the context of decentralization, seems to work out differently from what any appeal to a transnational government centered in international institutions such as the World Bank or the International Monetary Fund might suggest. It works its magic by making centralized forms of governance seem unappealing, even unnecessary. Indeed, its promise lies in the ways it makes subjects means of their own subjection.

The emergence of subjects and their complicity in projects of rule is precisely the potential that decentralized government seeks to realize so as to nullify the threat humans might pose to nature. This chapter has argued that to imagine the residents of Kumaon as environmental subjects capable of government—not just as acquiescent objects of rule in central projects of the government of nature but also as thinking and self-regulating subjects—the project of power had to recognize their humanity. The humanity of the object of government is the ground on which the promise of decentralization government rests. Who else can govern but the human?

To the extent centralized forms of government of nature recognize humans, they inevitably see them as threats to the survival of nature. Humans are considered especially threatening as a collective. Populations and their growth continue to be portrayed by most scholars of the environment as principal sources of concern in relation to environmental governance. The failure of exclusionary forms of government, whether as national parks, protected forests, or other forms of territorial seclusion, is in part what has led many environmentalists to experiment with attempts to involve humans in the government of nature. Environmental subjects as holders of beliefs and desires, and as enactors of actions consistent with the beliefs and desires they hold, become reasonable targets of responsible government through changes in their beliefs and desires and through constraints on their self-oriented actions.

Even as such experiments with decentralization have called into question earlier assumptions about the necessity of separating humans from nature to protect it, they have also been criticized as being little more than a new mechanism through which humans can be encouraged to exclude themselves from nature.

This view of decentralization as a ruse has something to recommend it, because indeed humans intimately implicated in decentralized technologies of rule seek to reduce their own levels of consumption and to encourage others to do the same. To see their actions just as a reflection of the aims of power or as an indication that the project of rule has succeeded would, however, be to miss the emergence of new subject positions that the exercise of power enables. If the creation of all subject positions is in part the result of the exercise of power, then surely not all exercise of power occurs to create victims or to negate freedom.

In this sense, my discussion has examined and advanced an approach to understanding relationships between nature and humans that takes neither as given, and the remaking of each through the exercise of power as a necessary point of departure. The coming together of different strategies of power—encoded in the bureaucratic structure of the colonial state, prevailing and changing understandings of what forests meant for different political actors, and subject positions of those whose livelihoods depend on forests—led to the outcomes I describe. At its core, I suggest, the study of environmental government is about the simultaneous redefinition of self and environment, and such redefinition is accomplished through the means of political economy. In this sense, the study of environmental government reflects on the nature of the relationship between regulation and the individual, policy and perceptions, state and community. Instead of seeing these concepts as oppositional, or as the opposite ends of a spectrum, it is far more rewarding to view them as occupying a necessarily reciprocal and mutually constitutive connection.

NOTES

1 As paid, direct appointees of the state, village headmen and other revenue officials had little leeway in interpreting the responsibilities they were supposed to discharge.

2 The vast literature on the common pool resources and local governance provides many guidelines, not always the same ones, to shape the use of resources. See Ostrom 1990 for a rigorous introduction to writings on the commons; and Crook and Manor 1998 for a comparative analysis of programs of decentralized development.

3 For a more detailed discussion of the committee's recommendations, see KFGC 1921. See also Agrawal 2005.

4 See Shrivastava 1996. This reliance by colonial conservation officials on existing local practices is also noted by Grove 1995, and it helps call into question the presumed watershed that colonial rule is often taken to mark.

5 The techniques through which villagers control their communities are visible in the records of the forest councils. Their reports on their meetings, local rule violations, the

identities of rule breakers, and the magnitude of financial transactions are remarkably informative. These records show that the protection villagers ensure, the policing tasks they undertake, and the monitoring mechanisms they have created have produced an imperfect but more comprehensive mechanism of regulation than that exercised by the Forest Department.

6 See Sivaramakrishnan 1999. Although his use of "modern forests" is primarily a reference to colonial Bengal, forms of modernity are always in flux, and the term is evocative of the emerging regimes of regulation in Kumaon as well.

7 I use *government* in a Foucauldian sense, but one should note that even in Foucault, and certainly in much of the scholarship based on his suggestive arguments, there is only an indication of *what* the term implies; there is little or no exploration of how government is accomplished, *how* changes in projects of rule combine with changes in subjectivities, and *how* one is to explain variations in transformations of subjects (Butler 1997).

8 *Resistance* would be a more appropriate term. The obvious popularity of idioms of resistance in the wake of James Scott's (1990) landmark study—and, in critical response to his analysis, of ideas of negotiation and engagement—would be an all-too-easy trap into which a historian of forested environments in Kumaon might fall. For studies that elaborate on these idioms, see Colburn 1989; and Haynes and Prakash 1992.

9 Without doubt, the process of decentralization and the reconfiguration of relationships between central governments, localities, and persons is also closely implicated in the production of the state itself. However, a discussion of how the state is itself reconfigured through the process of decentralization is beyond the scope of this chapter. For an extended treatment of the making of state and community in Kumaon, see Agrawal 2001.

10 As David Scott (1999) points out in his work on postcolonial criticism, "In the colonial world, the problem of *modern* power turned on the politico-ethical project of producing subjects and governing their conduct. . . . The political problem of modern colonial power was therefore not merely to contain resistance and encourage accommodation but to seek to ensure that *both* could *only* be defined in relation to the categories and structures of modern political rationalities" (52; emphasis in original).

11 In some ways, this part of the argument can be seen as an effort to examine how bureaucratic, scientific mechanisms of regulation reshape human agency (for a contrasting view, see James Scott 1990).

12 This is true even of Jon Elster, who, among those who have written from an institutionalist perspective, is perhaps the most alive to questions of changes in the self and subjectivities (see Elster, Offe, and Preuss 1998: 247–70; and Elster 1999).

13 Of course, there are other scholars whose work suggests that the turn to community has been incompletely accomplished, or who point to other fractures within community to suggest that state efforts to shift political power and resources toward communities benefit specific populations within communities rather than the community as a whole (see Bryant and Bailey 1997; Weaver, Rock, and Kusterer 1997; and Wolverkamp 1999).

Counting the Dead in the Cancer Trial

S. Lochlann Jain

IN ITS ATTEMPTS to recruit patients with late-stage and metastatic renal cancer, Oxford Biomedica's patient pamphlet takes the standard form of asking and answering an array of imagined patient questions. Among them is this one: "What happens if I get a placebo and TroVax® is then shown to work?" The answer: "If the study shows TroVax® prolongs survival and you received the placebo you will be given the opportunity to be treated with TroVax®, *following regulatory approval*" (Patient Information Leaflet 2007; my emphasis). The hopeful sentence of the now defunct trial writes progress as a given. The pamphlet might, after all, have had the imaginary patient ask, "What if I am in the TroVax® group and it is shown *not* to work, or to work but with impossibly brutal side effects?" But the tragic effect of the question and answer Oxford Biomedica gives lies in its elision of the simple but critical fact that a person with late-stage and metastatic renal cancer has virtually no hope of surviving long enough for this drug to come to market. While the hope of sidestepping that fact may well underwrite a patient's willingness to take part in the trial in search of a miracle cure, question and answer relies on a serious misrecognition and misrepresentation of the temporal scope of the trial in relation to its mortal subjects.

In this sense, the recruiting pamphlet offers insight into both the ways that cancer is constituted as a cultural object in the United States and how subjects are invited to live in a space organized through both hope and progress as virtually inescapable, ubiquitous tropes. In my research on cancer, I have come to believe that hope forms a central structure through which cancer is understood. Venues as distinct as marches for a cure, fundraisers for children's camps, and clinical interactions between doctor and patient parry around the concept of hope. The randomized control trial (RCT) plays a critical role in the infrastructures of hope. Offering the possibility of cure where there is otherwise none, it builds in and on a cultural presumption of progress in cancer treatment, and it provides the basis for highly protocol-driven treatments for cancer. The method offers a critical site in which the structures of hope and future-orientation are produced, represented, and deployed through the wider culture of cancer and its treatments.

The RCT plays the role of scientific flagship of hope for both patients and the culture at large. It also produces cancer culture through the creation of nearly ritual protocol- and population-driven treatment. Outlining the history of chemotherapy for lung cancer in which one or two subjects may survive for a couple of years but all die before the five and ten years, Helen Valier and Carsten Timmermans have noted how in the midst of incremental progress in cancer treatment, "participation in a clinical trial has turned into a symbol of hope for patients."[1] My ethnographic, literary, and historical research shows that the very form and fantasmic role of the trial structures experiences and understandings of cancer not only through statistics about risk and prognoses but also in how some people with cancer consider possible participation in future trials, in how people research their own and others' disease, in advertisements for cancer drugs, and in doctor-patient interactions.

Often slow growing and asymptomatic, often misdiagnosed, often cured, and often recurring, cancer rerenders notions of time. Even the clichéd refrain that cancer makes one value each moment and live each day to the fullest counters capitalist notions of hard work for future reward and capital accumulation that the possibility of recurrence can undermine. If hope orients one to and anticipates a future, the results of the research trial look backward, counting and accounting for deaths and recurrences. Hope for a positive outcome offers what will be for many patients a counterfactual future. Trial results, on the other hand, purport to find reasons for what did happen, for who died and how their death related to their treatment.[2]

A lecture given in 2007 at the annual San Antonio Breast Cancer Conference strikingly captured the temporal fissure central to my analysis. Introducing his research with a roundabout acknowledgement of the subjects, Mitchell Dowsett (2007) declared, "1,050 people would have to relapse before we had data." It is not just Dowsett's translation of lives into data, or the third-person "would have to" that so startles, nor is it simply the transference of people's lives into terms of ownership over data. Most surprising is the disjuncture of the counterfactual created by the temporal shiftiness: one only knows afterward that 1,050 recurrences were suffered. Yet Dowsett's phrasing sounds as though he knew in advance that there would be 1,050 recurrences, or at the very least, a group of recurrences and deaths. A subject in the trial may have hoped to be in the nonrecurrence group, yet after the data were collected, one would know which group one had been in. How do we wrap our minds around these central, structuring temporal paradoxes of cancer culture: its inevitability, its predictability, the possibility and impossibility of early detection, the mystery of relapse: its counterfactual hopes and histories made so vivid in these different views on the trial?

The RCT replicates and proliferates temporal paradoxes, which I believe are central to how cancer is produced as a cultural and material object, that I aim to unpack. My analysis aims to better understand the material-making of cancer and its cultures and economies. Thus I want to try in this chapter a thought experiment: What happens if we suspend this future orientation of the promise of cancer treatments, even as it is utterly embedded in RCT-based protocol? My hypothesis is that this temporal suspension will allow us to focus on the subject positions required by the RCT. Taking out the relentless future orientation (in terms of results, better treatments, cure) may allow us to view the RCT as an actual, material, *present* structure—as a representational form—in and through which people live and die and eke out forms of understanding about the disease (even as these understandings create the disease), medicine, and mortality. In making this conceptual shift, in attempting to better understand the centrality of RCTs as one primary material practice through which cancer patients are constituted as certain kinds of material and conceptual objects and subjects, I aim to better understand how cancer is lived and reproduced in the United States.

Futurity so centrally informs American understandings of cancer research, fund-raising, survivorship, and treatment that the argument I pose here may seem both counterintuitive and in some ways abhorrent. As I have witnessed many times in talks and academic reviews, hope as a charitable emotion, as a life raft, or as a habit is not dispensed with easily. One dispenses with it personally, analytically, and politically at one's own peril regardless of survivor-status not only because of its obvious attraction but because of the identity politics that adheres to efforts to speak and write about cancer. I propose here that the politics of the disease both informs and exceeds any given experience with it.

Thus, I outline with care what I am not doing. My argument does not question the intent of oncologists. Like practitioners of many professions, oncologists perform their craft with various complementary and contradictory intents and with greater and lesser skill, and my goal here is neither to question nor affirm those. Similarly, I remain neither antihope, nor antisurvival, nor antitreatment. I point no fingers at researchers, at people choosing among a sparse set of treatments, or at those raising money for more research, camps, awareness, or rides to the hospital. Many patients, caretakers, and doctors tell their stories sincerely and sympathetically albeit with a great deal of anger, trust, frustration, resignation, and grief, and this affect and these emotions remain central to any possibility of understanding the cultural traumas of cancer and the high stakes in this mode of critique. Nevertheless, I take seriously an aspect of oncology rarely considered in the social science literature: cancer as a disease is constituted in the midst of much medical and scientific uncertainty and failure.

Focusing on the widely acknowledged though somewhat unpleasant aspect of the scientific mystery of cancer forces us to consider the materiality produced by the slippery term *cancer*, so often an umbrella not only for the disease of dividing cells but for the dangerous and often injurious treatments. The vastness of the events described by *cancer* enables treatment injury to go unremarked, making the ways patients take on risk and injury and the ways they and others understand risk and injury virtually invisible. The ways in which treatment injury is occluded matters, not only because unpacking them can give us a better understanding of the conditions under which people decide to undergo often dangerous and injurious treatments, but also because these choices may lead to better, more carefully thought-out research and policy. Treatment injury is also central to the making of the shock and anger, illness and suffering all around us. In other words, I aim to unpack the assumptions that have undergirded cancer treatments for centuries. Today these assumptions include the belief that chemotherapy, the toxic chemicals used to treat patients, even without extensive animal studies, are wholly justified against the "toxic cost of cancer" (Rothman and Edgar 1992).[3] What assumptions lie behind these equations and how do they take on broader significance in cancer culture?

With more than half a million deaths a year, 12 million survivors, and with 1 in 39 people under the age of 40 diagnosed with cancer, virtually everyone in the United States has lived through it (the cliché is that they have been "touched by cancer"), in varied forms and in closer or further proximity. Yet very few languages of structural understanding attempt to grapple with this central trauma of American life. As a multibillion-dollar industry, proliferating cancer cultures demand anthropological analysis. The way cancer is understood within this morass of big money and big suffering matters, and while tropes of hope, charity, the good death, and cure may be of use in certain circumstances, their hegemony in cancer culture seriously misrepresents, obscures, and downplays the deeply political character of the disease.

In the TroVax® pamphlet cited above, one does not read about how difficult it is to get into trials, or what it is like to be presented a series of chemotherapy options and survival statistics by a physician in a clinical setting and asked to choose one. One does not hear about the people with their oxygen tanks flying to Texas or Argentina for treatment in their last months and weeks, or taking the carefully researched stacks of trial reports and trial numbers inscribed on a folded sheet of paper into the doctor's office and hearing the physician say: "Oh, no one followed that up," or "That's just not what we do here," or, "There were not enough people in the trial to draw any conclusions," or, "Yes, but those results are controversial so we don't give that treatment," or, "Yes, but the population was too varied to be of use in your case," or, "Yes, but your insurance will not pay for that treatment." These stories I have collected, but their confusion and heartbreak is only the latest in a long history of the rise and fall of "miracle" cures—whose legions have included radium pills, letrozole, interferon, and GC-MAF—and the hundreds of thousands of patients who have taken them, often at great physical and financial cost. The stories demonstrate the excruciating positions inhabited by both patients and physicians who live, represent, manage, and attempt to communicate, on a daily level, information and speculation about diseases and potential treatments under conditions in which very little is known and very much is hoped for.

If, on the one hand, these stories make evident the vast rifts in the ideals of cancer treatment and trials and the fantasmatic role they play for cancer patients—to the extent that "I need a trial" sometimes substitutes for "I need a cure"—on the other, they attest to the centrality of the trial format to the experience and culture of cancer.[4] In this chapter, then, I do not present new ethnographic data about how trials are run and experienced; rather, I aim to shift the conceptual lens through which we understand how their logics underpin cancer culture.

THE GOLD STANDARD

The randomized control trial, as the gold standard of evidentiary medicine, is an experimental method in which two similar groups given different treatments are compared to measure the efficacy of the treatment. In human trials, a group of people with something to be treated or measured will enter a trial that may have controls for age, race, or disease characteristics. They are then randomized into two different groups, one which takes a placebo or standard of care treatment, and the other that receives the new treatment (Rothman and Edgar 1992). After a predetermined amount of time, data from the groups is compared using highly specialized and often controversial statistical methods.

The method is taken to be so intuitively correct that even to unpack it to examine how it produces scientific facts, or to understand how the method determines what kinds of research are possible, invites the response by scientists that there is simply nothing better, that the objectification of the patient is an unfortunate but necessary by-product of the method (Oakley 2005). And, as physicians sometimes note, RCTs have led to improved patient care: survival rates for several types of cancers have skyrocketed thanks not only to new treatments but as a result of the RCT's ability to establish that new treatments are, in fact, better.

My project intersects with but diverges from current literature on RCTs, which tends to fall into four categories: (1) the RCT's historical rise, (2) its dependence on statistical thinking and methods, (3) its emergence from agricultural fields, and (4) its use in studying many treatments. Anthropologists have examined the cultural specificity of the trials and the outsourcing of trials in the search for treatment-naive populations. Others have focused on the ethics of the trials and the treatment of subjects, and a burgeoning literature addresses the on-the-ground efficacy of trials in terms of the slippages between theory and practice, the value of different statistical models, and the politics of pharmaceutical funding (Fisher 2009; Petryna 2009). By unpacking how late-stage cancer trials set up subject positions in the context of the certain, and possibly even required, deaths of their subjects, I aim to open a space for a question that contemporary cancer scholarship has stopped short of asking: How can the decades and centuries of intensely dangerous, risky, and often horrific treatments that cancer patients have undergone, and continue to undergo, be understood?

A growing number of historians have traced the rise and fall of various cancer treatments. Each examine in different ways how the bodies of cancer patients have been caught up and used in struggles that relate often only marginally to a larger cultural effort to find a cure for cancer. Sometimes well-intentioned local attempts to treat individual cases have had disastrous effects. Barron Lerner (2001) describes the use of more and more radical surgeries that cut out huge margins of the body through the mid-twentieth century. Eileen Welsome (2000) and Gerard Kutcher (2006) write about experimentation with massive doses of radiation or the injection of radioactive elements. And Elizabeth Toon (2009) traces out how bodies with cancer were caught in big professional shifts, such as the movement by radiologists to have radiation treatments added to the protocol despite major debates about the treatments' efficacy.

In his remarkable history of breast cancer treatments, James Olson (2002) describes the women who had access to the latest, most aggressive treatments of their age, in his term, a "sisterhood of guinea pigs." Such treatments included the removal of the adrenal and pituitary glands, cracking open the sternum to remove the internal mammary chain, cauterization with hot irons, huge doses of radiation and X-rays, and surgeries that in some cases included the removal of ribs, collarbones, and shoulders following the discovery of tumors of under one centimeter. Using this phrase carries the implication that these people were used, according to the *OED*, "like a guinea-pig as the subject of an experiment." Unlike many treatments which are tested using hired subjects or that are contracted overseas, experimental late-stage cancer treatments are often offered to Americans. Patients often request the most aggressive treatments. Indeed, many people describe the period after the chemotherapy is over as the hardest part of treatment, since there is then nothing to do but wait. This space between what is presented as the most aggressive treatment and what is assumed to be the most effective treatment provides one critical place to better understand and theorize the structures through which the contests between cancer the disease (nature) and treatments (technology) are made material through human bodies and how these human bodies fare semiotically and materially in that process.

To be sure, oncology as a professional field has virtually been defined by the RCT and its use to test chemotherapy, pharmaceuticals, radiation, and various surgical techniques. The rise of the profession and its stature coincided not with big improvements in survivorship, which has increased by only 6 percent since 1975 (a rate often compared to much larger improvements in heart disease); not with the huge gains one might expect in early detection or better treatments (the declining rates of tobacco-related cancers providing the one exception); but rather with more aggressive treatments, people staying in treatment for longer and having more rounds of chemotherapy, and more and bigger trials (Harrington and Smith 2008). Thus, as a central mode through which oncology is practiced, propagated, and even explained to patients in educated settings, RCTs offers a central structure through which cancer is or will be inhabited by everyone, even though only a small percentage of patients are actually enrolled in them. As Nicholas Christakis (2001) writes in his study on prognosis in medicine, the "booming industry in clinical trials . . . supports increasing interest in the development and use of various prognostic staging systems and clinical markers." The constant reporting of their results in the news media suggests that they centrally shape American understandings of risk and causation, to the extent that people feel the most excruciating guilt and talk in the most crushing ways about being blamed for their cancers, as if their cancer were a result of their drinking too much milk or letting their stress go uncontrolled: as if the cancer were the victims' fault. As one twenty-seven-year-old, three-time cancer survivor said to me, "I hate it when people talk like that, it makes me feel bad and it's *too late for me.*"

The logic of the randomized control trial offers an elegant simplicity, one so beyond reproach in its commonsensical grounding that, even as the relevance of results and specific trials are hotly contested, the method itself serves as a tightly shut black box in medical discussions and debates. While some accounts credit the first use of the RCT with having eradicated scurvy by leading to the introduction of limes, the historian Harry Marks (1997) traces the contemporary hegemony of the method in medical research to agricultural studies, where it was developed by a geneticist and statistician, R. A. Fischer. In searching for a way to measure whether new agricultural treatments were an improvement, the most reliable data were found by dividing the land into strips and alternating a specific treatment—fertilizer, say—with none. This method, by producing multiple replications of a comparison, averaged out—thus canceling—random factors such as moisture or sun exposure, that might affect one patch of land more than the other. By comparing two large patches of land over time, the efficacy of the fertilizer could be judged against the other factors. In this way, the individual chance that the fertilizer would work on any individual sunny or windy patch of land could be recast as population probability that the fertilizer would work on many of the land patches, with sun and wind factored out of the equation. Thus, taken up in human trials the method is celebrated for precisely this ability to eliminate any factor other than the one being tested.

RCTS are used to study many things, from the potential benefits of physical exercise and eating greens to the proper dosing of medications. They have stood so firmly as the evidentiary standard for cancer chemotherapy trials—both have grown explosively since the Second World War—that the method itself barely requires comment in the scientific literature. The common sense of the trial holds that a new drug will be tested on a randomly selected group of people who have a particular disease against another group who have the same disease and are given either a placebo or the previous standard of care. It would be unethical, for example, to conduct a trial that compared a group given a new chemotherapy to a group given none if chemotherapy were the standard of care. Similarly, it would be unethical to let most types of cancers grow for very long simply to "see" if they were fast- or slow-growing cancers. Ideally a series of controls such as age, gender, or stage of disease will narrow the random factors, but often the quest for subjects requires that few controls are put on a group, affecting the clinical value of trial results, which requires comparing the population in the trial to the actual patient. Moving from phase 1 to phase 3 trials requires moving to progressively larger groups of people. At each phase, so long as the factor to be compared is correctly identified, the variations among people will, in theory, cancel each other out—so the larger the group, the more accurate the trial is thought to be. As the neurologist Lesley Fellows told me, however, "the larger the trial needs to be, the less obvious the efficacy of a treatment—if a treatment really worked, we know with five patients" (interview, March 23, 2009). The fact that individual prognosis cannot be determined with cancer except in cases of significant metastasis for most cancers confounds the question. Since no one knows who would experience a recurrence without the treatment, trials virtually have to be population based. This uncertainty also lies at the heart of historical controversies over survival in increments of survival time after treatment.

The RCT literature assumes remarkably lightly and without comment that patches of land can translate into the self-evident unit of a person; that the disease can become a category with as much certainty as an agricultural pest or the natural course of the growth of peas; and that the treatment of mobile, complicated individuals can be understood as unproblematically as fertilizer on land. I personally consider the facility of these translations a happy coincidence, rather like the fact that the visibly obvious boiling point of water makes the perfect cup of tea, that the Moon fits perfectly under the Earth's shadow during an eclipse; or that popcorn is cheap, not unhealthy, and delicious. The current common sense of trials, however, hides shifts in structures of knowledge collection such as the growth of statistics and what Ted Porter (1995) has called the "trust in numbers" over experience and other forms of knowledge. Other historians have traced the professional battles and debates that came to favor the RCT methods. In short, belief in the RCT reflects a medical philosophy and culture of health quite different than that of the nineteenth century, when an individual's physical and emotional constitution influenced the course of the disease more than particular disease characteristics (Rosenberg 2002). A nineteenth-century physician may not have understood the logic of the RCT, let alone taken it for granted as the primary—practically exclusive—means to medical evidence. Indeed, because of their commitment to ideas of clinical excellence rather than statistics, several oncologists in the 1970s refused to give up the Halsted radical mastectomy despite trial evidence that, for all its brutality, removing muscle, tissue, and sometimes ribs, it lowered risk of recurrence no more than a simple mastectomy. This fundamental belief in clinical care over statistics demonstrates how trust in these numbers had to be cultivated, as did the techniques of collection. Nonetheless, clinicians sometimes resist treating their patients based on trial results.

The RCT offers five simple facts, which bear noting as background information to my argument. First, despite the billions of dollars being spent and the thousands of trials being undertaken at any given moment, survival rates for most cancers have improved incrementally at best, and the recent declines in overall cancer deaths in the United States (300 fewer in 2003–4; 2,600 fewer in 2004–5 out of about 500,000) are accounted for nearly universally by reduced smoking rates, earlier detection for some cancers, or expected statistical anomalies. Stage for stage, however, cancer death rates are similar to what they were thirty years ago; that is, if diagnosed right this minute, one is as likely to live for ten years with a stage III (nearly any cancer except testicular or certain leukemias) as one would have been if diagnosed twenty years ago. Incidence rates are increasing for certain cancers, especially among children and young adults, and cancers are still caught at criminally late stages for some demographics: people of color, queers, and young adults.[5]

Second, RCT logic seems utterly immutable—so beyond reproach, so objective, that it stands up even against the parade of obvious flaws that may derail any study, which are simply ignored in the data collection. For example, often whole categories of terms such as what counts under "relapse free survival" will vary from study to study or even within studies and among medical centers. This makes studies virtually impossible to compare, as oncologists readily admit. Often people in the treatment group are not treated: the category is "intent to treat," rather than "actually treated" (Rettig et al. 2007). Look for a history of RCTs for any cancer you like, and you will find promising phase 1 and 2 trials for inexpensive drugs that were simply never picked up again, or multimillion-dollar phase 3 trials testing for incremental survival benefits.

Third, since cancer treatments offer high profit margins, debates rage around certain high profile trials. For example, the Food and Drug Administration (FDA) recently approved the expensive drug Avastin for breast cancer ($100,000/patient/year) after the second application by its manufacturer, Genentech. Controversy raged around the fact that Genentech was able to provide evidence of a short extension in disease-free survival but no evidence of overall survival with the drug. In other words, the patient would die by having a treatment with many side effects that would slow a cancer's growth briefly before it came roaring back to kill the host. One Genentech oncologist explained to me that this disease-free survival period opened the possibility that other treatments could be tried and developed. Some activists decried the use of expensive drugs and the lack of more efficacious treatments. Genentech stock increased in value by 9 percent on the day of approval, and it was explicitly priced in accordance with what people would pay rather than what it cost to develop and manufacture. By managing such trials and protocols, oncology has been promoted from a backwater medical practice in which most of the patients died to one of the highest-paid medical specialties, working in some cities' shiniest buildings, in which most of the patients die. While oncologists by necessity recognize this fact, others complain that it is not nice to note this truth, as if to note it is to blame someone.

Fourth, my research has turned up several ways that ethnographic slippage takes place, potentially rendering the data unreliable. In a discussion of one such slippage at a cancer retreat I recently attended, several people compared their experiences with radiation treatment, which was described as "one of the most alienating experiences of treatment, even worse than having red chemicals pumped into me." The reason for this alienation was the obvious disconnect between the "big science" of the machinery and the seeming lack of precision exhibited by technicians who seemed to approximate the proper positioning of people's bodies and arms, going so far even to ask the patient if "this felt like the right position." There are also the clear institutional limits to delivery: while the treatment protocol is for delivery every day, in fact, people are not treated on weekends, and, as one doctor told a patient in laying out the treatment plan, "We'll skip Easter, too, since the technicians aren't working." This kind of evidence complicates the purported precision of big cancer science, the exactitude of trials, and the actual delivery of treatment. Of the three people in the discussion at the cancer retreat, one had quit treatment early, the second had changed the scheduling, and the third felt humiliated by and had lost faith in the entire process.[6] Another example of this type of slippage came in an email discussion group recently, in which one person claimed that she would take a drug for a metastatic recurrence, and if a trial came along which required subjects who had not taken that drug, she would simply say she had not taken the drug in order to get into the trial. People manage their treatments and stories in relation to the medical industrial complex.

Fifth, the RCT is not in itself science; that is, it cannot offer a cure for cancer or come up with a better treatment, though it is often presented to patients as if it could. It can only compare treatments that are being developed or have been developed for other uses and are now being tested for new markets (and patients). It is easy to forget, as one moves around the enormous halls of oncology conferences, that the massive numbers of RCTs and the huge amount of money spent on running them have to some large extent become their own industry, completely separated from actual survival rates. It is easy to lose track of the fact that counting deaths for an RCT may render them in some small sense significant—it makes no promise it can keep to reduce future deaths. Even if errors are made (group or disease characteristics are not similar enough to lead to actual treatment protocols—a matter of constant confusion), the method will by definition elicit some numerical data. Ironically, then, this self-propagating hum of RCTs generates statistics that can be endlessly analyzed. The trickiness and politics of RCT research in light of incremental differences between drugs was hinted at by another doctor at the 2007 San Antonio Breast Cancer Conference who observed: "It is a great time to be a statistician" (Brenner 2007). The statistician was referring to the notorious difficulties in comparing RCTs and how easily results can be manipulated because of the variety of statistical methods.

THE MORTALITY EFFECT

RCT logic reflects such a structuring principle of our time that some of its key paradoxes barely register: two groups compete, one wins. It is the logic of war: two sides competing to see which can kill or injure the other; it is the logic of sport: two sides competing for goals, points, or marks. One might say that the RCT participant partakes in a competition to "out heal," or to beat his prognosis. Yet there is a good reason that the word *patient* contains mixed meanings of "able to wait calmly; quietly expectant," a person "under the care of another," a "person suffering without complaint," "a person who or thing which undergoes some action, or to which something is done; a (passive) recipient. Chiefly in contrast with *agent*." If patients have agency, it is best spent putting themselves in what Talcott Parsons called the "sick role," or the position of trying to get better. This typically entails taking on the social and physical role of patient.

In the RCT, patients compete in a contest that exceeds their ability to compete; they will not even know which treatment they are getting. Indeed, any question of their own agency and the incredible efforts required of them and their caretakers will be elided and the success or failure of the treatment attributed solely to the treatment itself.[7] The spectacle of the competition, in the RCT, lies only in the result, not in the life and death dramas it enfolds. In that sense, it stands at the crux of a counterfactual paradox: it relies on the elision of its conditions of possibility (the deaths of its human subjects). It steadies itself in this paradox by legitimating its dead through the future promise of a cure. Recall Dowsett: "1,050 people would have to relapse before we had data." The doctor overseeing the RCT stands in wait for relapses that he presumes would have happened regardless of his aggregation. One might draw an analogy to the person waitlisted for a liver, waiting for someone else's fatal car accident or brain aneurism. One dies so that another might live.

In this way, the self-evident logic of the RCT manages the possibility—the virtual requirement—of the ill subject's death, for nearly all of the subjects in trials of treatments for late-stage cancers will die. The RCT thus asks its subjects to partake in the higher calling of what Foucault (1994) might have called "collective living on" (see also Murray 2006). He writes this paradox of individual sacrifice for the vision of a social form: "Go get slaughtered and we promise you a long and pleasant life." This critical disjuncture, the confusion between one's own mortality and the longevity of the social, so often missed by cancer scholars who inscribe themselves in the position of survivor-researcher, is central to grasping cancer culture and its collective living on—it may even be central to the reproduction of cancer's conditions of possibility, or at least the conditions of the flourishing industry it has produced.

I witnessed exactly this disjuncture at a lunch for cancer activists sponsored by Genentech. The representatives and scientists were attempting to recruit subjects, and they claimed that the success of leukemia drugs and survival rates in the 1960s and 1970s was because of the high rate of leukemia patients enrolled in trials (70 percent)—as opposed to only 3 percent of breast cancer patients enrolled in trials. There are many reasons why leukemia treatments succeed, the most critical of which is that chemotherapy simply was and remains much more efficacious for liquid than for solid tumors. But the point for this analysis is that Genentech's representatives were cajoling audience members not to let their diseases go uncounted, wasted, as missed opportunities. Work in the service of "your" disease, Genentech representatives essentially exhorted the audience, thus using the future collective both to rally patients' alliance and further Genentech's interest.

The RCT asks cancer patients to undergo hardship for future patients, for a slim hope of a cure, or do one's bit for science and humanity. One person described to me how her mother participated in a trial for years, collecting and freezing her waste, explicitly as a noble endeavor done in the interest of future generations. This model relies on the promise of future progress and depends on an alliance of patients with their particular illness and future patients with that illness. If the statement that "our ancestors died for this historic day" provides a way to mark the teleological culmination of history at a presidential inauguration, the request to participate in the RCT mirrors this standard political truism in U.S. politics. The RCT offers the opportunity to have one's disease and death serve a higher goal.

The RCT works in the service—or, depending how cynical you are, the lip service—of collective living on, but who and what do we miss by moving to that endpoint so quickly? Bodies lent to science suffer, and in many cases greatly, from cancer treatments, both standard and experimental. Through its future-counterfactual promise, the RCT also dispenses with the questions of its own forms of violence. Who corals its logics and into the service of what—science, capital, professional advancement—are the deaths and illnesses it oversees pressed?

Margaret Edson's play *Wit* (1999), which documents the brutal experimental chemotherapy treatment and death of Vivian Bearing, an English professor, from ovarian cancer, captures a set of miscommunications between doctor and patient that illustrate one facet of the paradox I am aiming to unpack. The success of the play (which was made into a film), its resonance for so many who had been involved in the cancer complex, lay in how it captured the physical and emotional costs of the logical mismatch between the objective account of the doctors and the required but disavowed subjective experience of the patient—herself having to come to terms in the play with her own misrecognition of this mismatch in her professorial career. The story of this mismatch between accounts is one I have heard over and over again in cancer retreats and support groups; it is central to the trauma of cancer.

The point of the play is not that Bearing should have been cared for more empathetically or more respectfully by the treating physicians. Rather, the play explores the fact that even if the medical community had treated Bearing more compassionately, the system would paradoxically count individual mortality through the immortal logic of the science itself. Bearing's doctors simply did not need to know anything about her except whether or not she would survive the experimental chemotherapy. She could have been anyone with ovarian cancer—the doctors did not care that she was Vivian Bearing, or why her cancer was diagnosed so late, or if she was among the one in seven Americans who live near a Superfund site. Regardless of whether she lived or died, useful data would be produced.

In exchange for the deaths, the researcher renders them significant: he counts them. In counting them he conjures a future—on the one hand absorbing the individual into a yearned-for advantage, and on the other hand further institutionalizing that fantasy of hope for the next generation of subjects. At the same time, the researcher will need to justify a new round of grant funding and consolidate his or her professional reputation: necessary aspects of the practice of science that help or hinder the effort to find the cure. When that data is written up, not only will we not remember Bearing's name and profession, we will not know her blood type, whether or not she smoked, whether the treatment was administered in the correct way, or even, likely, what may turn out for future researchers to be critical details of the cancer she had. Everything about her, except a tick in the box for her cancer and another in that for her treatment, will be gone.

Thus, something of a commodity logic underpins the RCT model (all pig meat is priced equivalently and is thus considered to be equally tasty regardless of which pig the meat comes from). In thinking about the RCT as a version of commodification, I do not mean that patients should join a system akin to what Gayle Rubin (1975) describes as a "traffic in women," in which a kind of objectification and exchange takes place. Rather, I mean to understand this version of objectification in terms of a separate ontological framework, one that asks RCT subjects to join a system in which they are profoundly *in* an individual body as a system of disease, flesh, and treatment at the same time as they embody an abstraction of those very entities. The deaths in the trial swing both ways. Dowsett's 1,050 relapses were tallied from both groups: members of both the treatment and placebo groups died (Jain 2006).

In her analysis of war, Elaine Scarry (1985) offers a unique insight into the political stakes of how death can be separated from material, fleshy bodies. As she notes, bodies on both the winning and losing sides of the Civil War have been consolidated and explained as the price of freedom; in that sense, killed bodies gain a mobility of attribution. She notes that the non-referential character of the dead body "gives it a frightening freedom of referential activity, one whose direction is no longer limited and controlled by the original contexts of personhood and motive." This point is particularly salient in thinking through the nonreferential character of deaths in RCTs for several reasons. First, we see this over and over again in how the statistics are rerun and debated, and the results are used for protocol, redone, or ignored. Second, where survival (and thus death) is the endpoint of the trial, the question of quality of life and quality of death rides in this framework of nonreferentiality.

When a person counts only insofar as he or she lives or dies, the medical descriptions of suffering shift nearly invisibly and often not consciously or vindictively, but simply because they are not seen, are not made to count. The injuries, then, gain a frightening nonreferentiality and an ease of misrecognition in the name of future progress. Current suffering and the questions it raises are simply illegible: Is the suffering due to the initial (natural?) cancer or the treatment? Are people dying of cancer or chemotherapy? To what extent is it acceptable and who should decide? How are people living with, and dying of, cancer? The elision of these issues makes it easier to divert attention away from other aspects of cancer production in the United States—misdiagnosis, environmental causes, and early detection—only tangentially associated with the profession of oncology.

In this immutability the RCT shields its own god-trick, its contingency on a sort of double-logic of survivorship. In counting out the dead from each side, the RCT logic poses as if it simply offered an accounting: the 1,050 recurrences that were needed for the data were lives and deaths that were presumably going to happen anyway. The researcher has merely arranged these lives to figure out which treatments would be more promising, which pharmaceuticals more profitable. Having no time for the life and death dramas it enfolds and depends on, the RCT promises a final statistic that will be bloodlessly inscribed by an omniscient observer, someone to weigh out the benefits and costs of a new treatment. Future cancer patients will be invited to stare at these statistics and attempt to slot themselves in to one side or the other in making decisions about treatments or whether to save money.

Over and above the shock and confusion generated by survival prognoses, one finds the violence and grieving of such elisions everywhere in patient-generated literature on cancer treatments. Anatole Broyard (1991), writing as he was dying of prostate cancer, illuminates part of the issue: "While he inevitably feels superior to me because he is the doctor and I am the patient, . . . I feel superior to him too, that he is my patient also and I have my diagnosis of him." Broyard diagnoses not only the fallacy of the objectivist stance of the one who expects to survive the trial but the false sense of superiority marking the previvor, that space before fleshiness catches up to the physician. To Broyard, the physician is like the priest who decried sin in the face of black death before himself falling.[8]

But Broyard's feeling of superiority that may be a sort of high that comes with a first-hand knowledge of mortality does not quite explain the position demanded of the researcher, the counter of the dead. In big cancer trials the lifespan of the trial will exceed that of nearly everyone in it, and by necessity the survivors cannot be predicted in advance. Even in one of the most successful cancer treatments ever, the use of Herceptin for a subset of breast cancers, many physicians expected another failure and expressed shock at the survival rates (Bazell 1998). Horrific as it may sound, the investigator simply needs the deaths of subject groups to complete the study. The doctor thus is in the horrible position of making his living through, of needing, the deaths of his subjects. Elias Canetti (1960) might describe the principle investigator of a large cancer trial as the ultimate survivor: "He is, as it were, an *innocent* hero, for none of the corpses are of his killing. But he is in the midst of the putrefaction and must endure it. It does not strike him down; on the contrary, one could say it is this which keeps him upright." Cancer deaths support the research and the researcher; they are productive; they support whole industries and economies. Indeed, the more people die, the more the science becomes self-referential: the bigger problem cancer becomes, the more trials we need. That is the mortality effect. The desire to have one's dead body thrown onto the steps of the FDA, as one activist requested, is an attempt at interruption, an attempt to reanimate the concerns of the dead.

Shifting the question in this way enables several critical interventions. First, we begin to see how the RCT creates not just a mortal hierarchy between the dying and the survivors but also a temporal hierarchy, since the mortality of some patients props up, allows, the survival of the others. This mortality effect, however inevitable, critical, and central to the RCT method, comes with a politics. Second, its perceived objectivity and self-evidence erases whole cultures of cancer and how it is produced by the RCT. Who is this patient coming into the clinic full of hope against hope of getting into a trial? How do people locate themselves within the RCT results and prognoses? These and many others are questions that the RCT provokes and elides.

An ideology of progress is so strongly inscribed in the trial form that its manifest failures are nearly unthinkable, rendered invisible in the name of continued progress. Thus, one finds very few analyses of cancer treatments and their histories, and of how and why they became and stay protocols. Where such histories exist, we find often that treatments remain standard not because they are the best treatments, but for many other political reasons.[9] In cancer treatments these questions are particularly relevant not only because of their brutality but because of the moral cast of the treatments, as if to refuse them were suicide.

NOTES

I would like to thank audiences at the University of California, San Francisco; the University of Michigan; and Harvard. I am also grateful to Jake Kosek, Sharon Kaufman, Gail Hershatter, Fred Turner, Kate Zaloom, Michelle Murphy, Elizabeth Roberts, Elaine Scarry, Derek Simons, Sylvia Sokol, Miriam Ticktin, and the many other people who have discussed cancer with me from so many angles. This chapter is dedicated to the memory of Eve Kosofsky Sedgwick.

1   Cancer trials have often "delivered at best marginal benefits," with controversial endpoints and success difficult to assess. "Nevertheless, such controversy did not undermine the progress of the clinical trial as an increasingly essential feature of clinical bio-medical research" (Valier and Timmermans 2008: 501–2).

2   Hope offers perhaps the central trope through which cancer is understood in the United States. This country's future bias in cancer treatment often holds out an implicit trade-off between present misery and future health on the individual level, and present expense or pain and a future cure on the social level. The RCT, no matter what it is testing (such as water from Los Angeles versus water from Texas) offers the hope that one thing will be found to be better than another; the form of the RCT is central to how cancer is understood in the United States.

3   "Can it be more ethical to deny the possible good effects to most, by avoiding all toxicity in order to do no harm to one? The unmitigated disease must be calculated as a toxic cost of cancer. Under dosing, in an attempt to avoid toxicity, is far more deadly" (James Holland of New York City's Mount Sinai Hospital, quoted in Rothman and Edgar 1992: 196).

4   Only recently have patient advocacy groups been allowed to attend oncology conferences, and their admission is strictly regulated. They certainly do not participate in any

real sense. At the San Antonio oncology meetings every December, for example, patient advocates can listen each evening to a panel of medical experts who translate the events of the day into lay language. The week I attended the tone was sometimes condescending and other times simply explanatory, but the forum was never taken as an open exchange among knowledgeable participants in the cancer complex.

5   When I attended a camp for young adult survivors of cancer (20–40 years old), I heard stories of tumors growing to enormous sizes—6, 7.5, and 10 centimeters—before being diagnosed. One person told me he returned to the doctor three times with a tumor literally sticking out of his neck before it was diagnosed. Another person told me her teacher wanted to fail her on her final exams because she was hospitalized during the time they were scheduled.

6   Over the four years of my ethnographic data collection, which included participation in several week-long and day-long retreats, support groups, and interviews, many of the same issues, such as these experiences with radiation, come up over and over again— across age, geography, treating hospitals, and so on. This indicates, I think, the deep institutionalization of cancer treatments driven by highly standardized protocols, as well as the physical, social, and material making of cancer survivorship.

7   It is fascinating to note that this is in direct opposition to the "survivor" rhetoric, which fetishizes the role of individual agency. I find it no accident that both of these versions of agency take place in the context of a natural and social history of confusion about the causes and mechanisms of cancer.

8   Diagnosis and value-laden terms, such as *patient*, might fall under the term perlocutionary speech, as described by linguistic philosopher J. L. Austin (1975). Such speech acts bring one—by the very act of declaration—into a new subject position requiring a different set of customs, laws, ethics, and regulations—the same nearly unavoidable violence as the RCT.

9   Perhaps the best known of many such examples is the existence of the Pap smear decades before it became standard practice. When it came into general use it reduced cervical cancer from the most deadly cancer to one of the least deadly forms of the disease.

Moral Commitments and Ethical Dilemmas of Humanitarianism

Didier Fassin

> Thus for the ordinary, everyday man, the value of life rests solely on the fact that he regards himself more highly than he does the world. The great lack of imagination from which he suffers means he is unable to feel his way into other beings and thus he participates as little as possible in their fortunes and sufferings. *He*, on the other hand, who really could participate in them would have to despair of the value of life; if he succeeded in encompassing and feeling within himself the total consciousness of mankind he would collapse with a curse on existence.
>
> —FRIEDRICH NIETZSCHE, *Human, All Too Human*

HUMANITARIANISM has become a major component of contemporary government on the global and local scenes of affliction, whether in contexts of war, disasters, famines, epidemics, or poverty. Humanitarian agents are present on battlefields and in refugee camps, in the aftermath of earthquakes or floods, and in clinics for undocumented immigrants and homeless citizens. They treat the wounded and the sick, they develop food supplementation projects against malnutrition in African villages and risk-reduction programs for drug users in American inner cities, they negotiate international corridors to bring assistance to civilian populations in the former Yugoslavia and national legislation in favor of universal access to health care in France. Humanitarian actions are conducted by nongovernmental organizations (NGOs) bringing assistance to populations in distress, in the tradition invented by the Red Cross and reformulated by Doctors without Borders (Médecins sans Frontières [MSF]), but also more and more by states intervening with troops in other countries in the name of humanitarian rights or to prevent humanitarian crises, from Somalia to Kosovo (Fassin and Pandolfi 2009). They have long been considered as an exclusive prerogative of Western institutions and nations, but they are claimed also by Islamic organizations and states.

Beyond this extreme diversity of agents and actions, what is humanitarianism? It is both a moral discourse (based on responsibility toward victims) and a political resource (serving specific interests) to justify action considered to be in favor of others exposed to a vital danger, action taken in the name of a shared humanity. Its ambition is thus indivisible (it includes all human beings without distinction of race, class, religion, ideology), but its implementation is always situated (where others are thought to be in need of assistance). In this text I want to analyze the ultimate practical implications of these characteristics.

Two sets of concepts are in tension in this definition of humanitarianism. The first one involves a politics of life and an evaluation of humanity: What sort of life is implied for which human beings? The second one implies a practice of difference and an ideal of universality: Under which conditions may a different other be assisted through universal values? My main thesis is that the tensions between the ideal of universality (the abstract principle of treating everyone in the same way) and the practice of difference (the concrete confrontation to the distant other) are expressed—often invisibly—in terms of politics of life (the values and meanings attributed to lives) which is related to an implicit evaluation of humanity (the distinct worthiness of human beings). More precisely, humanitarianism is founded on an inequality of lives and hierarchies of humanity. This profound contradiction between the noble goals of humanitarian action (saving endangered others and alleviating suffering everywhere in an indiscriminate manner) and the concrete terms under which humanitarian agents have to operate (producing inequalities and hierarchies) is not the result of dysfunction of the humanitarian organizations or misbehavior of their agents: it is an aporia of humanitarian governmentality (Fassin 2007a). This is probably the most painful reality many humanitarian agents experience in their work.

The critique I am trying to develop here is not from above, as have been many ideological attacks on humanitarianism: it comes from its very heart. By this expression, I mean two things. On the one hand, I believe the contradictions I analyze are intrinsic to humanitarian intervention as such: so my point is not to denounce the wrongdoings of humanitarian agents (which they often denounce themselves either as self-criticism or as critique of others, two sorts of games that many of them practice with delight); it is to enter into the contradictions of humanitarianism as such. On the other hand, I base my analysis on my own practice as an insider: having been personally involved as a fellow traveler with several NGOs and more directly as a member of the administrative board of one of them, I build my discussion on issues raised within them (rather than from outside them); many humanitarian agents are themselves conscious of these issues, even though their debates rarely enter very far into these painful territories of reflexivity. So I am not interested in the psychological analysis of humanitarianism, not even in its political science variations studying the motivations of humanitarian agents (Dauvin and Siméant 2002). Neither am I willing to enter into ethical considerations about humanitarian intervention, trying to decide when and where it is desirable or acceptable to intervene (Holzgrefe and Keohane 2003). Nor do I try to give a picture of the new international order, as some political scientists describe it (Suhrke and Klusmeyer 2004). Although I consider these approaches relevant, my aim is different. I intend to explore, from an anthropological perspective, the moral economy of a globally enacted humanitarianism.

The focus of this study is war situations, although humanitarian action is not limited to military conflicts. But I hypothesize that the battlefield, where humanitarianism was born, in Solferino in 1859, when the Red Cross initiated the first age of humanitarianism, and reborn, in Biafra in 1969, when MSF inaugurated its second age, is of special meaning, because humanitarianism is, in Rony Brauman's (2005) words, a "school of dilemmas." Through these dilemmas, illustrated with exemplary case studies from Angola, Iraq, and Palestine, I will distinguish three different types of life which are at stake in these extreme situations: lives to be saved, lives to be exposed, and lives to be told. In each of these cases, where the "cause of the victims" (Fassin 2004) has to be defended, I will attempt to make explicit the sorts of inequalities and processes of evaluation which underlie the corresponding paradigms of humanity.

SAVING LIVES: THE POLITICS OF RESCUE

With these grandiloquent phrases, Jean-Hervé Bradol (2003), the president of MSF, delivers his conception of the humanitarian politics of life.

> When the humanitarian spirit is stripped of the illusion that humanity is inexorably progressing toward an ideal society, it can actively resist the very human temptation to accept the death of part of our global community so the "common good" may prevail. The undeniable failure of the humanitarian project resides for many in the allegiance of humanitarian actors to institutional political authorities who have the power to condone human sacrifice, to divide the governed between those who should live and those who are expendable. Humanitarian action can still oppose the elimination of part of humanity by exemplifying an art of living founded on the pleasure of unconditionally offering people at risk of death the assistance that will allow them to survive. Doing so makes victories over the most lethal form of politics possible. The twenty thousand children saved from starvation by Médecins sans Frontières in Angola in 2002 provide a shining example.

In a world where many die because of criminal or indifferent governments, humanitarian agents make it their duty to rescue "those that society sacrifices," as he also writes in the same text (Bradol 2003). For, according to Bradol, sacrifices are not only active, as a result of wars in which populations are exterminated, they are also passive, as a result of either (or both) a lack of will displayed by powerful states which privilege international realpolitik over people's survival or a lack of interest by rich countries which abandon the sick inhabiting deprived areas with no treatment for their lethal diseases. In Michel Foucault's (1991 [1978]) terms, to the "sovereign power" of states which have "the right to decide life and death" or, more precisely, "the right to take life and let live," humanitarian organizations thus oppose the supreme power to save lives. They confront this sovereign power of the states by stopping its murderous arm, by preventing it from taking lives, by depriving it of its absolute "right to kill." The obligation to save may be seen simultaneously as different from and more than "biopower," which is "a power to foster life or disallow it to the point of death," or in other words "the techniques for achieving the subjugation of bodies or control of populations." It is not merely a biopolitics, in the sense of a set of technologies of regulation, it is a politics of life (Fassin 2007b) which qualifies and measures the value and worth of lives.

Here humanitarian medicine distinguishes itself from the clinical art as it emerges at the end of the eighteenth century: not only does it treat individual "bodies"; it intervenes on large "populations." Thus it does not just save a few lives; it spares tens of thousands of them. If the object of humanitarianism is "life in crisis," as Peter Redfield (2005) suggests, the difference between this form of intervention and "ordinary" medicine is apparently more quantitative than qualitative. Whereas the hospital doctor may believe that a life is saved once in a while thanks to her or his work, the refugee camp physician has the everyday evidence of tens of existences snatched from death. But this numeric difference is in turn not merely quantitative; it introduces a qualitative change from "persons" to "populations," using a notion invented with public hygiene in the early nineteenth century. The confined space of the camp, the specific knowledge of epidemiology with its statistics and tests, the elementary technologies of nutrition, rehydration, and immunization, with their remarkable efficiency, produce a new form of practice which is neither clinical medicine nor public health: from the former it borrows its curative objective; from the latter it takes the collective basis. The specificity of its instruments and the hybridity of its references together contribute to the accomplishment of a politics of massive rescue which gives humanitarian organizations such practical and symbolic efficacy.

Angola is indeed an exemplary case study. After a twenty-seven-year civil war which culminated between 1998 and 2002 with extreme levels of violence between the Popular Movement for the Liberation of Angola (Movimento Popular da Libertação de Angola [MPLA]), and the National Union for the Total Independence of Angola (União Nacional para a Independência Total de Angola [UNITA]) and ended with the signing of a cease-fire, MSF, like many other humanitarian organizations, finally got access to populations which had been trapped between the belligerents and had suffered massive killings and displacements. Confronted with a famine, 174 voluntary expatriates from all over the world and 2,260 national personnel were mobilized in what became MSF's largest operation ever: "at 23 intensive feeding centres, more than 16,000 children have been able to escape certain death," the organization commented in its report significantly titled, *Angola: Sacrifice of a People* (MSF 2002: 5). Not only did MSF implement this program, it publicly stigmatized Western governments for being complicit with Luanda and with U.N. institutions in their slow reaction to the emergency, thus initiating a polemic in the field of humanitarianism. However, MSF itself was not exempt from difficulties and errors with dramatic consequences. Faced with external as well as internal critiques that his organization's work was undermined by its arrogance, the president finally admitted frankly in his 2003 annual report: "Priority given to food programmes have had negative consequences for the sick, especially tuberculosis patients and abused women. We could not do everything and we had to choose. We are very proud of what we have done to feed the children and their families. We saved thousands of people. But on the frontline we have felt it very painful to have to choose between categories of victims" (MSF 2003: 6). In spite of these "hard choices" (Moore 1998), Angola was a watershed event for MSF that for years to come will continue to give highest justification to MSF's action and clearest legitimization to its agents: there, lives had been saved in numbers. For many doctors who have long shared the humanitarian saga, and in particular for the MSF president, Angola is a sort of redemption from the nightmare of the genocide in Rwanda, where humanitarian agents had watched helplessly as people were exterminated before their eyes.

Speaking of a humanitarian "way of life," as Bradol does when referring to the act of saving lives, can be seen as an ironic although probably involuntary counterpoint to what Michael Ignatieff (2000) calls "the new American way of war." Reviewing a series of publications on recent conflicts, from the first Gulf War to the bombings of Kosovo, the Canadian journalist and politician analyzes what was defined as "the revolution in military affairs." His interest is less in the justification of war (calling it "humanitarian" rather than "just") or the technological "improvement" in weapons as such than in the consequences of the latter as a reinforcement of the former: the possibility of minimizing human losses in the military intervention makes the intervention acceptable by public opinions in democracies where the death of soldiers has begun to threaten governments. However, as Ignatieff remarks, there is a hidden dimension to this apparently felicitous evolution of warfare: "The central difficulty of the American way of war in Kosovo was that avoiding 'collateral damage' to civilians and to nonmilitary targets and avoiding pilot loss were conflicting. If pilots fly high, they cannot identify targets accurately and the risks of horrifying accidents increase. Flying low improves accuracy but the risk to pilots is significantly increased. There was no loss of North Atlantic Treaty Organization (NATO) lives but the bombing claimed between 488 and 527 civilian lives." Clearly choices were made by the military staff to privilege "zero [military] death" over the reality of "collateral [civilian] damage." These decisions—which have to do with flight altitude or the use of certain weapons—imply a practical evaluation of lives: five hundred Kosovar men, women, and children weigh less than one American or British soldier. Under the moral economy of Western armies, the sacrifice of civilians is the undesired but necessary burden of, at best, establishing human rights or exporting democracy or, at worst, of protecting private and national interests. In the case of Kosovo, it should not be forgotten that the war was described as "humanitarian" by the prime minister of Great Britain and the president of the Czech Republic, and that MSF published a report on the crimes committed by the Serbs a few days after the initiation of the bombings, providing NATO with unexpected support for its military intervention.

In contrast with these "human sacrifices," the humanitarian organizations can claim the sacredness of all lives. Whereas Western armies consider life sacred only when it is on their side, MSF and its colleague organizations defend the universal value of lives. Against the military politics of sacrificed lives they assert a humanitarian politics of saving lives. In both cases, the type of life which is either sacrificed or saved is very strictly defined. It is what Giorgio Agamben (1998) calls "bare life," the physical existence of individuals abandoned to death or snatched from it. There is no social or political dimension to it. Just as the Angolan refugees quoted by MSF in its report seem to talk only of "hunger" and "suffering," the humanitarian agents, who often consider themselves "rescuers," inscribe their intervention on bodies—malnourished, sick, and wounded. But the humanitarians' rhetorical opposition to the military forces has one blind spot. Giving themselves the noble role on the battlefield and often denouncing what Bradol (2003) calls the "cannibal order" of the mighty, they omit one fact: if soldiers expose their lives on the battlefield, humanitarian agents demand pacified spaces to intervene, precisely to avoid exposing their lives. This is a limit some of these agents tried to overcome in Iraq.

EXPOSING LIVES: THE POLITICS OF SACRIFICE

In the May 2003 issue of the MSF journal *Infos*, François Calas tells the story of his abduction.

> At 10:30 p.m. on April 2, individuals claiming they belonged to the Iraqi intelligence services knocked at our door and asked us to follow them. They took us handcuffed to the central prison of Abu Ghraib. We were two in each tiny cell, without light. Bombings were continuous; we could hear the progression of the American army. After three days, we were transferred to the infamous jail of Al Faluja. No more separate rooms, but a common space where the sanitary conditions were awful. We stayed there two and a half days without going out or being able to lie down. The lack of movement and of privacy raised tensions among the detainees. "This is the kind of place one never gets out of," they would say.

In March 2002, a few days after the beginning of the U.S. attack on Iraq, the French doctor had been kidnapped with a Sudanese colleague and an Iraqi chauffeur. They were members of a small MSF team that had decided to stay in Baghdad despite the obvious danger, which they thought would come from bombings rather than abduction. For several days MSF could get no information about what had happened to them. In the unstable conditions brought on by the invasion of Iraq, the worst could have occurred. Finally they were released as the battle for Baghdad was ending. The U.S. army was entering the Iraqi capital, and humanitarian organizations were coming in behind it. The French section of MSF decided then to leave the country, criticizing the lack of autonomy for doing their work but also shocked by the recent events. They left without having treated a single patient.

This episode is highly revealing of the effort by humanitarian agents to reintroduce a certain level of equivalence between lives, that is, between their own and local ones. Whereas everyday the world differentiates between lives worthy to be lived and what Zygmunt Bauman (2004) calls "wasted lives"—not only through military means, as we have seen, but also through economic, social, medical, and judicial decisions—humanitarian organizations constantly reassert that every life is valuable. They refuse to take sides in conflicts in the countries where they intervene, offering help to the entire population. The insistence on this stance was crucially reaffirmed during the crisis of the "boat people" fleeing Vietnam and resulted in ideological dissensions within the humanitarian movement, since the leftist background of many made it difficult to admit that one could be oppressed by a communist regime, as Rony Brauman (2000) recalls. Born from this crisis, Doctors of the World (Médecins du Monde [MDM]) gave itself the motto, "We rescue the victims, all the victims." But beyond a refusal to distinguish among victims, these organizations also seek to overcome the obvious distinction within humanitarian action between those who assist and those who are assisted. They recognize that humanitarian workers, who come of their own choosing and remain in missions less than six months, on average, before returning to the safety and comfort of their homelands, do not share the same social condition and life expectancy as the persons for whom they intervene. By risking their lives, the members of MSF who decided to stay in Iraq after March 18, when U.S. President George W. Bush told all foreigners to leave the country, were counterbalancing the structural inequality of humanitarian aid with their courageous decision. This decision was not only hard for the team in Baghdad to make but also difficult for headquarters in Paris to accept and ratify.

The monthly meeting of the administrative board which took place on March 28 was the most impassioned in years. Everybody remembered it afterward as one of the turning points in the thirty-year history of MSF. A few days earlier, the discussion among the permanent salaried staff had been heated, with the majority in favor of the decision and a minority against it. Taking place a week after the beginning of the bombing of Iraq, the public debate with the administrators came too late to change anything. The democratic life of the organization, however, required this performance, which mimicked deliberation when decisions had already been made. The dilemma lay in balancing the evident risk of being under the U.S. bombs in Baghdad and the much less obvious utility of this presence on the battlefield. The two dimensions of the argument were partly linked: because it was so dangerous, movement and therefore activity were necessarily restricted. But even more than that, the efficacy seemed compromised by the size of the team (six people: among them a physician, a surgeon, and an anesthesiologist), in comparison with the hundreds of well-trained Iraqi doctors present in the thirty-five well-equipped hospitals in the capital (sixty doctors and seventeen operating rooms in the hospital where the team was to be based).

Why be there, then? An answer could have been: precisely to be there, that is, to stay as witnesses to the expected humanitarian crisis and human rights violations and thus be able to deliver public testimony. But the official position was different: the team would not take such risks if it were not specifically to help the population, treat the sick, heal the wounded, alleviate suffering, and, in the end, save lives. So however little credibility the argument seemed to have for the audience, of the two self-defined mandates of humanitarian organizations—to assist and to testify—the latter was dismissed and the former invoked as the only reason to stay. Later events put the argument to a painful test. The abduction of the three members of the team blocked all action. Their release was followed by MSF's departure from the country after what the head of the local mission, who was one of the kidnapped, described in the August 2003 issue of the internal journal *DazibAG* as a "very precipitous decision . . . justified afterward by fallacious arguments," in other words by humanitarian organizations' lack of autonomy. This was a cruel acknowledgment for him: not a single Iraqi life had been saved, but six lives of humanitarian agents had been put at risk.

This episode reveals a profound truth about humanitarianism. In the context of global injustice and violence, MSF as well as other organizations of its kind demonstrate their solidarity with the victims. However, the Iraqi story reveals the impossibility of finding a way out of the inequality of lives which structures the humanitarian world in particular, as well as contemporary societies in general: the inequality between those whose life is sacred and those whose life may be sacrificed. In the end, the effort to break this logic of inequality fails as the sacrifice remains too high a price to pay. Analyzing the recent transformations in the international political order, Adi Ophir (2005) asserts that the sovereignty of the states is challenged by two new actors who confront their politics of life: the "humanitarian" and the "terrorist." Besides the obvious distinction he recognizes in their actions of saving or killing people, another difference merits attention: terrorists (especially suicide bombers) stake their own lives; humanitarians do not. The former reject the sacredness of life—theirs and others'. The latter claim it as a supreme value—definitely for the distant others, but even more so for themselves.

This claim, however, follows a complex path. First, against the evidence to the contrary on the battlefield, humanitarian agents assert that all lives are sacred and deserve to be saved. Still, there remains the difference between those who are protected in their pacified spaces and those who remain under the bombs. Therefore, second, in a heroic attempt to break this disequilibrium, the humanitarian agents expose themselves to the same fate as the populations they assist by staying among them in spite of the danger, putting their own lives at risk. Obviously, the rule is not the same on both sides, since the humanitarian agents can freely decide to stay, while the Iraqis are not expected to have a choice, but by risking their lives humanitarian agents hope to abolish the distance. However, third, as violence becomes reality, they rediscover the asymmetry of the relation, since not only is it the Iraqis who kidnap them, but the abduction reveals the vulnerability of the French organization, which is paralyzed and finally abandons the field. The initial difference in the evaluation of lives is still present. In spite of all efforts, a line remains between "us" and "them" as a reminder that humanitarianism is always about "saving strangers," as Nicholas Wheeler (2000) writes. Whatever fraternity the humanitarian agents display in their activity, this distinction persists.

A further fact has remained unnoticed by those who have commented on this episode. In all the news reports referring to it, whether in the press or even within the humanitarian organization, hesitation was perceptible: How many MSF members had been abducted? Sometimes the number given was two, sometimes it was three. In fact, two persons were strictly speaking members of the organization, a French doctor and a Sudanese logistician; the third abductee was an Iraqi salaried worker, thus not considered as belonging to the organization. This distinction, which exists in most humanitarian as well as development institutions, has been a recurrent theme of discussion within MSF. The difference of status means also unequal remuneration, contract stability, and rights to decide and vote. It implies that humanitarian organizations identify two types of persons working for them, those who have a moral involvement in the humanitarian project, who are called "volunteers" but receive a regular salary, and those who are not related to the humanitarian saga, since they are simply "employed" by the organization. This distinction between agents supposedly motivated by altruism and others supposedly motivated by money, between those who have a deep "desire for humanitarianism," as Gilles Brücker (1993), former president of MDM, expresses it, and those for whom it is just a job, suggests that humanitarian organizations are run in the field by foreign "missionaries" and local "mercenaries." In their everyday work, the distinction has long been accepted as inevitable by the international staff (who often do not know they are making it) but criticized as intolerable by national personnel (who frequently see themselves as no less morally involved than their Western colleagues).

This difference of status and image may also have tragic consequences in situations of war, since the foreign workers are protected by their alien status and a sort of symbolic but also political aura since they come mostly from Western countries, while the local workers cannot benefit from humanitarian immunity since they do not even belong to the organization. Belligerents act with full knowledge of this distinction: they kidnap the "expatriates," whose life, they suppose, will justify a good ransom; but they usually kill "nationals," who they know have little exchange value and who are often caught up in the local political or ethnic issues. The assassination of seventeen persons working with Action against Hunger in Sri Lanka in August 2006 can only be understood through this distinction: conversely to what has been often said and written, the victims were not "members" of the organization but mere salaried local workers, moreover clearly identified as Tamils. The massacre of hundreds of employees of international agencies and NGOs during the 1994 genocide in Rwanda follows the same logic: they were considered as Tutsis rather than as "members" of these institutions. Bradol (2004), who headed the MSF mission in Kigali during this period, admitted afterward: "We have not been very effective in protecting, or even motivated to protect, our Tutsi colleagues, who were employees just like us in humanitarian organizations. I have seen honorable conduct but also simple abandonment. The lack of protection of our Tutsi colleagues is representative of the relationships between expatriates and local workers." Of course, I do not mean that these Tutsis were killed because they were not seen as belonging to the humanitarian world. I mean that belligerents distinguish in their criminal projects between the lives of "expatriates," who are protected and for whom they can get money, and the lives of "nationals," who are unprotected and whom they may simply eliminate. In Sri Lanka and Rwanda, things are tragically simple. Belonging to the humanitarian world implies a political life which has to be spared. Being on its margins reduces individuals to the biological life of ethnic cleansing. The challenge for humanitarian organizations is to transform this dialectic of the biological and the political. This is what has been at stake in Palestine.

TELLING LIVES: THE POLITICS OF TESTIMONY

The MSF psychiatrists Marie-Rose Moro and Christian Lachal (2002), who lead a mental health program in the Palestinian Territories, have used the stories that their colleagues, mostly physicians and psychologists, collected during the second intifada in order to make public statements about the suffering of the Palestinian people.

> Empathy, our capacity to put ourselves in the other's place, is a mental attitude which is mainly emotional. Public opinion mobilizes through empathy, on the basis of information it received as scenarios to read or see. After some time, it gets tired of it, not because of moral deficiency or because of affective laziness, but because empathy is ephemeral. Telling the traumatic events, for instance what inhabitants of the Gaza strip have experienced since the beginning of the second intifada, describing them, documenting them, distinguishing facts and what is amplified or transformed by fear, is useful as testimony. The narration of events is sometimes at the interface between our approach and that of the media.

After MSF's exploratory mission to the Palestinian Territories in 2000, two things were clear: first, MSF wanted to be present by the side of the population under Israeli occupation and oppression; second, Palestinian health infrastructures and professionals were perfectly capable of facing the consequences of the conflict in terms of medicine and surgery. This apparent contradiction was solved by developing a mental health program based on trauma.

During the following years, trauma was presented both as a psychic symptom justifying the presence of the medical organization in a highly politicized field and as the clinical evidence attesting the violence of the conflict (Fassin and Rechtman 2009). In fact, as it soon appeared that the practical conditions of practicing psychotherapy on the front lines were not met since it was impossible to spend the proper time in the proper space with patients, telling Palestinians' stories came to be seen not only as an instrument for constructing public testimonies but also as a tool with psychological benefits. As Pierre Salignon, Fouad Ismael, and Elena Sgorbati (2002) express it: "Faced with their suffering, it is our duty to describe the effects of war on Palestinian families. This implies narrating what we witness in the Territories. And this appears to be highly important for them from a therapeutic perspective." The same choices had been simultaneously made by MDM, with the same arguments. The inscription of trauma in testimonies represents an innovation in the construction of political causes: arousing international indignation through the description of people's symptoms which psychiatrists and psychologists are able to relate to violence, it transforms the emotional involvement of the public from a sense of injustice to a sentiment of compassion. But this new form of denunciation also underlines a different phenomenon which has a general meaning: when lives cannot be saved, they can still be told. Instead of being rescuers, humanitarian agents may become spokesmen, and they may do so within the framework of their medical competencies.

This shift from saving lives to telling lives is part of a recent change in the humanitarian world. It is, at least partially, the consequence of a situation much more common than generally admitted: there are no lives to be rescued but still a presence to justify for the donors and more broadly to the public. Not all humanitarian interventions are Angola. One could even assert that it was the exception. In many crises on the planet, humanitarian organizations are not in the position of rescuers, either because the spaces of their intervention are not protected, because they arrive too long after the civil security is already at work bringing useful assistance, or because the national actors have the technical capacity to cope with the medical consequences of the conflicts. Medical humanitarianism was invented to assist the wounded and the sick when they were abandoned—under a status of exception which allowed doctors to go on the battlefield with the protection of the belligerents. While they continue to intervene in these traditional contexts, humanitarian organizations today are also increasingly confronted with new configurations where they have to develop new roles. This was obviously the case in Palestine, where MSF and MDM have both been present for a long time, where they cannot claim to have saved a single life, but where medical assistance remains the official reason for their being there, in spite of the local presence of well-trained professionals and well-equipped facilities.

Here, two historical facts converge to delineate a distinct politics of life. On the one hand, humanitarian testimony has become crucial to the public defense of the causes of victims. It is often said that the second generation of humanitarian organizations in the early 1970s emerged in response to the silence of the Red Cross, from Auschwitz to Biafra, as Fiona Terry

(2002) recalls. Even if the genesis of the movement is somewhat more complex, its emergence identified a new function of humanitarianism: to bear witness in the face of a world of violence and injustice, to speak out amid a general indifference to the suffering of distant others. To give more weight to humanitarian testimony, one had to include narratives by the victims. Their words brought additional evidence to the stories told by humanitarian agents. Today, all reports are punctuated with quotes from survivors of the conflicts.

On the other hand, humanitarian psychiatry occupies an increasingly important place within the organizations. If psychiatrists have been present at the margins and even within militaries since the end of the nineteenth century, their introduction on the humanitarian scenes is quite recent. It can even be precisely dated to the aftermath of the 1988 earthquake in Armenia. Fifteen years later, it has become one of the major components of humanitarian interventions in many sites. Not only do mental health specialists emphasize the importance of their curative action, they also claim their share of the public testimony. Trauma has been a part of psychiatric nosology for a long time, but as Allan Young (1995) has shown, it was revived in the early 1980s through posttraumatic stress disorder. It occupies a special place here, since it contributes to the definition of the object of humanitarian psychiatry simultaneously as sign of the suffering to be treated and proof of the violence to be denounced.

What makes human life properly human, explains Hannah Arendt (1958), is that it can be told: "the chief characteristic of this specifically human life is that it is itself always full of events which ultimately can be told as a story, establish a biography." For her, "this life, *bios*," which makes men and women distinct from animals, can be "distinguished from mere *zoe*," which is common to all living beings. Making one's life into a biography implies two specifically human qualities: making sense of events which have occurred and using language to transmit it to others. In the case of populations exposed to violence and injustice, narrating stories, which means telling lives, implies changing the politics of biological life to be rescued into a politics of biographical life to be heard. Here again it is to make the others closer to oneself: they are not just bodies to be saved but individuals, and these individuals are not passively inscribed in a story but possess a unique perspective on this story. In the move from biology to biography, politics is supposedly brought back to the victims of wars and disasters.

Again, things are not so simple. This politics of narrated lives remains asymmetrical, just like the politics of saved lives for which it acts as substitute. It distinguishes those whose lives can be told from those who can tell them. This difference is not only relational: it constructs the narratives—and consequently the lives—in a specific manner. For the humanitarian organizations, the men and women they deal with are victims. To defend their cause for an international audience, they have to emphasize the pathos of their situations. Of course, these situations are often tragic, but they also have complex genealogies and sociologies. The victims may also be combatants, or terrorists, or simply farmers. In his study of the first intifada, John Collins (2004) has shown how each institution, each actor defined publicly the "children of the stones" in a distinct manner: for some they were heroes, for others they were martyrs; some insisted on their courage, others on their suffering. In these discourses, the psychological element has taken an increasingly important place, not only under the influence of humanitarian psychiatry but also as a consequence of the presence of Palestinian psychiatrists and psychologists generally trained in Europe or North America and well aware of the symptomatology of posttraumatic stress disorder.

The humanitarian construction of suffering others—especially through psychiatry—has two consequences. The first is the abstraction of the figures of the victims from the larger context of the war. This is especially evident in the two consecutive reports that MDM published in 2003 under the joint title *Israeli and Palestinian Civilians: Victims of an Endless Conflict* (*Les Civils israéliens et palestiniens victimes d'un conflit sans fin*). One analyzes the Palestinian victims of the Israeli army, and the other studies the Israeli victims of the Palestinian bombings. The extreme application of the principle of neutrality, but also the political divisions existing within the organization, led the authors to present a "balanced" view of both situations. The result was a reification of victims, made possible by the existence of trauma on both sides: the historical and political asymmetry of the conflict disappeared as all civilians were exposed to intolerable suffering attested to by clinical symptoms. The second consequence of this innovation is the isolation of trauma in the narratives of victims. It is particularly clear in MSF's *Palestinian Chronicles*, which was published in 2002 and received a great deal of exposure, as it was published and discussed in several countries including Palestine and Israel. It consists of a collection of brief observations by physicians and psychologists in Hebron and Gaza. Rather than narratives making sense of the biography of the persons encountered, they are illustrations of the psychic consequences of the experience of humiliation, fear, and loss. Thus a rebel adolescent throwing stones at the occupation army becomes a child wetting his bed at night, and a man arrested and beaten by enemy soldiers appears as a catatonic patient affected by seizures. The logic of the testimony creates an obligation to prove the causal relation between events and symptoms, rejecting more complex determinism made familiar to us not just by psychoanalysis but also by sociology. All that we know of the persons in these narratives is that they are traumatized victims. The short narrative fragments collected resemble clinical vignettes rather than biographical excerpts.

Several years ago, Annette Wieviorka (1998) asserted that we had entered the era of the witness. She was referring to the multiplication of individual testimonies in the public sphere. Although the phenomenon was of a larger scale, she was interested in the case of the survivors of the Holocaust. These testimonies were written in the first person. By contrast, what humanitarian organizations propose are testimonies written in the third person. The humanitarian agents are the witnesses and they tell the stories. Moreover, they tend to underline the psychological dimension of the experience, leaving aside the historical and political dimensions often so important for the populations enduring war. Victims hardly speak; they have spokespeople. They are not political subjects but moral objects. A few Palestinians protest against the reduction of their condition to that of traumatized victims. Most of them, however, express their gratitude to humanitarians who at least allow them to exist on the international scene.

CONCLUSION

Humanity is a recent invention. It supposes that human beings belong not only to the same biological community but above all to the same moral one. It implies that others can no longer be included in categories which have historically divided the human world between "us" and "them," the former being more human than the latter, who could even sometimes be cast out of the human world. But humanity is an abstract notion. It becomes concrete in real situations through action on behalf of these others, which reveals an underlying politics of life. From this perspective, when we seek to understand humanitarianism, we are best informed not by the ideal principles declared in its charters but by its interventions, and sometimes by its abstentions.

On the battlefield, humanitarian agents are confronted with two main kinds of politics of life: one of exclusion, the other of indifference. Belligerents may seek the elimination of the enemy or even the extermination of others, as we have seen in ethnic cleansing and ultimately genocide: this was the case for the Serbs in Bosnia and the Hutus in Rwanda. Or belligerents may rather desire the defeat of the enemy and simply consider as negligible the loss of even large numbers of civilian lives: this was the case for NATO in Kosovo and the United States in Iraq. In the first case, others must be suppressed. In the second, they are simply insignificant. Both are founded on unequal valuations of lives and hierarchies of humanity.

To these principles, humanitarian organizations oppose their own politics. These are of three kinds. The humanitarians' main claim is saving others' lives. Sometimes they may also expose their own lives. Recently they have developed a strategy of telling lives. The three politics—of rescue, sacrifice, and testimony—presuppose the equivalence of lives against armies which attribute lesser value to others—through either exclusion or indifference. However, these operations cannot restore equality. Inequalities of lives and hierarchies of humanity surreptitiously reappear—in spite of the humanitarian agents and often without their knowing it—between the persons who intervene and the persons they assist, or even between foreigners and nationals within the organizations. These inequalities and hierarchies do not result from theoretical premises or from individual prejudices. They are structural aporias of humanitarianism which are grounded in the asymmetry of the objective risk of death and of the subjective relation of compassion. These aporias are more generally characteristic of contemporary societies, especially in the Western world from which most members of humanitarian organizations originate.

Analyzing these politics of life and attempting to give an explicit intelligibility to a reality which remains largely implicit does not condemn the works of humanitarianism. On the contrary, it might contribute to making its agents more reflective, more modest—more human. After all, the best one can expect from them is less that they will promote humanity as an abstract concept or an empty sentiment and more that they will simply produce acts which both reduce the inequality of lives and recognize its existence as a political fact.

THE POLITICS OF EXPERIMENTALITY ⟶

Adriana Petryna

IN THE PAST TWO decades, human experimentation has moved out of the more exclusive domains of academic medicine and has
expanded into sites of everyday medical care.
With biotechnology and genetics on the cusp
of revolutionizing medicine, more people in the
United States and elsewhere are ready to take
unprecedented risks. Against the background
of ongoing pandemics such as HIV/AIDS, vaccine research takes place globally and in contexts where experiments have become the only
survival option. Where acute and chronic diseases mix with political transitions, civil wars,
civil unrest, and poverty, the language of crisis
has become instrumental, granting legitimacy
to experimentation when it otherwise might
have none. Some claim that experiments and experimental treatment can only do good in such
desperate contexts, and research has come to fill
the vacuum where state agencies furnish limited or no health care. Whether in the regulated
confines of the clinic or in the experimental
crapshoots in which lives are wagered in many
unsettled parts of the world, the criteria by
which to judge differences between experimental and standard treatments are being constantly
troubled. No single standard, regulation, law,

or oversight mechanism exists to keep up with the diversity of contexts in which experiments take place.

This chapter considers the new geographies of capital and power that allow pharmaceutical companies to export their research enterprise to middle- and low-income countries, and the complicated ways trials have become integral to public health and medical care in these contexts. The landscape of pharmaceutical research and trial participation is changing. How it changes, and how ethics configures alongside it to justify a massive expansion of commercialized human-subjects research, forms the core of this inquiry. How is the line between experimental and standard treatments shifting? How are hierarchies of differentiated humans and human subjects being implicated in a predominantly for-profit medical field? In the absence of other forms of health care, have clinical trials become the "preferential treatment option for the poor"? What implications would this have for justice and governance (Farmer 2002a)? As the merchants of trials operate transparently, their practices mark the place where politics fails to account for the risks that accompany global experimentality.

Fortune 500 lists the pharmaceutical industry as one of the five most profitable industries in the United States. By 2008 the world market for pharmaceuticals reached US$900 billion. This phenomenal growth of markets has been coupled with an equally unprecedented surge in the number of people participating in drug research. According to the Food and Drug Administration (FDA), the principal agency regulating drugs, medical devices, and biological products used in the United States, 6,079 new studies were started in the period 1981–85, 16,435 new studies in 1991–95, and 36,839 new studies in 2001–4 (CenterWatch 2005).

An American entrepreneur who coordinates trials for drug companies abroad characterized the link between pharmaceutical market growth and clinical research growth in terms of a convoluted economic dependency: "If a doctor or nurse asked you if you were willing to put a family member in a clinical trial and if it was not a life or death issue, would you do it? The answer would most likely be no. The fact is that all of us, drug researchers and consumers, are economically dependent on other people being willing to say yes." New populations within the United States are being pursued as research subjects. Researchers are also looking outside the country, to poorer contexts where people facing insurmountable forms of deprivation and health-care crises are also willing to say yes. Landscapes of experimentation evolve in a kind of give-and-take where people with unmet medical needs are willing to say yes to the movement of global capital and scientific and medical commodities.

Clinical trials involving new drugs are typically divided into four phases. In phase 1 trials, researchers determine the safety and safe dose range of experimental drugs and detect their toxicological side effects in a small group (20–80) of healthy volunteers. In phase 2 trials, one hundred to three hundred people are recruited to assess the drug's efficacy and to further evaluate its safety. In phase 3 trials, the study drug is administered to between one thousand and three thousand people to confirm its effectiveness, scrutinize side effects, compare it to other treatments, and collect information on optimal use. These trials are commonly coordinated across various centers which, increasingly, are located worldwide. Phase 4 trials, also known as postmarketing surveillance, are primarily observational and nonexperimental studies in which companies and regulators collate data on the drug's risks and benefits once it enters the market. Postmarketing surveillance involves millions of people, but in practice it remains vastly underdeveloped (USNIH 2007).

Clinical trials accounted for over forty percent of industry research and development (R&D) spending in 2008.[1] As research expands, the chain of entrepreneurial stakeholders is getting longer and more decentralized. Pharmaceutical drug trial sponsors depend on networks of outsourced partners to carry out clinical development.[2] The "clinical trials industry" includes everything from patient recruitment firms to investigative sites, investigative site management organizations to academic research organizations, and patient data-mining companies to for-profit institutional review boards (IRBs). It is a booming business—accounting for roughly one-third of all clinical development expenditures and outpacing the pharmaceutical industry in terms of growth (see Parexel 2005: 35; and CenterWatch 2005: 162).[3] The bulk of outsourced activities takes place in the second and third phases of drug development; these phases are by far the most time consuming and expensive. As one clinical trials industry executive put it to me, "About 60 percent of all clinical development costs are spent on phase 1 and phase 3 trials. So the big money is there."

Precise figures of the number of trial participants and clinical trials carried out in the United States, let alone worldwide, are hard to come by. This is in part because the FDA is unable to identify all ongoing clinical trials and their associated trial sites (OIG 2007).[4] As of 2008, 65,755 trials sponsored by federal agencies and private industry were listed on ClinicalTrials.gov, a service of the U.S. National Institutes of Health (NIH) designed to provide up-to-date information for those interested in locating clinical trials. It is estimated that each year, more than 2.3 million people participate in clinical trials throughout the country. Between 2000 and 2005, the FDA audited less than 1 percent of the 350,000 trial sites that the Office of Inspector General has estimated are active worldwide (ibid.: 19). In the meantime, a global field of experimental activity is thriving—with its scope and reach largely unknown.

In the first part of this chapter, I address some of the regulatory, economic, and medical realities underlying the offshoring of clinical trials. The concept of arbitrage in trials markets, fueled by variable regulations across national boundaries and continents, is central here. Mobility is a defining feature of the clinical trial industry. As I show, a largely uncharted field of global experimental activity has been taking form over the past decades—sometimes beyond what established regulations can control or even keep track of. In the second part of the chapter, I address the circumstances that opened up a field of experimentality globally. I show how the "experimentalization" of everyday life in the United States (among some populations) is intimately linked to the globalization of the experiment in other parts of the world. At stake in this analysis is not just a general invocation of predatory capitalism and its legal or regulatory voids but also a detailed examination of the concrete sites of an expanding and restructuring research enterprise—and how it moves.[5]

In looking at this locomotive phenomenon, I work somewhere in between what Michael Fischer (2003: 35) terms the "interactive effects of . . . the hidden machineries of [large-scale] technologies" and Bruno Latour's (2005) call for "making things public." In a "global" age of markets, science, technology, ecological crisis, and terrorism, people are interconnected, but they are not necessarily "assembled" by any common politics or nationality. Our task, Latour states, is to make politics with the right objects—to make a political assembly out of all the various assemblages in which we are already enmeshed, interpret those assemblies, and identify alternative political possibilities. Conversely, as we standardize and stabilize novel objects of research in the life sciences, we should ask what practices can turn them into largely depoliticized public goods. How does governance take shape as an ethical proposition in the varied global environments in which new technologies take root (Adams, Novotny, and Leslie 2008)? What work is to be done locally to guarantee accountability and to link human subjects to regimes of protection?[6]

FROM OFFSHORING TO EXPERIMENTALITY

The decisions about whether to carry out clinical trials, where, and how are as scientific as they are economic and political.[7] This political economy has deep roots in tropical medicine and colonial health services, experimentation in "island nations," Cold War population science, and international development in Africa, Asia, and Latin America since the Second World War. From the Walter Reed's Yellow Fever Commission in Cuba, to the experimental eradication of malaria from Cuba and Mauritius in the 1960s, to present AIDS and malarial vaccine research and clinical trials, most of these efforts have involved government sponsorship and have actively blurred lines between research experiment and provision of health services (see, e.g., Packard 2007; Geissler et al. 2008; and Whyte et al. 2006).[8] This political economy also bears the stamp of a set of practices inherent to the pharmaceutical industry as it has evolved in North America in the twentieth century. Specifically, I have in mind the history of research among minorities and so-called cooperative patients and professional guinea pigs. I also have in mind the power the industry exerts over evidence-making and drug regulatory policy.[9]

As I tracked their scientific evidence-making practices, my informants detailed, often with surprising candor, the challenges and uncertainties that compromise the integrity of their experiments. The former director of a large contract research organizations (CRO) told me in 2005 that, "given the cost of drug development and the financial risks involved, we don't even go to the clinical trial stage unless we are sure that a drug works. ... There's nothing worse than 'killing' a drug late." His main scientific adviser questioned the mechanics of this evidence-gathering process: "Companies can now pick and choose populations in order to get a most pronounced drug benefit signal as well as a 'no-harm' signal." Picking and choosing subjects who allegedly have not been diagnosed or treated for the condition under study creates efficient results, free of statistical noise. But even here, my CRO informants express serious doubts about the generalizability of data— for example, how well can results derived from treatment-naive groups be generalized to populations in treatment-saturated markets?

As their comments suggest, experiments are not just instruments for hypothesis testing but multisided and locomotive phenomena and operative environments. Experimentality, the process through which populations as objects of experiments are reconfigured, affects not only the poor but also the consuming rich. In picking and choosing "idealized" subjects, data on the "real-life patient" is often missing, and consumers have become unwitting experimental extensions of engineered trials that brought ineffective or unsafe drugs to the market. As a mode of gathering (of distinct biological resources) and as a mode of distribution (of distinct benefits and risks), experimentality is not exclusive to crisis contexts. Institutionalized state withdrawals make it possible, favoring economic interests over strictly regulated systems of patient or consumer protection—even if only for a certain (profitable) time period.

Experimentality also provokes questions about how exactly the boundaries between research and practice are negotiated in various health settings. This complicated animal transcends any artificial separation between the controlled conditions of testing (the "lab") and the public (the "field"). It has a certain mechanical advantage over and above what ethical responses have accounted for until now. Its quality is dependent not only on standardized compliances or techniques of data processing but also on how commercial, scientific, regulatory, and ethical criteria are set (Abraham 2007: 41). These criteria call forth categories of human subjects to whom human rights and dignity are either allocated or denied.

In the Tuskegee syphilis study, which ran for four decades (1932–72), the U.S. Public Health Service withheld standard treatments from four hundred African American men infected with syphilis as a matter of "good" science, and so that scientists could observe the natural course of subjects' untreated disease. This scandal, among others that came to light in the 1960s and 1970s, redefined vulnerable persons in need of protection and led to dramatic changes in the regulation of research conduct in the United States. More recently, devastating pandemics have proven that given regulations do not always hold up in crises. For example, in 1987, investigational drug regulations were revised to expand patient access to experimental AIDS treatments.[10] Regulations that would have defined these patient groups as vulnerable, and thus would have barred them from becoming experimental test subjects for unproven therapies, were overturned by those very same groups.[11] Patients themselves judged the acceptability of the risks they took as a matter of their human rights. Yet this instance of patients' resetting the terms of allowable experimentation may be an outlier in the history of human experimentation. More often than not, political actors, economic interests, scientific practices, and law, rather than patients, "have repeatedly redrawn the line between that which is experimental and that which is non-experimental (accepted, routine)" (Marks 2002), thus resetting the terms by which the rights of human subjects are recognized, protected, or violated.

In probing how experimentality came to be and the many values that it assumes, I take the operations of CROs as a window into the contemporary offshored environments of industry-sponsored human-subjects research. CROs are highly competitive transnational businesses that make up a globalized industry specializing in investigator and subject recruitment and drug research. They are the largest and most profitable players in the "clinical trials industry."[12] Pharmaceutical, biotechnology, and medical device companies often rely on CROs to implement and manage global clinical trials according to a given research protocol. In coordinating clinical trials in the United States and abroad, these firms guide their clients through complex regulatory and legal environments and provide data management and statistical services. CROs also offer on-the-ground monitoring services to assure their clients and regulators that clinical research is conducted according to accepted technical standards, that it complies with national and international ethical guidelines concerning biomedical research in humans, and that the data has integrity and is free from fraud.

In 2000 I began tracking the operations of two contract research organizations in the U.S. Northeast pharmaceutical "corridor," which extends from Washington, D.C., to Boston—this region is home to one of the largest concentrations of pharmaceutical companies and their outsourced service providers in the world. Since then, I have spoken with executives, researchers, and clinical trials staff involved in CRO operations. I have also interviewed and collected professional histories from former regulatory officials and other key players in the pharmaceutical industry. In doing so, I have produced a recent history of the clinical trials industry, tracing it back to the postwar boom in pharmaceutical production and to regulatory and health care system changes in the United States. I have also inquired into this industry's specific scientific and technical expertise, the legal and ethical precepts that govern its activities, how it is organized and responds to evolving regulatory and scientific constraints, and the channels through which it operates and moves to other countries (otherwise known as off-shoring). In charting the activities and strategies of the global trials business, I also illuminate the motivations of the diverse actors who have high stakes in making it thrive. I am particularly concerned with the kinds of medical science, ethical reflections, and critiques that emerge from this novel experimental and social terrain—both in terms of global corporate governance and local decision making.

HOW PROTOCOLS FLOAT: ETHICAL VARIABILITY

The clinical trial industry provides a snapshot into the "massive arbitrage" that "is really the definition of globalisation" (Garnier 2005: 2). Bureaucrats, evidence gatherers, and entrepreneurs are all enmeshed in what one industry consultant described to me in 2005 as "cutthroat commodity work." Offshoring, according to the CEO of a leading pharmaceutical firm, reflects the "real challenge of globalization [. . . , which] is of course that it allows you to consider the transformation of your enterprise, in other words, you can de-aggregate all the core processes of the company, whether it's financial services, manufacturing, R&D, and rebuild them" elsewhere. You can "obtain access to pools of low-cost resources as well as high-value skilled laborers, wherever they may be found" (Garnier 2005: 2). This executive's sense of offshoring—in which drug development is likened to automobile parts production or any other industrial process—is animated by arbitrage. Arbitrage is a hedged investment meant to derive profit from differences in price; it is a form of riskless profit.[13] Deaggregating core industrial processes and rebuilding them elsewhere allows companies "to take full advantage of the massive *arbitrage* that is really the definition of globalisation, *arbitrage* in labour cost, in financial cost, but also in pools of skilled employees and in regulatory and administrative hurdles" (ibid.). For example, GlaxoSmith-Kline announced its objective goal of offshoring a full third of its clinical trials to lower-cost countries like India and Poland. As its CEO explained, "We do about 60,000 patients in total trials each year—so the savings per person if you switch, say 20,000 of those patients to India is in excess of US$10,000 per patient. So that's a savings of US$200 million right there" (Capell 2004).

The variability that arbitrage exploits is a far cry from the comforting relativisms of an earlier age. In the field of medical anthropology, reliance on culture to explain differences in global health practices has been a central project for decades.¹⁴ Knowledge of cultural differences as translated into the health-care arena tends to focus on "unbridgeable" moral divides between Western and non-Western groups. In the ethical imperialism versus relativism debate (Macklin 1999), anthropologists working in health-care arenas and elsewhere have been faulted for an alleged blind defense of local cultural tradition, making them susceptible to the "moral and intellectual consequences that are commonly supposed to flow from relativism—subjectivism, nihilism, incoherence, Machiavellianism, ethical idiocy, esthetic blindness, and so on" (Geertz 2000 [1984]: 42).¹⁵

As the world becomes a series of interlocking laboratories and data producing sites, ethical variability has become central to the development and testing of pharmaceuticals. It takes the specificities of local context and lived experience as a given and as a basis on which to consolidate a cost-effective variability in ethical standards in human research. In defining new research frontiers and in comparing their "local" levels of care and demands, ethical variability can bypass international standards of care and evolves as a commercial tactic in mobilizing human-subjects research and in the movement of trials worldwide. Deliberations over the ethics of research are set against, even eclipsed by, the market ethics of industry scientists and regulators. "There are so many places we can work in that we just bypass [ethical debate] all together," one CRO founder told me.

As an illustration of ethical variability, an industry entrepreneur whom I call Evan described the fate of one study which he said was "impossible-to-run" in the United States. The study protocol involved administering regular injections of a cancer-imaging agent to children. The product was approved for adult use, and the manufacturer wanted to have the product approved for use in children. The FDA required the manufacturer to run a trial on healthy children (aged six months to two years) to determine appropriate dosaging. "But what parent in the U.S. would put their own healthy child in a cancer-imaging agent trial?" Evan asked me rhetorically. "Sometimes the FDA is a bit disconnected in its demands from what institutional review boards are willing to accept." He told me that American researchers rejected the study, as they believed it involved an agent "that could be detrimental to children's health." Evan then sent the protocol to his Russian colleagues. They also rejected it. "If the protocol is rejected in Russia, where does it go next?" I asked him. He said he did not know. He suspected that the agent would continue to be used "off-label"—that is, prescribed for children's use without ever being systematically studied in children.

Evan counted on the fact that risks are measured differently depending on location, and, as his example shows, U.S. regulatory norms anticipate an unequal geography of clinical research for their fulfillment. The FDA encourages drug companies to study medical compounds in children. The FDA Modernization Act's Pediatric Studies Incentive, for example, affords certain drug applications an additional six months of patent exclusivity if a sponsor tests a drug on pediatric populations. In some ways, the FDA's effort to generate such data can be viewed as commendable. But whose children will be tested? The agency has yet to systemically investigate how its incentives and evidentiary rules are actually applied in global settings. Here, it is enough to say that, given the challenges and opportunities that U.S. drug regulation poses, location becomes a key economic decision and business asset.

To get an on-the-ground understanding of the offshoring of clinical trials, I interviewed national regulators, public health administrators, and investigators and their clinical trial monitors in Eastern Europe and Latin America. In some countries, trials have become a public health-care surrogate and have changed the quality of medical care. During the summers from 2003 to 2006, I carried out fieldwork in southern Brazil among industry-sponsored researchers and with doctors carrying out trials in public hospitals. Also, executives of one U.S.-based CRO allowed me to observe the operations of their affiliate in Poland and Russia; I carried out this part of the research in the summer of 2005. By working with business administrators and their local research partners, I observed some of the more troubling aspects of trial offshoring, especially in the stepped-up search for trial subjects in needy contexts. The turf war is not only about the numbers of subjects a given company can recruit. It is also about recruiting subjects quickly. As one veteran recruiter told me, "It's really a problem. I don't know anybody who has really cracked the code. Sometimes you get lucky and you fill the study quickly, but for the most part, patients are really difficult to find, and they are difficult to find because everybody is looking for them."

CROs find Eastern European countries attractive because the unmet demand for specialized care tends to hasten patient enrollment. High literacy rates in this region mean that subjects offer more "meaningful" informed consent, thus minimizing potential problems with auditors. As one industry executive told me, CROs compete over "who gets patients, who I can sign up to be in my alliance so that when I do attract a sponsor, I can say, 'I can line up five hundred cancer patients for you tomorrow morning.'" Eastern Europe is also known for its seemingly widespread absence of treatment for common and uncommon diseases. I say "seemingly" because people in low-income countries, just like people in affluent ones, might be consuming several drugs or treatments, often unsystematically. This anthropological fact has not deterred companies from identifying particular sites in which they think the "naive" (i.e., those who have not been diagnosed or treated for the condition under study) might be found—in a poorer region or hospital, for example. As one researcher told me in 2004, these populations "offer a more likely prospect of minimizing the number of variables affecting results and a better chance of showing drug effectiveness."

THE SCIENCE OF EXPECTED FAILURES

What animates the search for larger pools of human subjects? First, the sheer number of trials being run. R&D investments in research-based pharmaceutical companies grew from US$1.1 billion in 1975 to US$38.8 billion in 2003, and more new chemical entities are available for clinical testing than ever before (Parexel 2005: 46). The advent of blockbuster drugs with sales of over US$1 billion annually has led to the profitable and highly competitive "me-too" drugs business. With minimal pharmacological alteration, these drugs build on or mimic blockbuster drugs and exploit well-established markets. Trials for me-too drugs require large numbers of patients and often produce little or no evidence of additional therapeutic gain.

The second factor impelling the search for human subjects is the need for larger patient populations. To satisfy U.S. regulatory demands regarding the long-term safety of a new drug, ever larger numbers of patients must be included in clinical trials, especially of drugs designed to be widely prescribed. "If a few years ago you needed five hundred people to make a better aspirin, today you need five thousand," a clinical researcher for one of the country's largest CROs told me in 2002. "Three adverse events in a population of three thousand is enough for the FDA to tell you that you need more research. The bigger the population you have tested upfront, the better your chances of speeding the drug's regulatory approval."

The third factor is the rapid growth of particular drug therapies. Some therapeutic areas, like antihypertensives to control blood pressure and statins to control cholesterol, are expanding. New compounds and their competitors are being developed almost concurrently. The race to be the first to get drugs approved and to bring them to market makes the search for subjects particularly fierce. "When a therapeutic area gets hot," one researcher told me, "it's like a 'cattle stampede' for human volunteers."

The fourth factor is a "drug pipeline explosion." The U.S. Patent Office is being inundated with patent applications for new compounds that have yet to be clinically tested.

Changes in the science of drug development also impact subject recruitment. As new molecules are discovered, more experiments are taking place (before the formal phases of human testing) in order to accelerate the "discovery-to-clinic transition" (Parexel 2005: 61). Indeed, more compounds are coming into clinical testing than ever before, but fewer are making it through to phase 3 trials (46). A manager of clinical trial operations for a major CRO operating in eighteen countries explained this seeming anomaly: "It used to be that 90 percent of the novel compounds introduced got filtered out in animal testing. Now that rate is dropping to below 50 percent. This is partially due to the fact that there are more therapeutic targets. But it is also because we can't filter things out pre-clinically like we used to [toxicity, for example]. You might be able to make a better gerbil . . . but the real guinea pigs will be human."

Unfortunately, humans also are in short supply. The available pool of human subjects in major Western pharmaceutical markets is shrinking.[16] Relatively affluent populations are using too many drugs. And this treatment saturation is making Americans and Western Europeans increasingly unusable as research subjects. As one clinical trials industry executive put it to me: "People live on pills in the West. You have the fifty-year-old who takes four or five different medications. Someone living in Eastern Europe may be on one medication for high blood pressure or whatever, but certainly not four or five." In other words, our pharmaceuticalized bodies produce too many drug-drug interactions.[17] They are less and less able to show specific drug effectiveness, making test results less statistically valid.

Regardless of how many of us are ready—owing to therapeutic need, belief in medical progress, or altruism—to become human subjects, there will never be enough Americans to satisfy the current demand for subjects in U.S. private-sector science. This is pushing the human-subjects research enterprise to other shores. Other (compensating) factors also animate this globalizing trend. As the above-mentioned points suggest, the dominant business model of drug development (with its tendency toward me-too or copycat drugs and biased sampling to maximize drug benefit) is inefficient and subject to the loss of surplus-producing energy. This was most clearly evident in the recent case of Vioxx, a widely prescribed antiarthritic drug shown to increase risk of heart disease. The FDA gave Vioxx's investigational new drug application rapid "priority" FDA review. In initial evaluations, however, "the use of small, short-term trials, the exclusion of high-risk patients, and the methodologic inattention to cardiovascular events all minimized the possibility of uncovering evidence of cardiovascular harm" (Psaty and Furberg 2005: 1134). Highly screened ("biologically edited") subjects of clinical trials were tested over real-life patients, who are often much sicker than study subjects. This biasing compounded the experimental aspects of drug use in the postmarketing phase (Gilhooley 2007).

Revelations of postmarketing adverse drug effects and lawsuits have forced companies to invest in legal strategies to combat litigation. But remediation is not just legal in form. A senior research scientist suggested to me in 2004 that the current clinical trial operational model routinely underestimates adverse drug effects or risk; it operates within what he called "the paradigm of expected failure." For example, he told me, "In any industrial system, if you spend ten times as much on repair of data as on prevention, you are just going to live in a continued cycle of loss. For every dollar spent on an investigation, ten dollars are spent on going back and fixing the data after the fact." Meanwhile, pharmaceutical companies are trying to get what they can out of the paradigm while continuing to sell pharmaceuticals as a preeminent social good. In its offshoring mode, pharma exports a paradigm of expected failure, which is affecting any number of scales and institutions (state, legal, regulatory, and medical) and necessitating complicated and politically fraught modes of reform (Petryna 2009).

While the pool of U.S. human subjects has been shrinking from an industry standpoint, in the past two decades we have witnessed a strong mobilization by medical reformers for the inclusion of underrepresented groups (based on gender, race or ethnicity, and age) in scientific research. This came along with the mobilization of patient advocacy groups around AIDS and other life-threatening diseases, for example, to demand access to experimental therapies (see Epstein 1996; Lowy 2000; Hilts 2004; and Daemmrich 2004). Medical reformers have questioned the generalizability of biomedical data, arguing that variation contributes to disease vulnerability and treatment outcomes. Many federal initiatives have been launched to encourage or mandate the inclusion of representatives of designated subgroup populations in research to make it more relevant.[18]

The NIH have enhanced diversity in clinical trials, but it is much less clear how this policy of inclusion has been interpreted by the industry and how it is taken up in offshore research. One scientist, for example, described the demography of her company's Russian research population as age-diverse, and this diversity facilitated drug approval: "Different pollution profiles, different ways of regulating (or not regulating) air pollution, and high rates of lung cancers and respiratory diseases mean shorter life spans. There you have people getting cancer who are a lot younger. Younger people are more desirable from the perspective of trials because they are a better bet to be responsive to a therapy. And we have more data upfront for different age groups, which is good for approval." Here, the rhetoric of diversity seemed to shore up the profitable and interminable search for available subjects, themselves trapped in sick environments and highly unequal social relations. For many of my industry contacts, however, this rhetoric of efficacy trumped the rhetoric of diversity. They invoked the search for valuable "treatment naive" subjects with fewer conflicting variables in order to minimize "noise" and maximize drug-benefit signal, for example. Through strategic protocol design and subject selection, the industry deploys a trial science that "may swamp any differences potentially detectable between subgroups" (S. Epstein 2007: 285).

NORMAL VOLUNTEERS

The risk-benefit approach that characterizes modern drug development also provides a venue for experimentality in its many forms: as a form of new capital and as a potentially dangerous blurring of lines between the subjects of drug research and real patients and consumers.[19] The beginnings of a mobile and specialized drug-testing industry with expertise in human-subjects recruitment and research are traceable to the post–Second World War pharmaceutical boom in the United States. During this period a fee-for-service industry evolved in response to a demand for more safety testing in animals and humans. It became common for pharmaceutical companies to contract out about a third of their initial toxicological testing (today it is about half). Another point of origin for the expansion of human-subjects recruitment lies in the early 1970s, when the use of prisoner subjects in the United States was exposed and then severely limited. The scale of this prison-based research was impressive: an estimated 90 percent of drugs licensed in the United States prior to the 1970s were first tested on prison populations here (Harkness 1996). In 1980 the use of prisoners for particular phases of drug testing was finally banned, and pharmaceutical companies lost a major source of human volunteers. But by then they had shifted a good deal of their research elsewhere—namely, to countries such as England and Sweden, where, according to one founder of the contract research industry, "regulation did not necessarily hinder initiating trials."

This former physician was one of the first to establish a clinical development company dedicated to the conduct of global clinical trials in the mid-1970s. When I pushed him to say more about the prisoner-research scandal and how it affected his enterprise, he told me that he "was on the side of the people who said you really have to find a patient population that is more informed, that has a true free will, and that can walk away from the research at any moment they want to, which in a prison setting was not so easy." He paused and finished his train of thought, "And we really went after what we called normal volunteers."

By the early to mid-1980s, U.S. pharmaceutical companies were routinely outsourcing laboratory and clinical services, including the monitoring of investigational sites, data production, and preclinical bioassays (the latter are used to assess the activity of a chemical, mainly in animal models). By the early 1990s, drug development had become a globalized endeavor, in part under the aegis of the International Conference on Harmonization (ICH), in which the Food and Drug Administration played a key initiating role.[20] The ICH brought regulatory authorities from Europe, Japan, and the United States together with industry experts, creating international standards for ensuring and assessing the safety and quality of testing procedures for experimental compounds, including "good clinical practice" guidelines for investigators and the implementation of internal review boards (IRBs). Most important for the clinical trials industry, ICH standards opened up new experimental terrains and made clinical data from international research sites transferable and acceptable to regulatory bodies in these major markets (and particularly to the FDA).[21] The global trials industry was here to stay.

Today, CROs are rapidly expanding into the Third World and the former Second World of Eastern Europe, carving out new populations for larger and more complicated trials to meet the requirements for drug safety and efficacy demanded by U.S. regulators and consumers. When I asked one clinical trials manager how he would respond to a critique that his catchment strategy was exploitative, he argued that trial expansion has had overall "positive effects" as experiments themselves have become social goods: "We provide health care where there is none and medical relief for participants." Even if the trend in drug trial expansion can be justified in terms of potential health benefits, exposing disadvantaged populations that have no legal recourse to potential harms is ethically troubling. Well-intentioned local investigators, IRB members, and CRO workers have convinced themselves that they have little power to negotiate with pharmaceutical sponsors for better protection and care of trial subjects—for fear that trials might move to another country, another medical institution, or another CRO. Whether this fear is grounded is highly debatable. Here, it is enough to point out that rather than evening the starting conditions in which global human-subjects research is conducted, ethics as ethical variability itself becomes the industry norm.

The discursive (and somewhat illusory) condition of "treatment naiveté" speaks to differentiated human experiences and risks across the globe. The allegedly "purest" subjects are also often the poorest and most disenfranchised. Drug developers are now focusing on populations experiencing chronic health-care problems—populations whose life expectancies increased and whose incidence of infectious disease and mortality rates decreased under the "health transition" but whose lives are still shorter, more chronically diseased, and less socially protected. The public health tactic of demarcating disease to prevent disease (involving epidemiology, prevention, and medical access) is now used to carve out new catchment areas of human subjects who are targeted precisely because of their "naiveté." This move may appear problematic in itself, but the pharmaceutical industry argues that it is positive insofar as, in these regions, clinical trials have become social goods in themselves. And they may well be providing health care where there is little (Whyte et al. 2006) and allowing medical relief for participants' specific ailments for the duration of the trial.

Elements considered in cost-effective trial siting include population disease profiles, mortality rates, local levels of unemployment, per-patient trial costs, and potential for future marketing of the drug to be approved. CROS investigate the host country's regulatory environment. They ask whether universal access to health care is in place. They assess the regulatory priorities and capacities of host countries (e.g., efficacy of local ethical review boards and outlooks on and regulation of placebo use).

Such cost-effective modeling of research sites betrays the very purpose of a four-phase model of drug evaluation, which was instituted in the late 1960s on the heels of the scandal over thalidomide (a drug found to cause severe birth defects). The U.S. Congress mandated that all new drug applications submitted to the FDA for approval be based on the randomized controlled trial. Randomization, a process of assigning trial subjects to treatment or control groups, uses an element of chance to reduce bias of selection and thus increase the reliability of results. This statistical bias-reduction strategy came from a progressive impulse to reduce false beliefs and limit business interests in medicine (Marks 1997). In the context of global trials, this strategy is applied, but it is also circumvented. There is now bias-induction in both the recruitment of epidemiologically convenient populations and in protocol design, as the chief scientific officer of a midsized CRO told me: "In my recruitment strategy, I can use subject inclusion criteria that are so selective that I can 'engineer out' the possibility of adverse events being seen. Or, I can demonstrate that my new drug is better by 'engineering up' a side effect in another drug [by doubling its dose, for example]. That is the big game of clinical trials."

This officer heads a "triage committee" with other physicians. They review pharmaceutical research protocols and decide which ones their CRO should bid on. He told me that the pool of preferred patients in clinical trials is becoming much more targeted—"biologically edited," to use his precise phrasing. "We are seeing many more protocols with subject inclusion and exclusion criteria that are too difficult to meet, like advanced untreated diabetes," he said. His committee avoided bidding on some of these trials "because it is too dangerous and costly for us to monitor patients. The experiment becomes too difficult to control on the ground."[22]

As I learned in my ethnographic forays, CROS have different standard operating procedures with respect to accepting and implementing riskier protocols and potential liabilities. This officer also felt that the bias built into recruitment strategies and protocol design was increasing chances of ineffective and even unsafe drugs gaining FDA approval. Indeed, the global expansion of clinical trials goes hand in hand with new strategies of the demonstration of efficacy that carry, alongside prospective benefits, their own forms of harm.

EXPERIMENTS AS "SOCIAL GOODS"

There is, it seems, no place of stasis or stability in experimentality against which to measure exceptions. In discerning emergent lines of political re-structuring, work is required in places where the demands for "invisibility and visibility confront each other" (Sivaramakrishnan 2005: 326). Comparative analysis—across regions and different systems of accountability and law—is required in order to reveal the "rifts and gaps" and "enormous deficiencies" in public information and that thwart understandings of the total phenomenon (Malinowski 1961: 13). Such work can also shed light on alternative fields of social and scientific innovation.

In an earlier essay (Petryna 2005), I took the controversy over placebo use in Africa in 1994 during trials of short-course AZT treatment to halt perinatal transmission of HIV—a focal point in the debate over ethical standards in global clinical research—as a watershed in the expansion of the globalized clinical trial. I traced the relation between regulation and the evolution of ethical standards in human research, and how subject popula-tions are created at the intersection of regulatory deliberation, commercial interest, and crises (upon crises) of public health. I argued that the after-math of the AZT trials demonstrates how connected these universes are, and how transnational regulatory debates are implicated in the emergence of "local" and differentiated experimental terrains. I also argued, within the context of the ethics of the placebo debate, how the regulatory premium on untreated subjects was publicized.

The impact of the debate over the ethics of placebo use on "what is actu-ally done" was insignificant. A 2004 review, "Clinical Trials in Sub-Saharan Africa and Established Standards of Care," found that, "in general, patients with HIV disease enrolled in trials received care that did not conform to clinical guidelines; neither control nor intervention groups received 'best current' antiretroviral therapy, even when they had symptomatic or ad-vanced disease. . . . A likely explanation for these findings is that investi-gators who design and conduct these studies, and the ethics committees who review and approve them, consider trial design in the context of the local level of care rather than the international standard of care" (Kent et al. 2004: 240–41). Of the thirty-four trials that studied various aspects of HIV disease, for example, only one met the "best current" treatment guidelines for HIV, and this single study happened to be industry-sponsored. In zones of crisis, protection and safety considerations are at times weighed against immediate health benefits or the scientific knowledge to be gained. Ethics and method are thus modified to fit the local context and experimental data required.

In the early 1990s, a few years before the controversial AZT trials, contexts of data production got even more convoluted. The FDA began to actively promote the globalization of clinical trials, declaring "that the search for sites and sources of data are part of its mandate to determine . . . safety and efficacy" through the establishment of the ICH (OIG 2001: 42). Eager to attract new investments and participate in the booming production of global pharmaceuticals, many countries in the World Trade Organization had incorporated the agreement on Trade-Related Aspects of Intellectual Property Rights (TRIPS) into their national laws. By agreeing to implement ICH standards, these countries began the costly work of setting up national agencies that could standardize and monitor the conduct and performance of trials in their territories, as well as implement ethical review boards to ensure the rights and protection of patients. Full implementation varied from country to country, but the number of subjects involved in international clinical trials grew enormously, from four thousand in 1995 to four hundred thousand in 1999.[23] These numbers refer to new drug applications only, that is, applications made to the FDA to license and market drugs after they have been tested in animals and humans. Note that some clinical research does not require registration of preclinical and postmarketing studies (studies of new uses for already existing drugs). Trials leading to rejected drug applications are also not counted by the FDA.

By 2000, when I began this research, the largest documented increase in clinical trial participation had occurred in Eastern Europe and Latin America (recently, India and China have become major areas of outsourced drug development).[24] This global growth brought with it a new set of unknowns related to the circumstances of research and concerns about possible exploitation of foreign subjects. New institutions and a host of new acronyms—ICH, TRIPS, IRBs—provided the technical and legal bare minimum for clinical trials to globalize, but large-scale regulatory frameworks for registering global clinical trials or monitoring their conduct still do not exist. Proposals for improving the system of monitoring are plentiful. Most favor refinements of an IRB-based model. For instance, in 1999, the Office of the Inspector General, a periodic auditor of the FDA, found that "in spite of its active promotion of the search for sites and subjects elsewhere," the FDA has not been able to protect these subjects.[25] To address this failure, the inspector general recommended that the FDA support and, in some cases, help to construct local ethical review boards.[26]

This approach involves more monitoring and more reliance on local ethics committees, and it leans heavily toward what Iris Young (2004) called a "liability model" of accountability: Let regulators name the responsible local parties (in some cases, this would mean first creating such oversight bodies) and surely those parties can gather information and make the right decisions, surely they can stop inappropriate research from taking place. This approach presupposes a working and fair legal system (among other things). Much is also assumed about who is and is not the agent of abuse (most typically defined as the individual investigator). The fact is that certain conditions have to be met before a liability model can effectively protect research subjects: states themselves need to act as protectors and not abusers, transnational corporations need to respect the rights and dignity of all research subjects and recognize that different situations elicit different levels of coercion, and international ethics codes must be enforceable. In short, what I am pointing to is a political and ethical milieu lying beyond a procedural one governing investigator conduct.

As the rapid growth of clinical trials was under way, scandals arose that exposed the structural flaws and absences of institutionalized protective structures in a now-globalized system. Consider the now infamous case of industry-sponsored research in Nigeria for Trovan, a drug manufactured by Pfizer. One of the most widely prescribed antibiotics in the United States, Trovan was taken off the market in 1999 because it was found to produce serious liver-related side effects. In 1996, during the drug's clinical development stage, a Pfizer researcher and his team traveled to the city of Kano, in northern Nigeria, to test Trovan on pediatric victims of a bacterial meningitis outbreak. Nigeria was undergoing a period of massive civil unrest under the dictatorship of General Sani Abacha. Doctors without Borders was already injecting children with a fast-acting antibiotic (ceftriaxone), proven effective in treating bacterial meningitis, at a local city hospital.

The Pfizer research protocol aimed to show that an oral version of Trovan would work as well as ceftriaxone. The protocol was not approved by a U.S. ethics committee and received inadequate review in Nigeria. Legal documents show that informed consent forms used in Pfizer's defense are backdated. The Pfizer team arrived at Kano Infectious Diseases Hospital and selected two hundred children who were waiting in line to receive ceftriaxone. Some of these children were given Trovan in the oral form never tested on humans before; others were given a dose of ceftriaxone at a dose lower than that of the standard of care for meningitis. The Pfizer team is alleged not to have explained the experimental nature of Trovan to subjects; parents believed their children were receiving a proven treatment. According to the complaint filed by a New York law firm on behalf of the parents, the lower dosage allowed Pfizer researchers to show that Trovan was more efficacious (Lewin 2001). According to the parents, this low dosing also resulted in the deaths of eleven children.

This is one of the first cases brought by foreign subjects or citizens against a U.S.-based pharmaceutical company. The plaintiffs' lawyers suggested that a chain of complicity in making the children available for research included Nigeria's military rulers, state officials, Ministry of Health officials, and local hospital administrators; U.S. FDA regulators who authorized an unapproved drug's export to Nigeria for "humanitarian" purposes; and Pfizer researchers who, from a line of children waiting for standard treatments, selected subjects for their own trial. All were involved, lawyers claimed, in violating principles of the Nuremberg Code and other codes of human-subjects protection, referred to in the plaintiffs' court documents as "customary laws" that are "made up of fundamental principles of a civil society that are so widely held that they constitute binding norms on the community of nations" (*Rabi Abdullahi et al. v. Pfizer Inc.*, 01 Civ. 8118, 6 [2003]).[27]

The defendant's lawyers, by contrast, downplayed the authority of the code and stated that it and other such guidelines "are not treaties." (In some domestic cases, federal judges have ruled that internationally accepted codes of human-subjects protection, in this case the Nuremberg Code and the Helsinki declaration, cannot be relied on as the basis of civil suits in U.S. courts.) The defense situated Pfizer researchers' activities in the context of a "massive epidemic killing more than 11,000 people," whose outbreak they attribute to "woefully inadequate" sanitary conditions. By suggesting that their experimental treatment could only do good in such a desperate context, the defense troubled the criteria by which to judge the difference between experimental and standard of care treatment. It stated that it would be "paternalistic" for an American court to adjudicate the appropriate conduct of medical research in a country undergoing a public health crisis, and it echoed the ethically relativizing stance already familiar in the African AZT case (*Rabi Abdullahi et al. v. Pfizer Inc.*, 1).

In this brief sketch of the legal parrying, one point is worth stressing. As much as one would like to see the Kano case as an instance of the "dubious" or the "para" (paralegal, pararegulatory, paraethical), an interlocking set of regulatory, commercial, and state interests is at play that can potentially introduce uncertainty with respect to the observability of international ethics codes in local contexts or even suspend the relevance of such ethics altogether.[28] In this case, a functional ethical review of U.S. industry-sponsored research would have been necessary and might even have prevented this tragedy. But at the site of experimentation, interests were not on the side of protection but overwhelmingly on the side of making populations accessible to research. Pfizer argued that the case should be adjudicated in Nigerian courts. The Southern District of New York court agreed (but, after many efforts, a ruling has reinstated the U.S. lawsuit).

The case exemplifies how contextual factors (crisis and its humanitarianisms) and defenses fold into and construct new experimental scenarios and groups, what I term *expedient experimentality*. In other words, the crisis provided a ready-made scenario for bioscientific research.[29] Ethical positions, particularly those revealed by the AZT case, that relativize decision making over appropriate conduct of research to its local context inform a legal defense strategy which makes acts of experimentation—particularly those enacted in public health crises—either reachable or unreachable by international ethics codes.[30] What appears as scandalous activity with respect to global human-subjects research may, in fact, be seen as legitimate under evolving ethical and legal notions of fair play.

A humanitarian crisis creates a space that appears to be "ethics free" precisely because it is disastrous, beyond the reach of regulation. With the sudden suspension of normalcy, whole groups of people actually or potentially become experimental subjects.[31] This case also demonstrates the erosion of consent processes and of citizens' trust in state systems of public health and protection.

Experimentality is a flexible, transnational form of governance; it relies on the trope of humanity to, as the editors of this volume write, bypass "other ways of dividing up government." It "creates" human subjects differently under different conditions (e.g., those who are cared for in crisis, those who are increasingly medicated, those who are subject to the experiment as a "normal" part of health delivery, those who are formed through ethical variability, etc.). Ethics is used tactically by all actors in a chain of interests involved in human-subjects research. Such chains now function in states where the lives of citizens are not adequately protected by traditional health or welfare systems. The biological indicators of whole groups—however formed or damaged by social and economic context—can be enfolded into regimes of international and local forms of protection, where ethics becomes a "workable document."

RESEARCH SUBJECTS OF THE FUTURE

The "experimentalization" of everyday life in the United States (among some populations) is intimately linked to the globalization of the experiment in other parts of the world. In the 1970s and 1980s, drugs were tested largely on civilian, noninstitutionalized populations in the United States and Western Europe, in academic medical settings. Although, as I have noted, the use of prisoner subjects for nontherapeutic research in the United States had been banned by 1980, the continuation of prison research had strong advocates. Louis Lasagna (1977), cofounder of the Tufts Center for the Study of Drug Development, made the scientific case that shutting down the prison-testing infrastructure deprived U.S. researchers of the ability to test for adverse reactions to drugs. Prisoners, especially recidivists, made long-term safety studies possible. Referring to the closing of a Kentucky prison-related addiction research center, Lasagna wrote, "Without such a facility, this work is unlikely to be done elsewhere, and the sick public will become the unwilling (and unconsenting) research subject of the future."

In the early 1990s, the bulk of clinical trials still occurred in Western nations. With the "drug pipeline explosion" I referred to earlier producing an overdemand for investigational sites, U.S. pharmaceutical companies and CROs began to tap and even to prefer medical group practices and primary care centers to the tried and true academic medical centers. The number of group physicians and primary care doctors interested in integrating their practices into the clinical trials market steadily increased, and then fell during the past decade. Initial interest came, in part, as a response to lowered Medicare reimbursements and changes in the structure of payments from health management organizations; physicians saw clinical trials as an additional source of income. But profits often did not materialize, due to the many uncompensated or "hidden costs" related to study startup, regulatory compliance costs, and management and reporting of adverse events (Parexel 2005: 125). These economics also inform the intractable problem of what my CRO informants call *floater sites*—these are "fly-by-night" operations that promise many patients, routinely underbid for contracts, and are not particularly concerned with full regulatory compliance. They make their money and then disappear from the clinical trial food chain. Their existence lowers the profitability of clinical research in the United States.[32]

Consider this story. A researcher told me that a manufacturer once approached his company to test its drug (now withdrawn from the market) for additional uses. The protocol was designed to show that the drug could treat, among other things, infections due to ruptured appendixes. The researcher explained why his CRO lost and another CRO won the contract: "Whereas we went to the tried and true academic sites for patient enrollment, they went to the southwestern United States, to a ring of facilities in order to enroll trial subjects. By going to a southwestern hospital chain treating Hispanics with little or no medical insurance, this CRO far outstripped us in enrollment."

The reality of "rescue" research adds another layer of complexity to the ways domestic trends inform the global movement of industry-sponsored research. The term *rescue* applies to a study that begins in one location but, because of poor recruitment, is shifted to another location midway through the trial. Some trials initially launched in Western Europe, for example, were shifted to Eastern European countries (which were considered "rescue countries" in the early to mid-1990s). The term can also apply to a study that takes place when the life cycle of a new drug is suddenly cut short. This requires rapid patient enrollments and a quick setup. Rescue studies of this sort can result from unforeseen product failures (owing to adverse drug effects, for example). Both modes of rescue inform a significant amount of clinical research "gone global."

This view into the ordinary practices of human research illuminates the broader question of how commercial pressures change the very forms of scientific experimentation; and how potential systemic harms are generated through everyday practices that can elude the dictates of written protocols. Auditing mechanisms have not expanded to meet the proliferation of floater sites; there are thus concerns about the reliability of the data produced there. One very real factor pushing experimentality to countries is this phenomenon—whether it is to pursue more floaters elsewhere or as an escape from the economic constraints the phenomenon imposes here. Countries like Poland, for example, bid their research services as a more reliable alternative to floater sites. But, much to their dismay, Polish researchers cannot shed their reputation and attraction as rescue researchers in the global experimental economy.

"PHARMACEUTICALS ARE THE NEW GOLD"

As experiments redefine the distinction between experimentation and therapeutics and alter medical care in both rich and poor contexts, public institutions are pressured to mediate therapeutic markets and people's access to new technologies. Researchers in the newly built Unit of Clinical Research of University Hospital in Porto Alegre, Brazil, have been working hard to undo the potential harms of experimentality. The team, led by Paulo Picon, a cardiologist and public health expert, is very critical of the ways pharmaceutical companies and CROs are influencing the course of medical research and public health in Brazil. Picon and his team analyze the efficacy and dosage requirements of new drugs entering the market. They were particularly concerned with drugs that promise, not to cure or extend life, but simply to lower some nonclinical indicator, such as the reduced virological response promised by the hepatitis C drug, Peginterferon. Some new drugs cost twenty times more than existing treatments, and these researchers are showing that their efficacy is not much better.

"The industry is setting the state to purchase these drugs," Picon said. "Pharmaceuticals are the new gold." The industry mobilizes desperate patients, who use their right to universal health care, guaranteed by the Brazilian constitution, to pressure the government to buy these drugs. The industry and the patients model their efforts in part after successful movements by AIDS patients in Brazil and the United States. According to João Biehl (2006, 2007), this combination of patient activism and pharmaceutical-industry interests is leading to "an incremental change in the concept of public health from prevention and clinical care to community based care and drugging—that is, public health is increasingly decentralized and pharmaceuticalized" (Biehl 2006: 223). Drugging and experimentation, as

I have shown, cut both ways, in both rich and poor settings, as "health-conscious, well-insured, educated people in the United States and in other wealthy countries have come to take being medicated for granted . . . to the delight of pharmaceutical manufacturers" (Gorman 2004). In Brazil, this "pharmaceuticalization" raises vital questions about public health priorities and their financing, and the role of equity in the human right to health.

The researchers in Porto Alegre are creating a kind of counterscience, designing study protocols that show that less intensive doses of some heavily marketed new drugs work equally well and cost less. Testing drugs at lower-than-recommended doses can be highly problematic: disastrously unethical, as in the case of Trovan, because the best standard of care was already available in Kano, Nigeria; or controversial, as in the case of AZT treatment, which was tested at a less intensive dose for affordability and feasibility in Africa and elsewhere (Shaffer et al. 1999; Wiktor et al. 1999). New drugs are heavily marketed, and manufacturers often recommend the highest dose as the best standard of care. Boundaries between science and commerce blur in medicine and all too often the evidence base for making well-informed medical decisions is compromised: "All that is left for us is to follow the recommendations," Picon said.

In their effort to ascertain the most efficacious doses for their patients, Picon and his colleagues engage in a kind of "reverse engineering" of privatization (Bowker and Star 1999), applying a moral acid test to the sedimented political and social interests that allow pharmaceuticalization to maintain its hold. In the process, they have been beset by pharmaceutical lobbyists, threatened with lawsuits, and denounced as violators of human rights. They are partnering with local prosecutors and educating judges to make sure that their alternative evidence has some legal weight.

In 2005 I learned of a case in another hospital in which this business model failed, placing trial patients and investigators in an impossible position. Doctors were conducting a trial to test a new therapy for a rare inherited disorder. Advanced-stage patients who had never received any treatment were recruited, according to the study's strict inclusion criteria. The director of the service wanted the trial because of the resources it would bring. Without his colleagues' knowledge, he agreed to the sponsor's demand to reserve the right to withdraw the drug *at any time*—this was written into the consent forms that the patients signed. Informally, however, the company agreed to provide medication for two years, and it continued to do so for a third year. The drug worked well. But, without notice, the company pulled the study drug. A company representative hinted to the clinicians that Brazil was too slow in registering the drug. Company lawyers had contacted the patients to form a patient activist group to pressure the government to buy these drugs (which can cost up to US$200,000 per patient annually). This effort failed. Later, I learned that the company running the trial had been sold. Whatever had led to the withdrawal, the clinicians involved had no institutional recourse. There was no more treatment. Within four years, their advanced-stage patients would most likely die.

A middle-aged man whom I will call Inácio Santos told me that he had symptoms of the disease since adolescence. He lived in the Brazilian interior and in the early eighties, after migrating to Porto Alegre and going to college, he was able to interest an endocrinologist in private practice in his case. "When I had the money I paid," Inácio said, "and when I didn't have it, he saw me anyway." Inácio found a steady job as a public servant and from then on half of his medical expenses were paid. "The doctor taught me how to live with the disease."

But Inácio also began to be studied as his doctor participated in medical research at a local hospital. "I went religiously to his office twice a year. I had to do all kinds of exams and biopsies, sometimes I went three or four times a year there." He treated himself with pain killers and an elastic stocking to take care of the swelling in the legs, he said. Finally, one day in the late 1990s, "the doctor called me and declared, 'I discovered what you have. It is genetic. There is no treatment yet. But people are doing studies and some people from the hospital will contact you.'"

"The die was cast," said Inácio, who was in his forties and knew that he had already lived "beyond the average of people with the disease. Most people with the disease at my age were already dead or had killed themselves." I asked him whether the enzyme replacement therapy had improved the quality of his life. His answer was, "I have survived. I made a choice to enter the study. I could have chosen not to do anything, and maybe I would not be talking to you today. But there is no way I can know the actual impact of the study."

Inácio couched his trial subject agency in a complicated web of expectations, financial calculations, inducements, and abiding medical trust: "We do many things based on trust. We trust in the hospital and the staff, who we know are upright people. The only document I remember signing said that I was not responsible for paying the bill for anything. Everything they gave us, we signed. Company representatives made copies of the documents and after all this, nothing [no treatment]. In the beginning . . . and for two years they even gave me a full tank of gas. They gave me around fifty liters of gas to come here for the research."

As far as Inácio recalled, in case the treatment worked, "those patients who were willing to continue were going to have maintenance for the rest of their lives." Inácio and other patients, he said, could not understand how a company had been allowed to begin a trial and now be exempted from the legal responsibility to provide the treatment. "We exposed ourselves to the drug without knowing if it was or was not going to work. Some benefits the company had. We didn't die."

Inácio, like others on the trial, struggled to make sense of the new medical and legal configuration he had been thrown into as trial subjects without experimental therapies now engaging the judiciary at the state and federal levels. It took him way beyond the disease he once knew how to inhabit. Who was responsible for treatment access? Who would pay? Whom should he be loyal to? How was he actually doing medically? Who would help him?

As clinicians expressed their concerns over patient care, they highlighted the contractual uncertainties that pervade the world's clinical trial scene, and they showed how an obligation to minimize harm can be undercut. The ability to withdraw medication at any time illustrates the production of different and unexpected hierarchies of protection (some get experimental treatment, some get only partial or temporary treatment which can be stopped at any moment, some get no treatment, some depend on trials as their basic medical care, etc.). For many severely compromised patients like Inácio, life chances are now punctuated by the monopolistic power over new therapies and by public health experiments that are trying to attenuate, if not break, that power.

This case illuminates the unevenness of institutional powers in the now global landscape of experimentation. The local research unit lacked business savvy and was not able to negotiate its contracts and rights effectively; not wanting to lose the rare opportunity to treat patients and to foster medical know-how, its members simply agreed to the drug company's terms. While the methods of and benefits from the trial had been thought out in advance by the various parties involved, one element was not clearly articulated: the harm that could occur if the study treatment was withdrawn. Moreover, no one other than the pharmaceutical industry directly helped patients to formalize their interests. A modeling of the value of the patient in such trials would be helpful, particularly for discussions of benefit sharing.

Now a worldwide data-making enterprise, experimentality has thorny and sometimes contradictory value consequences. It may contribute to health benefits, but in leaving behind partial scientific evidence, unforeseen harms, and new medical and legal realities, it may also carry the seeds of its own failure. In September 2007 the inspector general of the Department of Health and Human Services published a report highlighting the FDA's failure to provide adequate oversight of clinical trials in the United States. The FDA, the document charges, is "unable to identify all ongoing trials and their associated trial sites," and "uncertainty of timing and lack of coordination impede FDA's ability to conduct . . . inspections" (OIG 2007: ii). The report estimates that the agency inspected only 1 percent of clinical trial sites between 2000 and 2005. Moreover, the FDA's guidance and regulations "do not reflect current clinical trial practices" (ibid.). Writing in response to this scathing report, the bioethicist Arthur Caplan (2007) asks, "How can it be that we know how many pigs, frogs, rats and monkeys are used in research and who uses them without knowing what is going on with respect to human beings?" The inspector general's report recommends improving information systems, creating a clinical trial database and an institutional review board registry, and establishing postauditing feedback mechanisms. Caplan agrees that such technical fixes are long overdue, but he notes that without political will and adequate funding from Congress, the FDA will not be able to remediate its failings or close loopholes.

When the focus of the experiment is on portability of data, the uncertainties of context and patient-related variables are engineered out. And this in itself, as some of my CRO informants suggest, is a risk that may show up later as harm. Institutional and personal risks and benefits deriving from this expansion are unevenly distributed; they favor industry's immediate goals. Moreover, current institutional ideas about patient protection remain rather narrowly conceived, and the ideas about harm (how it is produced in the broader contexts of experimentation) need specification amid the systematic uncertainties built into research.

The offshoring of clinical research is one particularly salient anthropological arm of the pharmaceutical industry inasmuch as it bounds and compares places and inasmuch as it makes its experimentality work. At stake is not just the moral relationship governing researcher and researched but the polities and citizens that are empirically in the making and that ethnography can chart and critique, particularly in relation to how people live with the new experimental investments that draw value from them. As it troubles the line between the experimental and the therapeutic, experimentality swamps central problems of inequality and creates new hierarchies of human vulnerability. Failures to protect the most vulnerable are almost assured owing to asymmetries of knowledge described in the cases I have described here. Bioethical critiques of such convoluted contexts of data production dwell too heavily on procedural issues—clinical conduct and informed consent—as if harm could be located exclusively within a traditional model of physician-induced harm.[33] The question of human-subjects protection moves beyond scripted procedures of informed consent into questions of legal capacities and aggregate values (Marks 2000). And, once more knowledge about the contexts of the production of pharmaceuticals evolves—the kinds of experiments, human participants, benefits, and harms they entail—we may be in a better position to rethink the criteria we use to define therapeutic value and, in the process, redirect our economic and scientific investments.

NOTES

I am grateful to Miriam Ticktin and Ilana Feldman for their invitation and feedback, and I thank the participants of the Government and Humanity workshop for their lively engagement and probing questions. I am also grateful to João Biehl for his insights and commentaries, as well as for the suggestions of the anonymous reviewers.

1   Spending by the top ten biopharmaceutical companies represents roughly 60 percent of total industry R&D spending. By 2008, industry R&D spending by the top ten biopharmaceutical companies reached US$65 billion. See Pharmbiosys 2007.

2   The pharmaceutical industry outsources not only R&D, but also manufacturing, packaging, distribution, and sales and marketing activities.

3   Outsourced clinical development expenditures reached US$23 billion in 2008, doubling from US$11.2 billion in 2003.

4   On the changing geography of clinical research, see OIG 2001.

5   Corporate evasion of regulation is a key focus in the new field studies of regulation. For an overview of field-based scholarship on law and the social sciences, see Greenhouse 2006.

6   Anthropological work on the ethics of biotechnology and new medical technologies has deepened the analysis of new biomedical technologies as they affect patterns of civic, medical, and commercial organization (Biehl 2007; Cohen 1999; DelVecchio Good

2001; Dumit 2000; Lock 2001; Petryna 2002; Rapp 1999; Scheper-Hughes 2004). New technologies raise new contexts of decision making over doing what is right; thus, beyond defining instances of moral certainty, ethics also involves a set of tactics that can generate new human conditions and events (Fischer 2003; Rabinow 2003; Sunder Rajan 2006).

7   See Harry Marks's (1997: 13) discussion of clinical trials as social institutions.

8   On AIDS as a domain of expansion of transnational medicine, see Dodier 2005. Arguably, one of the first global trials linked to "population science" and with explicit industry ties began in 1956, when Searle, a British pharmaceutical company, launched worldwide trials for their oral contraceptive pill Enovid (Lara Marks 2001). Initial field studies of the pill were carried out in Puerto Rico, believed to be well suited because it was outside the jurisdiction of the Comstock laws, which made the testing of contraceptives illegal in most U.S. states (ibid.: 265). Moreover, it was an island with a stable population, excellent for monitoring research; and it hosted a large family planning movement with networks of birthing clinics, excellent for attracting trial participants. As Lara Marks shows in her important book, *Sexual Chemistry*, research on the oral contraceptive—the century's first "lifestyle" drug—combined charity and international development efforts with pharmaceutical market expansion. Similar public-private patterns and partnerships continue today in the context of AIDS philanthropy (Biehl 2007).

9   For overviews and case studies of research abuses among minorities and other disadvantaged groups, see, e.g., Reverby 2000; Jones 1993 [1981]; Lederer 1997; Moreno 2000; and Rothman 1991. For critiques of the U.S. system for developing, testing, and using prescription drugs, see Angell 2005; Goozner 2005; Avorn 2004; Abramson 2004; Kassirer 2004; and Moynihan and Cassels 2005.

10   The new regulations also included other patients with serious diseases that had no alternative therapies.

11   Steven Epstein (1996) has written eloquently on social mobilization around AIDS and AIDS treatments.

12   The CRO market size is estimated at US$10 billion and growing. Revenue is increasing at an annual rate of 14–16 percent (ACRO 2008). Hundreds of CROs operate worldwide and employ a labor force of nearly one hundred thousand professionals (Rettig 2000). The move toward outsourcing increased dramatically in the 1990s. By 2004, nearly 42 percent of all pharmaceutical drug development expenditures had been committed to outsourcing; that compared with only 4 percent in the early 1990s (ARCO 2008).

13   Definition from http://www.investopedia.com/.

14   My use of "variability" is not meant to evoke the notion of cultural relativism here, although it has been considered in such terms (Christakis 1992).

15   Medical anthropologists more recently contend that a focus on cultural and moral difference in health care has become dangerous to the very people and practices that anthropologists have sought to explain, particularly in the contexts of massive epidemics and debates over treatment access. As the anthropologist and physician Paul Farmer and others point out, culture has been used to explain "why" the poor are somehow

less responsible regarding treatment regimes. The alarmingly slow development of the anti-HIV drug market in Africa, for example, has been attributed to the allegedly unreliable medical and economic behaviors of that continent's desperately poor HIV sufferers. These characteristics are said to heighten investment risk that in turn justifies limited access to low-cost drugs. The anthropologist and physician Jim Yong Kim and colleagues (2003) have exposed the way moral assumptions in health planning can further entrench inequality, justifying some interventions while disallowing others. Other medical anthropologists have shown how the local trajectories of pandemics are influenced by the logic of international policy and choices (Das 1999; Cohen 1999; Biehl 2007). This latter body of work explores how differences in the organization of institutions authorized to deal with health problems (state bureaucracies, welfare agencies, insurance companies, medical facilities, and religious and humanitarian organizations) result in distinct programs and policies. These not only differ greatly in form and content, they also can shape different courses of health and disease and influence the outcomes of both (Petryna and Kleinman 2006). These works move beyond emphasis on difference in the health arena and point to the kinds of empirical work required to address the moral, ethical, and cultural realities of emergent global drug markets.

16 Among the ten leading global pharmaceutical markets, the United States ranks first, holding a 60.5 percent share of pharmaceutical markets. Germany, France, Italy, the United Kingdom, Spain, and Belgium also rank among the top ten. Combined, they hold a 21 percent share, followed by Japan (15.1 percent), Canada (2.4 percent), and Australia (1.1 percent) (IMS Health 2009).

17 For further discussion on the "pill-taking life," see Gorman 2004, which characterizes this treatment saturation as a "kind of leap into the posthuman future. [The] jump is biochemical, mediated by proton-pump inhibitors, serotonin boosters and other drugs that have become permanent additives to many human bloodstreams. Over the past half-century, health-conscious, well-insured, educated people in the United States and in other wealthy countries have come to take being medicated for granted. More people shift to the pill-taking life every year, to the delight of pharmaceutical manufacturers."

18 In his landmark study *Inclusion* (2007), the sociologist Steven Epstein shows that the institutionalization of the U.S. inclusion-and-difference paradigm has led, among other things, to the reification of identity categories, thus drawing attention away from the inequalities that are rooted not in biology but society (281). Statistics speak to the importance of enhancing diversity. For example, in 1996, African American patients represented 11 percent of all cancer trial participants; by 2002 that number declined to 7.9 percent. Hispanics, who make up 9.1 percent of the U.S. population, made up only 3 percent of participants in clinical trials in 2002, down from 3.7 percent in 1996 (Murthy, Krumholz, and Gross 2004).

19 I am grateful to Harry Marks for pointing me to these issues and, specifically, to experimentality at work at the outset of modern drug regulation, which he illustrates in Marks 1997. On experimentality and HIV treatment programs, see Nguyen (2009).

20 The full name of this initiative is the International Conference on Harmonization of Technical Requirements for Registration of Pharmaceuticals for Human Use.

21 Testing requirements are typically established by national regulatory agencies and can differ from country to country; duplicate testing threatened to delay foreign market access and affect the global trade in pharmaceuticals. Japan, perceived to be a potential and large consumer market for U.S. pharmaceuticals, is famous for its intransigent regulatory system. See Applbaum 2006.

22 As a result, investigators and trial monitors have to be more careful so as not to include patients who are too sick or who are ineligible. "You may be providing treatment to someone who may not need it," as this informant put it.

23 According to the Office of the Inspector General (2001), these are partial estimates.

24 "Among the countries that have experienced the largest growth in clinical investigators [for commercially sponsored trials] are Russia and countries in Eastern Europe and Latin America" (ibid.: i).

25 The OIG's (2004) mission statement reads as follows: "The mission of the Office of Inspector General, as mandated by Public Law 95–452 (as amended), is to protect the integrity of Department of Health and Human Services (HHS) programs, as well as the health and welfare of the beneficiaries of those programs. The OIG has a responsibility to report both to the Secretary and to the Congress program and management problems and recommendations to correct them. The OIG's duties are carried out through a nationwide network of audits, investigations, inspections and other mission-related functions performed by OIG components."

26 The regulatory preference for the expansion of the IRB model was reflected in a recent National Bioethics Advisory Commission (2000) report recommending that studies submitted to the FDA receive ethical committee review both in the United States and in the country where research is being carried out (as opposed to the present situation, in which only foreign ethical review and approval is required). The report endorsed the idea of dual review with the provision that, if host countries have working ethical review committees, then only approval of those committees is required.

27 The Nuremberg Code was established as a response to Nazi medical experiments on prisoners in concentration camps. The code instituted norms of protection for subjects of scientific research experiments in the form of informed and voluntary consent and human rights guarantees.

28 For another instance of lawyers attempting to eliminate ethical restrictions, rather than to assert them, see Alden 2004.

29 This "expedient" experimentality first caught my attention in the context of the scientific management of the Chernobyl nuclear crisis. Here, too, the language of crisis became instrumental, granting legitimacy to experimentation when it otherwise might have had none. See Petryna 2002.

30 The domain of international law in remunerating human subjects violations is beyond the scope of this article. This problematic has been outlined in Veena Das's (1995) consideration of the Bhopal Union Carbide case.

31 While the RHGM-CSF trials were taking place in a clinic in Moscow, in Vienna, delegations of Soviet, European, and U.S. nuclear industry officials met to decide how to portray the scope of the disaster to the world. In their press release, they announced that

thirty-one clean-up workers had died in the course of work in the zone. As the officials were negotiating over this number, hundreds of thousands of workers were being sent into the zone in a massive, ongoing effort to contain the flames and radioactivity of a burning reactor. Humanitarianism in the form of scientific cooperation provided the Soviet state some protection in organizing this massive labor recruitment. The numbers of deaths are not known because of lax monitoring and medical follow-up (Petryna 2002).

32 There is currently a move to license sites just like one would a dentist's office, but the industry is strongly resisting this.

33 The ethics committee model for monitoring the conduct of research, as sociologists and anthropologists of bioethics have noted, turns the ethical universe in which researchers operate into an essentially procedural one. See Bosk 1999, 2002, 2005; Bosk and de Vries 2004; de Vries 2004; and Guillemin 1998. This deflects attention from structural circumstances that can contribute to increased risk and injustice. See Farmer 2002a; Macklin 1999; Chambliss 1996; and Marshall and Koenig 2004.

Biomimesis and the Weaponization of Life

Charles Zerner

"These [military robots] are amazing," he said breath-
lessly. "They don't complain, like our regular soldiers do.
They don't cry. They're not scared. This robot has no fear,
which is a good supplement to the United States Army."
—STEVE FEATHERSTONE, "The Coming Robot Army"

No agency admits to having deployed insect-size spy
drones. But a number of U.S. government and private entities acknowledge that they are trying. . . . The robobugs
could follow suspects, guide missiles to targets or navigate the crannies of collapsed buildings to find survivors.
—RICK WEISS, "Dragonfly or Insect Spy?"

What import these silent nods and gestures
Which stealthwise thou exchangest with her?
—FRIEDRICH VON SCHILLER (trans. S. T. Coleridge),
The Death of Wallenstein

WHAT STATES of nature do we dream? What
kinds of governance and powers over nature
do we wish to legitimize, empower, and enact?
What varieties of life—organismic, machinic,
or somewhere in between—will we fashion
and shape into new ecologies? Which states
of nature will we ratify as legitimate polities?
How will the creation of machinic organisms—
cyborgian creatures—be judged or regulated?

Can we begin to create an ethical, moral, and political language that lays the groundwork for judging and critically assessing interventions in the structure of the organic world, while avoiding the pitfalls of a fantasized, green, sacralized pristine nature, on the one hand, or an uncritical celebration of polymorphous hybridity, on the other hand? Can we fashion a discourse that does not elevate cyborgian creatures to the status of icon or fetish? I hope that this chapter provokes reflection on these questions.

It is a truism in the world of environmental studies, and in the world of conservation and environmental management programs, to observe that nature is irremediably fused with culture. Nevertheless, recent books with apocalyptic titles by influential environmental pundits and conservation biologists signal an alarmist and deeply nostalgic vision of the nature of nature, including Bill McKibben's *The End of Nature* (1989) and John Terborgh's *Requiem for Nature* (1999). In 2003 McKibben issued another shot across the bow of contemporary developments in engineering and biology titled *Enough: Staying Human in an Engineered Age.* Underlying these continuing salvos against the extraordinary growth of knowledge and capacity in the biological and engineering sciences is a fundamental faith in the moral wisdom of leaving an imagined pristine state of nature—whether embryos, human bodies, or whole landscapes—untouched.[1]

In dialogue with these proponents of an unchanged nature are the historical counternarratives and critiques of William Cronon, Charles Mann, and Michael Pollan. Cronon's (1995) critique of the American wilderness fetish, and his masterful historicization of the shifting boundaries and uses of the idea of untouched nature, set off a seismic charge in the emerging field of environmental history. Mann's (2005) masterful documentation of a tableau of humanly induced, richly productive modifications of habitat throughout the Americas added empirical depth to Cronon's history of the idea of nature. Pollan's (1991) witty accounts of nature's indeterminacy, on the one hand, and his comic-ironic tales of the human urge to shape, improve, and master nature through gardening, on the other, injected an appreciation for humane, ethically informed interventions (as well as human perversities in landscape and livestock management) in what might be called "the natural course of things."

In the late 1980s and early 1990s, Donna Haraway and her cyborg aficionado Chris Hables Gray argued persuasively for a deeper appreciation of the myriad forms of machine-organism fusions, to the point of considering the possibility of civil rights and liberties for cyborgian forms of life.

Arguing for a more plural, generous vision of kinship with an engineered nature, Haraway and Gray have been, simultaneously, more curious and more at peace with a variegated vision of biological citizenship and being in the world. In this catholic vision of life-forms, Gray and Haraway gesture toward all manner of cyborg creatures, offering eligibility for some form of citizenship in their newly imagined bio-cyber-human polity (see Haraway 1991; and Gray 2001).[2]

This chapter is written within and against a landscape of contentious debate about the proper place of robotic creatures and robotic nature on this planet, and the proper place of human, indeed humane interventions in the structure of life. Situated within a larger, longer conversation about the role of "the machine in the garden," to use Leo Marx's evocative phrase, neither the retrovision of an untouchable pristine nature nor an uncritical celebration of polymorphous cyber-creatures seems adequate to the task of making useful distinctions or analysis. This chapter aims to articulate some of the social implications that military cyber-creatures may have for societies at war and at peace in the early twenty-first century.

A variety of actors are engaged in the creation of robots and cyborgs. I focus here on the governmental, public, and private sectors. This includes the military as well as academic researchers engaged in making robotic and cyborg creatures for surveillance and possibly for attack on the battlefield. Many researchers are focused on the design of robots or other engineered mechanisms whose features are modeled on biochemical processes, entities, and structures found in "nature." Other researchers are engaged in designing and producing true cyborgs: creatures that involve, to greater or lesser degrees, the integration of cybernetic mechanisms with living organisms.

The Defense Advanced Research Program Agency (DARPA) funded the development of vivisystems and robots modeled on living organisms. How will these programs inform, in ways subtle and not so subtle, our ideas of nature, landscape, and the natural environment? Are threats—to humanity, to democratic process in times of war and peace, and to the quality of life and privacy in a civil society—at stake in the developments described here? Will the existence of these machinic-organismic interventions shape our behavior? How will the use of "smart robots" and vivisystems affect the "feel" of surveillance, targeting, and killing in war zones? How will these emerging forms affect our behavior as citizens in peacetime? How might the material existence of these organism-artifacts, as well as their presence as a cultural imaginary in times of political terror, affect the perceived boundaries of public and private realms? DARPA's "warbots" embody emerging visions of warfare "with a click," a vision that brings the human cost of fighting wars (on "our" side) down to the level of replacing robotic bodies on the battle-field (see Featherstone 2007). DARPA's insects, "robolobsters," "roboscor-pions" "ravens," and "swifts," and the rest of the uncanny menagerie being created at universities and in the laboratories of private corporations in the United States, Japan, and Europe, embody a vision of "command and con-trol" governance in sites of conflict by remote surveillance, targeting, and aggression. On screens and simulacra, these technoscience practices have implications for the constitution of future politics and the prosecution of future wars by remote control. These creatures embody a spuriously seduc-tive vision of wartime and peacetime "governance" that is cheaper, easier, and less costly: wars without bodies, blood, or human suffering.[3]

While raising questions about the political, ethical, and practical con-sequences of disembodied, robotic mediation of human and nonhuman environmental threats, in times of war and peace, at a moment when the tropes of "at home" and "abroad" seem increasingly less useful, I also hope to disturb our ideas about essentializing the nature and consequences of robots and cyber-organisms.

STEALTH NATURE: ROBOTS IN THE GARDEN OF CIVIL SOCIETY AND THE LANDSCAPES OF WAR

The world of systemic insecticides is a weird world, surpassing the imaginings of the brothers Grimm—perhaps most closely akin to the cartoon world of Charles Adams. It is a world where the enchanted forest of the fairy tales has become the poisonous forest in which an insect that chews a leaf or sucks the sap of a plant is doomed.—RACHEL CARSON, *Silent Spring*

There are also three great types of weapons that progress in importance through the course of the ages, in the age-old duel between offensive and defensive forces: weapons of obstruction (ditches, ramparts, bastions, armor and fortresses of all sorts); weapons of destruction (lances, bows, cannons, machine-guns, missiles, etc.); and finally weapons of communications (lookout towers and signals, infor-mation and transport carriers, optical telegraph, wireless, telephone, radar and satellites, among others).—PAUL VIRILIO, *Desert Screen*

Lurking Lizards often lodge, by Stealth,

Within the Suburbs, and purloin their Wealth.

—VIRGIL (trans. John Dryden), *Georgics* IV

The U.S. military is now engaged in stimulating the conceptualization and creation of smart "insects"—or cybugs, if you will—that can "see," "hear," sense," and potentially "attack" in remote battlefields. For centuries in Euro-American popular culture and science, insects have been "good to think with," configured as images of social organization charged with a multiplicity of valences ranging from the utopian to dystopian (see Brown 2006). In the entomological rhapsodies of the nineteenth- and early twentieth-century French entomologist Jean-Henri Fabre, insects are moral beings, endowed with the "wisdom of instinct" and exquisitely calibrated motor skills.[4] In the mid-twentieth century, especially during the Second World War and in the decades following in the United States, insect representations were reconfigured (Russell 2001). Edmund Russell tracks the literature of the American armed forces as well as the propaganda of Japanese and German masters of information to show how insects, including cockroaches and mosquitoes, became infrahuman, insectivorous aliens that merited extermination. The mid-1950s witnessed the appearance, "on film, screen, and television," as the expression goes, of gigantic insects whose Academy Award–winning appearances and dimensions were caused by radiation from nuclear testing (see Masco 2004). In E.O. Wilson's scientific work during the 1960s and 1970s, ant behaviors provided a model for communication and caste in complex, evolving societies.[5] In the last decade of the twentieth century, and especially since the attacks of September 11, 2001, insects as well as microorganisms have been increasingly represented, in popular mediations, as objects of fear and contamination, on the one hand, and, on the other, as we shall see below, as instruments of surveillance, of "seeing" and remote visibility, in landscapes of war.[6]

In the examples below, I consider how design and research supported by what President Dwight D. Eisenhower in his farewell speech of 1961 perceptively called the "military-industrial complex," and what we might, in the world since September 11, call the "military-surveillance" complex, are engaged in the design of *stealth nature*. Ancient meanings of the word *stealth* associate the concept with theft, with taking or stealing secretly and wrongly. Stealth was, at least by the seventeenth century, associated with furtive or underhanded actions, acts accomplished by eluding observation or discovery. Contemporary notions of stealth incorporate these older meanings and add to them the idea of stealth as a branch of technology concerned with rendering aircraft and other weapons-delivery platforms hard to detect by radar. The creation of "smart," variable fusions of organisms and engineering into military "vivisystems"—hybrid creations that can move, fly, hover, creep, crawl, and scale vertical walls that only a gecko lizard might negotiate with impunity—are stealthy in both senses. These creatures are difficult to detect, due to their scale, mode of operation, or appearance or structure in specific contexts. In this sense, stealthy vivisystems are undetectable in the same ways that chameleons, butterflies, and walking sticks are stealthy. At the same time, these vivisystems and robotic "organisms" are stealthy creatures in the older sense of stealth as stealing: vivisystems and insectlike robots are stealing in plain view: they are sensing and absorbing information and images of persons, processes, and territories in the twenty-first-century battlespace. The data gathered by these cyber-creatures are transformed and relayed to specialized, restricted audiences at remote locations: places where operators are making real-time battlefield decisions.

The concept of stealth nature, as I use it in describing DARPA's endeavors, has two senses. The primary sense of stealth nature I intend are those attributes of organisms, developed through evolutionary processes, that aid in making an organism less detectable or invisible, although "in plain sight." Stealth nature in this sense refers to those built-in evolutionary processes that result in an organism's capacity, in relation to other organisms in its environment—its significant "public," if you will—for concealment or disguise or deception by varying its appearance, form, or behavior. DARPA, in this sense of stealth nature, is involved in a mimetic mode or, more precisely, a biomimetic mode, imitating not only the structure or appearance of specific organisms but the evolutionary strategy of stealth nature. The second sense of stealth nature arises through the discrepancy in scale between insects and humans: it is an attribute that merges only when the scale of the insect is put alongside the scale of the human. DARPA's programs fund and fashion stealth nature through both biomimetic evolutionary and relational strategies (see Whyte 1951).

Interventions in nature involving the design and weaponization of insects and microorganisms lead us to question whether it is useful to speak of the militarization of nature or what I call the weaponization of life. Is the use of natural structures, electrochemical processes, or the creation of true cybugs—cybernetic organisms that integrate living forms and human-made electro-chemo-mechanical structures for military-surveillance purposes—different from the appropriation of other natural structures or processes for military-industrial purposes? How might the weaponization of nature affect the ways scientists, engineers, military officials, and scientific elites, as well as nature conservationists and environmental ethicists, view the nature of nature?

At the level of mediation, we need to ask how these developments, often sponsored by DARPA and executed by private corporations and university-affiliated scientists, are described, imagined, and imaged in emergent rhetorical formations, Web sites, advertisements, the popular press, and the scientific literature. There are also questions of public response and mobilization: What accounts for the striking absence of environmental and social resistance, or even response(s), to these programs of nature fashioning of hybrid entities and threat creation?[7] What accounts for the absence of critique, countertactics, and resistance to the use of living organisms, appended to silicon circuits, for military purposes?

We know that insect societies have a long and varied history as social imaginaries. Insect republics, whether totalitarian or democratic, reactionary or left-wing, have been imagined as models of efficiency, societies characterized by elaborate hierarchies and ruthlessly precise social division. What kind of a republic of insects was Jonathan Schell imagining when his bleak assessments of the states of a post–nuclear holocaust nature and society appeared in 1982? Arguing eloquently in *The Fate of the Earth* against the proliferation of nuclear arms, Schell's republic of insects was a profoundly dystopian vision of an ecologically devastated planet. On a degraded planet contaminated by radiation, disoriented insects, incapable of receiving and interpreting ultraviolet spectrum, were disabled. They were rendered incapable of locating and pollinating plants. And the failure of plants to be fertilized by insects resulted in the death of our ecologically interconnected green and blue planet. A radiation-saturated planet resulted, for Schell, in fatal ruptures in the ecological web.

It was not images of a postapocalyptic insect republic, however, that appeared in March 2006 on DARPA's Web pages. What appeared was a request for proposals to create cyborgs, or "vivisystems," that could fly, hop, move, "carry payloads," and see on the battlefield: "vivisystems" that could function as innocuous inhabitants of the natural world. Since 2006 DARPA has been sponsoring research programs on the uses of biological systems for military purposes. To date, the program has invested about $12 million in projects at MIT, the University of Michigan, the Boyce Thompson Institute for Plant Research, the University of Arizona, and Washington University in St. Louis, among other sites at universities and private sector corporations across the United States. Joseph Masco (2004: 537) describes the tripartite character of these programs:

> The DOD (Department of Defense) research on controlled biological systems currently takes the form of three novel deployments of nature: (1) vivisystems, the use of insects (bees and moths) and other animals as "environmental sentinels" (currently tracking chemical weapons, explosives, and radioactive materials in the environment); (2) hybrid biosystems, an effort to create cyborg bugs and animals for surveillance or, as the project puts it, to "integrate living and nonliving components for novel device applications"; and (3) biomimetics, building mechanical devices that mimic the abilities and structures of living beings, particularly insects.

Masco offers a cogent reflection on DARPA's vivisystems, hybrid biosystems, and biomimetics programs: "Combining insects and nanotechnology for surveillance promises a whole new kind of cyborg creature, remote controlled and deployable for surveillance in the literal form of the fly on the wall" (ibid.).

This chapter engages with the fashioning of insects and other living creatures in two modes: (1) the creation of vivisystems, in which microsystems are integrated within the bodies of living insects to augment, "scavenge," or amplify and extend their capacities (true cybugs), and (2) the fashioning of "smart" robots whose anatomy and circuitry, or other anatomical-electrical-biochemical aspects, are the source for engineering that robot's bodily capacities. I focus below on one form of DARPA research on living systems, the effort to create cyborg insects known as Hybrid-Microelectromechanical Systems (HI-MEMS; see Lal 2006b). In March 2006 DARPA published a "presolicitation bid" for HI-MEMS which stated:

> DARPA seeks innovative proposals to develop technology to create insect-cyborgs, possibly enabled by intimately integrating microsystems within

insects, during their early stages of metamorphoses. The healing processes from one metamorphic stage to the next stage are expected to yield more reliable bio-electromechanical interface to insects, as compared to adhesively bonded systems to adult insects. Once these platforms are integrated, various *microsystem payloads can be mounted on the platforms with the goal of controlling insect locomotion, sense local environment, and to scavenge power.* (DARPA 2006; my emphasis)

Since this request for proposals for HI-MEMS, DARPA grantees have been working with living forms of insects—especially with insects in the pupal stage—in or on which governmental hands will be inserting chips and sensors. These insect-machine hybrids are now only what we might call "insect dreams"—the aspirations of a military-security apparatus focused on generating remote forms of relatively mobile surveillance devices that can see and sense with low probability that they (the insect-cyborgs) will be seen or sensed—the proverbial "fly on the wall."

According to DARPA, the vision underlying this program is the creation of "technology to reliably integrate microsystems payloads on insects to enable insect cyborgs" (Lal 2006a). The objectives of the HI-MEMS program are to "develop technology to enable highly coupled electro-mechanical interfaces to insect anatomy" and to "demonstrate MEMS platforms for electronic locomotion, control power harvesting from insect, and eliminate extraneous biological functions" (ibid.).[8]

> Cornell University researchers have succeeded in implanting electronic circuit probes into tobacco hornworms as early pupae. The hornworms pass through the chrysalis stage to mature into moths whose muscles can be controlled with the implanted electronics.

> The pupal insertion state is shown in insert "i" in the picture seen above. The successful emergence of a microsystem controlled insect is shown in insert "ii;" the microsystem platform is shown held with tweezers. The X-ray image (A) shows the probes inserted into the dorsoventral and dorsolongitudinal flight muscles. CT images (B) show components of high absorbance indicating tissue growth around the probe. (Christenson 2008)

The DARPA discourse lucidly articulates the basis for HI-MEMS "insects" by asking rhetorically: "Why not use insects directly?" Insects were used in attempts at behavior modification in "bee training" and in the use of nonsurgically altered insects with "insect backpacks" attached. Natural creatures were neither sufficiently predictable nor controllable to the desired degree. DARPA explains: "In previous exploratory research to manipulate insects, it was found that the instinctive behaviors for feeding and mating—and also responding to temperature changes, prevented them [the bees] from performing reliably."

We are witnessing not only a mutant ecology, to use Joseph Masco's (2004) apt phrase, but also a new, instrumentalized, industrialized, and managerial conception of species, their behavior, and ecosystemic functioning. How will the HI-MEMS cyborgs be evaluated? DARPA tells us: "The final demonstration goal of the HI-MEMS program is the delivery of an insect within five meters of a specific target located at hundred meters away, using electronic remote control and/or global positioning system (GPS)" (Lal 2006a).

The performance specifications of this insect-machine design are clear. The optical scanning and telemetric capacities of the desired, successful HI-MEMS creature are laid out crisply: "The insect must be able to transmit data either indefinitely or until *otherwise instructed*. The insect-cyborg must also be able to transmit data from DOD [Department of Defense] relevant sensors, *yielding information about the local environment*. These sensors can include gas sensors, microphones, video, etc." (ibid.; my emphasis).

Nature, at least nature in the form of a DARPA-made technoscience-insect cyborg, is to be something "instructed." As publications recounting DARPA-funded research illustrate, nature's living bodies are also the objects of incisions, invasions, and insertions at certain critical moments in their life cycle (see Alper Bozkurt et al. 2009). The DARPA cyborg insect will "obey" remote commands and must compliantly yield "information about the local environment. . . . Although flying insects are of great interest (e.g. moths and dragonflies), hopping and swimming insects could also meet final demonstration goals" (Lal 2006a).

One portion of the DARPA prospectus for insect cyborgs emphasizes their automaton-like characteristics: in conjunction with delivery, the insect must remain stationary indefinitely or until otherwise instructed (ibid.). Other portions of the DARPA documents emphasize their biological advantages, suggesting the vampire-like character of mechanical systems dependent on the "heat and mechanical power" of living insects. In a passage worthy of *Aliens!*, the DARPA writer tells us that HI-MEMS platforms must "demonstrate technologies to *scavenge power from insects*. During lo-comotion, insect thorax (*sic*) generates heat and mechanical power, which may be harnessed to power the microsystem payload. This capability may eliminate the need for batteries, and make the HI-MEMS self powered" (ibid.; my emphasis).

In this passage, DARPA employs the familiar image and understanding of a parasite as a living creature that derives sustenance from another living creature, the host organism. In this DARPA version of nature, military imagineers propose the creation of microelectronic mechanisms that drain, like alien parasites, the energy from a living system.[9] In this vision, the microelectronic mechanical component becomes the parasite "harvesting" or, more darkly, "scavenging" energy from living organisms. A distinct version of the alien-invasion narrative is sketched: Nature is drained of its life-giving energy by mechanisms.

How are these imagined forms of insect-cyborg nature conceptualized and valued? What are some of the constituent values that inform a militarized lens on nature? DARPA Web sites provide answers: There are "insect advantages" on the battlefield. DARPA tells us that insect cyborgs offer "resilient flight" and "built-in stealth." The monarch butterfly, for example, offers advantages of "size, speed, distance, and height [altitude]." Like a perverse Mark Trail, the nature guide of the 1950s syndicated comic strip, genially providing entertaining anecdotes as he walks the wooded trail, DARPA informs us that "monarchs can travel for 3000 miles without feeding for 75 days," therefore a cyborg monarch butterfly would offer the possibility of "long-distance missions."[10] DARPA emphasizes the speed of dragonflies as another military asset: "Dragonflies can travel at 45 mph for 2–3 hours," thus offering the military virtue of "fast missions." A particular species of butterfly indigenous to Brazil, *Thysania Agrippina*, offers the military advantage of being able to carry "huge payloads." Another butterfly, *Cocytius duponchel*, collected at the altitude of eleven thousand feet, offers the possibility of high-altitude "airborne missions" (Lal 2006b).

DARPA's documents reveal a world in which new kinds of electro-chemical-mechanical interventions are made in the structure of nature, inserted, etched, or inscribed within individual organisms. They also reveal a shift in the ways members of the military, the strategic policy community, and some scientific experts gaze on nature and its potentialities. The dream of HI-MEMS as instruments of warfare, indeed biological warfare, constitutes a conceptualization and body of environmentally interventionist practices that are radically different from earlier attempts at using biological systems and processes as weapons, such as the use of malaria-saturated blankets deployed against Native Americans in the eighteenth century or the earlier use of corpses, flung over the ramparts of medieval castles.[11] DARPA's militarized nature is robotic yet living, responsive to orders, visually and electronically well endowed, physically mobile, and docile, a nature responsive to government orders.

THE NATIONAL GEOGRAPHIC TOUR: IN THE LAND OF NATURE'S WARRIORS

In an era of military triumphalism that entertains a fantasy of a risk-reduced, remote-controlled battlefield mediated in part by cyborg insects, it is not surprising to learn that living species are seen as potential military assets. In the pages of *National Geographic*, a paragon of enthusiasm for the conservation of pristine nature, we can find nationalism fused with a celebratory view of the HI-MEMS insect world and the cyber-battlefield. In the television trailer for the National Geographic Explorer special titled "Secret Weapons," nature is configured as an arms race: "For millions of years, a kind of *arms race has been raging under our noses.* Its soldiers can walk on water, defy gravity, render themselves invisible to enemy eyes, and detect a heat signature several miles away. These are *nature's warriors—animals and plants that have survived in a harsh world by evolving an arsenal of remarkable abilities and weapons*" (National Geographic 2005; my emphasis). Thomas Hobbes's notorious formulation "Nature red in tooth and claw" is here supplanted with an image of the natural world as an armed camp, a landscape of internecine strife in which animals and plants are reconfigured as "nature's warriors," equipped with "an arsenal of remarkable abilities and weapons" and engaged in an "arms race." Barely a decade ago, scientists, especially conservation biologists and environmental nongovernmental advocacy groups, were asking the citizenry of global civil society to conserve the rainforest because it might offer the next round of antibiotics or cures for cancer.[12] During the administration of George W. Bush, Americans saw an instrumentalist vision of nature's options for protecting an American army increasingly stretched across the globe by providing teams of stealthy cyber-insects and increasing numbers of remotely piloted drone aircraft. Engaged in what administration officials cast as "the long war," nature, at least in some quarters, was now cast as an "inspiration" and a resource for "advantage" to the U.S. military: "Now the U.S. military is taking inspiration from nature to gain advantage on the modern battlefront. Scientists are harnessing the strength and flexibility of spider silk to develop an ultralight body armor that may increase protection from bullets and shrapnel. Others are looking to butterfly wings as they *design sophisticated camouflage that will allow troops and vehicles to blend imperceptibly into a changing landscape and be undetectable to heat-seeking sensors*" (ibid.; my emphasis). The humble beetle observed by Fabre at L'Harmas, his overgrown, weed-infested garden in southwestern France, has become an object of the entomological-military sublime for U.S. forces and DOD/DARPA grantees: "Even a tiny beetle has something to offer—its natural heat-seeking ability is helping scientists develop lightweight infrared detectors that may one day change the shape of nighttime warfare" (ibid.).

During the Obama administration, the use of uninhabited aerial drones, including the Predator, has increased significantly. Jane Mayer (2009) reports:

> The number of drone strikes has risen dramatically since Obama became President. During his first nine and a half months in office, he has authorized as many C.I.A. aerial attacks in Pakistan as George W. Bush did in his final three years in office. The study's authors, Peter Bergen and Katherine Tiedemann, report that the Obama Administration has sanctioned at least forty-one C.I.A. missile strikes in Pakistan since taking office—a rate of approximately one bombing a week. So far this year, various estimates suggest, the C.I.A. attacks have killed between 326 and 538 people. Critics say that many of the victims have been innocent bystanders, including children.[13]

For *National Geographic*, a holy alliance of "U.S. forces and innovative scientists and engineers" are allied to venture "into battle zones and cutting-edge labs," along with the Geographic Explorer staff, "to see how emerging technologies inspired by some of nature's most amazing designs may one day help protect troops and civilians" (National Geographic 2005). Whereas biologists like E. O. Wilson (1994) once wandered in a state of near-religious transport in the tropical rainforests of Indonesia, transfixed and inspired by nature's complexity, beauty, and aesthetic variety, nature is rapidly becoming a source of technical inspiration for the military-industrial complex. Nature's capacity for biological and chemical inventiveness will now be tapped for its use-value on the battlefield. A new species of the romantic vision? Nature as a source of military awe.

Donna Haraway's articulation of the figure of the cyborg, that fusion of machine and organism catapulted to academic notoriety in a textual frisson of praise, awe, and irony, is both celebratory and ambiguous, as Hugh Gusterson reminds us:

> Haraway's thought is built around the central figure of the cyborg, which she deploys as an *ambiguously utopian figure that dramatizes the dangers and possibilities of life in a globalizing technoscientific age.* . . . Haraway embraces the hybrid figure of the cyborg as her icon and, to use her own word, as her "kin." For her, a cyborg is not just a combination of human and machine, but, more elusively, any hybrid entity that *rewrites our sense of the possible, by reworking relationships between any combination of animal, human, vegetable, and machine.* (Gusterson 2005: 121; my emphasis)

SENSES OF SIGHT AND STEALTH:
CAMOUFLAGE, SUBTERFUGE, SURVEILLANCE

How does the question of visibility and invisibility fit into this tale of insects and machines? Although these are creatures that can be seen, they are unobtrusive. HI-MEMS insects are difficult to see not only because they are small but because they look as if they are part of the fabric of nature.

There is, however, another sense in which visual perception and strategies of visibility (or invisibility) are key dimensions of the HI-MEMS: HI-MEMS vivisystems are forms of life that are designed to see, scan, and survey a landscape and to relay features of the landscape deemed significant back to remotely situated human beings. These cybugs are conceptualized as part of an emerging landscape of nature, surveillance, and global governance through monitoring. What is the imagined landscape? People sitting at screens, possibly halfway around the world, at remote terminals, scanning the visual information being transmitted and making decisions about whether to attack or change the trajectory, speed, and altitude of the reconnoitering cyborg creature. These creatures' "eyes" and other sensory

1 Lobster-inspired robot, mine sweeper. Invented by Don Massa and Joseph Ayers. "Robo-Lobster, a 7-lb., 2-ft.-long crustacean made of industrial-strength plastic, has a bigger job to do: detecting and destroying mines buried in the surf zone. At least, that's how the U.S. Navy plans to use the robot once developers at Massa Products deliver their final version next year. The current prototype mimics a real lobster's movements to negotiate all types of coastal terrain. The plastic antennas sense obstacles; the eight legs can propel it in any direction; the two claws and tail keep it stable in turbulent water" (*Time.com* N.d.). Photo courtesy of Don Massa and Joseph Ayers.

"organs" are relaying visions and information that may become part of a battle plan or actual strike. Whether with "natural eyes," humanly created "eyes," or cyborgian hybrid "eyes," these creatures are patrolling landscapes (and seascapes) where it is too dangerous or difficult for a human being to walk or swim (see fig. 1).

While nongovernmental environmental organizations, artists, and writers are working on strategies of visibility, technologies of exposure of threats to the public, the gaze of these cyborg creatures set loose in the air, in the water, and on the ground of the potential battlefield is to be invisible and, at the same time, to surveil: to be the eye above that looks down on the scene, and to expose the alien, the enemy, the threat, to the remote human scanner.

These cyborg bees, swarms of hornets, wasps, dragonflies, and butterflies, moreover, will not be sending signals back to a remote yet potentially enormous citizenry if their bioengineers succeed. This is not an act of public communication. Their telemetry is for a restricted viewing audience—perhaps a group of human monitors working in secret, hidden, "safe" environments, in contrast to the embodied tactics of street performers and environmental mediators. HI-MEMS insects may well become part of a military-intelligence apparatus that was broadly expanded in the years following the attacks of September 11, 2001.

On November 17, 2006, the *Sydney Morning Herald* published a story about an insect-like robot under the headline "Israel Developing Killer Bionic Hornet" (Reuters 2006). The article suggested the emerging capacities of warbots: "Israel is using nanotechnology to try to create a robot no bigger than a hornet that would be able to chase, photograph and kill its targets, an Israeli newspaper reported. The flying robot, nicknamed the 'bionic hornet,' would be able to navigate its way down narrow alleyways to target otherwise unreachable enemies such as rocket launchers, the daily *Yedioth Ahronoth* said."

Descriptions of these flying machines blur mechanical and biological realms, producing a sense of the uncanny.[14] While the Reuters story describes a robot, it merges cyborg capacities with biological imagery, conjuring up a marvel or a monster of sorts: the bionic hornet. About a year later, in October 2007, a story in the *Washington Post* recounted a sighting of flying cyborg-insects on a surveillance mission in the public square:

> Vanessa Alarcon saw them while working at an antiwar rally in Lafayette Square last month. "I hear someone say, 'Oh my god, look at those,'" the college senior from New York recalled. "I look up and I'm like, 'What the hell is that?' They looked kind of like dragonflies or little helicopters. But I mean, those are *not* insects." This is just one of the questions hovering over a handful of similar sightings at political events in Washington and New York. Some suspect the insect like drones are high-tech surveillance tools, perhaps deployed by the Department of Homeland Security. Others think they are, well dragonflies—an ancient order of insects that even biologists concede look about as robotic as living creatures can look. (Weiss 2007)

As of this writing, it is hard to pin down the status of these reports. Are these stories intentional releases of information organized by government press agencies, defense business updates, or sightings of vivisystems being tested? While many robotic insects, marine crustaceans, and birds are in various stages of feasibility, no controllable insect vivisystems are yet viable. It is possible, if not probable, that many of these sightings represent an emerging cultural imaginary rather than an already existent empirical reality. It is a truism about American society since September 11 that images of potential terror as well as pervasive surveillance in governmental discourse, programs, and funding flows have dominated popular culture, news, and fiction.[15] Bioterror feature films and novels have proliferated, augmenting and amplifying political rhetoric. Sightings of cyberbugs may constitute a phenomenon parallel to the sightings of UFOs during the 1950s and 1960s, when fulminating anxieties about the Cold War and fallout from nuclear testing spread across the nation.

In another vein, we might ask whether citizens are about to be "faced"— in public spaces, alleys, streets, doorways, or hovering over whole landscapes—with the specter of a potentially lethal gaze of the cyber-insect or the pure drone, a remotely operated form of emerging life-mechanism whose "eye in the sky" scans the terrain for targets.[16] What will a human being, viewing her computer or television screen on the other side of the world, see, think, or feel when viewing images transmitted from a "bionic hornet" or the cyborg butterfly hovering in an alley in the Middle East, or in a ghetto district of Los Angeles? How will the mediation of killing through "point and click" technologies, linked to hovering cyborgs or warbots, affect the act of killing other human beings? Given the speed at which these technologies are developing, the expression "a lethal gaze" may no longer be a metaphor.[17]

Are the questions posed here an indictment of robots? Are they a bill of particulars against cyborgs? I argue, rather, that questions of human intentions, context, and agency in evaluating robotic and cybernetic interventions are critical. In the final section of this chapter we turn to the story of an ur-cyborg, the Golem.

ENGINEERING ENVIRONMENTAL VISIBILITY: ARTS OF RESISTANCE IN AN ERA OF BIOCYBERNETIC REPRODUCTION

In times of shock resulting from massive technological change, Walter Benjamin asserts, the human sensory system reverses its historic role and, instead of enabling the body to receive and respond to new stimuli, its goal becomes aesthesis, a numbing of the organism, a deadening of the senses and repression of memory. Reflecting on the technologically induced incapacity to register sensory stimuli, the environmental ethnographer Joseph Masco (2006: 12) offers this question: "What might be the social consequences of living in a world where the everyday has been so thoroughly colonized by the possibility of annihilation that, for most, it has become simply banal? . . . If in fact people can be so anesthetized by the possibility of extinction that it no longer seems to register, how do we now regain our senses in order to ever begin to answer such questions?"

The invisibility of lethal environmental risks—whether mutagenic radioactivity or toxic compounds in air, water, soil, or our own bodies—has bedeviled environmentalists since the inception of global and local activist movements. In a world of toxic, invisible realities, the problem becomes how concerned artists, scientists, and groups of lay persons, organized in local, national, as well as transnational nongovernmental networks, can create strategies of visibility, forms of mediation that embody and render accessible to the senses the toxic environmental substances and forms of energy that cross ecological boundaries and penetrate human bodies with impunity, causing multigenerational harm.

Many of the lethal compounds produced by contemporary industry and government-sponsored facilities are not accessible to the senses. Human beings are not biologically equipped to sense the hazards of radioactivity; nor do they perceive, under normal circumstances and levels of contamination, the presence of chemical compounds or radioactive materials that are significant causes of disease, debility, and mortality in human and nonhuman populations. These risks are not literally visible—they cannot be seen—and in a broader metaphoric sense they are not accessible to any of our senses. Our bodies are, in some profound sense, not equipped to perceive and respond to these emerging dangers (Beck 1992). At the same time, our bodies register, concentrate, and eventually constitute a tangible record of environmental toxicity. Many chemical and radiological threats, moreover, only become visible beyond normal human temporal scales: certain mutations only become perceptible on a multigenerational scale.

The problem and the challenge for a variety of differently situated citizens—artists, local residents, writers, scientists, and public policy experts, as well as a panoply of local, regional, and nongovernmental environmental advocacy organizations—is how to render "visible," or accessible to our sensory apparatus in its broadest sense, the nature and immanence of these

toxic and radiological threats: How are regional and transnational solidarities creating and deploying "strategies of visibility" and "tactics of sensibility"—techniques of translation and mediation that engage our capacities to perceive and respond to sensory stimuli—in order to create more
fully informed, alert, and engaged publics? An archaic meaning of *sensibility* is readiness to respond to suffering or to the pathetic. How do strategies of visibility create possibilities for awareness, empathy, and informed
interventions?

Designers of "strategies of visibility" face a second problem: Contemporary environmental risks are not only inaccessible to normal sensory perception. Strategists of visibility must reckon with the nature of an image-
saturated society. Marketing and advertising bombard citizens with images.
We are immersed in the world of the simulacrum, the imitation. The proliferation of imagery—on Web sites, advertisements, on all communicative
networks—creates the prospect of an anaesthetized public, stupefied, sated,
and incapable of significant response. Since September 11, 2001, moreover,
society is actively reorganizing politics and imagery circulated in the public
sphere: to the extent the state can manipulate citizens, the themes of terror
and state security dominate the imagination, dwarfing prior concerns for
human and planetary health. In addition, decades of apocalyptic imagery
in environmental campaigns complicate the efforts of strategists of environmental visibility. Current attempts to render environmental risks visible are thus compounded by histories of inflammatory rhetoric generated
by environmentalists, Hollywood, and, more recently, the state security
apparatus.

In the preceding section I examined the ways actors from the governmental, public, and private sectors make visible the hazards, targets, and
environmental risks to "our" soldiers operating on remote battlefields. Robotics, cybernetics, and telemetry are also being deployed by artists, engineers, writers, filmmakers, video and performance artists, and nongovernmental activists who are making invisible environmental threats accessible,
as sensuous phenomena, to varied publics. Their inventive restructuring
and deployments of robotic, cybernetic, and biological mediations of environmental threats to public well-being are often ingenious, provocative
uses of the same technologies being developed and deployed by the military. While the military robots and vivisystems are being deployed in simu-
lations and "battle-space," contemporary artist-engineers are intervening in
contemporary equivalents of the agora, the public sphere par excellence,

on and within their bodies, in varied media and through varied forms of mediation (Catts and Zurr 2002, 2004–5; Hirsch 2005).[18] What bridges military and artistic uses of robotics and biological organisms? How are artists and engineers using robots as tools of surveillance, discovery, and resistance to threats generated by industry and government? How are artists using emerging design and fabrication techniques and technologies, actual organisms and human bodies, cybernetics and telemetry to form strategies of visibility? In which contexts are these technologies deployed, at which publics are they aimed, and for what purposes is the information transmitted? The animated inventions of one artist-engineer, Natalie Jeremijenko, provide one illustration of use of robotics, remote sensing, and cybernetic technologies in the service of the public and the public sphere.

STRATEGIES AND TACTICS OF VISIBILITY: THE ARTS AND MOBILE TECHNOLOGIES OF NATALIE JEREMIJENKO

> What would happen if radioactivity itched? Nuclear policy, as well as dealings with modern mega-hazards in general, would confront a completely changed situation: the object being disputed and negotiated would be culturally perceptible.—ULRICH BECK, *Risk Society: Towards a New Modernity*

Almost half a century ago, Rachel Carson, a meticulous marine biologist, created a revolution in public consciousness—and, to a lesser extent, in the practices of industry and governmental oversight—by publishing *Silent Spring* (1994 [1962]).[19] Her book was a critique of the consequences of invisible, undetected releases of the chemo-industrial complex on the health of human and nonhuman life. At the same time, the book was an intoxicating paean to the interconnectedness of living systems, human and nonhuman, and the ecological substrate on which all living systems depend. How are we to understand the worldwide provocation and subsequent mobilization that *Silent Spring* precipitated? Carson's book challenged industry with its fastidious and, within the limitations of her time, comprehensive compilation of a massive scientific literature, culled from journals, newspapers, and the testimony of scientific colleagues. It was also shocking because scientific evidence was woven into and mediated through prose that was alternately rhapsodic, moralistic, and saturated with disturbing and devastatingly effective tropes. Images of invisible poisons, likened to nuclear radiation, yet penetrating our soils and stored below the kitchen sink, stimulated a sense of the uncanny. Fears of the Atomic Age were coupled with a new source of invisible threats—chemical compounds—and these fears reverberated throughout the American public and beyond.

In the post–*Silent Spring* era, we continue to be inundated by chemicals that disrupt our immune and reproductive systems. And we are, at least in certain zones of the globe and society, inundated by scientific information.[20] Surf the Web. At the same time, popular films saturated with special effects have rendered banal the image of planetary catastrophes. The tropes of *Silent Spring*—the homely images of an imagined 1950s suburban community—no longer have the capacity to move audiences.

The problem then becomes determining what forms of mediation can possibly make information accessible to the communities most affected by the chemo-industrial complex, the nuclear-business complex, and the global warming industries? How can the findings of science be mediated in ways that can inform, move, and mobilize communities for effective political action? How can access to environments and environmental information important to our health be rendered visible and affect differently positioned publics? If aesthetics is the domain of knowledge that shows how we are viscerally affected by objects and environments (how we feel what we feel, how our sensorium registers and responds to stimuli) as opposed to the anesthetics (substances that render us incapable of feeling) then one of the key questions for contemporary environmental artists and activists is how to mediate the findings of science in ways that activate and provoke, that reach the body as well as the mind, to create the conditions for mobilization.

Natalie Jeremijenko's experiments at the juncture of engineering-art-environmental staging, her creation of scientifically legible, sensuous, mediagenic performances, her attempts to make the findings of science moving, even mobilizing, in the early twenty-first century, are an attempt to ask and to probe this question: What are the conditions of contemporary environmental mobilization?[21] Jeremijenko is engaged in performance, the politics of visibility, and making significant dimensions of our environment accessible to multiple publics and a broad spectrum of the senses. In "The Trouble with Wilderness; or, Getting Back to the Wrong Nature," the environmental historian William Cronon reminds us of the appalling costs of the American dichotomization of the "wild," located outside the metropolis, and the world of the city, imagined as a zone of pure culture. To

2 Dog tag for a feral robot named Chuzi. Photo courtesy of Natalie Jeremijenko.

the degree that we imagine, write, and draw this dichotomy in our environmental plans, we create pure sanctuaries of "untouched nature" and pure urban spaces devoid of oxygen, islands of pure garbage, and rivers saturated with invisible, toxic pollutants. Jeremijenko's projects, including *Amphibious Architecture*, are directed at reinvigorating the living edge of our human interactions with the natural world. While her interventions have a wonderfully ludic, performative quality that suggests mime, political theater, and environmental "happenings," her work is linked to the earlier, profoundly destabilizing work of Rachel Carson. Jeremijenko's robotic dogs are cybernetic instruments intentionally structured to sense, track, and locate sites of environmental danger—radioactivity or chemical toxicity—in rural and urban environments.

Jeremijenko's *Toxic Feral Dog Release* interventions are about making the frightening explicit, about locating danger in the landscape, and about specifying, rendering accessible to public view and investigation, the toxic threats of the industrial and postindustrial chemo-nuclear industrial techno-complex (see fig. 2). Like a court jester in Shakespearean play—the one person permitted to point, in the play within a play, toward the poison, or the malefactor—Jeremijenko's *Feral Robotic Dog Pack* constitutes an antic and deadly serious drama about nature and its corruption. Rather than

3 Jeremijenko's students releasing "feral dogs" in Arizona. Photo courtesy of
   Natalie Jeremijenko.

handing out tired, moralistic environmental placards with slogans painted
onto boards, Jeremijenko works with young collaborators, children in the
Bronx and in the American Southwest, as well as their teachers, to repro-
gram the dogs so they function in new ways attuned to their locally pol-
luted, toxified, or irradiated sites. Commercial, mass-produced, robotic
toys—expensive automata performing banal actions—are thus elevated to
environmental tools: mobilized, environmentally smart prostheses.

Jeremijenko sets the hounds running. She and the kids that live in the
neighborhood of toxic sites release the pink and yellow feral robotic dog
pack, each wired canine outfitted with sensors capable of detecting and
tracking the trajectory of particular, toxic chemical signatures. The dog
pack has detected military waste when roaming over regions of Florida. In
south Phoenix the pack has located chemical hazards in the American desert outback and reared up on its hind legs (see fig. 3).

At the offending source point, the mechano-hounds are programmed
to bay, rear, and gesture with their bodies. Rather than cornering the proverbial raccoon up the tree, children from the Bronx and their mechano
pack have treed the offending polluter. The dogs rear up and point in the
direction of environmental (in)justice. As director, Jeremijenko releases the

management of the robotic dog pack into the hands of the young—who are not typically included in public processes of environmental assessment and monitoring, or the discovery of health-affecting environmental facts. African American and Hispanic children, the historic victims, or the children of victims of toxic releases, become environmental investigators. The release of the toxic dog pack joins futuristic robotics with a version of the southern hunt with hounds. But in Jeremijenko's hands the event may include the great-granddaughters of former slaves, or the children of Caribbean migrants whose ancestors once labored and died in the cane fields, or the grandchildren of Mexican braceros, in holding, managing, and releasing the dogs to sniff out the traces of poisons designed, manufactured, and released—dumped, spilled, leaked, or leached into the soils of the Bronx, the wetlands of New Jersey, or the bombed and mined landscape of the American Southwest, which Valerie Kuletz (1998) has called a "landscape of national sacrifice."[22] While her techno-dogs are temporarily "kenneled" in art museums throughout the country, Jeremijenko releases them into the hands of the dispossessed, the marginal, the information-poor in the information age—those whose bodies have carried the burden, since the Second World War, of the American environment—waters, air, soil, food, and communities that have been irradiated and saturated with toxins, transmogrified through "Better Living through Chemistry" and a Walt Disney fantasy world of "Our Friend the Atom." Rather than the Environmental Protection Agency, it is the local children who, in Jeremijenko's artful, irreverent environmental dramas, are releasing important information about toxins and their sites in our neighborhoods. "Although these dogs cannot bite," Jeremijenko asserts, "they can bark! They can begin to expose the problem and insist on media attention to it."[23]

On her roller skates in New York City, or wheeling around her high-technology lab at the University of California, San Diego, with her engineering students, Jeremijenko is often likened to the figure of the mime and the court jester, covered in sparkles while her children and graduate students play. Pleasure and play are indeed part of her performative strategies and political calculus. The ludic is disarming. But Jeremijenko's environmental interventions are, at the same moment, deadly serious. This engineer–environmental director–artist is fashioning novel forms of social interaction, in collaboration with marginal communities, engineering cultures, nonhuman engineered creatures, as well as the media world, at the sites of invisible, lethal pollution that we breathe and ingest on a daily basis. Part of Jeremijenko's power is her capacity to fashion such playful, disarming interventions. Carsonian homilies and kitchen-saturated metaphors just do not work these days. Whether Jeremijenko's scripts and dramas will affect public consciousness in significant ways is an open question. Does it matter how we position her, or name her métier, or specify her primary performance genre? Theater director? Performance artist? Information specialist? Techno-provocateur? Earthworker? Environmental artist? In a post-Carsonian world, in which environmental terror, as material reality and as spectacle—in television ads, subway posters, and movie theaters—is shockingly commonplace, Jeremijenko's environmental-engineering dramas and interventions are ironic, amusing, and surprising attempts to make threats visible, to disseminate important information, and to mobilize publics in aesthetically moving ways. One hopes that her dramas, and the information they make accessible to wider publics, may become, in James Scott's words, ingeniously effective "weapons of the weak."

REFLECTIONS

In Jewish legend, [the Golem is] a figure made of clay, etc., and supernaturally brought to life; in extended use, an automaton, a robot.
—*Oxford English Dictionary*

Scientists discover the world that exists; engineers create the world that never was.—THEODORE VON KARMAN, HI-MEMS Proposers Day, March 14, 2006

So it was not humanoid automata that formed the new armies but synthetic insects (synsects)—ceramic microcrustacea, titanium annelids, and flying pseudohymenoptera with nerve centers made of arsenic compounds and with stingers of heavy, fissionable elements.—STANISLAW LEM, *The Upside-Down Evolution*

The Baal-Shem smiled when he was told that the official version of the *Golem*'s work proclaimed that "the accident was caused by a red bolt of lightning, which killed the people and destroyed the building."—HENRY ILIOWIZI, *In the Pale: Stories and Legends of the Russian Jews*

In the euphemistic geek-speak of the U.S. military, the Total Urban Dominance Layer System will encompass "long hover and loiter propulsions systems, multidiscriminate sensors and seekers, mini- and micro-air vehicles, mini-lethal and non-lethal warheads, autonomous and man-in-the loop control algorithms, and a strong interface with a battlespace information network." Entirely robotic attack aircraft or "dominators" are already under development by the U.S. Air Force. As the blurb from one manufacturer puts it, "these dominators will be capable of completing the entire kill chain with minimal human involvement."

—STEPHEN GRAHAM, "Cities and the 'War on Terror'"

"Talmudic lore," Stefan Helmreich (1998: 5) recounts, "tells us of a Rabbi Low of Prague who, in 1580, fashioned a creature of clay called the Golem, which he brought to life by breathing into its mouth the ineffable name of God, an act that appropriated the divine creative power of the word." The story of the Golem can be read as a story about human arrogance, ingenuity, and craft in fashioning an artificial being, a man of clay who will do man's bidding: a creature under a regime of "command and control." The tale of the Golem may also be read as a story of technology or nature gone out of control: a parable on the limits of human capacities to control the world of artifice or the world of nature.

Many film versions of the Golem tale contain a creature that is ugly, ungainly, and crude: a monster that runs amok and must be destroyed. In contemporary laboratories across the country, however, a more exalted view of the biological world, and of human ingenuity in fashioning things from nonliving substances as well as living creatures, modeling complex mechanisms on natural structures and processes, is widespread. Yoseph Bar-Cohen (2006: v), a physicist who has specialized in using electroactive materials and mechanisms to mimic natural processes and structures, a procedure known as biomimesis, asserts: "Over the 3.8 billion years since life is estimated to have begun to appear on Earth, evolution has resolved many of nature's challenges leading to lasting solutions with maximal performance using minimal resources. Nature's inventions have always inspired human achievement and have led to effective algorithms, methods, materials, processes, structures, tools, mechanisms, and systems."

Bar-Cohen's reverence for biological structures and processes reflects a recent branch in the long genealogy of scientific inspiration from natural structure and operations (see Bar-Cohen 2006). It is linked to Fabre's meditative gaze at the structure and behaviors of spiders, wasps, and mantises. It is related to Leonardo da Vinci's observations on and drawings of the flight of birds: awe at a world ingeniously constructed and pulsating with the quickening contact of life. The exquisitely fashioned camouflage of a butterfly's wings. The mosaic dome of a dragonfly's eye. The brilliantly calibrated grace of a walking stick's slender legs.

In the eighteenth century Romantic poets sought out manifestations of the world of wild nature. For William Wordsworth and Samuel Taylor Coleridge, among others, the experience of being in the presence of wild nature provoked a powerful, disturbing sense of something alien, profound, and even terrifying.[24] In the late twentieth century, wild nature was still a sight and a site for the sublime. In his autobiography, the biologist E. O. Wilson (1999) testified to the transports he experienced in what he believed to be the pristine wilderness of tropical rainforests.[25] In an interview with David Takacs (1996), an environmental historian who has tracked the development of the idea of biological diversity, Wilson offered a few reflections: "When I pick up another species of *Pheidole* [an ant genus], for me it's like seeing the creation: I'm the first to see this species. I'm the first to see why it's different, what's unique about it, and so on. And that gives me immense pleasure in just dealing with the fine detail. God is in the details: that's really what it comes down to. So I've always had that feeling."

William Cronon (1995) tells us, however, that until the beginning of the eighteenth century it was nature, and not the world of clever, humanly made artifice, which provoked anxiety, fear, even terror.[26] In the early twenty-first century, another turn is being made in the history of the gaze on the natural world and on the human landscape: A world of "roboflies" and robots that may resemble (or be) walking sticks, dragonflies, beetles, or birds, where "microfliers reach for the skies" and Israeli bionic hornets "navigate . . . down narrow alleyways to target otherwise unreachable enemies" and "DARPA solicits bids for insect cyborgs," where resting butterflies' sensory capacities may be augmented by undetectable "backpacks" carrying micro-electromechanical components (Lal 2006b). When the "insect advantages" of "resilient flight," "built-in stealth," and "efficient actuators" are installed into micro-robots or vivisystems that look like, act, and seem like real insects, what feelings may be aroused as we walk along the shore and a praying mantis alights on a nearby bayberry branch (ibid.)? When the DARPA program using "object insertion ability into butterfly pupas to reliably insert microsystems for insect control" creates microflyers that are successful cyborg-microsystems, how will we regard nature? With awe or suspicion? With an instrumental eye for what we can garner, harvest, or, in DARPA-speak, "scavenge"? With an eye for weaponry? With an ear for the grinding of gears? Will citizens eyeball the merest bug for signs of telemetry?

It is not only *our* gaze that is important here. When that exquisitely camouflaged monarch butterfly alights on a branch beside our park bench in the center of Manhattan, *its* gaze is equally important. What information is it sending by telemetric or other forms of electronic signaling, and where and to whom is this information being sent? What are the political and practical implications of these strategies of invisibility? In this emerging biotechnological environment, the boundaries between mechanism and organism are increasingly and intentionally blurred.

I call the newly constituted species of cyborg nature and the landscape in which they are situated "stealth nature": a nature that surveils, that itself is hidden in plain sight. Stealth nature is camouflaged by and through its everyday form. Surveillance, as scholars of the public sphere and politics increasingly inform us, has multiplied in the cities, centers of population and terror.[27] Nature, whether in the country or the city, can no longer be thought of as an unambiguous site of repose, calm, and the tamed aesthetics of the sublime. In the late eighteenth century and throughout the nineteenth, contact with the wild, before intense storms and fantastic mountains, stimulated a sense of the sublime, the alien, and an anxiety so intense as to sometimes rise to the level of terror. In the twenty-first century and beyond, will certain geographic regions become sites of apprehension? Will species of a certain kind stimulate anxiety? In a moment of incredible creativity in the biological and engineering sciences, well-known species—the black widow spider or the coral snake—may not be the only harbingers of danger. Given DARPA's enthusiasm for avian and insectoid forms of stealth nature, arachnid and avian anxieties may proliferate. If the dreams of DARPA's bioengineers come true, stealth nature will be equipped with sensors and linked to command and control centers near and distant. On the battlefield, stealth nature may save lives but may also bring the eye of military intelligence, danger, and even death (Christenson 2009).

Surveillance and spying are not new in the history of civilization or in the history of military operations. After September 11, 2001, surveillance instruments bristled on the surfaces of governmental and private buildings (Parenti 2003). These instruments proliferated in subway systems and on public roads, walls, entrances, and exits. Like the natural camouflage on a butterfly's wings, stealth nature vivisystems provide their own natural cover.

Unlike stationary camera "eyes" affixed to subway entrances, vivisystem eyes in the sky will follow us. Will there be creatures looking at us in the alley, on the street, in the subway, in Grand Central Station, in the great outdoor public park near the wondrous public library? Will they follow us? Nature, after all, is everywhere.

And so is humanity. If the realm of the human is made, in part, by differentiation from the animal, then how does and how will the constitution of a weaponized other affect our idea of the human? How will these new forms of nature remake the social? What happens when the other (the animal), against which the human is continually defined, is radically remade through weaponization and cyborgization? As efforts are undertaken to "borg" the human soldier-body (Shachtman 2003), on the one hand, and to dissolve rigidly maintained boundaries, affective and cognitive, between the human and the animal (Pepperberg 1999, 2008), on the other hand, it is time to examine redefinitions of the idea of humanity and the social.

Might the weaponization of the insect other facilitate a new normal for the idea of humanity? It is commonplace to assert that we are already cyborgs: pacemakers, psychotropic drugs, and cybernetic limbs constitute part of a new bodily and psychological normal (Gray, Mentor, and Figuroa-Sarriera 1995). Alterations in the body of the diminutive alien, the six-legged insect, may ease the transition to a norm of weaponized personhood: not the Terminator whose innards are steel and circuitry but a weaponized Borg whose flayed skin may reveal the pulsing heart and viscera of a human being. What if the experiments to create weaponized stealth nature, as well as ongoing efforts to engineer fully integrated cyborgian soldiers, constitute a technosocial trajectory leading to a fully roboticized armed force? How will these material changes in the soldier's body affect thinking about the body, self, personhood, or human agency? The question *What happens to the social in an era of weaponized life?* becomes more concrete when we ask: "What happens to the idea and practice of a representative democracy when the price of war is no longer paid in bodily terms—the blood, limbs, and lives of citizens?"

Are shifts in the ways we imagine stealth nature affecting the ways soldiers in Afghanistan and Iraq, in the theater of operations, think about and model the enemy? Is the enemy still being conceptualized in insectoid terms, as it was imagined and imaged during the Second World War (Russell 2001)? How is the proliferation of entomological analogies like "swarming," for example, affecting images of the political and the human as well as the reconceptualization of military tactics?

Whether we are observing swarms of mechanical-looking dragonflies hovering over protests in the public square or tracking the manic movements of Jeremijenko's feral robotic dogs homing in on toxic vapor trails in the south Bronx, we are situated in what the art critic and philosopher W. T. J. Mitchell calls "the age of biocybernetic reproduction." On the power of the biocybernetic figure, Mitchell (2005: 316) observes: "Films like *Blade Runner*, *Alien*, *The Matrix*, *Videodrome*, *The Fly*, *The Sixth Day*, *AI*, and *Jurassic Park* have made clear the host of fantasies and phobias that cluster around biocybernetics: the specter of the 'living machine,' the reanimation of dead matter and extinct organisms, the destabilizing of species identity and difference, the proliferation of prosthetic organs and perceptual apparatuses, and the infinite malleability of the human mind and body have become commonplaces of popular culture."

Hugh Gusterson (2005: 122) reminds us in his meditation on the poetics and politics of the rhetoric of Frankenfood—genetically modified forms of agricultural crops—that we cannot afford the luxury of being techno-fundamentalists, cyberphobes who unilaterally reject these amazing, astonishing life-forms: "The 'natural,' then, is a fiction, a word that freezes the world around us, unnaturally, at a moment in time, after—or maybe before—the last set of changes we made, a way of erasing the traces of our own agency in our environment." The insect-cyborg we reject may be the very creature that, by ascending the walls of a nuclear reactor with gecko-like feet, may prevent another Chernobyl-like nuclear meltdown from happening. Cyborg-cell forms may constitute the next technoscience wave of interventions in cardiology or oncology.[28] Like the Golem, an ambiguous, polyvalent figure, threatening to go out of control,[29] cyborgs are deeply ambiguous, structured in ever more complex ways, deployed in a bewildering variety of contexts, made to function on many scales. While we cannot afford to be phobic or paranoid about these boundary-rupturing creatures, we should not be sanguine about their existence, either.[30]

Perhaps it would be more prudent to ask, case by case, in situ and in vivo, what kinds of insects we wish to create, and to impregnate with the technical embryos of our civilization. Hybrid creatures deserve mixed metaphors and provoke mixed feelings. What intentions animate our insertions of the machinic in the most intricate structures of life—whether at microbiological levels of organization, at the level of the human body, or within entire ecosystems? Neither the rabbi nor the Golem, neither the engineer nor the microbiologist, neither the artist, the activist, the anthropologist, nor the Pentagon planner should be immune from scrutiny. These are questions about the co-constitution of humanity and nature. These are questions as much about the social world we will inhabit as the idea of the animal. These are questions concerning the mediation and manipulation of life and the choice of technologies of war: how we observe, track, target, and kill human beings. These are questions about the intentions which animate our gaze on nature and the nature that, in turn, gazes on us: the nature we create.

What human interventions in the structure of the world—in the body of nature and within our own bodies, in the body social and within the body politic—at war and at peace, in public and in private, will we recognize as humane or inhumane? As welcome additions to species-being? These are questions implicating culture and technology, politics and biology, engineering and design, as well as ethics, which cut across these domains of knowledge. As military-funded biologists and engineers engage in that extraordinary process we call biomimesis, gazing thoughtfully at the natural world, we might ask, with Schiller: "What import these silent nods and gestures / Which stealthwise thou exchangest with her?" The existence of these insects as fantasy, and their potential materialization, provokes curiosity, awe, and repulsion. At the same time, they jolt us with a frisson of the uncanny. Vivisystems and biomimetic robots will not only inhabit a new nature. They constitute elements in new ecologies and bio-cyber-mechanical landscapes.

The existence and continuing development and deployment of vivisystems for military, civilian-governmental, and commercial purposes will affect ideas about freedom of expression in the public sphere and the boundaries between the public and private. As biomimetic and robotic technologies develop, they will be increasingly deployed, accelerating the roboticization of combat. The use of these biocybernetic technologies will alter the dynamics of assault, complicating the sequence of decision-making links in what military technocrats call the "kill chain." The use of these biocybernetic devices will alter practices of surveillance and crowd control on the "home front" as well as combat in remote "theaters of operation." What happens if the algorithms governing the biomimetic robot, or the armed vivisystem, fail to effectively distinguish between combatant and noncombatant, committing, if one may appropriately use the vocabulary of agency, a massacre? Who is responsible? Is anyone responsible? Can one even speak of responsibility? Would this be a violation of the Geneva Convention or a product-liability case? Is it any kind of "case" at all? The near-term reality of vivisystems and their biomimetic robotic kin, in scenes of combat and "homeland" security operations, is a specter—unsettling how we imagine and wage war, how we fashion nature and the social, haunting the landscape of the present.

NOTES

Several colleagues generously offered insightful comments on earlier drafts of this chapter, including Tania Munz, Jake Kosek, Stefan Helmreich, Bob Desjarlais, Joseph Masco, Elizabeth Hartmann, and Toby Volkman. I gratefully acknowledge their contributions. Thanks also to research assistants Angela Galli and Sharlane "Charlie" Prasad for help in preparing this manuscript. I am grateful to Miriam Ticktin and Ilana Feldman, who invited me to participate in the workshop "On Government and Humanity" at New York University and to contribute to this volume. Earlier versions of this chapter were presented at the 2007 Annual Meetings of the Society for the Social Study of Science in Montreal, at the panel "War and Weapons" and at the 2008 meetings of the American Anthropology Association in San Francisco. A earlier version of the section on Natalie Jeremijenko appeared as "Engineering the Arts of Environmental Seduction: The Arts and Technologies of Natalie Jeremijenko," *New Media Caucus* 2(3) (2006): 38–43.

1 In 1964, Leo Marx painted a portrait of American ambivalence toward the machine and industrialism in his masterwork, *The Machine in the Garden: Technology and the Pastoral Ideal in America*. Marx's reflections were merely a mid-twentieth-century *compte rendu* in a conversation that can be traced back to Virgil's *Eclogues*.

2 For a view of the landscape of cyborg scholarship in the mid-1990s, see Gray, Mentor, and Figuroa-Sarreira 1995.

3 On cybernetically mediated war, see der Derian 2001; and Gray 2001. See also Gray, Mentor, and Figuroa-Sarreira 1995. For a useful description of recent efforts to fashion combat-ready robots, and the questions raised about responsibility for killing by robot in the battlespace of the twenty-first century, see Featherstone 2007. On the effort of the Bush administration's "war on terror" to "rework imaginative geographies separating the urban places of the U.S. 'homeland' and those Arab cities purported to be sources of 'terrorist' threats against U.S. national interest," see Graham 2006.

4 On Fabre's *Souvenirs entomologiques: Etudes sur l'instinct et les moeurs des insectes*, see also Fabre and Miall 1914. Fabre's portraiture of insects and their behaviors was far more various than might be inferred from this assertion. While his characterizations of insect personalities and behaviors were deeply romantic, his portraiture runs the gamut from the demonic (cf. his essay on the praying mantis) to the pastoral, humble domestic, and familial (cf. his portrait of the dung beetle). See Pressly 1973; and Caillois, Frank, and Naish 2003 for analyses of figure of the praying mantis in art and literature.

5   I am indebted to Tania Munz for bringing my attention to this issue. See E. O. Wilson 1971; see also Wilson and Orster 1979; as well as the corpus of Wilson's earlier work on ants.

6   Both *Them!* (Douglas 1954), in which irradiated, giant ants pose a dire threat to humanity (and sugar factories), and *Mimic* (del Toro 1997), in which human-size, morphing insects are enhanced by genetic engineering as well as natural processes of mutation, embody fears of the outcomes of technoscience interventions in natural bodies and processes. "In Manhattan, cockroaches are spreading a deadly disease that is claiming hundreds of the city's children. Entomologist Susan Tyler (Mira Sorvino) uses genetic engineering to create what she and her colleague (and husband) Peter Mann (Jeremy Northam) call the Judas Breed, a large insect (looking like a cross between a termite and a praying mantis) that releases an enzyme that kills off the disease-carrying roaches by speeding up their metabolism. The Judas Breed work spectacularly and the crisis is abated. Since the Judas Breed have also been designed to only produce one male able to breed, and they keep it in their care, the hybrid species should die out in a matter of months. Some years later, people begin to go missing in the subways and tunnels under the city. Susan, Peter, and their staff learn that they severely underestimated the Judas Breed's ability to adapt to its conditions. The Judas Breed has found a way to reproduce and has evolved in order to better hunt a new food source. To everyone's horror, they discover that the Judas' new food source is humans, and now the insects have grown to be as big as people and can mimic the appearance and behavior of humans with uncanny accuracy. Susan and Peter have learned that huge swarms of the Judas Breed are living beneath the city in the subway system, and with the help of Leonard (Charles S. Dutton), a transit system police officer, they search out the insects, whose quick evolution (one fertile male and hordes of females) also made them humanoid, before they can take over the city and from there the world" (Wikipedia 2009).

7   In contrast to the absence of a critical scholarly literature or social movements linked to stealth nature, the literature as well as public comment on genetic engineering in the nongovernmental sector is vast and often intemperate. In the United States and in Europe, the transnational literature of genetically modified organisms often focuses on their "unnatural," hybrid nature. See Gusterson 2005, and Haraway 1991. On Haraway's views on genetic engineering, see Myerson 2000.

8   One cannot help but wonder what "extraneous biological functions" are and what conception of nature this phrase means to suggest.

9   The term *imagineers* was coined by the Walt Disney Corporation to describe its employees who imagine and engineer theme parks and other projects. "Walt Disney Imagineers come in all forms; artists, writers, architects, landscape architects, engineers, model builders, construction managers, technicians, designers and a whole range of others" (Wikipedia 2007).

10 Apparently Mark Trail was a tougher character than I remembered: "*Mark Trail* was a daily newspaper comic strip created by the American cartoonist Ed Dodd. Introduced on April 15, 1946, the strip centers on environmental and ecological themes. Mark Trail, the main character, was a photojournalist and magazine writer whose assignments

lead him into danger and adventure. His assignments inevitably lead him to discover environmental misdeeds, most often solved with a crushing right cross" (Wikipedia 2008).

11   On the history of biological warfare, see Miller, Engelberg, and Broad 2001; and Guillemin 2005.

12   See Greene 2003 for an ironic account of the fetishizing of tropical forests and the aura of traditional medicinal knowledge. For a less critical account, see Balick, Elisabetsky, and Laird 1996.

13   On the risks of using drones, and the Pentagon's plans to create an increasingly roboticized army, see P. W. Singer (2009) and Noel Sharkey (2008a, 2008b, 2008c).

14   Amit Lal, the director of the DARPA HI-MEMS project, credited *Sparrowhawk* (1990), a science-fiction novel by the biology professor Tom Easton, as his inspiration for DARPA HI-MEMS. Easton's novel describes animals enlarged by genetic engineering and "outfitted with implanted control systems." See Christenson 2009.

15   On the emergence of terror talk and the terror imaginary, see Orr 2005. On the production and proliferation of bioterror, see Sarasin 2006.

16   On the increasing role of surveillance technologies, networks, and robotic components in the "revolution in military affairs," the work of Stephen Graham (2007a, 2007b) is particularly relevant.

17   On speed and its relationships to wide-ranging societal changes, see Virilio 2006; see also Virilio 1989.

18   See W. J. T. Mitchell 2005 for an astute tour of emerging forms of art that engage biological and cybernetic materials, technologies, and processes. For divergent views on the ethics of contemporary uses of biological materials and organisms in the arts, see Lynch 2003; see also Baker 2005.

19   See Carson 1994. On the origins and efficacy of Carson's tropes, and their relationship to the larger technoscience and environmental context, see Lutts 1985. See also McCay 1993.

20   On the accessibility and intelligibility of environmental information in Web-based mediations, see Fortun 2004. See also PERI 2007, which seeks to render Environmental Protection Agency data more understandable and useful to members of the lay public seeking to understand emissions levels from industrial sites in their area.

21   On the environmental arts of Natalie Jeremijenko, see Gertz 2004; Case 2004; and KQED-TV 2003. See also Make Audiozine 2005. For a more detailed description of the Amphibious Architecture Project, see http://www.nyu.edu/projects/xdesign/ (accessed February 18, 2010).

22   On the nuclear landscape of the American Southwest, see also Masco 2006.

23   Author interview with Natalie Jeremijenko, June 14, 2008.

24   By the early twentieth century, William Cronon (1995) asserts, "the terrifying character of the wild had been tamed, managed, and safely bounded with a system of National Parks. For mid-twentieth century Americans, at least, nature was no long wild in tooth and claw, but rather, the object of postcards, auto tours, and panoramas viewed from horseback."

25 See also Lewis 2003. See Takacs 1996 for a full-scale exposition of the philosophies and animating assumptions of several prime movers in the history of the idea and value of biological diversity.

26 Alternately regarded as an automaton, as a serf or servant of human intention, or as a human figure brought to life through the divine intervention of God or the esoteric knowledge of men, Golems and Golem narratives reveal an intense ambivalence. See Wiener 1964 for an account of the myth of the Golem and its relationship to the development of cybernetics in the 1940s.

27 See Mann, Nolan, and Wellman 2003; and Parenti 2003 for discussions of surveillance, civil liberties, and countersurveillance.

28 Eugene Thacker (2009) contrasts the capacities of MEMS with bio-BioMEMS in the following terms: "While MEMS have generally found application in everything from airbags in cars to digital processing, one of the leading fields of MEMS research has been in biotech development include: in vivo blood pressure sensors (with wireless telemetry), oligonucleotide microarrays (DNA chips), and microfluidics stations (labs on a chip)." On the possibilities of nanotechnology, see Feynman 1992; for a later reassessment of Feynman's views on nanotechnological possibilities, see Roukes 2001.

29 For one of the earliest and, now, classic reflections on the ambiguous nature of the cyborg, see Wiener 1964.

30 Paul Virilio's comments on "technical essentialism" or a "cybercult" are acute: "Just as there is religious 'essentialism,' there is a technical 'essentialism' through technical fundamentalism, just as frightening as religious fundamentalism" (in der Derian N.d.).

BIBLIOGRAPHY 〜

Aaseng, Nathan. 1992. *The Peace Seekers: The Nobel Peace Prize*. Minneapolis: Lerner.

Abadia-Barrero, C. E., and Castro A. 2006. "Experiences of Stigma and Access to HAART in Children and Adolescents Living with HIV/AIDS in Brazil." *Social Science and Medicine* 62(5): 1219–28.

Abélès, Marc. 2006. "Globalization, Power, and Survival: An Anthropological Perspective." *Anthropological Quarterly* 79(2): 483–508.

Abraham, John. 2007. "Drug Trials and Evidence Bases in International Regulatory Context." *Biosocieties* 2:41–57.

Abramson, John. 2004. *Overdo$ed America: The Broken Promise of American Medicine*. New York: Harper Perennial.

Adams, Vinceanne, with Thomas E. Novotny and Hannah Leslie. 2008. "Global Health Diplomacy." *Medical Anthropology* 27(4): 315–23.

Adato, Allison. 1998. "Kids' Pictures to God: What Children Want God to See." *Life*, March.

Adelman, G. 1987. *Heart of Darkness: Search for the Unconscious*. Boston: Twayne.

Agamben, Giorgio. 1992. *Stanzas: Word and Phantasm in Western Culture*. Trans. Ronald L. Martinez. Minneapolis: University of Minnesota Press.

———. 1998. *Homo Sacer: Sovereign Power and Bare Life*. Trans. Daniel Heller-Roazen. Stanford, Calif.: Stanford University Press.

———. 2004. *The Open: Man and Animal*. Trans. Kevin Attell. Stanford, Calif.: Stanford University Press.

Agrawal, Arun. 2001. "State Formation in Community Spaces: The Forest Councils of Kumaon." *Journal of Asian Studies* 60(1): 1–32.

———. 2005. *Environmentality: Technologies of Government and the Making of Subjectivities*. Durham, N.C.: Duke University Press.

Agrawal, Arun, and Elinor Ostrom. 2001. "Collective Action, Property Rights, and Decentralization in Resource Use in India and Nepal." *Politics and Society* 29(4): 485–514.

Alden, Edward. 2004. "U.S. Interrogation Debate: Dismay at Attempt to Find Legal Justification for Torture." *Financial Times*, June 10.

Allen, James, with Jon Lewis, Leon F. Litwack, and Hilton Als. 2000. *Without Sanctuary: Lynching Photography in America*. Santa Fe, N.M.: Twin Palms.

Alley, Kelly D., and Daniel Meadows. 2004. "Workers' Rights and Pollution Control in Delhi." "Environmental Rights," special issue of *Human Rights Dialogue* 2, no. 11. www.cceia.org/index.html (accessed December 15, 2009).

Althusser, Louis. 1969. "Marxism and Humanism." *For Marx*, 219–47. Trans. Ben Brewster. London: Penguin.

———. 1976. *Essays in Self Criticism*. Trans. Graham Locke. London: New Left.

Amadi, Elechi. 1991. *The Concubine*. London: Heinemann.

Amman, Diane Marie. 1999. "*Prosecutor v. Akayesu*: Case ICTR-96–4-T." *American Journal of International Law* 93(1): 195–99.

Anderson, Benedict. 1991. *Imagined Communities: Reflections on the Origin and Spread of Nationalism*. Rev. and extended edn. London: Verso.

Anderson, David, and Richard Grove, eds. 1987. *Conservation in Africa: People, Policies, and Practice*. Cambridge: Cambridge University Press.

Ang, Ien. 2001. "I'm a feminist but . . . : 'Other' Women and Postnational Feminism." *Feminism and "Race,"* ed. Kum-Kum Bhavnani, 394–409. Oxford: Oxford University Press.

Angell, Marcia. 2005. *The Truth about the Drug Companies: How They Deceive Us and What to Do about It*. New York: Random House.

Anglund, Joan Walsh. 1993. *Peace Is a Circle of Love*. New York: Gulliver, Harcourt Brace.

Appadurai, Arjun. 2006. *Fear of Small Numbers: An Essay on the Geography of Anger*. Durham, N.C.: Duke University Press.

———, ed. 2001. *Globalization*. Durham, N.C.: Duke University Press.

Applbaum, Kalman. 2006. "American Pharmaceutical Companies and the Adoption of SSRI's in Japan." *Global Pharmaceuticals: Ethics, Markets, Practices*, ed. Adriana Petryna, Andrew Lakoff, and Arthur Kleinman, 85–111. Durham, N.C.: Duke University Press.

Aranguren, José Luis. 1966. "Openness to the World: An Approach to World Peace." *Daedalus* 95(2): 590–606.

Arendt, Hannah. 1951. *Origins of Totalitarianism*. New York: Meridian.

———. 1958. *The Human Condition*. Chicago: University of Chicago Press.

———. 1959. "Reflections on Little Rock," *Dissent* 6(1): 45–56.

———. 1961. *Between Past and Future*. New York: Viking.

————. 1970. *On Violence*. New York: Houghton Mifflin Harcourt.

————. 1973 [1951]. *The Origins of Totalitarianism*. New York: Harvest/HBK/ Harcourt, Brace.

————. 1996. *Love and Saint Augustine*. Chicago: University of Chicago Press.

————. 2002. *Denktagebuch: 1950 bis 1973*. Muenchen: Piper.

Ariès, Philippe. 1962. *Centuries of Childhood*. Trans. Robert Baldick. London: Jonathan Cape.

Aristotle. 1953. *Generation of Animals*. Trans. A. L. Peck. Cambridge, Mass.: Harvard University Press.

————. 1957. *Aristotle Politica*. Ed. W. D. Ross. Oxford: Clarendon.

————. 1998. *Politics*. Trans. C. D. C. Reeve. Indianapolis: Hackett.

Asad, Talal. 2003. *Formations of the Secular*. Stanford, Calif.: Stanford University Press.

————. 2007. *On Suicide Bombing*. New York: Columbia University Press.

Association of Clinical Research Organizations (ACRO). 2008. "CRO Industry at a Glance." http://www.acrohealth.org/ (accessed December 21, 2009).

Augustine, Saint. 1984. *The City of God*. New York: Penguin.

Austin, J. L. 1975. *How to Do Things with Words*. Cambridge, Mass.: Harvard University Press.

Avorn, Jerry. 2004. *Powerful Medicines: The Benefits, Risks, and Costs of Prescription Drugs*. New York: Knopf.

Babylonian Talmud. 1978. Ed. Isidore Epstein. Brooklyn: Soncino Press.

Bains, Paul. 2001. "Umwelten." *Semiotica* 134(1/4): 137–67.

Baker, G. Sherston, ed. 1908. *Halleck's International Law or Rules Regulating the Intercourse of States in Peace and War*, vol. 1. London: Kegan Paul, Trench, Trubner & Co.

Baker, Tom. 2005. *The Medical Malpractice Myth*. Chicago: University of Chicago Press.

Balibar, Etienne. 2004. *We, the People of Europe? Reflections on Transnational Citizenship*. Princeton, N.J.: Princeton University Press.

Balibar, Etienne, and Immanuel Wallerstein. 1992. *Race, Nation, Class: Ambiguous Identities*. London: Verso.

Balick, Michael J., Elaine Elisabetsky, and Sarah A. Laird. 1996. *Medicinal Resources of the Tropical Forest: Biodiversity and Its Importance to Human Health*. New York: Columbia University Press.

Bar-Cohen, Yoseph. 2006. *Biomimetics: Biologically Inspired Technologies*. New York: Taylor and Francis.

Barthes, Roland. 2001 [1957]. *Mythologies*. New York: Hill and Wang.

Bastos, Cristiana. 1999. *Global Responses to AIDS: Science in Emergency*. Bloomington: Indiana University Press.

Bauman, Zygmunt. 2004. *Wasted Lives: Modernity and Its Outcasts*. Cambridge: Polity.

Bayart, Jean-François. 1989. *L'Etat en Afrique: La politique du ventre*. Paris: Artheme Fayard.

———. 1993. *The State in Africa: The Politics of the Belly*. London: Longman.

Bayart, Jean-François, Stephen Ellis, and Beatrice Hibou. 1997. *La criminalisation de l'Etat en Afrique*. Espace International. Bruxelles: Complexe.

Bazell, Robert. 1998. *Her-2: The Making of Herceptin, a Revolutionary Treatment for Breast Cancer*. New York: Random House.

Beck, Ulrich. 1992. *Risk Society: Towards a New Modernity*. Trans. Mark Ritter. London: Sage.

Beck, Ulrich, and Natan Sznaider. 2006. "A Literature on Cosmopolitanism: An Overview." *British Journal of Sociology* 57(1): 153–64.

Benedek, Elissa. 1990. "Response to the Presidential Address: Our Children, Our Future." *American Journal of Psychiatry* 147(9): 1120–25.

Benhabib, Seyla. 2007. "Twilight of Sovereignty or the Emergence of Cosmopolitan Norms? Rethinking Citizenship in Volatile Times." *Citizenship Studies* 11(1): 19–36.

Benjamin, Walter. 1999. "Old Toys." *Walter Benjamin: Selected Writings*, vol. 2, *1927–1934*, ed. Michael W. Jennings, Howard Eiland, and Gary Smith, trans. Rodney Livingstone and others, 98–102. Cambridge, Mass.: Belknap.

Berkman, A., J. Garcia, M. Muñoz-Laboy, V. Paiva, and R. Parker. 2005. "A Critical Analysis of the Brazilian Response to HIV/AIDS: Lessons Learned for Controlling and Mitigating the Epidemic in Developing Countries." *American Journal of Public Health* 95(7): 1162–72.

Berman, Marshall. 1993. "Children of the Future." *Dissent* 40(2): 221–25.

Bermudez, J. A. Z., R. Epsztein, M. A. Oliveira, and L. Hasenclever. 2000. *O acordo TRIPS da OMC e a proteção patentária no Brasil: Mudanças recentes e implicações para a produção local e o acesso da população aos medicamentos*. Rio de Janeiro: Escola Nacional de Saúde Pública, Fundação Oswaldo Cruz/Organização Mundial da Saúde.

Berry, Sara. 1989. "Social Institutions and Access to Resources." *Africa* 59: 41–55.

———. 1992. "Hegemony on a Shoestring: Indirect Rule and Access to Agricultural Land." *Africa* 62(3): 327–55.

Bhabha, Homi K. 1994. "Signs Taken for Wonders." *The Location of Culture*, 102–22. New York: Routledge.

———, ed. 1990. *Nation and Narration*. New York: Routledge.

Biehl, João. 2004. "The Activist State: Global Pharmaceuticals, AIDS, and Citizenship in Brazil." *Social Text*, no. 80: 105–32.

———. 2005a. "Technologies of Invisibility: The Politics of Life and Social Inequality." *Anthropologies of Modernity: Foucault, Governmentality, and Life Politics*, ed. Jonathan Xavier Inda, 248–71. London: Blackwell.

———. 2005b. *Vita: Life in a Zone of Social Abandonment*. Berkeley: University of California Press.

———. 2006. "Pharmaceutical Governance." *Global Pharmaceuticals: Ethics, Markets, Practices*, ed. Adriana Petryna, Andrew Lakoff, and Arthur Kleinman, 206–40. Durham, N.C.: Duke University Press.

———. 2007. *Will to Live: AIDS Therapies and the Politics of Survival*. Princeton, N.J.: Princeton University Press.

Bigo, Didier. 1988. *Pouvoir et obéissance en Centrafrique*. Paris: Karthala.

Blake, William. 1992 [ca. 1826]. *Songs of Innocence and Songs of Experience*. New York: Dover.

Bloch, Ernst. 1986. *The Principle of Hope*, vols. 1–3. Cambridge, Mass.: MIT Press.

Blunt, Peter, and D. Michael Warren. 1996. *Indigenous Organizations and Development*. London: Intermediate Technology.

Borneman, John, ed. 2004. *The Case of Ariel Sharon and the Fate of Universal Jurisdiction*. Princeton, N.J.: Princeton Institute for International and Regional Studies Monograph Series.

Bornstein, Erica. 2003. *The Spirit of Development: Protestant NGOs, Morality, and Economics in Zimbabwe*. New York: Routledge.

Bosk, Charles. 1999. "Professional Ethicist Available: Logical, Secular, Friendly—Bioethics and Beyond." *Daedalus* 128(4): 47–68.

———. 2002. "Now That We Have the Data, What Was the Question?" *American Journal of Bioethics* 2(4): 21–23.

———. 2005. *What Would You Do? The Collision of Ethnography and Ethics*. Chicago: University of Chicago Press.

Bosk, Charles, and Raymond de Vries. 2004. "Bureaucracies of Mass Deception: Institutional Review Boards and the Ethics of Ethnographic Research." *Annals of the American Academy of Political and Social Science* 595(1): 249–63.

Boutros-Ghali, Boutros. 1993. "Address by the Secretary-General of the United Nations at the opening of the World Conference on Human Rights," Vienna, June 14. United Nations, Office of the High Commission for Human Rights, http://www.ohchr.org/.

Bowker, Geoffrey C., and Susan Leigh Star. 1999. *Sorting Things Out: Classification and Its Consequences*. Cambridge, Mass.: MIT Press.

Boyden, Jo, and Joanna de Berry, eds. 2005. *Children and Youth on the Frontline: Ethnography, Armed Conflict, and Displacement*. New York: Berghahn.

Bozkurt, Alper, Robert F. Gilmour Jr., Auesa Sinah, David Stern, and Amit Lal. 2009. "Insect-Machine Interface Based Neurocybernetics." *IEE Transactions on Biomedical Engineering* 56(6): 1727–33.

Brace, Loring. 2005. *Race Is a Four-Letter Word: The Genesis of the Concept*. New York: Oxford University Press.

Bradol, Jean-Hervé. 2003. "L'ordre international cannibale et l'action humanitaire," *A l'ombre des guerres justes*, ed. Fabrice Weissman, 13–32. Paris: Flammarion.

———. 2004. "La commémoration amnésique des humanitaires." "Le génocide des Tutsis du Rwanda," special issue of *Humanitaire: Enjeux, pratiques, débats* 10:12–28.

Brandis, Dietrich. 1994 [1897]. *Forestry in India: Origins and Early Developments*. Dehradun: Natraj.

Brauman, Rony. 2000. *L'action humanitaire*. Paris: Flammarion.

————. 2005. "L'école des dilemmes." "Politique non gouvernementale," special issue of *Vacarme* 34:8–14.

Breckenridge, Carol, Sheldon Pollock, Homi K. Bhabha, and Dipesh Chakrabarty, eds. 2002. *Cosmopolitanism*. Durham, N.C.: Duke University Press.

Breed, Allen. 1990. "America's Future: The Necessity of Investing in Children." *Corrections Today* 52(1): 68–72.

Brenner, Barbara. 2007. "Barbara Brenner's Reflections on the 30th Annual San Antonio Breast Cancer Symposium—Day 2." Breast Cancer Action, http://bcaction.org/ (accessed March 6, 2008).

Brigido, L. F. M., with R. Rodrigues, J. Casseb, D. Oliveira, M. Rossetti, P. Menezes, and A. J. S. Duarte. 2001. "Impact of Adherence to Antiretroviral Therapy in HIV-1 Infected Patients at a University Public Service in Brazil." *AIDS Patient Care and STDs* 15(11): 587–93.

Brow, J. 1996. *Demons and Development: Hegemony and Experience*. Tucson: University of Arizona Press.

Brown, Eric C., ed. 2006. *Insect Poetics*. Minneapolis: University of Minnesota Press.

Browne, Thomas. 1922. *Religio Medici*. Ed. W. Murison. Cambridge: Cambridge University Press.

Broyard, Anatole. 1991. *Intoxicated by My Illness, and Other Writings on Life and Death*. New York: Clarkson Potter.

Brücker, Gilles. 1993. "L'humanitaire ou l'incessant questionnement sur l'humanité." "Le désir d'humanitaire," special issue of *Ingérences: Revue de Médecins du Monde* 1:3–8.

Bryant, Raymond, and Sinead Bailey. 1997. *Third World Political Ecology*. London: Routledge.

Burman, Erica. 1994. "Innocents Abroad: Western Fantasies of Childhood and the Iconography of Emergencies." *Disasters* 18(3): 238–53.

Butler, Judith. 1997. *The Psychic Life of Power: Theories in Subjection*. Stanford, Calif.: Stanford University Press.

Caillois, Roger, Claudine Frank, and Camille Naish. 2003. *The Edge of Surrealism: A Roger Caillois Reader*. Durham, N.C.: Duke University Press.

Calame, Claude. 1986. "Facing Otherness: The Tragic Mask in Ancient Greece." *History of Religions* 26(2): 125–42.

Callon, Michel. 1986. "The Sociology of an Actor-Network: The Case of the Electric Vehicle." *Mapping the Dynamics of Science and Technology: Sociology of Science in the Real World*, ed. Michel Callon, John Law, and Arie Rip, 19–34. London: Macmillan.

Callon, Michel, and Vololona Rabeharisoa. 2004. "Gino's Lesson on Humanity: Genetics, Mutual Entanglements and the Sociologist's Role." *Economy and Society* 33(1): 1–27.

Canetti, Elias. 1960. *Crowds and Power*. New York: Farrar, Strauss, Giroux.

Canguilhem, Georges. 1998. "The Decline of the Idea of Progress." *Economy and Society* 27(2/3): 313–29.

Capell, Kerry. 2004. "It's a Perfect Storm for Drugmakers" (interview with Jean-Pierre Garnier). *Bloomberg Businessweek*, October 4. www.businessweek.com/ (accessed December 21, 2009).

Caplan, Arthur. 2007. "Report Paints Grim Picture of Drug Trial Safety." *MSNBC. com*. September 28. http://www.msnbc.msn.com/ (accessed November 5, 2009).

Cardoso, Fernando Henrique. 1998. "Notas sobre a reforma do Estado." *Novos estudos do CEBRAP* 50:1–12.

Carson, Rachel. 1994 [1962]. *Silent Spring*. New York: Houghton-Mifflin.

Case, David. 2004. "An Engineer for the Avant-Garde." *Yale Alumni Magazine*, March–April. http://www.yalealumnimagazine.com/ (accessed December 22, 2009).

Cassier, M., and M. Correa. 2003. "Patents, Innovation and Public Health: Brazilian Public-Sector Laboratories' Experience in Copying AIDS Drugs." *Economics of AIDS and Access to HIV/AIDS Care in Developing Countries: Issues and Challenges*, ed. J. P. Moatti, B. Coriat, Y. Souteyrand, J. Dumoulin, and Y. A. Flori, 89–107. Paris: ANRS.

Castilho, Euclides, and Pedro Chequer. 1997. "A epidemia da AIDS no Brasil." *Epidemia da AIDS no Brasil: Situação e tendências*, 9–12. Brasília: Ministério da Saúde.

Catts, Oran, and Ionat Zurr. 2002. "Growing Semi-living Sculptures: The Tissue Culture and Art Project." *Leonardo* 35(4): 365–70.

———. 2004–5. "Ingestion/Disembodied Cuisine." *Cabinet Magazine* 16 (Winter).

Center for Tropical Forest Sciences (CTFS). 1997. "Inside the Center for Tropical Forest Science of the Smithsonian Tropical Research Institute: The ICBG Initiative." *Inside CTFS* (Summer): 7. (Barro Colorado Island, Panama: Center for Tropical Forest Science.)

CenterWatch. 2005. *State of the Clinical Trials Industry: A Sourcebook of Charts and Statistics*. Boston: Thomson CenterWatch.

Chambliss, Daniel F. 1996. *Beyond Caring: Hospitals, Nurses, and the Social Organization of Ethics*. Chicago: University of Chicago Press.

Chan, Stephanie. 1990. "Ambassadors to the Future." *Journal of Nutrition Education* 22(5): 240A.

Chatterjee, Partha. 1983. "More on Modes of Power and the Peasantry." *Subaltern Studies: Writings on South Asian History and Society*, vol. 2, ed. Ranajit Guha, 311–50. Delhi: Oxford University Press.

———. 1993. *The Nation and Its Fragments*. Princeton, N.J.: Princeton University Press.

Cheah, Pheng, and Bruce Robbins, eds. 1998. *Cosmopolitics: Thinking and Feeling beyond the Nation*. Minneapolis: University of Minnesota Press.

Children's Express. 1993. *Voices from the Future: Our Children Tell Us about Violence in America*, ed. Susan Goodwillie. New York: Crown.

Chomsky, Noam. 1999. *The Umbrella of U.S. Power: The Universal Declaration of Human Rights and the Contradictions of U.S. Policy*. Open Media Pamphlet Series 9. New York: Seven Stories.

Christakis, Nicholas. 1992. "Ethics Are Local: Engaging Cross-Cultural Variation in the Ethics for Clinical Research." *Social Science and Medicine* 35(9): 1079–91.

———. 2001. *Death Foretold: Prophecy and Prognosis in Medical Care.* Chicago: University of Chicago Press.

Christenson, Bill. 2008. "HI-MEMS: Control Circuits Embedded in Pupal Stage Successfully." Technovelgy, January 27. http://www.technovelgy.com/ (accessed February 23, 2008).

———. 2009. "Micro Air Vehicle Video Shows SF Style." Technovelgy, January 6. http://www.technovelgy.com/ (accessed December 22, 2009).

Cleaver, K. E. A., ed. 1992. *Conservation of West and Central African Rainforests.* Environment Paper no. 1. Washington, D.C.: World Bank and IUCN—World Conservation Union.

Coerr, Eleanor. 1977. *Sadako and the Thousand Paper Cranes.* New York: Dell.

Cohen, Lawrence. 1999. "Where It Hurts: Indian Material for an Ethics of Organ Transplantation." *Daedalus* 128(4): 135–65.

———. 2002. "The Other Kidney: Biopolitics beyond Recognition." *Commodifying Bodies,* ed. Nancy Scheper-Hughes and Loïc Wacquant, 9–30. London: Sage.

Colburn, F., ed. 1989. *Everyday Forms of Peasant Resistance.* Armonk, N.Y.: M. E. Sharpe.

Coles, Robert. 1986. *The Political Life of Children.* Boston: Atlantic Monthly Press.

Collier, Stephen, Andrew Lakoff, and Paul Rabinow. 2004. "Biosecurity: Towards an Anthropology of the Contemporary." *Anthropology Today* 20(5): 3–7.

Collins, John. 2004. *Occupied by Memory: The Intifada Generation and the Palestinian State of Emergency.* New York: New York University Press.

Colonna, Fanny. 1997. "Educating Conformity in French Colonial Algeria." *Tensions of Empire: Colonial Cultures in a Bourgeois World,* ed. Frederick Cooper and Ann Stoler, 346–72. Berkeley: University of California Press.

Comaroff, John, and Jean Comaroff. 1992. *Ethnography and the Historical Imagination.* Boulder, Colo.: Westview.

Conklin, Alice. 1997. *A Mission to Civilize: The Republican Idea of Empire in France and West Africa.* Stanford, Calif.: Stanford University Press.

Conrad, John. 1990. "The Future Is Almost Here." *Federal Probation* 54(1): 62–64.

Conrad, Joseph. 1983 [1910]. *"The Heart of Darkness" and "The Secret Sharer."* New York: New American Library Penguin.

Coronil, Fernando. 1997. *The Magical State: Nature, Money, and Modernity in Venezuela.* Chicago: University of Chicago Press.

Cosendey, M. A., J. A. Z. Bermudez, A. L. A. Reis, H. F. Silva, M. A. Oliveira, and V. L. Luiza. 2000. "Assistência farmacêutica na atenção básica de saúde: A experiência de três estados brasileiros." *Cadernos de saúde pública* 16(1): 171–82.

Coveney, Peter. 1957. *Poor Monkey: The Child in Literature.* London: Rockcliff, Salisbury Square.

Cronon, William. 1995. "The Trouble with Wilderness; or, Getting Back to the Wrong Nature." *Uncommon Ground: Toward Reinventing Nature,* ed. William Cronon, 69–90. New York: W. W. Norton.

Crook, Richard C., and James Manor. 1998. *Democracy and Decentralization in South Asia and West Africa: Participation, Accountability, and Performance*. Cambridge: Cambridge University Press.

Cruikshank, Barbara. 1999. *The Will to Empower: Democratic Citizens and Other Subjects*. Ithaca, N.Y.: Cornell University Press.

Daemmrich, Arthur A. 2004. *Pharmacopolitics: Drug Regulation in the United States and Germany*. Chapel Hill: University of North Carolina Press.

Dangwal, Dhirendra Datt. 1997. "State, Forests, and Graziers in the Hills of Uttar Pradesh: Impact of Colonial Forestry on Peasants, Gujars, and Bhotiyas." *Indian Economic and Social History Review* 34(4): 405–35.

Das, Veena. 1995. "Suffering, Legitimacy, and Healing: The Bhopal Case." *Critical Events: An Anthropological Perspective on Contemporary India*, 137–74. Delhi: Oxford University Press.

———. 1996. "Voices of Children." *Daedalus* 118(4): 262–94.

———. 1999. "Public Good, Ethics, and Everyday Life: Beyond the Boundaries of Bioethics." *Daedalus* 128(4): 99–134.

Dauvin, Pascal, and Johanna Siméant. 2002. *Le travail humanitaire: Les acteurs des ONG, du siège au terrain*. Paris: Presses de la Fondation de Sciences Politiques.

Davis, Mike. 2001. *Late Victorian Holocausts: El Nino Famines and the Making of the Third World*. London: Verso.

Defense Advanced Research Program Agency (DARPA). 2006. "Hybrid Insect MEMS (HI-MEMS)." Presolicitation notice. March 9. http://www.darpa.mil/mto/solicitations/baa06-22/ (accessed May 7, 2010).

De Landa, Manuel. 2006. *A New Philosophy of Society: Assemblage Theory and Social Complexity*. London: Continuum.

Deleuze, Gilles. 2006. *Two Regimes of Madness: Texts and Interviews, 1975–1995*. New York: Semiotext(e).

Deleuze, Gilles, and Félix Guattari. 1987. *A Thousand Plateaus: Capitalism and Schizophrenia*. Trans. Brian Massumi. Minneapolis: University of Minnesota Press.

del Toro, Guillermo, dir. 1997. *Mimic*. 105 min. Dimension Home Video. Distributed by Buena Vista Home Entertainment, New York.

Del Vecchio Good, Mary-Jo. 2001. "The Biotechnical Embrace." *Culture, Medicine and Psychiatry* 25(4): 395–410.

der Derian, James. 2001. *Virtuous War: Mapping the Military-Industrial-Media-Entertainment Network*. Boulder, Colo.: Westview.

———. N.d. "Dialogues: Future War: A Discussion with Paul Verilio." *InfoTechWar-Peace*, http://www.watsoninstitute.org/infopeace/index2.cfm.

Derrida, Jacques. 1974. *Of Grammatology*. Trans. Gayatri Chakravorty Spivak. Baltimore: Johns Hopkins University Press.

———. 1980. *Writing and Difference*. Trans. Alan Bass. Chicago: University of Chicago Press.

———. 1987. "Heidegger's Hand (*Geschlecht* II)." *Deconstruction and Philosophy*, ed. John Sallis, trans. John P. Leavey, Jr., 161–96. Chicago: University of Chicago Press.

————. 1989. *Of Spirit: Heidegger and the Question*. Chicago: University of Chicago Press.

————. 1989/1990. "Force of Law: The Mystical Foundation of Authority." *Cardozo Law Review* 11:920–1046.

————. 2002a. *Negotiations: Interventions and Interviews, 1971–2001*. Stanford, Calif.: Stanford University Press.

————. 2002b. "The Animal That Therefore I Am (More to Follow)." *Critical Inquiry* 28(2): 369–418.

————. 2005. *The Politics of Friendship*. London: Verso.

————. 2008 [1997]. *The Animal That Therefore I Am*. New York: Fordham University Press.

Descartes, René. 1985. "Discourse on the Method." *The Philosophical Writings of Descartes*, vol. 1, ed. and trans. John Cottingham, Robert Stroothoff, and Dugald Murdoch, 111–51. Cambridge: Cambridge University Press.

Devji, Faisal. 2008. *The Terrorist in Search of Humanity: Militant Islam and Global Politics*. New York: Columbia University Press.

DeVries, Dawn. 2001. "'Be Converted and Become as Little Children': Friedrich Schleiermacher on the Religious Significance of Childhood." *The Child in Christian Thought*, ed. Marcia Bunge, 329–49. Grand Rapids, Mich.: Eerdmans.

De Vries, Raymond. 2004. "How Can We Help? From 'Sociology in' to 'Sociology of' Bioethics." *Journal of Law, Medicine, and Ethics* 32(2): 279–93.

De Waal, Alex. 2004. "Tragedy in Darfur: On Understanding and Ending the Crisis." *Boston Review*, October/November.

d'Hertefelt, M. 1971. *Les clans du Rwanda ancien: Eléments d'ethnosociologie et ethnohistoire*. Tervuren, Belgium: Musée Royal de l'Afrique Centrale.

Djian, Jean-Michel. 2004. "La diplomatie culturelle de la France à vau-l'eau: Economisme ou volonté de 'rayonnement'?" *Le monde diplomatique*, June 28.

Dodier, Nicolas. 2005. "Transnational Medicine in Public Arenas: AIDS Treatment in the South." *Culture, Medicine, and Psychiatry* 29(3): 285–307.

Doimo, Ana Maria. 1995. *A vez e a voz do popular: Movimentos sociais e participação política no Brasil pós-70*. Rio de Janeiro: ANPOCS/Relume Dumará.

Douglas, Gordon, dir. 1954. *Them!* 94 min. Warner Bros. Pictures. New York.

Dourado, I., M. A. Veras, D. Barreira, and A. M. de Brito. 2006. "AIDS Epidemic Trends after the Introduction of Antiretroviral Therapy in Brazil." *Revista de saúde pública* 40 (supl.): 1–8.

Dowsett, Mitchell. 2007. "William L. McGuire Memorial Lecture: Biomarking the Oestrogen Dependence of Breast Cancer." Paper presented at the San Antonio Breast Cancer Conference, San Antonio, December 14.

Dubois, Laurent. 2000. "La République Métissée: Citizenship, Colonialism, and the Borders of French History." *Cultural Studies* 14(1): 15–34.

DuBois, Page. 1991. *Torture and Truth*. New York: Routledge.

————. 2003. *Slaves and Other Objects*. Chicago: University of Chicago Press.

Dumit, Joseph. 2000. "When Explanations Rest: 'Good Enough' Brain Science and the New Biomental Disorders." *Living and Working with the New Medical Technologies: Intersections of Inquiry*, ed. Margaret Lock, Alan Young, and Alberto Cambrosio, 209–33. Cambridge: Cambridge University Press.

———. 2004. *Picturing Personhood: Brain Scans and Biomedical Identity*. Princeton, N.J.: Princeton University Press.

Durrell, Ann, and Marilyn Sachs, eds. 1990. *The Big Book for Peace*. New York: Dutton Children's.

Easton, Tom. 1990. *Sparrowhawk*. Rockville, Md.: Wildside.

Economist. 2004. "Rwanda since the Genocide: The Road out of Hell." *Economist Special Report*, March 27.

Edson, Margaret. 1999. *Wit, a Play*. New York: Faber and Faber.

Elkins, Caroline. 2005. *Imperial Reckoning: The Untold Story of Britain's Gulag in Kenya*. New York: Henry Holt.

Ellenberger, Henri F. 1960. "Zoological Garden and Mental Hospital." *Canadian Psychiatric Association Journal* (July 5): 136–49.

Elshtain, Jean Bethke. 1994. "Political Children." *Criterion* 33(2): 2–15.

Elster, Jon. 1999. *Alchemies of the Mind: Rationality and the Emotions*. Cambridge: Cambridge University Press.

Elster, Jon, with Claus Offe and Ulrich K. Preuss. 1998. *Institutional Design in Postcommunist Societies: Rebuilding the Ship at Sea*. Cambridge: Cambridge University Press.

Eltringham, Nigel. 2004. *Accounting for Horror: Post-genocide Debates in Rwanda*. London: Pluto.

Epstein, Helen. 2007. *The Invisible Cure: Africa, the West, and the Fight against AIDS*. New York: Farrar, Strauss, and Giroux.

Epstein, Steven. 1996. *Impure Science: AIDS, Activism, and the Politics of Knowledge*. Berkeley: University of California Press.

———. 2007. *Inclusion: The Politics of Difference in Medical Research*. Chicago: University of Chicago Press.

Eriksen, Thomas. 1993. *Ethnicity and Nationalism: Anthropological Perspectives*. London: Pluto.

Esposito, Roberto. 2008. *Bios: Biopolitics and Philosophy*. Trans. Timothy Campbell. Minneapolis: University of Minnesota Press.

Exley, Richard, and Helen Exley. 1985. *My World/Peace: Thoughts and Illustrations from the Children of All Nations*. Lincolnwood, Ill.: Passport. Also published as *Dear World: "How I'd Put the World Right"—By the Children of over Fifty Nations*.

Fabian, Johannes. 2002 [1983]. *Time And The Other: How Anthropology Makes Its Object*. New York: Columbia University Press.

Fabre, Jean-Henri, and Bernard Miall. 1914. *Social Life in the Insect World*. New York: Century.

Fanon, Frantz. 1963. *The Wretched of the Earth*. New York: Grove.

Farmer, Paul. 2002a. "Can Transnational Research Be Ethical in the Developing World?" *Lancet* 60(9342): 1301–2.

————. 2002b. "Introducing ARVs in Resource-Poor Settings: Expected and Unexpected Challenges and Consequences." Partners in Health, http://www.pih.org/ (accessed December 15, 2009).

————. 2004. *Pathologies of Power: Health, Human Rights, and the New War on the Poor.* Berkeley: University of California Press.

Fassin, Didier. 2004. "La cause des victimes." "L'humanitaire," special issue of *Les temps modernes* 59(627): 73–91.

————. 2007a. "Humanitarianism as a Politics of Life." *Public Culture* 19(3): 499–520.

————. 2007b. "La biopolitique n'est pas la politique de la vie." "Michel Foucault et la sociologie," special issue of *Sociologie et sociétés* 38(2): 35–48.

Fassin, Didier, and Mariella Pandolfi, eds. 2009. *Contemporary States of Emergency: The Politics of Military and Humanitarian Interventions.* New York: Zone.

Fassin, Didier, and Richard Rechtman. 2009. *The Empire of Trauma: An Inquiry into the Condition of Victimhood.* Princeton, N.J.: Princeton University Press.

Featherstone, Steve. 2007. "The Coming Robot Army: Introducing America's Future Fighting Machines." *Harper's Magazine,* February.

Fecomme, R., and S. Singa Ndourou. 1995. "Procès-verbal de l'Assemblée Générale Constitutive de l'Association Nature Profonde (ANP): Statut de l'association et règlement intérieure." Unpublished document. Bangui, Central African Republic.

Feldman, Allen. 1991. *Formations of Violence: The Narrative of the Body and Political Terror in Northern Ireland.* Chicago: University of Chicago Press.

————. 1994. "On Cultural Anesthesia: From Desert Storm to Rodney King." *American Ethnologist* 21(2): 404–18.

————. 1997. "Violence and Vision: The Prosthetics and Aesthetics of Terror in Northern Ireland." *Public Culture* 10(1): 25–60.

————. 2001. "Philoctetes Revisited: White Public Space and the Political Geography of Public Safety." *Social Text* 19(3): 57–89.

————. 2003. "Strange Fruit: The South African Truth Commission and the Demonic Economies of Violence." *Social Analysis* 46(3): 234–65.

————. 2005. "The Actuarial Gaze: From 9/11 to Abu Ghraib." *Cultural Studies* 19(2): 203–26.

Feldman, Ilana. 2007a. "Difficult Distinctions: Refugee Law, Humanitarian Practice, and Political Identification in Gaza." *Cultural Anthropology* 22(1): 129–69.

————. 2007b. "The Quaker Way: Ethical Labor and Humanitarian Relief." *American Ethnologist* 34(4): 689–705.

————. 2008a. *Governing Gaza: Bureaucracy, Authority, and the Work of Rule, 1917–1967.* Durham, N.C.: Duke University Press.

————. 2008b. "Mercy Trains and Ration Rolls: Between Government and Humanitarianism in Gaza." *Interpreting Welfare and Relief in the Middle East,* ed. Inger Marie Okkenhaug and Nefissa Naguib, 175–94. Leiden: Brill.

Ferguson, James. 2004. *Global Shadows: Africa in the Neoliberal World Order.* Durham, N.C.: Duke University Press.

Ferguson, James, and Akhil Gupta. 2002. "Spatializing States: Toward an Ethnography of Neoliberal Governmentality." *American Ethnologist* 29(4): 981–1002.

Feynman, Richard P. 1992. "There's Plenty of Room at the Bottom." *Journal of Microelectromechanical Systems* 1(1): 60–66.

Filipovic, Zlata. 1994. *Zlata's Diary: A Child's Life in Sarajevo*. New York: Viking.

Fineberg, Jonathan. 1997. *The Innocent Eye: Children's Art and the Modern Artist*. Princeton, N.J.: Princeton University Press.

Fischer, Michael M. J. 2003. *Emergent Forms of Life and the Anthropological Voice*. Durham, N.C.: Duke University Press.

———. 2009. *Anthropological Futures*. Durham, N.C.: Duke University Press.

Fisher, Jill A. 2009. *Medical Research for Hire: The Political Economy of Pharmaceutical Clinical Trials*. New Brunswick, N.J.: Rutgers University Press.

Fisher, Philip. 2002. *The Vehement Passions*. Princeton, N.J.: Princeton University Press.

Food and Agriculture Organization (FAO). 1999. *Status and Progress in the Implementation of National Forest Programmes: Outcome of an FAO Worldwide Survey*. Mimeograph. Rome: FAO.

Fortmann, Louise. 1995. "Talking Claims: Discursive Strategies in Contesting Property." *World Development* 23(64): 1053.

Fortun, Kim. 2004. "Environmental Information Systems as Appropriate Technology." *Design Issues* 20(3): 54–65.

Foster, Robert. 1991. "Making National Cultures in the Global Ecumene." *Annual Review of Anthropology* 20: 235–60.

Foucault, Michel. 1979 [1975]. *Discipline and Punish: The Birth of the Prison*. New York: Vintage.

———. 1980. *The History of Sexuality*, vol. 1, *An Introduction*. New York: Vintage.

———. 1982. "The Subject and Power." *Michel Foucault: Beyond Structuralism and Hermeneutics*, Hubert L. Dreyfus and Paul Rabinow, 208–26. Chicago: University of Chicago Press.

———. 1984. "The Right of Death and Power over Life." *The Foucault Reader*, ed. Paul Rabinow. New York: Pantheon.

———. 1991 [1978]. "Governmentality." *The Foucault Effect: Studies in Governmentality: With Two Lectures by and an Interview with Michel Foucault*, ed. Graham Burchell, Colin Gordon, and Peter Miller, 87–104. Chicago: University of Chicago Press.

———. 1994. "The Political Technology of Individuals." *Power: The Essential Works of Michel Foucault, 1954–1984*, vol. 3., ed. James D. Faubion, 403–17. New York: New Press.

———. 1997. *Society Must Be Defended: Lectures at the Collège de France, 1975–1976*. New York: Picador.

———. 2003. *Abnormal: Lectures at the Collège de France, 1974–1975*. Ed. Valerio Marchetti and Antonella Salomoni, trans. Graham Burchell. New York: Picador.

———. 2006. *Madness and Civilization*. New York: Routledge.

————. 2007. *Security, Territory, Population: Lectures at the Collège de France, 1977–1978*. New York: Palgrave Macmillan.

Franklin, Sarah, and Margaret Lock. 2003. *Remaking Life and Death: Toward an Anthropology of the Biosciences*. Santa Fe, N.M.: School of American Research Press.

Freeman, Michael. 1991. "The Theory and Prevention of Genocide." *Holocaust and Genocide Studies* 6(2): 185–99.

Galvão, Jane. 2000. *A AIDS no Brasil: A agenda de construção de uma epidemia*. São Paulo: Editora 34.

————. 2002. "A política brasileira de distribuição e produção de medicamentos anti-retrovirais: Privilégio ou um direito?" *Cadernos de saúde pública* 18(1): 213–19.

Garnier, Jean-Pierre. 2005. "The Opportunities and Challenges of Globalisation: The Rise of India and China." Speech given at the conference "Advancing Enterprise," London, February 4. Available at HS Treasury, http://www.hm-treasury.gov.uk/ (accessed February 4, 2005).

Garrison, Jennifer, and Andrew Tubesing. 1995. *A Million Visions of Peace: Wisdom from the Friends of Old Turtle*. Duluth, Minn.: Pfeifer-Hamilton.

Geertz, Clifford. 2000 [1984]. "Anti Anti-relativism." *Available Light: Anthropological Reflections on Philosophical Topics*, 42–67. Princeton, N.J.: Princeton University Press.

Geissler, P. W., A. Kelly, B. Imoukhuede, and R. Pool. 2008. "'He is now like a brother, I can even give him some blood': Relational Ethics and Material Exchanges in a Malaria Vaccine 'Trial Community' in the Gambia." *Social Science and Medicine* 67(5): 696–707.

Gertz, Emily. 2004. "Natalie Jeremijenko: The WorldChanging Interview." *WorldChanging*, October 22. http://www.worldchanging.com/ (accessed December 22, 2009).

Gilhooley, Margaret. 2007. "Vioxx's History and the Need for Better Procedures and Better Testing." *Seton Hall Law Review* 37:941–56.

Gilroy, Paul. 1991. *"There ain't no black in the Union Jack": The Cultural Politics of Race and Nation*. Chicago: University of Chicago Press.

————. 2000. *Against Race: Imagining Political Culture beyond the Color Line*. Cambridge: Harvard University Press.

Goldberg, David Theo, ed. 1990. *The Anatomy of Racism*. Minneapolis: University of Minnesota Press.

Goozner, Merrill. 2005. *The $800 Million Pill: The Truth behind the Cost of New Drugs*. Berkeley: University of California Press.

Gorman, James. 2004. "The Altered Human Is Already Here." *New York Times*, April 6.

Gottlieb, Alma. 2004. *The Afterlife Is Where We Come From: The Culture of Infancy in West Africa*. Chicago: University of Chicago Press.

Goyemidé, Etienne. 1984. *Le silence de la forêt*. Paris: Hatier.

————. 1989. "Le théâtre existe." *Notre librairie* 96:87–92.

Graham, Stephen. 2006. "Cities and the 'War on Terror.'" *International Journal of Urban and Regional Research* 30(2): 255–76.

————. 2007a. "The City in the Crosshairs: A Conversation with Stephen Graham (Part 1)." *Subtopia: A Field Guide to Military Urbanism*, August 6. http://subtopia .blogspot.com/ (accessed December 29, 2007).

————. 2007b. "From Space to Street Corners: Global South Cities and U.S. Military Technophilia." Unpublished manuscript. http://www.geography.dur .ac.uk/information/staff/personal/graham/graham_documents/DOC%203.pdf (accessed June 1, 2008).

Gray, Chris Hables. 2001. *Cyborg Citizen: Politics in the Posthuman Age*. New York: Routledge.

Gray, Chris Hables, Steven Mentor, and Heidi J. Figuroa-Sarriera. 1995. *The Cyborg Handbook*. New York: Routledge.

Greene, Alex. 2003. "The Voice of Ix Chel: Fashioning Maya Tradition in the Belizean Rain Forest." *In Search of the Rainforest*, ed. Candace Slater, 101–32. Durham, N.C.: Duke University Press.

Greenhouse, Carol. 2006. "Fieldwork on Law." *Annual Review of Law and Social Science* 2: 187–210.

Greenwalt, Alexander. 1999. "Rethinking Genocidal Intent: The Case for a Knowledge-Based Interpretation." *Columbia Law Review* 99(8): 2259–94.

Grinker, Roy Richard. 1994. *Houses in the Rain Forest: Ethnicity and Inequality among Farmers and Foragers in Central Africa*. Berkeley: University of California Press.

Grove, Richard. 1995. *Green Imperialism: Colonial Expansion, Tropical Island Edens, and the Origins of Environmentalism, 1600–1860*. Delhi: Oxford University Press.

————. 1998. *Ecology, Climate and Empire: The Indian Legacy in Global Environmental History, 1400–1940*. Delhi: Oxford University Press.

Guillemin, Jeanne. 1998. "Bioethics and the Coming of the Corporation to Medicine." *Bioethics and Society*, ed. Raymond de Vries and Janardon Subedi, 60–77. Upper Saddle River, N.J.: Prentice Hall.

————. 2005. *Biological Weapons: From the Invention of State-Sponsored Programs to Conventional Bioterrorism*. New York: Columbia University Press.

Gupta, Akhil. 1995. "Blurred Boundaries: The Discourse of Corruption, the Culture of Politics, and the Imagined State." *American Ethnologist* 22(2): 375–402.

————. 2001. "Reliving Childhood? The Temporality of Childhood and Narratives of Reincarnation." *Ethnos* 67(1): 1–23.

Gusterson, Hugh. 2005. "Decoding the Debate on 'Frankenfood.'" *Making Threats: Biofears and Environmental Anxieties*, ed. Betsy Hartmann, Banu Subramaniam, and Charles Zerner, 109–34. Lanham, Md.: Rowman and Littlefield.

Guyer, Jane. 1995. *Money Matters: Instability, Values and Social Payments in the Modern History of West African Communities*. Portsmouth, N.H.: Heinemann.

Hall, Stuart. 1991. "The Local and the Global: Globalization and Ethnicity." *Culture, Globalization and the World-System: Contemporary Conditions for the Representation of Identity*, ed. Anthony D. King, 19–40. Binghamton: State University of New York Press.

Hall, Stuart, with Charles Critcher, Tony Jefferson, and John Clarke. 1978. *Policing the Crisis: Mugging, the State and Law and Order*. New York: Palgrave Macmillan.

Hamanaka, Sheila. 1995. *Peace Crane*. New York: HarperCollins.

Hannerz, Ulf. 1989. "Notes on the Global Ecumene." *Public Culture* 1(2): 66–75.

———. 1990. "Cosmopolitans and Locals in World Culture." *Theory, Culture and Society* 7(2/3): 237–51.

Haraway, Donna. 1991. "A Cyborg Manifesto: Science, Technology, and Socialist-Feminism in the Late Twentieth Century." *Simians, Cyborgs, and Women: The Reinvention of Nature*, 149–81. New York: Routledge.

———. 2007. *When Species Meet*. Minneapolis: University of Minnesota Press.

Hardin, Rebecca. 2000. "Translating the Forest: Tourism, Trophy Hunting, and the Transformation of Forest Use in Southwestern Central African Republic." PhD diss., Yale University.

Hardin, Rebecca, and M. Remis. 1997. *Séminaire: Recherches scientifiques et développement rural, réserve Dzangha Sangha, République Centrafricaine*. Sangha River Network Series. Yale Center for International and Area Studies. New Haven, Conn.: Yale University. Available at www.yale.edu/sangha (accessed February 16, 2010).

Harkness, Jon M. 1996. "Nuremberg and the Issue of Wartime Experiments on U.S. Prisoners: The Green Committee." *Journal of the American Medical Association* 276(20): 1672–75.

Harrington, Sarah Elizabeth, and Thomas J. Smith. 2008. "The Role of Chemotherapy at the End of Life: 'When is enough, enough?'" *Journal of the American Medical Association* 299(22): 2667–78.

Haskell, Thomas L. 1985. "Capitalism and the Origins of the Humanitarian Sensibility." Pts. I and II. *American Historical Review* 90(2): 339–61; 90(3): 547–66.

Hayden, Cori. 2003. *When Nature Goes Public: The Making and Unmaking of Bioprospecting in Mexico*. Princeton, N.J.: Princeton University Press.

Haynes, Douglas, and Gyan Prakash, eds. 1992. *Contesting Power: Resistance and Social Relations in South Asia*. Delhi: Oxford University Press.

Healy, David. 2004. *Let Them Eat Prozac: The Unhealthy Relationship between the Pharmaceutical Industry and Depression*. New York: New York University Press.

Hecketsweiler, Philippe. 1990. *La conservation des écosystèmes forestiers du Congo*, vol. 1. Gland, Switzerland: International Union for Conservation of Nature and Natural Resources.

Heidegger, Martin. 1971. "The Thing." *Poetry, Language, Thought*. Trans. Albert Hofstadter, 163–82. New York: Harper and Row.

———. 1977. *The Question Concerning Technology and Other Essays*. Trans. William Lovitt. New York: Harper Torchbooks.

———. 1995. *The Fundamental Concepts of Metaphysic: World, Finitude, Solitude*. Trans. William McNeill and Nicholas Walker. Bloomington: Indiana University Press.

———. 1998. *Pathmarks*. Ed. and trans. William McNeill. Cambridge: Cambridge University Press.

———. 2000. *Gesamtausgabe*, vol. 16, *Reden und andere Zeugnisse eines Lebensweges*. Frankfurt am Main: Vittorio Klostermann.

Held, David. 2004. *Global Covenant: The Social Democratic Alternative to the Washington Consensus*. Cambridge: Polity.

Helmreich, Stefan. 1998. *Silicon Second Nature: Culturing Artificial Life in a Digital World*. Berkeley: University of California Press.

———. 2009. *Alien Ocean: Anthropological Voyages in Microbial Seas*. Berkeley: University of California Press.

Hibou, B. 1998. "Retrait ou redéploiement de l'Etat." *Critique internationale* 1:151–68.

Higonnet, Anne. 1998. *Pictures of Innocence: The History and Crisis of Ideal Childhood*. London: Thames and Hudson.

Hilts, Philip. 2004. *Protecting America's Health: The FDA, Business, and One Hundred Years of Regulation*. Chapel Hill: University of North Carolina Press.

Hirsch, Robert. 2005. "The Strange Case of Steve Kurtz: Critical Art Ensemble and the Price of Freedom." *Afterimage* 32:22–32.

Hirschfeld, Lawrence. 2002. "Why Don't Anthropologists Like Children?" *American Anthropologist* 104(2): 611–27.

Hirschman, Albert. 1970. "The Search for Paradigms as a Hindrance to Understanding." *World Politics* 22(3): 329–43.

Hochschild, Adam. 1998. *King Leopold's Ghost: A Story of Greed, Terror, and Heroism in Colonial Africa*. Boston: Houghton Mifflin.

Holmstrom, Bengt. 1982. "Moral Hazard in Teams." *Bell Journal of Economics* 13(2): 324–40.

Holston, James. 2008. *Insurgent Citizenship: Disjunctions of Democracy and Modernity in Brazil*. Princeton, N.J.: Princeton University Press.

Holzgrefe, J. L., and Robert O. Keohane, eds. 2003. *Humanitarian Intervention: Ethical, Legal and Political Dilemmas*. Cambridge: Cambridge University Press.

Honig, Bonnie. 2001. *Democracy and the Foreigner*. Princeton, N.J.: Princeton University Press.

Hyndman, Jennifer. 2000. *Managing Displacement: Refugees and the Politics of Humanitarianism*. Minneapolis: University of Minnesota Press.

Ignatieff, Michael. 2000. "The New American Way of War." *New York Review of Books*, July 20.

Inguizeguino, Toutou E. 1994. "Projet: Office du Tourisme et création jardin animalier." Unpublished document. Bangui, Central African Republic.

Intercontinental Marketing Services (IMS Health). 2006. "IMS Health Reports Global Pharmaceutical Market Grew 7 Percent in 2005, to $602 Billion." Press release, March 21. http://www.imshealth.com/ (accessed on February 10, 2010).

Ivy, Marilyn. 1995. "Have You Seen Me? Recovering the Inner Child in Late Twentieth-Century America." *Children and the Politics of Culture*, ed. Sharon Stephens, 79–104. Princeton, N.J.: Princeton University Press.

Jain, Sarah Lochlann. 2006. "Living in Prognosis." *Representations* 98(1): 77–92.

James, Allison. 2004. "Understanding Childhood from an Interdisciplinary Perspective: Problems and Potentials." *Rethinking Childhood*, ed. Peter Pufall and Richard Unsworth, 25–37. New Brunswick, N.J.: Rutgers University Press.

James, Allison, and Alan Prout, eds. 1997. *Constructing and Reconstructing Childhood: Contemporary Issues in the Sociological Study of Childhood*. London: Falmer.

Janis, Mark. 2005. "Dred Scott and International Law." *Columbia Journal of Transnational Law* 43(3): 763–810.

Jenkins, Janis. 1991. "The State Construction of Affect: Political Ethos and Mental Health among Salvadoran Refugees." *Culture, Medicine, Psychiatry* 15:139–65.

Jenks, Chris. 1996. *Childhood*. New York: Routledge.

Jewsiwiecki, Bogumil. 1993. "Cheri Samba and the Postcolonial Reinvention of Modernity." *Callaloo* 16(4): 772–95.

Jones, James H. 1993 [1981]. *Bad Blood: The Tuskegee Syphilis Experiment*. New York: Free Press.

Kalyvas, Andreas. 2004. "From the Act to the Decision: Hannah Arendt and the Question of Decisionism." *Political Theory* 32(3): 320–46.

Kassirer, Jerome P. 2004. *On the Take: How Medicine's Complicity with Big Business Can Endanger Your Health*. Oxford: Oxford University Press.

Kennedy, David. 2004. *The Dark Sides of Virtue: Reassessing International Humanitarianism*. Princeton, N.J.: Princeton University Press.

Kent, David, with D. Mkaya Mwamburi, Michael L. Bennish, Bruce Kupelnick, and John P. Ioannidis. 2004. "Clinical Trials in Sub-Saharan Africa and Established Standards of Care: A Systematic Review of HIV, Tuberculosis, and Malaria Trials." *JAMA: Journal of American Medical Association* 292(2): 237–42.

Kent, G. 1991. "Our Children, Our Future." *Futures* 23(1): 32–50.

Kim, Jim Yong, Joia S. Mukherjee, Michael L. Rich, Kedar Mate, Jaime Bayona, and Mercedes C. Becerra. 2003. "From Multidrug-Resistant Tuberculosis to DOTS Expansion and Beyond: Making the Most of a Paradigm Shift." *Tuberculosis* 83(3): 59–65.

Kittichaisaree, Kriangsak. 2001. *International Criminal Law*. Oxford: Oxford University Press.

Kleinman, Arthur, and Joan Kleinman. 1996. "The Appeal of Experience; The Dismay of Images: Cultural Appropriates of Suffering in Our Times." *Daedalus* 125(1): 1–23.

Knight, Jack. 1992. *Institutions and Social Conflict*. Cambridge: Cambridge University Press.

Kohn, Eduardo. 2007. "How Dogs Dream: Amazonian Natures and the Politics of Transspecies Engagement." *American Ethnologist* 34(1): 3–24.

Korbin, Jill. 2003. "Children, Childhoods, and Violence." *Annual Review of Anthropology* 32:431–46.

Kosek, Jake. 2006. *Understories: The Political Life of Forests in Northern New Mexico*. Durham, N.C.: Duke University Press.

Koskenniemi, Martti. 2002. *The Gentle Civilizer of Nations: The Rise and Fall of International Law, 1870–1960*. Cambridge: Cambridge University Press.

Koulaninga, Abel. 1990. "L'éducation chez les pygmées de Centrafrique." PhD diss., Université de Paris V, Sorbonne.

KQED-TV. 2003. "Natalie Jeremijenko." *Spark*, broadcast April. http://www.kqed
.org/ (accessed December 22, 2009).

Kretsinger, Anna. 1993. *Recommendations for Further Integration of BaAka Interests in Project Policy, Dzanga Sangha Dense Forest Reserve*. Washington, D.C.: World Wide Fund for Nature.

Kriner, Stephanie. 2001. "President Bush Thanks Children at American Red Cross Headquarters." American Red Cross press release. http://www.redcross.org/ (accessed April 7, 2004).

Kuletz, Valerie. 1998. *The Tainted Desert: Environmental and Social Ruin in the American Southwest*. New York: Routledge.

Kumaon Forest Grievances Committee (KFGC). 1921. *Report of the Forest Grievances Committee for Kumaon*. Lucknow, India: Government of Uttar Pradesh.

Kurz, Kathleen, and Cynthia Prather. 1995. *Improving the Quality of Life of Girls*. New York and Washington, D.C.: United Nations Children's Fund and Association for Women in Development.

Kutcher, Gerald. 2006. "Cancer Clinical Trials and the Transfer of Knowledge: Metrology, Contestation and Local Practice." *Devices and Designs: Medical Technologies in Historical Perspective*, ed. Carston Timmermann and Julie Anderson, 212–29. Houndmills, U.K.: Palgrave MacMillan.

Lacan, Jacques. 1977. "The Subversion of the Subject and the Dialectic of Desire in the Freudian Unconscious." *Ecrits*. Trans. A. M. Sheridan, 281–312. New York: W. W. Norton.

Lal, Amit. 2006a. "Hybrid Insect MEMS (HI-MEMS) Proposer Information Pamphlet 01." March 9, 2006. http://www.darpa.mil/MTO/index.html (accessed December 7, 2009).

———. 2006b. "Hybrid Insect MEMS (HI-MEMS) Proposer's Day." May 24. DARPA-MTO, 10. http://www.darpa.mil/MTO/index.html (accessed December 7, 2009).

Laqueur, Thomas. 1989. "Bodies, Details and Humanitarian Narrative." *The New Cultural History*, ed. Lynn Hunt, 176–204. Berkeley: University of California Press.

———. 2009. "Mourning, Pity, and the Work of Narrative in the Making of 'Humanity.'" *Humanitarianism and Suffering: The Mobilization of Empathy*, ed. Richard Ashby Wilson and Richard D. Brown, 31–57. Cambridge: Cambridge University Press.

Lasagna, Louis. 1977. "Prisoner Subjects and Drug Testing." *Federation Proceedings* 36(10): 2349–51.

Las Casas, Bartolomé de. 1972. *The Tears of the Indians*. Trans. John Phillips. New York: Oriole.

Latour, Bruno. 1987. *Science in Action: How to Follow Scientists and Engineers through Society*. Milton Keynes: Open University Press.

———. 2004. *Politics of Nature: How to Bring the Sciences into Democracy*. Trans. Catherine Porter. Cambridge: Harvard University Press.

————. 2005. *Reassembling the Social: An Introduction to Actor-Network-Theory*. Oxford: Oxford University Press.

Law, John, and John Hassard, eds. 1999. *Actor Network Theory and After*. Oxford: Blackwell.

Lazreg, Marnia. 2007. *Torture and the Twilight of Empire: From Algiers to Baghdad*. Princeton, N.J.: Princeton University Press.

Lederer, Susan. 1997. *Subjected to Science: Human Experimentation in America before the Second World War*. Baltimore, Md.: Johns Hopkins University Press.

Leite, Fabiane. 2005. "Laboratórios apontam atraso de repasses." *Folha Online*, February 24, 2005. http://www1.folha.uol.com.br/ (accessed December 15, 2009).

Lemkin, Raphael. 1944. *Axis Rule in Occupied Europe: Analysis of Government, Proposals for Redress*. Washington, D.C.: Carnegie Endowment for World Peace.

Leonhardt, Alec. 2006. "Baka and the Magic of the State: Between Autochthony and Citizenship." *African Studies Review* 49(2): 69–94.

Lerner, Barron H. 2001. *The Breast Cancer Wars*. New York: Oxford University Press.

Levinas, Emmanuel. 1990. "The Name of the Dog, or Natural Rights." *Difficult Freedom: Essays on Judaism*. Trans. Seán Hand, 151–53. London: Athlone.

Lewin, Tamar. 2001. "Families Sue Pfizer on Test of Antibiotic." *New York Times*, August 30.

Lewis, Michael. 2003. *Inventing Global Ecology: Tracking the Biodiveristy Ideal in India, 1945–1997*. Hyderabad: Orient Longman.

Linden, Eugene. 1992. "The Last Eden: A Personal Journey to a Place No Human Has Seen." *Time*, July 13.

Lippit, Akira Mizuta. 2000. *Electric Animal: Toward a Rhetoric of Wildlife*. Minneapolis: University of Minnesota Press.

Lock, Margaret. 2001. *Twice Dead: Organ Transplants and the Reinvention of Death*. Berkeley: University of California Press.

Lowy, Ilana. 2000. "Trustworthy Knowledge and Desperate Patients: Clinical Tests for New Drugs from Cancer to AIDS." *Living and Working with the New Medical Technologies: Intersections of Inquiry*, ed. Margaret Lock, Alan Young, and Alberto Cambrosio, 49–82. Cambridge: Cambridge University Press.

Lutts, R. H. 1985. "Chemical Fallout: Rachel Carson's *Silent Spring*, Radioactive Fallout and the Environmental Movement." *Environmental Review* 9(3): 210–25.

Lynch, Lisa. 2003. "Trans-genesis: An Interview with Eduardo Kac." *New Formations* 49(Spring): 75–89.

Lynch, Owen, and Kirk Talbott. 1995. *Balancing Acts: Community-Based Forest Management and National Law in Asia and the Pacific*. Washington, D.C.: World Resources Institute.

Machel, Graca. 2002. *The Impact of War on Children: A Review of Progress since the 1995 United Nations Report on the Impact of Armed Conflict on Children*. New York: United Nations Publications.

MacIntyre, Alasdair. 1984. *After Virtue: A Study in Moral Theory*. Notre Dame: University of Notre Dame Press.

MacKenzie, John M. 1997. *The Empire of Nature: Hunting, Conservation, and British Imperialism*. Manchester: Manchester University Press.

Macklin, Ruth. 1999. *Against Relativism: Cultural Diversity and the Search for Ethical Universals in Medicine*. Oxford: Oxford University Press.

Mahfouz, Naguib. 1997. *Echoes of an Autobiography*. New York: Doubleday.

Magloire, Ambourhouet Bigmann. 1991. *Une littérature du silence*. Littérature gabonaise. *Notre librairie* 105. Paris: Clef.

Magnarella, Paul. 2000. *Justice in Africa: Rwanda's Genocide, Its Courts, and the UN Criminal Tribunal*. Brookfield, Vt.: Ashgate.

Make Audiozine. 2005. "Natalie Jeremijenko." August 9. http://odeo.com/ (accessed December 22, 2009).

Malinowski, Bronislaw. 1961. *Argonauts of the Western Pacific*. New York: E. P. Dutton.

Malkki, Liisa. 1994. "Citizens of Humanity: Internationalism and the Imagined Community of Nations." *Diaspora* 3(1): 41–68.

———. 1995. *Purity and Exile: Violence, Memory, and National Cosmology among Hutu Refugees in Tanzania*. Chicago: University of Chicago Press.

———. 1996. "Speechless Emissaries: Refugees, Humanitarianism, and Dehistoricization." *Cultural Anthropology* 11(3): 377–404.

———. 2007. "Professionalisme, internationalisme, universalisme." *Anthropologie et sociétés* 31(2): 45–63.

Mamdani, Mahmood. 1996. *Citizen and Subject: Contemporary Africa and the Legacy of Late Colonialism*. Princeton, N.J.: Princeton University Press.

———. 2001. *When Victims Become Killers: Colonialism, Nativism and Genocide in Rwanda*. Princeton, N.J.: Princeton University Press.

———. 2007. "The Politics of Naming: Genocide, Civil War, Insurgency." *London Review of Books*, March 8.

———. 2009. *Saviors and Survivors: Darfur, Politics, and the War on Terror*. New York: Pantheon.

Mann, Charles C. 2005. *1491: New Revelations of Americas before Columbus*. New York: Knopf.

Mann, Steve, Jason Nolan, and Barry Wellman. 2003. "Sousveillance: Inventing and Using Wearable Computing Devices for Data Collection in Surveillance Environments." *Surveillance and Society* 1(3): 331–55.

Manoussakis, John P. 2002. "From Exodus to Eschaton: On the God Who May Be." *Modern Theology* 18(1): 95–107.

Mansuri, G., and V. Rao. 2004. "Community-Based and Driven Development: A Critical Review." *World Bank Research Observer* 19(1): 1–39.

Marks, Harry M. 1997. *The Progress of Experiment: Science and Therapeutic Reform in the United States, 1900–1990*. Cambridge: Cambridge University Press.

———. 2000. "Where Do Ethics Come From? The Role of Disciplines and Institutions." Paper presented at the conference "Ethical Issues in Clinical Trials," University of Alabama at Birmingham, February 25.

————. 2002. "Commentary." Third Annual W. H. R. Rivers Workshop, Global Pharmaceuticals: Ethics, Markets, Practices. Harvard University, May 19–21.

Marks, Lara. 2001. *Sexual Chemistry: A History of the Contraceptive Pill.* New Haven, Conn.: Yale University Press.

Marrus, Michael R. 2009. "International Bystanders to the Holocaust and Humanitarian Intervention." *Humanitarianism and Suffering: The Mobilization of Empathy,* ed. Richard Ashby Wilson and Richard D. Brown, 156–74. Cambridge: Cambridge University Press.

Marshall, Patricia, and Barbara Koenig. 2004. "Accounting for Culture in a Globalized Ethics." *Journal of Law, Medicine, and Ethics* 32(2): 252–66.

Marx, Karl. 1978a. "Economic and Philosophical Manuscripts of 1844." *The Marx-Engels Reader,* 2nd edn., ed. Robert C. Tucker, 66–125. New York: Norton.

————. 1978b. "On the Jewish Question." *The Marx-Engels Reader,* 2nd edn., ed. Robert C. Tucker, 26–52. New York: Norton.

Marx, Leo. 1964. *The Machine in the Garden: Technology and the Pastoral Ideal in America.* New York: Oxford University Press.

Masco, Joseph. 2004. "Mutant Ecologies: Radioactive Life in Post–Cold War New Mexico." *Cultural Anthropology* 19(4): 491–550.

————. 2006. *Nuclear Borderlands: The Manhattan Project in Post–Cold War New Mexico.* Princeton, N.J.: Princeton University Press.

Mayer, Jane. 2009. "The Predator War: What Are The Risks of the CIA's Covert Drone Program?" *New Yorker,* October 26. http://www.newyorker.com/ (accessed February 18, 2010).

Mazower, Mark. 2002. "The Strange Triumph of Human Rights." *New Statesman,* February 4. http://www.newstatesman.com/ (accessed February 11, 2010).

Mbembe, Achille. 1992. "The Banality of Power and the Aesthetics of Vulgarity in the Postcolony." *Public Culture* 4(2): 1–30.

McCay, Mary A. 1993. "Conflict." *Rachel Carson,* 63–83. New York: Twayne.

McKibben, Bill. 1989. *The End of Nature.* New York: Anchor.

————. 2003. *Enough: Staying Human in an Engineered Age.* New York: Times.

Médecins du Monde (MDM). 2003. *Les Civils israéliens et palestiniens victimes d'un conflit sans fin,* Pt. I : "Opération 'Mur de protection', Naplouse," MDM-International Federation of Human Rights study mission, July 2002; Pt. II: "Les civils israéliens victimes des attaques des groupes armés palestiniens," Médecins du Monde. Report, July 2003.

Médecins sans Frontières (MSF). 2002. *Angola: Sacrifice of a People.* Report, October 20. London: MSF U.K. http://www.msf.org.uk/ (accessed December 20, 2009).

————. 2003. *Rapport Moral 2002–2003,* presented by Jean-Hervé Bradol, Paris: MSF France, http://www.msf.fr/ (accessed February 8, 2010)

Mehta, Uday Singh. 1999. *Liberalism and Empire: A Study in Nineteenth-Century British Liberal Thought.* Chicago: University of Chicago Press.

Melody, Cheryl. 1997. *WORLD PEACE: The Children's Dream! A Multicultural Musical for the Whole Family!* Compact disc. Hopkinton, Mass.: Cheryl Melody Productions.

Merry, Sally Engle. 2005. *Human Rights and Gender Violence: Translating International Law into Local Justice*. Chicago: University of Chicago Press.

Miller, Christopher L. 1993. "Nationalism as Resistance and Resistance to Nationalism in the Literature of Francophone Africa." *Yale French Studies* 82:62–100.

Miller, Gary. 1992. *Managerial Dilemmas: The Political Economy of Hierarchy*. New York: Cambridge University Press.

Miller, Judith, Stephen Engelberg, and William J. Broad. 2001. *Germs: Biological Weapons and America's Secret War*. New York: Simon and Schuster.

Mitchell, Timothy. 1999. "Society, Economy, and the State Effect." *State/Culture: State-Formation after the Cultural Turn*, ed. George Steinmatz, 76–97. Ithaca, N.Y.: Cornell University Press.

———. 2002. *Rule of Experts: Egypt, Techno-politics, Modernity*. Berkeley: University of California Press.

Mitchell, W. J. Thomas. 2005. "The Work of Art in the Age of Biocybernetic Reproduction." *What Do Pictures Want: The Lives and Loves of Images*, 309–32. Chicago: University of Chicago Press.

Moise, Robert. 1996. "Pygmies, Citizens and Others: A Study of Identity and Intercultural Relations in the Forests of the Central African Republic—Proposal for Research to be Conducted." RDS Project archives (Bangui, Central African Republic).

Mol, Annemarie. 2002. *The Body Multiple: Ontology in Medical Practice*. Durham, N.C.: Duke University Press.

Montagu, Ashley. 1997. *Man's Most Dangerous Myth: Fallacy of Race*, 5th edn. Lanham, Md.: Altamira.

Moore, Donald S., Jake Kosek, and Anand Pandian, eds. 2006. *Race, Nature, and the Politics of Difference*. Durham, N.C.: Duke University Press.

Moore, Jonathan. 1998. *Hard Choices: Moral Dilemmas in Humanitarianism*. New York: Rowman and Littlefield.

Moreno, Jonathan D. 2000. *Undue Risk: Secret State Experiments on Humans*. London: Routledge.

Moro, Marie-Rose, and Christian Lachal. 2002. "Remèdes à la mélancolie." *Chroniques palestiniennes*, July, 11–16.

Moynihan, Ray, and Alan Cassels. 2005. *Selling Sickness: How the World's Biggest Pharmaceutical Companies Are Turning Us All into Patients*. New York: Nation.

Mundis, Daryl. 2006. "The Judicial Effects of the Completion Strategies on the Ad Hoc International Criminal Tribunals." *American Journal of International Law* 99(1): 142–58.

Murray, Stuart J. 2006. "Thanatopolitics: On the Use of Death for Mobilizing Political Life." *Polygraph: An International Journal of Politics and Culture* 18:191–215.

Murthy, Vivek H., Harlan M. Krumholz, and Cary P. Gross. 2004. "Participation in Cancer Clinical Trials: Race-, Sex-, and Age-Based Disparities." *JAMA: Journal of the American Medical Association* 291(22): 2720–26.

Myerson, George. 2000. *Donna Haraway and GM Foods*. London: Icon.

Nagele, Rainer. 1991. *Theater, Theory, Speculation: Walter Benjamin and the Scenes of Modernity*. Baltimore, Md.: Johns Hopkins University Press.

Nakazawa, Keiji. 2004 [1987]. *Barefoot Gen: A Cartoon Story of Hiroshima*. San Francisco: Last Gasp.

National Bioethics Advisory Commission. 2000. *Ethical and Policy Issues in International Research: Clinical Trials in Developing Countries*. Bethesda, Md.: National Bioethics Advisory Commission.

National Geographic. 2005. "Premiere! Secret Weapons." *National Geographic Explorer Extra*. Television program, May 17.

Near, Holly. 1993. *The Great Peace March*. Lisa Desimini, illustrator. New York: Henry Holt.

Nemes, M., H. Carvalho, and M. Souza. 2004. "Antiretroviral Therapy Adherence Rates in Brazil." *AIDS* 18(suppl 3): S15–20.

Neumann, Roderick P. 1998. *Imposing Wilderness: Struggles over Livelihood and Nature Preservation in Africa*. Berkeley: University of California Press.

N'gouandjika, Mathias. 1989. "Le roman, entre le silence et le défi." *Notre librairie* 96:60–67.

Nguyen, Vinh-kim. 2005. "Antiretroviral Globalism, Biopolitics, and Therapeutic Citizenship." *Global Assemblages: Technology, Politics, and Ethics as Anthropological Problems*, ed. Stephen J. Collier and Aihwa Ong, 124–44. Malden, Mass.: Blackwell.

———. 2009. "Government-by-exception: Enrolment and Experimentality in Mass HIV Treatment Programmes in Africa." *Social Theory & Health* 7(3):196–217.

Nichols, Michael, and John Michael Fay. 2005. *The Last Place on Earth: Photographs by Michael Nichols with Mike Fay's African Megatransect Journals*. Washington, D.C.: National Geographic Books.

Nietzsche, Friedrich. 1983. *Thus Spoke Zarathustra*. Trans. Walter Kaufmann. Harmondsworth, U.K.: Penguin.

Nussbaum, Martha Craven. 2004. *Hiding from Humanity: Disgust, Shame, and the Law*. Princeton, N.J.: Princeton University Press.

Nygren, Anja. 2005. "Community-Based Forest Management within the Context of Institutional Decentralization in Honduras." *World Development* 33(4): 639–55.

Oakley, Ann. 2005. "Who's Afraid of the Randomized Controlled Trial? Some Dilemmas of the Scientific Method and 'Good' Research Practice." *The Ann Oakley Reader: Gender, Women and Social Science*, 233–44. Bristol, U.K.: Policy.

O'Connor, Karen. 1993. "They Believe That Children Are the Future." *Billboard* 105(7): C3.

Office of Inspector General, Department of Health and Human Services (OIG). 2001. "The Globalization of Clinical Trials: A Growing Challenge in Protecting Human Subjects. Boston: Office of Evaluation and Inspections." http://oig.hhs .gov/ (accessed December 7, 2009).

———. 2007. *The Food and Drug Administration's Oversight of Clinical Trials*. http://oig.hhs.gov/ (accessed December 7, 2009).

Okie, S. 2006. "Fighting HIV: Lessons from Brazil." *New England Journal of Medicine* 354(19): 1977–81.

Okri, Ben. 1991. *The Famished Road*. New York: Anchor Books.

———. 1996. *Dangerous Love*. London: Phoenix House.

Olson, James S. 2002. *Bathsheba's Breast: Women, Cancer, and History*. Baltimore, Md.: Johns Hopkins University Press.

Omenn, G. 1988. "Healthy Children: Investing in the Future." *Issues in Science and Technology* 5(1): 106.

Ong, Aihwa. 1999. *Flexible Citizenship: The Cultural Logics of Transnationality*. Durham, N.C.: Duke University Press.

———. 2006. *Neoliberalism as Exception: Mutations in Citizenship and Sovereignty*. Durham, N.C.: Duke University Press.

Ophir, Adi. 2005. "Le souverain, l'humanitaire et le terroriste." "Politique non gouvernementale," special issue of *Vacarme* 34:20–25.

Orokas, Jean. 1994. "TERE Village: Agence en communication culturelle et en promotion des activités artistiques et touristiques en Centrafrique." Unpublished document. Bangui, Central African Republic: Espace Lingatere.

Orr, Jackie. 2005. "Making Civilian Soldiers: The Militarization of Inner Space." *Making Threats: Biofears and Environmental Anxieties*, ed. Betsy Hartmann, Banu Subramaniam, and Charles Zerner, 47–70. Lanham, Md.: Rowman and Littlefield.

Ostrom, Elinor. 1990. *Governing the Commons: The Evolution of Institutions for Collective Action*. New York: Cambridge University Press.

Oxford Biomedica. 2007. "Patient Information Leaflet. FINALver.1.0, TroVax ® Renal Immunotherapy Survival Trial TRIST™." www.ack.org/trovax (accessed August 12, 2007).

Packard, Randall. 2007. *The Making of a Tropical Disease: A Short History of Malaria*. Baltimore, Md.: Johns Hopkins University Press.

Pandolfi, Mariella. 2003. "Contract of Mutual (In)Difference: Governance and the Humanitarian Apparatus in Contemporary Albania and Kosovo." *Indiana Journal of Global Legal Studies* 10(1): 369–81.

———. 2008. "Laboratory of Intervention: The Humanitarian Governance of the Postcommunist Balkan Territories." *Postcolonial Disorders*, ed. Mary-Jo Delvecchio Good, Sandra Hyde, Sarah Pinto, and Byron Good, 157–88. Berkeley: University of California Press.

Parenti, Christian. 2003. *The Soft Cage: Surveillance in America from Slavery to the War on Terror*. New York: Basic.

Parexel. 2005. *Pharmaceutical R&D Statistical Sourcebook, 2005/2006*. Waltham, Mass.: Parexel International.

Parker, Richard. 1994. *A construção da solidariedade: AIDS, sexualidade e política no Brasil*. Rio de Janeiro: Relume-Dumará, ABIA, IMS/UERJ.

———, ed. 1997. *Políticas, instituições e AIDS: Enfrentando a epidemia no Brasil*. Rio de Janeiro: Jorge Zahar/ABIA.

Partridge, Damani. 2009. "We Were Dancing in the Club, Not on the Berlin Wall: Hypersexed Bodies, Street Bureaucrats, and Exclusionary Incorporation into the New Europe." *Cultural Anthropology* 23(4): 660–87.

Patterson, Orlando. 1982. *Slavery and Social Death: A Comparative Study*. Cambridge, Mass.: Harvard University Press.

Peace Child Foundation. 1987. *Peace Child: A Musical Fantasy about Children Bringing Peace to the World*. Musical director's score. Music and lyrics by David Gordon. Arrangements by Steve Riffkin. Fairfax, Va.: Peace Child Foundation.

Peluso, Nancy Lee, and Peter Vandergeest. 2001. "Genealogies of the Political Forest and Customary Rights in Indonesia, Malaysia, and Thailand." *Journal of Asian Studies* 60(3): 761–812.

Pepperberg, Irene M. 1999. *The Alex Studies: Cognitive and Communicative Abilities of Grey Parrots*. Cambridge, Mass.: Harvard University Press.

———. 2008. *Alex and Me: How a Scientist and a Parrot Discovered a Hidden World of Animal Intelligence—and Formed a Deep Bond in the Process*. New York: Collins.

Peters, Krijn, and Paul Richards. 1998. "Fighting with Open Eyes: Young Combatants Talking about War in Sierra Leone." *Rethinking the Trauma of War*, ed. Patrick J. Bracken and Celia Petty, 76–111. New York: Free Association Press.

Petryna, Adriana. 2002. *Life Exposed: Biological Citizens after Chernobyl*. Princeton, N.J.: Princeton University Press.

———. 2005. "Ethical Variability: Drug Development and the Globalization of Clinical Trials." *American Ethnologist* 32(2): 183–97.

———. 2009. *When Experiments Travel: Clinical Trials and the Global Search for Human Subjects*. Princeton, N.J.: Princeton University Press.

Petryna, Adriana, and Arthur Kleinman. 2006. "The Pharmaceutical Nexus: An Introduction." *Global Pharmaceuticals: Ethics, Markets, Practices*, ed. Adriana Petryna, Andrew Lakoff, and Arthur Kleinman, 1–33. Durham, N.C.: Duke University Press.

Petryna, Adriana, Andrew Lakoff, and Arthur Kleinman, eds. 2006. *Global Pharmaceuticals: Ethics, Markets, Practices*. Durham, N.C.: Duke University Press.

Pharmbiosys. 2007. "Pharmaceutical Research and Development in the Twenty-First Century." http://www.pharmbiosys.com (accessed March 3, 2007).

Pinder, Mike. 1995. *A Planet with One Mind: Stories from around the World for the Child within Us All*. Audiocassette. One Step Records, BMI.

Platteau, Jean-Philippe, and Frédéric Gaspart. 2003. "The Risk of Resource Misappropriation in Community-Driven Development." *World Development* 31(10): 1687–1703.

Political Economy Research Institute (PERI). 2007. "Corporate Toxics Information Project." http://www.peri.umass.edu/ (accessed January 16, 2007).

Pollan, Michael. 1991. "The Idea of a Garden." *Second Nature: A Gardener's Education*, 209–238. New York: Delta.

Porter, Ted. 1995. *Trust in Numbers: The Pursuit of Objectivity*. Princeton, N.J.: Princeton University Press.

Power, Samantha. 2002. *A Problem from Hell: America and the Age of Genocide*. New York: Basic.

Prado, Paulo. 2005. "Brazil Again Seeks to Cut Cost of AIDS Drug." *New York Times*, August 19. http://www.nytimes.com/ (accessed December 15, 2009).

Pressly, William L. 1973. "The Praying Mantis in Surrealist Art." *Art Bulletin* 55(4): 600–615.

Prime Time Live. 1997. Special broadcast from northern Congo featuring Michael Fay, aired March 3. New York: ABC Television.

Psaty, B. M., and C. D. Furberg. 2005. "COX-2 Inhibitors—Lessons in Drug Safety." *New England Journal of Medicine* 352: 1135.

Rabinow, Paul. 2002. "Midst Anthropology's Problems." *Cultural Anthropology* 17(2): 135–49.

———. 2003. *Anthropos Today: Reflections on Modern Equipment.* Princeton, N.J.: Princeton University Press.

———. 2008. *Marking Time: On the Anthropology of the Contemporary.* Princeton, N.J.: Princeton University Press.

Raffles, Hugh. 2002. *In Amazonia: A Natural History.* Princeton, N.J.: Princeton University Press.

Ramiah, I., and Michael Reich. 2006. "Building Effective Public-Private Partnerships: Experiences and Lessons from the African Comprehensive HIV/AIDS Partnerships (ACHAP)." *Social Science and Medicine* 63(2): 397–408.

Rancière, Jacques. 2004a. "Introducing Disagreement." *Angelaki* 9(3): 1–8.

———. 2004b. "Who Is the Subject of the Rights of Man?" *South Atlantic Quarterly* 102(2–3): 297–310.

Rapp, Rayna. 1999. *Testing Women, Testing the Fetus: The Social Impact of Amniocentesis in America.* New York: Routledge.

Redfield, Peter. 2005. "Doctors, Borders, and Life in Crisis." *Cultural Anthropology* 20(3): 328–61.

———. 2006. "A Less Modest Witness: Collective Advocacy and Motivated Truth in a Medical Humanitarian Movement." *American Ethnologist* 33(1): 3–26.

Rettig, Richard. 2000. "The Industrialization of Clinical Research." *Health Affairs* 19(2): 129–46.

Rettig, Richard A., Peter D. Jacobson, Cynthia M. Farquhar, and Wade Aubry. 2007. *False Hope: Bone Marrow Transplantation for Breast Cancer.* New York: Oxford University Press.

Reuters. 2006. "Israel Developing Killer Bionic Hornet." *Sydney Morning Herald.* November 17. http://www.smh.com.au/ (accessed December 22, 2009).

Reverby, Susan, ed. 2000. *Tuskegee's Truths: Rethinking the Tuskegee Syphilis Study.* Chapel Hill: University of North Carolina Press.

Reynolds, Pamela. 1995. *Traditional Healers and Childhood in Zimbabwe.* Athens: Ohio University Press.

Riley, Denise. 1988. *Am I That Name? Feminism and the Category of "Women" in History.* Minneapolis: University of Minnesota Press.

Robbins, Bruce. 1998. "Introduction Part 1: Actually Existing Cosmopolitanism." *Cosmopolitics: Thinking and Feeling beyond the Nation*, ed. Pheng Cheah and Bruce Robbins, 1–19. Minneapolis: University of Minnesota Press.

Rodriguez-Pose, A., and N. Gill. 2003. "The Global Trend towards Devolution and Its Implications." *Environment and Planning C: Government and Policy* 21(3): 333–51.

Rose, Carole. 1991. "Property as Storytelling: Perspectives from Narrative, Game and Feminist Theory." *Yale Journal of Law and the Humanities* 2: 37–57.

Rose, Nikolas. 1999. *Powers of Freedom: Reframing Political Thought*. Cambridge: Cambridge University Press.

———. 2006. *The Politics of Life Itself: Biomedicine, Power and Subjectivity in the Twenty-First Century*. Princeton, N.J.: Princeton University Press.

Rose, Nikolas, and Carlos Novas. 2005. "Biological Citizenship." *Global Assemblages: Technology, Politics, and Ethics as Anthropological Problems*, ed. Aihwa Ong and Stephen J. Collier, 439–63. Oxford: Blackwell.

Rosen, David. 2005. *Armies of the Young: Child Soldiers in War and Terrorism*. Piscataway, N.J.: Rutgers University Press.

Rosenberg, Charles. 2002. "The Tyranny of Diagnosis: Specific Entities and Individual Experience." *Milbank Quarterly* 80(2): 237–60.

Rosenblum, Robert. 1988. *The Romantic Child: From Runge to Sendak*. New York: Thames and Hudson.

Rothman, David J. 1991. *Strangers at the Bedside: A History of How Law and Bioethics Transformed Medical Decision Making*. New York: Basic.

Rothman, David J., and Harold Edgar. 1992. "Scientific Rigor and Medical Realities: Placebo Trials in Cancer and AIDS Research." *AIDS: The Making of a Chronic Disease*, ed. Elizabeth Fee and Daniel M. Fox, 182–222. Berkeley: University of California Press.

Roukes, Michael. 2001. "Plenty of Room, Indeed." *Scientific American* 285:42–49.

Rousseau, Jean-Jacques. 1978 [1762]. *Emile; or, On Education*. Ed. Allan Bloom. New York: Basic.

Rubin, Gayle. 1975. "The Traffic in Women: Notes on the 'Political Economy' of Sex." *Toward an Anthropology of Women*, ed. Rayna Reiter, 283–308. New York: Monthly Review Press.

Russell, Edmund. 2001. *War and Nature: Fighting Humans and Insects with Chemicals from World War I to "Silent Spring."* Cambridge: Cambridge University Press.

Sahlins, Marshall. 1976. *Culture and Practical Reason*. Chicago: University of Chicago Press.

Salignon, Pierre, Fouad Ismael, and Elena Sgorbati. 2002. "Soigner l'esprit." *Chroniques palestiniennes*, July, 8–10.

Sarasin, Philipp. 2006. *Anthrax: Bioterror as Fact and Fantasy*. Cambridge, Mass.: Harvard University Press.

Sartre, Jean-Paul. 1995 [1946]. *Anti-Semite and Jew: An Exploration of the Etiology of Hate*. New York: Schocken.

Sassen, Saskia. 1998. *Globalization and Its Discontents*. New York: New Press.

———. 2006. *Territory, Authority, Rights: From Medieval to Global Assemblages*. Princeton, N.J.: Princeton University Press.

Scarry, Elaine. 1985. *The Body in Pain*. Oxford: Oxford University Press.

Schabas, William. 2000. *Genocide in International Law*. Cambridge: Cambridge University Press.

Schatzberg, Michael, ed. 1988. *The Dialectics of Oppression in Zaire*. Bloomington: Indiana University Press.

Schell, Jonathan. 1982. *The Fate of the Earth*. New York: Avon.

Scheper-Hughes, Nancy. 2004. "Parts Unknown: Undercover Ethnography of the Organs-Trafficking Underworld." *Ethnography* 5(1): 29–74.

Scheper-Hughes, Nancy, and Carolyn Sargent, eds. 1998. *Small Wars: The Cultural Politics of Childhood*. Berkeley: University of California Press.

Scheper-Hughes, Nancy, and Loïc J. D. Wacquant, eds. 2002. *Commodifying Bodies*. London: Sage.

Schmitt, Carl. 1996. *The Concept of the Political*. Chicago: University of Chicago Press.

———. 2007. *Political Theology: Four Chapters on the Concept of Sovereignty*. Trans. George Schwab. Chicago: University of Chicago Press.

Scholes, Katherine. 1990. *Peace Begins with You*. Robert Ingpen, illustrator. Boston: Little, Brown, Sierra Club Books.

Schopenhauer, Arthur. 1970. *Essays and Aphorisms*. New York: Penguin.

Schürmann, Reiner. 1984. "Legislation-Transgression: Strategies and Counter Strategies in the Transcendental Justification of Norms." *Man and World* 17:361–98.

Schweitzer, Albert. 1950. *Denken und Tat*. Ed. Rudolph Grabs. Hamburg: Richard Meiner.

Scott, David. 1999. *Refashioning Futures: Criticism after Postcoloniality*. Princeton, N.J.: Princeton University Press.

Scott, James C. 1990. *Domination and the Arts of Resistance: Hidden Transcripts*. New Haven, Conn.: Yale University Press.

Scott, Joan. 1996. *Paradoxes to Offer: French Feminists and the Rights of Man*. Cambridge, Mass.: Harvard University Press.

———. 2001. "Deconstructing Equality-versus-Difference; or, The Uses of Poststructuralist Theory for Feminism." *Theorizing Feminism: Parallel Trends in the Humanities and Social Sciences*, ed. Anne C. Herrmann and Abigail J. Stewart, 254–67. Boulder, Colo.: Westview.

Sen, Amartya. 1981. *Poverty and Famines: An Essay on Entitlement and Deprivation*. Oxford, New York: Oxford University Press.

Sendak, Maurice. 1981. *Outside over There*. New York: HarperCollins.

Sepúlveda, Juan. 1892. "Democrates Alter; or, On the Just Causes for War against the Indians." *Boletín de la Real Academia de la Historia* 21 (October 1892). Originally translated for *Introduction to Contemporary Civilization in the West*. New York: Columbia University Press, 1946, 1954, 1961.

Serra, José. 2004. *The Political Economy of the Struggle against AIDS in Brazil*. Princeton, N.J.: School of Social Science of the Institute for Advanced Studies, Occasional Papers.

Shepard, Todd. 2006. *The Invention of Decolonization: The Algerian War and the Remaking of France*. Ithaca, N.Y.: Cornell University Press.

Shachtman, Noah. 2009. "Uber-Soldier Needs Much Debugging." *Wired*, May 24. http://www.wired.com/ (accessed April 30, 2010).

Shaffer, N., R. Chuachoowong, P. A. Mock, et al. for the Bangkok Collaborative Perinatal HIV Transmission Study Group. 1999. "Short-Course Zidovudine for Perinatal HIV-1 Transmission in Bangkok, Thailand: A Randomised Controlled Trial." *Lancet* 353:773–80.

Sharkey, Noel E. 2008a. "Cassandra or the False Prophet of Doom: AI Robots and War." *IEEE Intelligent Systems* 23(4): 14–17.

———. 2008b. "The Ethical Frontiers of Robotics." *Science* 322:1800–1801.

———. 2008c. "Grounds for Discrimination: Autonomous Robot Weapons." *RUSI Defence Systems* 11(2): 86–89.

Shiva, Vandana. 1994. *Close to Home: Women Reconnect Ecology, Health, and Development Worldwide*. Philadelphia: New Society.

Shrivastava, Aseem. 1996. "Property Rights, Deforestation, and Community Forest Management in the Himalayas: An Analysis of Forest Policy in British Kumaon, 1815–1949." PhD diss., University of Massachusetts, Amherst.

Siamundelé, André. 1994. "Sociocritique du roman d'Afrique francophone." Paper presented in Yale French Department Graduate Colloquium, New Haven, April 1994.

Singa Ndourou, S. 1987. "Projet: Equipements destinés à promouvoir une intégration socio-culturelle des pygmées de la préfecture de la Sangha économique." Ministère Chargé du Secrétariat Général du Conseil des Ministres. Bangui, Central African Republic: MEEFCPT-CAR.

Singer, P. W. 2009. *Wired for War: The Robotics Revolution and 21st Century Conflict*. New York: Penguin.

Sivaramakrishnan, K. 1999. *Modern Forests: Statemaking and Environmental Change in Colonial Eastern India*. Stanford, Calif.: Stanford University Press.

———. 2005. Introduction to "Moral Economies, State Spaces, and Categorical Violence: Anthropological Engagements with the Work of James Scott." *American Anthropologist* 107(3): 321–30.

Slater, Candace, ed. 2003. *In Search of the Rain Forest*. Durham, N.C.: Duke University Press.

Spivak, Gayatri Chakravorty. 1988. "Can the Subaltern Speak?" *Marxism and the Interpretation of Culture*, ed. Cary Nelson and Larry Grossberg, 271–313. Urbana: University of Illinois Press.

Spurr, David. 1993. *The Rhetoric of Empire*. Durham, N.C.: Duke University Press.

Staub, Ervin. 1994 [1989]. *The Roots of Evil: The Origins of Genocide and Other Group Violence*. Cambridge: Cambridge University Press.

Steedman, Carolyn. 1995. *Strange Dislocations: Childhood and the Idea of Human Interiority, 1780–1930*. Cambridge, Mass.: Harvard University Press.

Stephens, Sharon. 1995. "Children and the Politics of Culture in 'Late Capitalism.'" *Children and the Politics of Culture*, ed. Sharon Stephens, 3–48. Princeton, N.J.: Princeton University Press.

Stoler, Ann Laura. 1997. "Sexual Affronts and Racial Frontiers: European Identities and the Cultural Politics of Exclusion in Colonial Southeast Asia." *Tensions of*

Empire, ed. Frederick Cooper and Ann Laura Stoler, 198–237. Berkeley: University of California Press.

———. 2004. "Affective States." *A Companion to the Anthropology of Politics*, ed. David Nugent and Joan Vincent, 4–20. Malden, Mass.: Blackwell.

Strathern, Marilyn. 1991. *Partial Connections*. Lanham, Md.: Rowman and Littlefield.

Subramaniam, Banu. 2001. "The Aliens Have Landed! Reflections on the Rhetoric of Biological Invasions." *Meridians: Feminism, Race, Transnationalism* 2(1): 26–40.

Suhrke, Astri, and Douglas Klusmeyer. 2004. "Between Principles and Politics: Lessons from Iraq for Humanitarian Action." *Journal of Refugee Studies* 17(3): 273–85.

Sunder Rajan, Kaushik. 2006. *Biocapital: The Constitution of Postgenomic Life*. Durham, N.C.: Duke University Press.

Takacs, David. 1996. *The Idea of Biodiversity: Philosophies of Paradise*. Baltimore, Md.: Johns Hopkins University Press.

Tambiah, Stanley J. 1985. *Culture, Thought, and Social Action: An Anthropological Perspective*. Cambridge, Mass.: Harvard University Press.

Taussig, Michael. 1987. *Shamanism, Colonialism, and the Wild Man: A Study in Terror and Healing*. Chicago: University of Chicago Press.

Teitel, Ruti. 2004. "For Humanity." *Journal of Human Rights* 3(2): 225–37.

———. 2005. "The Alien Tort and the Global Rule of Law." *ISSJ* (UNESCO) 185: 551–60.

Telesis Consulting Firm. 1991. *Sustainable Economic Development Options for the Dzanga Sangha Reserve, Central African Republic: Final Report*. Washington, D.C.: World Wildlife Fund, U.S., and the PVO/NMRS Project.

Terborgh, John. 1999. *Requiem for Nature*. Washington, D.C.: Island.

Terry, Fiona. 2002. *Condemned to Repeat? The Paradox of Humanitarian Action*. Ithaca, N.Y.: Cornell University Press.

Thacker, Eugene. 2009. Wet Data: Biomedia and BioMEMS. January 6, 2009. www.nettime.org.

Ticktin, Miriam. 2005. "Policing and Humanitarianism in France: Immigration and the Turn to Law as State of Exception." *Interventions: International Journal of Postcolonial Studies* 7(3): 347–68.

———. 2006a. "Medical Humanitarianism in and beyond France: Breaking Down or Patrolling Borders?" *Medicine at the Border: Disease, Globalization and Security, 1850 to the Present*, ed. Alison Bashford, 116–35. New York: Palgrave.

———. 2006b. "Where Ethics and Politics Meet: The Violence of Humanitarianism in France." *American Ethnologist* 33(1): 33–49.

Time.com. N.d. "Best Inventions 2003: Mine Sweeper." http://www.time.com/ (accessed February 26, 2010).

Toon, Elizabeth. 2009. *Breast Cancer Therapy and Experience in Postwar Britain*. New York: Palgrave Macmillan.

Torgovnick, Marianne. 1990. *Gone Primitive: Savage Intellects, Modern Lives*. Chicago: University of Chicago Press.

Tsing, Anna Lowenhaupt. 1993. *In the Realm of the Diamond Queen: Marginality in an Out-of-the-Way Place*. Princeton, N.J.: Princeton University Press.

———. 2005. *Friction: An Ethnography of Global Connection*. Princeton, N.J.: Princeton University Press.

Tsuchiya, Yukio. 1988 [1951]. *Faithful Elephants: A True Story of Animals, People and War*. Boston: Houghton Mifflin.

United Nations Children's Fund (UNICEF). 1994. *I Dream Of Peace: Images of War by Children of Former Yugoslavia*. New York: UNICEF/HarperCollins.

UNAIDS/WHO/UNICEF. 2008. *Towards Universal Access: Scaling up Priority HIV/AIDS Interventions in the Health Sector*. Progress report. Geneva: World Health Organization. http://www.who.int/ (accessed February 11, 2010).

U.S. National Institutes of Health (USNIH). 2007. "Understanding Clinical Trials." http://clinicaltrials.gov/ (accessed December 21, 2009).

Valentine, Gill. 1996. "Angels and Devils: Moral Landscapes of Childhood." *Environment and Planning D: Society and Space* 14(5): 581–99.

Valier, Helen, and Carsten Timmermans. 2008. "Clinical Trials and the Reorganization of Medical Research in Post–Second World War Britain." *Medical History* 52: 493–520.

Van Eys, Jan. 1981. *Humanity and Personhood: Personal Reaction to a World in Which Children Can Die*. Springfield, Ill.: Charles C. Thomas.

Vattel, Emmerich de. 2005 [1975, 1854, 1758]. *The Law of Nations; or, Principles of the Law of Nature, Applied to the Conduct and Affairs of Nations and Sovereigns*. Ed. Joseph Chitty. From the French of Monsieur de Vattel, with additional notes and references by Edward D. Ingraham, Esq. Clark, N.J.: Lawbook Exchange.

Veit, Peter G., and Catherine Benson. 2004. "When Parks and People Collide." "Environmental Rights," special issue of *Human Rights Dialogue* 2, no. 11. www.cceia.org/ (accessed March 15, 2008).

Verwimp, Philip. 2004. "Death and Survival during the 1994 Genocide in Rwanda." *Population Studies* 58(2): 233–45.

Vian, Boris. 1947. *L'écume des jours*. Paris: Gallimard.

Virilio, Paul. 1989. *War and Cinema: The Logistics of Perception*. London: Verso.

———. 2006. *Speed and Politics*. Los Angeles: Semiotext(e).

Vittachi, Varindra Tarzie. 1993. *Between the Guns: Children as a Zone of Peace*. London: Hodder and Stoughton.

Von Uexküll, Jakob. 2001. "An Introduction." *Umwelt Semiotica* 134(1/4): 107–10.

Wade, Robert. 1994. *Village Republics: Economic Conditions for Collective Action in South India*. San Francisco: ICS.

Wairagala, Wakabi. 2006. "Health Crisis Worsens in CAR." *Lancet* 367:1969–70.

Wall, John. 2004. "Fallen Angels: A Contemporary Christian Ethical Ontology of Childhood." *International Journal of Practical Theology* 8:160–84.

Wallerstein, Immanuel. 2004. *World Systems Analysis: An Introduction*. Durham, N.C.: Duke University Press.

Walton, D. A., with P. E. Farmer, W. Lambert, F. Léandre, S. P. Koenig, and J. S. Mukherjee. 2004. "Integrated HIV Prevention and Care Strengthens Primary

Health Care: Lessons from Rural Haiti." *Journal of Public Health Policy* 25(2): 137–58.

Wark, McKenzie. 1995. "Fresh Maimed Babies: The Uses of Innocence." *Transition* 65:36–47.

Weaver, James H., Michael T. Rock, and Kenneth Kusterer. 1997. *Achieving Broad-Based Sustainable Development: Governance, Environment, and Growth with Equity.* West Hartford, Conn.: Kumarian.

Weber, Max. 2000 [1930]. *The Protestant Ethic and the Spirit of Capitalism.* New York: Routledge.

Weedon, Chris. 2001. *Feminism, Theory, and the Politics of Difference.* Oxford: Blackwell.

Weiss, Rick. 2007. "Dragonfly or Insect Spy? Scientists at Work on Robobugs." *Washington Post*, October 9. http://www.washingtonpost.com/ (accessed December 22, 2009).

Weissman, Fabrice, and Joanne Myers. 2007. "The Darfur Crisis: Humanitarian Aid in the Balance." http://www.cceia.org/ (accessed December 7, 2009).

Weitz, Eric. 2003. *A Century of Genocide: Utopias of Race and Nation.* Princeton, N.J.: Princeton University Press.

Welsome, Eileen. 2000. *The Plutonium Files: America's Secret Medical Experiments in the Cold War.* New York: Delta.

West, Paige, and Dan Brockington. 2006. "An Anthropological Perspective on Some Unexpected Consequences of Protected Areas." *Conservation Biology* 20(5): 609–16.

Wheeler, Nicholas. 2000. *Saving Strangers: Humanitarian Intervention in International Society.* Oxford: Oxford University Press.

White, Hayden. 1990. *Content of the Form: Narrative Discourse and Historical Representation.* Baltimore: Johns Hopkins University Press.

———. 1998. Address to "Histories of the Future" Residential Research Group, University of California Humanities Research Institute, University of California, Irvine.

Whyte, Lancelot Law. 1951. "Animal Form in Relation to Appearance." *Aspects of Form: a Symposium on Form in Nature and Art*, 121–56. New York: Pellegrini and Cudahy.

Whyte, Susan Reynolds, Michael Whyte, Lotte Meinert, and Betty Kyaddondo. 2006. "Treating AIDS: Dilemmas of Unequal Access in Uganda." *Global Pharmaceuticals: Ethics, Markets, Practices*, ed. Adriana Petryna, Andrew Lakoff, and Arthur Kleinman, 240–62. Durham, N.C.: Duke University Press.

Wiener, Norbert. 1964. *God and Golem, Inc.: A Comment on Certain Points Where Cybernetics Impinges on Religion.* Cambridge, Mass.: MIT Press.

Wieviorka, Annette. 1998. *L'ère du témoin.* Paris: Hachette.

Wikipedia. 2007. "Walt Disney Imagineering." February 1. http://en.wikipedia.org/ (accessed December 7, 2009).

———. 2008. "Mark Trail." February 1. http://en.wikipedia.org/ (accessed December 7, 2009).

————. 2009. "Mimic (film)." November 28. http://en.wikipedia.org/ (accessed December 22, 2009).

Wiktor, S. Z., E. Ekpini, J. M. Karon, et al. 1999. "Short-Course Oral Zidovudine for Prevention of Mother-to-Child Transmission of HIV-1 in Abidjan, Côte d'Ivoire: A Randomised Trial." *Lancet* 353:781–85.

Williams, Raymond. 1985. *Marxism and Literature.* Oxford: Oxford University Press.

Wilson, Edward O. 1971. *The Insect Societies.* Cambridge, Mass.: Belknap Press of Harvard University Press.

————. 1994. *Naturalist.* Washington, D.C.: Island.

————. 1999. *The Diversity of Life.* New York: W. W. Norton.

Wilson, Edward O., and George F. Orster. 1979. *Caste and Ecology in the Social Insects.* Cambridge, Mass.: Belknap Press of Harvard University Press.

Wilson, Richard Ashby. 2005. "Judging History: The Historical Record of the International Criminal Tribunal for the Former Yugoslavia." *Human Rights Quarterly* 27(3): 908–42.

————, ed. 1997. *Human Rights, Culture and Context: Anthropological Perspectives.* London: Pluto.

Wilson, Richard Ashby, and Richard D. Brown, eds. 2009. *Humanitarianism and Suffering: The Mobilization of Empathy.* Cambridge: Cambridge University Press.

Wogart, J. P., and G. Calcagnotto. 2006. "Brazil's Fight against AIDS and Its Implications for Global Health Governance." *World Health and Population,* January, 1–16.

Wolverkamp, Paul, ed. 1999. *Forests for the Future: Local Strategies for Forest Protection, Economic Welfare and Social Justice.* London: Zed.

Yamazaki, James, with Louis Fleming. 1995. *Children of the Atomic Bomb: An American Physician's Memoir of Nagasaki, Hiroshima, and the Marshall Islands.* Durham, N.C.: Duke University Press.

Yanow, Dvora. 2003. *Constructing "Race" and "Ethnicity" in America: Category-Making in Public Policy and Administration.* Armonk, N.Y.: M. E. Sharpe.

Yoneyama, Lisa. 1999. *Hiroshima Traces: Time, Space, and the Dialectics of Memory.* Berkeley: University of California Press.

Young, Allan. 1995. *The Harmony of Illusions: Inventing Post-traumatic Stress Disorder.* Princeton, N.J.: Princeton University Press.

Young, Iris. 2004. "Responsibility and Historic Injustice." Paper presented at the School of Social Science Thursday Seminar, Institute for Advanced Study, Princeton, N.J., February 19.

Zelizer, Viviana. 1994. *Pricing the Priceless Child: The Changing Social Value of Children.* Princeton, N.J.: Princeton University Press.

CONTRIBUTORS ∽

ARUN AGRAWAL teaches environmental politics at the University of Michigan in the School of Natural Resources and Environment (SNRE). He is the associate dean for research at SNRE, and the coordinator of the International Forestry Resources and Institutions Network. His research interests include how power works in communities, self-governance, adaptation to climate change, and poverty and rural social life. He is the author of *Greener Pastures: Politics, Markets, and Community among a Migrant Pastoral People* (1999), and *Environmentality: Technologies of Government and the Making of Subjectivities* (2005). When not teaching, writing, and traveling, he hunts mushrooms, bakes bread, and learns French.

JOÃO BIEHL is Susan Dod Brown Professor of Anthropology and Woodrow Wilson School Faculty Associate at Princeton University. He is the author of *Vita: Life in a Zone of Social Abandonment* (2005), *Will to Live: AIDS Therapies and the Politics of Survival* (2007), and a co-editor of *Subjectivity: Ethnographic Investigations* (2007). His current research explores the social impact of large-scale treatment programs in resource-poor settings, and the role of the judiciary in administering public health.

DIDIER FASSIN is James Wolfensohn Professor of Social Science at the Institute for Advanced Study in Princeton, N.J., and director of studies in anthropology at the Ecole des Hautes Etudes en Sciences Sociales (EHESS). He directs the Interdisciplinary Research Institute for Social Sciences (CNRS / Inserm / EHESS /

Université de Paris–Nord). Trained as a medical doctor, he has been vice-president of Médecins sans Frontières and is currently president of the Comité Médical pour les Exilés. Among other books, he is the author of *When Bodies Remember: Experience and Politics of AIDS in South Africa* (2007), and co-editor of *Contemporary States of Emergency. The Politics of Military and Humanitarian Interventions* (2010).

ALLEN FELDMAN is a cultural anthropologist and associate professor at New York University where he teaches visual culture, the anthropology of the body, and philosophy of media. He is the author of *Formations of Violence: The Narrative of the Body and Political Terror in Northern Ireland* (1991), numerous articles on the visual and performance culture of violence, and the forthcoming book *Archives of the Insensible: War, Terror, and Violence as Dead Memory* (2011).

ILANA FELDMAN is an assistant professor of anthropology and international affairs at George Washington University. Her current research examines the Palestinian experience of humanitarianism since 1948, exploring both how this aid apparatus has shaped Palestinian social and political life and how the Palestinian experience has influenced broader postwar humanitarian practice. She is the author of *Governing Gaza: Bureaucracy, Authority, and the Work of Rule, 1917–1967* (2008).

REBECCA HARDIN is an associate professor at the University of Michigan in the School of Natural Resources and Environment. Her research, published in journals such as *American Anthropologist* and *Conservation Biology*, focuses on the Sangha River region, where Cameroon, the Central African Republic, and the Democratic Republic of the Congo meet. Her book *Concessionary Politics: Regional Rivalry and Territorial Identity in the Use of Africa's Natural Resources* is forthcoming.

S. LOCHLANN JAIN is an associate professor of anthropology at Stanford University. The author of *Injury: Design and Litigation in the United States* (2006), she is currently at work on two book manuscripts that analyze the distribution of everyday violence in the United States: "Commodity Violence: American Automobility" and "Cancer Culture." Her recent essays have been published in *Cultural Anthropology* and *Representations*. She was awarded the Cultural Horizons Prize by the Society for Cultural Anthropology for best article published in *Cultural Anthropology* in 2004.

LIISA MALKKI is an associate professor of anthropology at Stanford University. Her research interests include the politics of nationalism, internationalism, cosmopolitanism, and human rights discourses as transnational cultural forms; the social production of historical memory and the uses of history; political violence, exile, and displacement; the ethics and politics of humanitarian aid; child research; and visual culture. She is the author of *Purity and Exile: Violence, Memory, and National Cosmology among Hutu Refugees in Tanzania* (1995).

ADRIANA PETRYNA is a professor of anthropology at the University of Pennsylvania. Her research addresses the social dimensions of scientific knowledge in contexts of crisis and in U.S.-based pharmaceutical research. She is the author of *Life*

Exposed: Biological Citizens after Chernobyl (2002) and a coeditor of *Global Pharmaceuticals: Ethics, Markets, Practices* (2006). Her recently published book, *When Experiments Travel: Clinical Trials and the Global Search for Human Subjects* (2009), explores patient protections in the context of global clinical trials.

MIRIAM TICKTIN is an assistant professor of anthropology at the New School for Social Research. Her research interests include the anthropology of the human, post-human, and humanitarianism; migration, camps, and borders; sexual violence and violence against women; and the anthropology of science, medicine, and ethics. She has published essays in journals such as *American Ethnologist* and *SIGNS*. Her book *Pathologies for Papers: Humanitarianism, Sexual Violence and the Politics of Immigration in France* is forthcoming.

RICHARD ASHBY WILSON is the Gladstein Chair of Human Rights, professor of anthropology and law, and director of the Human Rights Institute at the University of Connecticut. He is the author or editor of numerous works on human rights, truth commissions, and international criminal tribunals, including *The Politics of Truth and Reconciliation in South Africa* (2001), and *Humanitarianism and Suffering: The Mobilization of Empathy* (2009, coedited with Richard D. Brown). His book *Writing History in International Criminal Trials* is forthcoming.

CHARLES ZERNER is the Barbara B. and Bertram J. Cohn Professor of Environmental Studies at Sarah Lawrence College and director of the Environmental Studies/Science, Technology, and Society Colloquium Series *Intersections*. His earlier research focused on environmental justice and rights issues in Southeast Asian environments. In the post–September 11 security context, he is particularly interested in the relations between affect, imagery, bio-technology, and military strategy. He is contributing editor of *Culture and the Question of Rights: Forests, Coasts, and Seas in Southeast Asia* (2003), and a coeditor of *Making Threats: Bio-fears and Environmental Anxieties* (2005).

INDEX ∽

Page numbers in italics refer to illustrations.

Abélès, Marc, 189n4

Abraham, John, 261, 286n9

Actus reus (proscribed act), 33

Africa. *See* CAR (Central African Republic); ICTR (International Criminal Tribunal for Rwanda); Rwanda; *Le silence de la forêt* (Goyemidé)

African Americans, 18, 116, 125, 261, 287n18

Agamben, Giorgio: on bare life, 139, 143, 165, 244; on bestialization, 120; on biopolitics, 165; on biopower, 123, 124, 125; *homo sacer*, 9, 165; on life as *hypokeimenon*, 123; *logos/phoné* theorem and, 121–22, 149n3; on the thanatopolitical, 122–23; *zoé/bios* (bare life/political existence), 75, 113n16, 119–23, 125, 131–32, 143–44, 149n3, 165, 244. *See also* Animal and animality

Agrawal, Arun, 20, 24, 194, 196, 210

AIDS patients, *163, 182*; AZT drugs and, 182, 273–74, 279; dependence by, on medication, 181–83; drug resistance and, 176; exclusion of other patients by, 181; first-line treatments for, 176–77; identification with medication and, 179, 182; NGOs assistance to, 185–86; as patient-citizens, 166; religion adopted by, 162; resocialization of, 162; self-sufficiency of, 179, 181, 185; social stigma and, 163; treatment adherence of, 157, 159–60, 162, 163, 184; triage of, 184, 187; under-served

AIDS patients (*cont.*)
population of, 151, 155, 187; will to live
of, 156, 179, 181–83, 185, 186. *See also*
Caasah residents
AIDS policies in Brazil: access to medica-
tion, 18–19, 152, 280; generic pharma-
ceuticals, 157, 168–71, 177; outsourcing
of care to private sector, 170; rising
costs of, 176–77; success of, 172–73;
sustainability and, 174–76; UNAIDS,
158, 171, 174
Aka communities, 104
Akayesu, Jean-Paul, 36–37, 38–41, 52–53
Akayesu judgment, 34–41, 52–53
al-Qaeda, 24
Althusser, Louis, 10, 123, 149n5
America's Fund for Afghan Children, 72
Amman, Diane, 43
Amphibious Architecture (Jeremijenko),
211
Anderson, Benedict, 90
Anderson, David, 190, 198
Ang, Ien, 8
Angell, Marcia, 286n9
Angolan civil war, 242, 243, 251
Animal and animality: animal ethics, 119,
149n1; *animal laborans*, 165; animal
voice, 122; autobiography of, 133–34,
135–36; in biopolitical theory, 143–44;
critique of anthropologization, 141–42;
dehumanization of, 115, 116–17; in dehumanizing contexts, 21–22, 116; gaze
of, 119, 135–36, 137, 144–45; Gnat and
the Sovereign (Talmudic story), 147–
49; as limit of white racial respect-
ability, 126; lynchings and, 125, 126; as
metaphors for slaves, 149n2; nakedness and, 136–38; natality and, 119, 127–
34, 145, 146, 150n6; as *Nebenmensch*,
134, 135; nonhuman abjection and,
126–27; ontological privation of, 139–
40; *phoné*, 121, 122, 149n3; political
animality, 116–18; *prosopon*, 143, 144,
145, 146, 147; in *Le silence de la forêt*

(Goyemidé), 98; suffering animals, 67;
Umwelt, 139; vocality, 121–23; *zoé/bios*
(bare life/political existence), 75, 113n16,
119–23, 125, 131–32, 143–44, 149n3,
165, 244
Anthropologists: returning to the field,
178–79
Anthropology, 116; critique of anthro-
pologization (Foucault), 141–42;
natality's influence on, 131
Antihumanism, 10–11
Antihumanitarianism, 30–31, 277
Antiracisms, 78–80
ANVISA (National Health Surveillance Agency, [Agência Nacional de
Vigilância Sanitária]), 177
Appadurai, Arjun, 5, 23
Araújo, Jorge, 159, 160–62
Arbitrage: in drug development, 263–64,
286n15
Arendt, Hannah: on animals, 15, 132, 143,
165; on *bios*, 131–32, 252; on the cate-
gory of man in the Declaration of the
Rights of Man and Citizen, 7, 25n5;
on children as political beings, 80–81;
on denaturalization of people, 9; on
natality, 119, 127–33; on political ac-
tion, 128–29; on political v. private,
164–65; on slavery, 25n5, 129, 132–33.
See also Animal and animality
Aristotle, 6, 118, 121, 129, 130, 132
Arusha Peace Agreement, 34–35
ARVs (antiretroviral drugs): access to, 151,
157, 173–74, 280; changes in distribution policies for, 179; pricing for, 157,
170–71, 176; sustainability of program
for, 176; universal distribution of, 152,
170–71
Asad, Talal, 9, 14
Augustine, Saint, 60, 128
Autopsia, 141

Balibar, Etienne, 7, 59
Balick, Michael J., 323n12

Bangui, 94, 105–6

Bar-Cohen, Yoseph, 315

Bare life (*zoé* [Agamben]), 75, 113n16, 119–23, 125, 127–28, 131–32, 143–44, 149n3, 165, 244

Barthes, Roland, 59, 78

Bauman, Zygmunt, 245

Bayart, Jean-François, 91, 92, 93

Bazell, Robert, 235

Beck, Ulrich, 12, 24, 309

Becker, Gary, 74–75

Benjamin, Walter, 62, 81, 306

Benumbedness, 140, 148

Berkman, A. J., 152, 156

Bermudez, J. A. Z., 168, 174

Bhabha, Homi K., 88, 96–97, 112n4

Biehl, João, 18, 19, 24, 25n3, 152–53, 280, 285n6. *See also AIDS headings; Brazil headings; Caasah headings*

Biology and biotechnology: biodiversity monitoring, 112n3; cyborg insects and, 298–306, 316, 320, 321n3, 322n6. *See also* Forests; Pharmaceutical industry

Biomimesis, 295, 297, 315–16, 320

Biopolitics, 120, 122–23, 136, 143–44, 165, 231, 241–42

Biopower theory, 123–25, 127, 130, 241

Biosemiotics, 138–39

Bios (political existence), 120–21, 122, 123, 125, 131, 252

Bloch, Ernest, 76, 77

Bokassa, Jean Bédel, 94, 112n6

Bornstein, Erica, 75, 76, 83

Bosk, Charles, 289n33

Bosnia, 65–66, 244, 255

Boutros-Ghali, Boutros, 67–68

Bowker, Geoffrey C., 281

Braai (barbecue) interrogations, 116

Bradol, Jean-Hervé, 241, 243, 249

Brandis, Dietrich, 199, 200

Brauman, Rony, 240, 246

Brazil: incidence of AIDS in, 156–57; off-shore clinical trials in, 265; pharmaceutical market in, 157, 168–71, 172–73, 177, 280–81; policy-making initiatives in, 167–68; policy of drugs for all in, 157–58; pressure from patients to buy drugs and, 280; price reductions on AIDS drugs in, 157; private-sector activism in, 170; success of AIDS program in, 167–68

Breast cancer, 220, 224, 230, 231, 235, 236n4

Bryant, Raymond, 217n13

Burman, Erica, 59, 64–65

Butler, Judith, 217n7

Butterflies, 300, 302, 304–5, 316

Caasah, 160, *161*, 189n1; AIDS orphans in, 179, 181; as biocommunity, 164; field interviews at, 162; founding of, 161–62; redesign of, 178; as short-term care facility, 178. *See also* AIDS patients

Caasah residents, *163*, *164*, *182*, *183*; dependence of, on medication, 181–83; moral reasoning of, 181, 186; religion adopted by, 162; resocialization process of, 162; self-sufficiency of, 179, 181, 185; will to live, 181–83, 185, 186

Callon, Michel, 11, 16

Cancer patients: access of, to experimental treatments, 261, 268–69; advocacy for, 157, 173–74, 229, 235, 236n4, 268–69, 280; agency of, 222, 230–31, 237n7; death and, 222, 228, 231, 234, 235–36, 282–83; decision of, to undergo treatment, 181–83, 221–22, 236n3, 282–83; detection in young adults, 228, 237n5; guilt feelings of, 225; healing of, as competitive, 230–31, 237n7; human rights of, 261–62; incidence of relapse and, 220, 231; mortal hierarchy in RCT, 222, 227, 228, 231–36; objectification of, 220, 223, 224, 227, 232–33; participation of, in drug trial, 218–19; request by, for aggressive treatments, 225; retreats for, 229, 237n6, 237n9; self-management of

Cancer patients (*cont.*)
treatments by, 229; use of term, 230–31, 237n7

Cancer treatments: cost effectiveness of, 228–29; patient-generated literature on, 235; radical surgery and, 224; survival of, 228–29

Canetti, Elias, 115, 235

Canguilhem, Georges, 171

Cannibalism, 94, 116

Caplan, Arthur, 284

Captivation, 140

CAR (Central African Republic): civil servants in, 105–6; educational opportunity in, 110, 111; environmental governance in, 105–6; forests in, 98–99; national literature of, 96; opportunities for innovation in, 107; political stability of, 90. *See also* Forests; Goyemidé, Etienne; Pygmies

Cardoso, Fernando Henrique, 167, 168, 169, 170

Care. *See* AIDS patients; Caasah; Cancer patients; Clinical trials; Forest councils; Forests

Caricature (Italian term), 127

Carson, Rachel, 293, 309, 311, 323n19

Casa de apoio (house of support). *See* Caasah

Cassels, Alan, 286n9

Catts, Oran, 309

Chambliss, Daniel, 264, 288n33

Charitable organizations, 64–65, 72, 82–83; representational use of children, 75–76

Chatterjee, Partha, 10, 192

Chemotherapy, 222, 236n3; leukemia treatments, 231; objectification of patients of, 232–33; RCT (randomized control trial), 225; in *Wit*, 232–33

Chernobyl nuclear crisis, 288n29, 288n31, 319

Children and childhood: in abuse cases, 69–70; age-based models of, 81–82; as blank slate (*tabula rasa*), 61, 75; child soldiers, 14–15, 63, 81; as credible witnesses, 69–70; in drug trials, 264–65, 275, 276; as environmental investigators, 22, 23, 312–13; environmental toxicity and, 22–23; ethnic identity of, in Rwanda, 43; genocide and, 55n10; girls as representative of all children, 78–79; humanitarian representation of, 14, 59, 73–74; infantilization of calls for peace, 71–73; as innocent, 60–66, 68–69, 82, 84n2; media images of, 76–77, 84n7; in Palestinian territories, 63, 253, 254; peace as subject of children's books, 70–71, 85n9; personhood of, 63–65, 64–65, 69–70, 71–72, 79, 80; as political beings, 80–81; as sufferers, 64–65; United Nations initiatives for, 59, 68, 74, 81; violent crimes by, 63

Christakis, Nicholas, 225, 286n14

Christenson, Bill, 317, 323n14

Christian tradition, 60, 61, 75–76

Citoyen, 93, 97

Clinical trials: advanced-stage patients in, 281–82; arbitrage in drug development, 263–64, 286n15; auditing mechanisms for, 275–76, 278–79, 280; AZT trials, 182, 273–74, 279; benefits of, 219, 236n1; biased sampling in, 268; children in, 264–65, 275, 276; corporate evasion of regulation and, 285n5, 286n8; cost-effective modeling of research sites, 272; costs of, 258, 285n1; design of, and local levels of care, 273–74; drug-drug interactions and, 267, 287n17; ethical variability in, 257–58, 264–65, 271, 273–74, 281–82, 286n15; of experimental AIDS treatments, 261–62; hierarchies of differentiated humans and human subjects in, 256; ICH (International Conference on Harmonization), 270–71, 274; international standards for, 270–71; IRBs (internal review boards), 270, 275, 288n26; legal implications of, 275, 283; lower-than-recommended doses of drugs, 281; for "me-too" drugs, 266, 268; monitoring of, 258–59, 274, 275, 284, 288n33; off-label treatments and, 265; on oral contraceptives, 286n8; paradigm of expected failure in, 267, 268, 287n17; phases of, 226–27, 258, 272, 274; placebos in, 223, 233, 273–74; primary care doctors' involvement in, 278–79; providing heath care through, 271; rescue research, 279–80; in response to humanitarian crisis, 276–77; as social good, 271, 276–77; termination of, 283–84; treatment-naive populations for, 224, 260, 266, 269, 271; TRIPS (Trade-Related Aspects of Intellectual Property Rights treaty), 168, 169, 171, 274; Trovan trials in Nigeria, 275–76, 281; underrepresented groups in, 268–69, 287n18. See also CRO (contract research organizations); Data; FDA (Food and Drug Administration); Offshore clinical trials; RCT (randomized control trial); Recruitment of research subjects

Clinton administration: response of, to Rwandan genocide, 36

Coerr, Eleanor, 66

Cohen, Lawrence, 16, 285n6, 287n15

Coles, Robert, 81

Collier, Stephen, 6

Collins, John, 253

Colonialism: betterment of humanity and, 8, 25n4; as dehumanization, 26n7; despotic decentralization and, 92; exclusionary practices of, 10; forest policies of, 20, 195, 199, 200; group classification influenced by, 40, 47, 99; resource management and extraction and, 92; tropes of rainforest exploration and, 89

Comaroff, Jean, 90

Comaroff, John, 90

Community members: desire of, for self-government, 199; distribution of burden of regulation, 191–92, 210–13; fires set by, 20, 194–95, 208; forest guards hired by, 196–97, 204, 205, 206, 209–10; formation of environmental subjects and, 193, 207–10, 213–14, 217n10; monitoring mechanisms for, 204, 205–7; responsibility of, for forest management and use, 199–200, 209–10, 216n5; sanctions against offenders, 203–4, 206, 208

Compassion: and access to medication, 18–19, 152, 280; and limits of humanitarian aid, 2, 15, 238–39, 241, 243, 245–48, 253, 255, 277, 288n29, 288n31; suffering and, 28–29, 64, 65, 66, 67, 82. See also Caasah; Doctors without Borders (Médecins sans Frontières); Humanitarian agents; Humanity

Conceição, Dona Macedo, 158–60, 159, 186–87

Conrad, Joseph, 94, 95, 101

Cosmopolitanism, 11–12, 24, 32, 49–50, 53, 111

Coveney, Peter, 60, 61

Cox, Simon, 56n21

CRO (contract research organizations): clinical trials in Brazil and, 280; expansion of, 271; influence of, 262, 286n12; medical office sites for (floater sites), 278–79, 280; personal risks of, in clinical trials, 284; recruitment strategies of, 260, 272; selection of drug trials, 272–73

Cronon, William, 291, 310–11, 316, 323n24

Crook, Richard C., 216n2

Cruikshank, Barbara, 203

Cybercult, 324n30

Cyborg insects: battlefield deployments of, 300, 320, 321n3; bionic hornets, 305, 316; butterflies, 300, 302, 304–5, 316;

Cyborg insects (*cont.*)
DARPA (Defense Advanced Research Program Agency), 22, 292, 293, 295, 296–97, 300, 302, 316; HI-MEMS, 297–98, 299, 300, 301, 302, 303–4, 324n28; integration of microsystems payloads on insects, 298; movie images of, 299, 322n6; parasitic behaviors of, 299–300; predictability of, 298–99, 322n6; pupal-stage manipulation and, 298, 316; reports of public sightings of, 305–6; speed of, 300

Cyborgs, 11, 22, 290, 318; citizenship for, 292; civil rights for, 291; DARPA research programs for, 296–97, 316; social benefits of, 319–20

Cybugs, 22, 290, 294, 296, 304, 305

Dallaire, Roméo, 36, 56n21

Darfur, 2, 25n1

DARPA (Defense Advanced Research Program Agency), 22, 292, 293, 295, 296–97, 300, 302, 316

Das, Veena, 75, 287n15, 288n30

Dasein, 118–19, 139, 144

Data: death as needed statistic in RCT (randomized control trial), 233–35; ethnographic slippage and reliability of, 229; impact of selection of research subjects on, 260–61, 268, 286n9; objectification of the patient, 220, 223, 224, 227; patient data-mining companies, 258

da Vinci, Leonardo, 315–16

Death: cancer and, 222, 228, 231, 234, 235–36; as common good, 241; *Dasein*, 118–19, 139, 144; legitimation of, for promise of a cure, 222, 228, 231–36, 282–83; as needed statistic in RCT (randomized control trial), 233–35; privileging of military deaths v. civilian damage, 244; thanatopolitics, 120, 121, 122–23, 140, 141, 231. *See also* Mortality

Decentralization: collective decision-making, 192; critics of, 212–13, 215–16; of environmental policy, 198–99; formation of environmental subjects, 193, 207–10, 213–14, 217n10; individual involvement in, 211, 214; moving the tasks of government to the governed, 205, 211; necessity of separating humans from nature, 214; state-local relations, 192–93, 201–2; transnationality, 214–15; variables for involvement in, 211, 214. *See also* Forest councils; Offshore clinical trails

Declaration of the Rights of Man and Citizen, 7

"Declaration of the Rights of Woman and the Female Citizen," 7–8

Defense Advanced Research Program Agency (DARPA), 22, 292, 293, 295, 296–97, 300, 302, 316

de Gouges, Olympe, 7–8

Dehumanization, 115, 116–17

Deleuze, Gilles, 154–55

Del Vecchio Good, Mary-Jo, 285n6

Department of Health and Human Services, 284

Department of Homeland Security, 305

Derrida, Jacques: on animal ethics, 119, 149n1; on animal hospitality, 119; on animality, 136–37, 141; on anthropological thresholds, 142–43; autobiography of animal, 133–34, 135–36; on benumbedness, 140; cat of, 119, 135–36, 137; on Foucault's understanding of madness, 137; on gaze, 119, 135–36, 137, 141, 144–45; on human/animal checkpoint, 133–34, 135–36; on nudity, 137, 144–45; zoo-spectacle of, 142

de Vattel, Emmerich, 28

Doctors of the World (Médecins Du Monde [MDM]), 246, 251, 253

Doctors without Borders (Médecins sans Frontières): abduction of staff

members of, in Iraq, 15, 245–46; in
Angola, 242, 251; antibiotic treat-
ments in Nigeria and, 275; as expert
witnesses, 56n21; founding of, 239;
humanitarian action and, 239, 241;
in Palestinian territories, 250–51; in
Rwanda, 249; salaried employees of,
248, 249; on Serbian atrocities, 244
DOD (Department of Defense), 297, 299
Dolus specialis (special intent), 33, 37, 51
Dowsett, Mitchell, 220, 231, 233
Dragonflies, 22, 300, 304–5, 316
Dubois, Page, 149nn2–3
Dumit, Joseph, 16, 286n6

Eastern Europe: offshore drug trials in,
263, 265–66, 270, 274, 279, 288n24
Easton, Tom, 323n14
Ecotourism, 86, 105
L'ecume des jours (Vian), 98
Edgar, Harold, 222, 223
Ellenberger, Henri, 120
Ellis, Stephen, 93
Elshtain, Jean Bethke, 80–81
Elster, John, 217n12
Eltringham, Nigel, 41, 48–49, 56n31
The End of the Poem (Agamben), 121–22
Enemies, 12, 24, 26n9, 247–48
Environmental activism. *See* Jeremijenko,
Natalie
Environmental governance: of central-
ized forms of government of nature,
215; double roles in, 91; fusion of na-
ture and culture in, 291; by national
agencies, 91; of rainforests, 89. *See also*
Decentralization; Forest councils;
Forests
Environmental history, 291
Epstein, Steven, 269, 286n11, 287n18
Eskerod, Torben, 158, 162, 178
Esposito, Roberto, 125
Ethical variability, 257–58, 264–65, 271,
273–74, 281–82, 286n15

Ethics: and access to medication and
treatment, 18–19, 152, 157, 173–74, 261,
268–69, 280–83; animal hospitality and, 119, 145; ethical variability
in clinical trials, 257–58, 264–65,
271, 273–74, 281–82, 286n15. *See also*
Slaves
Ethnic groups: colonial precedents in,
40; cosmopolitan jurists on, 50; definitions of, 34, 37–39, 45; identification cards establishing membership in,
39, 40, 45, 48; objective approach to,
45, 46, 52; subjectivist view of, 41, 44,
45, 52; Tutsi as, 37, 44, 48
Experimental drug treatments, 261–62,
268–69, 287n18

Fabre, Jean-Henri, 294, 302, 315, 321n4
Fanon, Franz, 26n7
Farmer, Paul, 153, 175, 189n3, 257, 286n15,
289n33
Fassin, Didier, 15, 23–24, 239, 240, 242,
250
Fay, J. Michael, 106, 108
FDA (Food and Drug Administration):
children in drug trials, 264–65; clinical trials monitored by, 258–59, 274,
284; drug reviews of, 228, 268, 272–73;
International Conference on Harmo-
nization (ICH), 270–71, 274; IRBS
(internal review boards), 270, 275,
288n26; large patient populations
required by, 266; mandated random-
ized control trials, 272; promotion of
offshore clinical trials, 274; protection
of subjects by, 235, 275, 284, 288n27
Featherstone, Steve, 290, 293, 321n3
Fecomme, Andre, 105–6
Feldman, Allen, 21–22, 24, 116, 117, 141–42
Feldman, Ilana, 5, 13
Feral Robotic Dog Pack (Jeremijenko), 311
Ferguson, James, 5, 6, 106, 154
Feynman, Richard, 324n28

Fields, Lesley, 227

Figeroa-Sarriera, Heidi J., 318, 321nn2–3

Filipovic, Zlata, 68, 79

Fischer, Michael M. J., 259, 286n6

Food and Agriculture Organization, 198

Forest councils: as agents of regulation, 204; allocation regimes, 210; formation of, 193, 199, 202–3, 292; participatory democracy, 197–98, 211–14; records of, 202, 216n5; rules of, 196–98, 199, 201, 203; sanctions against offenders, 203–4, 206, 208

Forests: Africanness represented by, 98; animal dwellers in, 99; changing relationships with, 208; colonial policies, 20, 195, 199, 200; fires set by villagers, 20, 194–95, 208; foreign aid, 94; Gonada's identification with, 95, 97, 101–2; guards for, 196–97, 204, 205, 206, 209–10; historical sources for control of, 91, 112n5; as origin of Africanness, 98–99; rainforests, 88, 89, 316; relation of, to nature, 208; social identities of residents, 91–93; state actors in, 93–94; tropical forests as fetishes, 323n12. See also *Le silence de la forêt* (Goyemidé)

Foucault, Michel: on animality, 124–25, 137, 140; biopolitics of, 136; on biopower, 124–25; on collective living, 231; critique by, of anthropologization, 141–42; on disciplinary power, 203; on governmentality, 25n2, 154, 207, 217n7; monsters of, 124, 125; on population, 153–54; on power relations, 210; production of forms-of-life, 120; on sovereign power, 26n9, 241; *Umwelt*, 138–39, 140

France, 35, 89, 92, 112n2

Frank, Anne, 68, 69, 79

Gabon, 95–96, 108

Galvão, Jane, 152, 157

Gaze: of animal, 119, 135–36, 137, 144–45; camera, 126; captivation, 139; of communal regulatory authority, 204; Derrida on, 119, 135–36, 137, 141, 144–45; as disenfranchisement of humanity, 137; the face and, 143–48; involuntary exhibition, 139; as lethal, 306; nakedness and, 120, 121, 136–38, 141, 143–44; *prosopon*, 143, 144, 145, 146, 147; shame and, 138–39, 141

Geertz, Clifford, 264

Generic pharmaceuticals, 157, 169–70, 177

Geneva Convention for the Amelioration of the Wounded (1864), 29

Génocidaires, 31, 35, 38, 41

Genocide: acknowledgment of, by international community, 35–36; *Akayesu* judgment, 38–41, 52–53; collective victim in, 49–50; as crimes against humanity, 32; Darfur, 2, 25n1; definitions of, 33, 36, 37, 39–41, 48, 55n10; discriminatory intent, 42, 43, 56n25; *dolus specialis* (special intent) for conviction of, 33, 37, 51; establishment of guilt and, 33, 36–37, 55n10; Genocide Convention (1948), 33, 34, 37, 38; perpetrators of, 33, 44, 48, 49, 52; romanticism of, 31–32, 50; sentiment of universal disgust, 14

Gnat and the Sovereign, the (Talmudic story), 147–49

Golem, 306, 314, 319, 324n26

Gomes, Celeste, 161, 162, 178, 179, 184

Gonada (character in *Le silence de la forêt*): appropriation of Pygmies by, 100–101; colonial exploration motifs of, 100; on ethnography, 101, 113n15; forest characterized by, 97; identity role reversal of, 97, 113n11; lack of knowledge about forests, 99; Pygmalion (wife of Gonada), 101–2; relations of, with indigenous peoples, 96–97; relations with Manga the Pygmy, 21, 97,

98, 111; scientism, 100; transition from European colonial heritage, 99–101, 113n12

Gorgonean, 143

Gorman, James, 281, 287n17

Governance: experimentality, 277–78. *See also* Decentralization; Forest councils

Governmentalization of localities. *See* Decentralization; Forest councils; Villagers of Kumaon, India

Goyemidé, Etienne: career of, 87, 103, 107, 108–9; in CAR national literature, 96; European textual conventions used by, 99–100, 108; forest narrative of, 91; lack of knowledge about forests of, 99; social distinctions in the forest, 93; on whiteness, 98; on women, 100–102. See also *Le silence de la forêt* (Goyemidé)

Graham, Stephen, 314–15, 323n16

Grammata, 122

Gray, Chris Hables, 291–92, 318, 321nn2–3

Greenhouse, Carol, 285n5

Group identity, 39; accusations of genocide, 33, 55n10; birth as defining factor in, 39; categories based on fixity and facticity, 51, 52; identification cards establishing, 39, 40, 45, 48; kinship and, 47; permanence as defining, 39–42, 51–52; stability in definition of, 39; subjectivity in construction of, 41–46

Grove, Richard, 190, 198, 199

Guillemin, Jeanne, 289n33

Gupta, Akhil, 6, 64, 75, 154

Gusterson, Hugh, 303, 319, 322n7

Habyarimana, Juvénal, 34–35, 48

Hague II Conventions, 29

Hall, Stuart, 78

Hamitic myth, 47–48

Haraway, Donna, 11, 135, 137, 291–92, 303, 322n7

Hardin, Rebecca, 20–21, 24, 93

Haskell, Thomas L., 79, 83

Hayden, Cori, 19, 114n18

Heart of Darkness (Conrad), 94, 112n7

Hecketsweiler, Philippe, 89

Hegel, Georg Wilhelm Friedrich, 123, 129, 149n5

Heidegger, Martin: on animality, 118, 120, 132, 133, 143; on animal perishing, 126; biosemiotics of, 138; on impoverished animality, 148, 150n11; *Umwelt*, 138–39, 140

Held, David, 53

Helmreich, Stefan, 11, 315

Herder, Johann Gottfried von, 48, 50

Higonnet, Anne, 63

Hirsch, Robert, 309

Hirschfeld, Lawrence, 82

Hirschman, Albert O., 153

HIV, 117, 156–57, 273–74

Hochschild, Adam, 10

Holocaust, 29–30, 118, 251, 254

Holzgrefe, J. L., 240

Homeless people, 117, 159–60, 181

Honig, Bonnie, 88

Hope, 218–19, 221, 222–23, 232, 236n2

Houses of support. *See* Caasah

Humanitarian agents: assassination of, 249; Christian sponsorship of, 75–76; conflicts in courses of action and, 2; Doctors of the World (Médecins Du Monde [MDM]), 246, 251, 253; environmental subjects and, 193, 207–10, 213–14, 217n10; forest councils as, 203–4, 206, 208; hierarchies of lives, 15, 239, 241, 244, 245–48, 253, 255; production of inequalities by, 238–39, 243; protected space of, 251; salaried employees and, 248, 249; as spokesmen, 251; suspension of normalcy in humanitarian crisis, 277, 288n29, 288n31; terrorists compared with, 247–48. *See also* Doctors without Borders (Médecins sans Frontières)

Humanity: antihumanism, 10–11; antihumanitarianism, 30–31, 277; bare life (*zoé*), 75, 113n16, 119–23, 125, 127–28, 131–32, 143–44, 149n3, 165, 244; as biological object, 16, 17–18, 220, 223, 224, 227; *bios*, 131–32, 252; colonial interventions on behalf of, 8, 25n4; cosmopolitanism and, 11–12, 24, 32, 49–50, 53, 111; Declaration of the Rights of Man and Citizen, 7; decolonialization and, 26n7; defining, 1–2, 4, 6–7, 28; dehumanization, 115, 116–17; of enemies, 12, 24, 26n9, 247–48; environment and, 20–21; exclusion/inclusion in production of, 8–10, 103, 181; homelessness as criteria in definition of, 18–19; *homo sacer*, 9, 165; inhumanization, 4–5, 22, 116–18, 126; military interventions on behalf of, 12, 29–30; modernity as threat to nature of, 21, 97, 98, 111; natality, 119, 127–34, 145, 146, 150n6; natural law and, 27, 28, 54n2; as negative category, 28–29; of Pygmies, 20–21; of rainforest residents, 88; of targets of power, 199; as threat, 6, 12, 21, 214–15; the unhuman and, 19–20; weaponized other, 22, 318, 322n7. *See also* Animal and animality; Ethics; Gaze; Slaves; Visibility

Human rights. *See* AIDS patients; Cancer patients; Clinical trials; ICTR (International Criminal Tribunal for Rwanda); ICTY (International Criminal Tribunal for the former Yugoslavia)

Hutu Power: *génocidaires*, 31, 35, 38; Hamitic myth, 47–48; mass murder by, 35; opposition of, to Arusha agreement, 35; RPF defeat of, 35

Hutus: atrocities of, 255; ethnic classification and, 38, 47–48

Hutu/Tutsi distinction: terms of, 47–48

Hybrid biosystems. *See* Cyborg insects

Hybrid-Microelectromechanical Systems (HI-MEMS), 297–98, 299, 300, 301, 302, 303–4, 324n28

ICC (International Criminal Court), 30, 43, 74

ICH (International Conference on Harmonization), 270–71, 274

ICTR (International Criminal Tribunal for Rwanda): *Akayesu* judgment, 38–41, 52–53; categorization of massacres by, 32; construction of group classifications by, 31, 41–46; colonial precedents and, 40; creation of, 34; crimes against humanity defined by, 43; discriminatory intent in crimes against humanity, 42–43; establishment of, 36; on ethnic group identity, 37, 38, 46–47; expert witnesses at, 51–52, 56n21; historical course of genocide, 34; individual criminal responsibility as principle of, 32; *Kayishema* judgment, 40, 43–45; perpetrators' intent considered by, 33, 44, 48, 49, 52; *Prosecutor v. Alfred Musema*, 50, 56n28; *Prosecutor v. Georges Anderson Rutuganda*, 45; rejection of racial categorization by, 38; social categories of collective identity established by, 34; status of the Tutsi determined by, 31. *See also* Genocide

ICTY (International Criminal Tribunal for the former Yugoslavia): establishment of group classifications by, 47; individual criminal responsibility as principle of, 32; *Jelisić* judgment, 42, 56n25; negative/positive stigmatization distinguished by, 42; subjectivity in construction of group classifications and, 41–46

I Dream of Peace; Images of War by Children of Former Yugoslavia, 68–69

Ignatieff, Michael, 243

Iliowizi, Henry, 314
IMS Health, 172
Inguizeguino, Toutou, 105
Inhumanization, 4–5, 22, 116–18, 126
Insect cyborgs. *See* Cyborg insects
Insects: behavior of, 294, 321n4; behavior modification and, 298–99; genetic engineering of, 322n6; historical images of, 294; as instruments of surveillance, 294, 296, 304, 305; as moral beings, 294
Institutionalism, 210–11, 217n12
International Conference on Harmonization (ICH), 270–71, 274
International Convention on the Elimination of All Forms of Racial Discrimination, 31, 34
International jurists, 31, 34, 38, 50–51
International law: individual criminal responsibility as principle of, 32; *jus cogens*, 30, 55n6; permanence of group identity/classification and, 39–42, 51–52; romanticism and, 31–32
International Monetary Fund, 215
IRA hunger strikers, 116, 120
Iraq: abductions in, 245–46; Doctors without Borders (Médecins sans Frontières) in, 15, 245
IRBS (internal review boards), 270, 275, 288n26
Islamic militants, 23–24
Ismael, Fouad, 250
Isonomia, 130, 132, 133
Israel, 253
Ivy, Marilyn, 80

Jain, S. Lochlann, 16, 24
James, Allison, 60, 80
Jameson, Fredric, 101, 112n7
Jelisić, Goran, 42, 56n25
Jeremijenko, Natalie, *311, 312*; feral dog robots of, 23, 311–14, 319; politics of visibility and, 210; robotics in art of, 309, 311

Jewsiwiecki, Bogumil, 98
Jones, James H., 286n9
Le journal de Zlata Filipovic, 68
Jus cogens, 30, 32, 55n6

Kalyvas, Andreas, 130
Kant, Immanuel, 12, 50, 53
Karemera case, 53
Kassirer, Jerome P., 286n9
Kayishema judgment, 40, 43–45
Kent, G., 85n16
Keohane, Robert O., 240
Kim, Jim Yong, 287n15
Kim Phuc, 79
King, Rodney, 116, 120
Kinship networks, 47, 92, 211
Kittichaisaree, Kriangsak, 50
Kleinman, Arthur, 16, 287n15
Koenig, Barbara, 288n33
Kohn, Eduardo, 19
Kolinga administration, 93
Korbin, Jill, 63
Kosek, Jake, 19
Koskenniemi, Martti, 12
Kosovo, 243, 255
Koulaninga, Abel, 105
Kuletz, Valerie, 313
Kumaon, India. *See* Decentralization; Forest headings; Villagers of Kumaon, India
Kutcher, Gerard, 224
Kyoto Protocol, 9

Lacan, Jacques, 118, 150n8
Lachal, Christian, 250
Laird, Sarah A., 323n12
Lakoff, Andrew, 6
Lal, Amit, 297, 298, 299, 300, 316
Laqueur, Thomas, 4, 14
Lasagna, Louis, 278
Latour, Bruno, 11, 19, 259
Lederer, Susan, 286n9
Lemkin, Raphael, 40–41, 50
Lemogali, Adolph, 86, 87, 88, 90, 107, 111

Levinas, Emmanuel, 118, 119, 143–44, 146
Lewin, Tamar, 276
Lewis, Michael, 324n25
Linden, Eugene, 113n13
Lindgren, Astrid, 79
Lippit, Akira Mizuta, 118
Lobster-inspired robot, *304*
Local empowerment. *See* Decentralization; Forest councils; Villagers of Kumaon, India
Lock, Margaret, 16, 286n6
Logos: phoné, 121, 149n3
Lotrowska, Michel, 176
Lula da Silva, Luis Inácio, 167, 176

Machine in the Garden: Technology and the Pastoral Ideal in America (Marx), 292, 321n1
Macklin, Ruth, 264, 288n33
Magloire, Ambourhouet Bigmann, 95–96
Malinowski, Bronislaw, 273
Malkki, Liisa, 13, 14–15, 24
Mamdani, Mahmood, 93
Marks, Harry, 226, 272, 285
Marks, Lara, 286n8
Mark Trail (Dodd), 300, 322n10
Marrus, Michael, 29–30
Marshall, Patricia, 288n33
Marx, Karl, 10, 129
Marx, Leo, 292, 321n1
Masco, Joseph, 6, 294, 297, 299, 307
Mass murder, 35; motivations for, 44–45
Mbembe, Achille, 94, 101–2
Médecins Du Monde (Doctors of the World), 246, 251, 253
Médecins sans Frontières (Doctors without Borders). *See* Doctors without Borders (Médecins sans Frontières)
Media: campaigns for drug cost reductions, 157; on conservation, 107; images of the forest in, 91; insect imagery in, 294; RCT (randomized

control trial) in, 225; strategies of visibility in, 308; weaponization of nature in, 296
Medical anthropology, 264, 286n15
Medicare reimbursements, 278–79
Mehta, Uday Singh, 3, 26n6
MEMS, 324n28
Mens rea (awareness), 33, 37
Mental health program: in Palestinian territories, 251–52
Mentor, Steven, 318, 321nn2–3
"Me-too" drug industry, 266, 268
Military: interference in aid delivery, 2; Israeli army, 253
Military interventions, 295; ethical dilemmas of, 244; rhetoric of humanity justifying, 29–30; surveillance, 294, 295
Miller, Christopher L., 92, 112n9
Mimesis, 122, 123, 295, 297, 315–16, 322n6
Mimic (del Toro), 322n6
Minority populations: AIDS patients and, 151, 155, 187; children as environmental investigators, 312–13; in environmental politics, 213–14; exploitation of, 281–83; as research subjects, 260, 271, 279, 286n9, 286n15; underrepresented groups in clinical trials, 268–69, 287n18
Miracle cure: search for, 218–19, 222–23
Mitchell, Timothy, 5, 20
Mitchell, W. J. T., 319, 323n18
Modernization Act's Pediatric Studies Incentive, 265
Monitoring mechanisms, 112n3, 205–7, 258–59, 284, 288n33
Moreno, Jonathan D., 286n9
Mortality: animals and, 118; legitimation of, 231–33, 231–34, 235; longevity of the social and, 222, 228, 231–34; perishing vs. dying, 118; in RCT for future good, 222, 228, 231–34
MSF (Médecins sans Frontières): abduction of staff members of, in Iraq, 15, 245–46; in Angola, 242, 251; antibiotic

treatments in Nigeria and, 275; as expert witnesses, 56n21; founding of, 239; humanitarian action and, 239, 241; inequality between expatriate and local employees of, 247–49; in Palestinian territories, 250–51; in Rwanda, 249; salaried employees of, 248, 249; on Serbian atrocities, 244

Mugesera, Léon, 48, 57n32

Nagele, Rainer, 142
Nakedness, 136–38, 141, 143–44
Naked voice, 120, 121
Nanotechnology, 297, 305, 324n28
Narrative of reversal, 95
Natality, 119, 127–34, 130, 131, 132, 133, 145, 146, 150n6
National Assembly of Saint-Domingue, 8
National Bioethics Advisory Commission, 288n26
National Geographic Society, 108, 301, 302
National groups, 39, 41, 42, 45
National Health Surveillance Agency (Agência Nacional de Vigilância Sanitária), 177
National literature, 95–96, 112n9
National minorities: protection of, 41
NATO, 30, 244, 255
Natural law, 27, 28, 54n2
Nature: American wilderness fetish, 291; animal voice, 122; children and, 61–62, 65; humanity as threat to, 214–125; idea of untouched nature, 291; as inspiration for military use, 301–3; militarization of, 301–2; pristine nature, 291, 292, 293, 301, 317; Pygmies identified with, 20–21; Romantic poets on wild nature, 316; Rousseau on, 61–62; trophy hunting, 86, 91, 105, 107; weaponization of, 22, 295–96, 322n7; wild nature, 316, 323n24. *See also* Cyborg insects; Forests

Nauruzbayeva, Zhanara, 72–73, 85n11

Nazism, 49, 80–81, 118
Nebenmensch, 134, 135
Neumann, Roderick, 198
NGOs: AIDS treatment and, 157; Caasah as, 161; environmental management and, 105, 109; Médecins Du Monde (Doctors of the World), 246, 251, 253; operation of, 5–6; poor AIDS patients requests for assistance from, 185–86; production of global natural patrimony, 89; Red Cross, 29, 240, 251; state actors and, 93. *See also* Doctors without Borders (Médecins sans Frontières)
N'gouandjika, Mathias, 96
Nguyen, Vinh-Kim, 155
Nietzsche, Friedrich, 118, 142, 238
Nigeria: Trovan trials in, 275–76, 281
Nonhuman abjection, 126–27
Nuclear arms, 22, 66, 296
Nuremberg Charter, 32
Nuremberg Code, 276, 288n27
Nuremberg trials, 29, 32
Nussbaum, Martha Craven, 14

Offshore clinical trials: in China, 288n24; of contraceptives, 286n8; in Eastern Europe, 263, 265–66, 270, 274, 279, 288n24; ethical variability and, 257–58, 264–65, 271, 273–74, 281–82, 284–85, 286n15; ICH (International Conference on Harmonization), 270–71, 274; in India, 263, 288n24; international standards for, 270–71; in Latin America, 265, 270, 274, 280, 281, 288n24; litigation and, 276, 277–78; oversight of, 275–76; paradigm of expected failure, 268; providing health care through, 271; rescue research, 279–80
OIG (Office of the Inspector General), 258, 259, 275, 284, 288n25
Ong, Aihwa, 5, 6, 25n3, 168
Ophir, Adi, 247

Ostrum, Elinor, 190, 194, 216n2
Oxfam, 82

Palestinian territories: children in, 63, 253, 254; first intifada, 63, 253, 254; humanitarian psychiatry, 250–54; testimonies of Palestinians, 250–54
Pandolfi, Mariella, 13, 239
Panopticon, 203
Partners in Health. *See* Farmer, Paul
Patterson, Orlando, 132, 133
Peluso, Nancy Lee, 190, 198
Performance art. *See* Jeremijenko, Natalie
Persecution, crime of, 42, 55n9, 56n25
Petryna, Adriana, 17–18, 24, 166, 224, 268, 286n6, 287n15, 288n29
Pharmaceutical industry: access to medication and, 18–19, 152, 157, 173–74, 261, 268–69, 280–83; activist policy makers and, 177; ARVs (antiretroviral drugs), 157, 170–71, 173–74, 176, 179, 280; Avastin, 228; Brazilian market, 157, 168–69, 168–71, 172–73, 177, 280–81; ceftriaxone, 275, 276; drug regulatory policy influenced by, 260, 286n9; early termination of drug trial, 281–82; Efavirenz, 177; Enovid (oral contraceptives), 286n8; Genentech, 228–29, 231–32; GlaxoSmith-Kline, 263; Herceptin, 235; intellectual property protection and, 168, 173; Kaletra (rescue drug), 177; litigation by, 268, 276, 277–78; Merck, 177; Oxford Biomedica, 218; patent protections and, 168, 169, 171, 173, 177; Peginterferon, 280; Pfizer, 275–76; pill-taking lifestyle in United States, 267, 280–81, 287n17; profitability of, 228–29, 257, 266; relations with public institutions of, 177; rescue drugs, 176, 177; Roche, 176; Searle, 286n8; T-20 (Fuzeon), 176–77; thalidomide, 272; TroVax, 218, 222; Vioxx, 268; WHO relations with, 174; withdrawal of medication, 283–84. *See*

also Clinical trials; CRO (contract research organizations); Offshore clinical trials
Phoné, 121, 122, 149n3
Physical territory (*terroir*), 91, 92
Picon, Paulo, 177, 280, 281
Pillay, Navanethem, 37, 38, 41
Pippi Longstocking (Lindgren), 79
Posttraumatic stress disorder, 252, 253
Predator (uninhabited aerial drones), 302
Pressly, William L., 321n4
Prisoners, 116, 117, 278, 279
Private-sector development of vivisystems, 296, 297, 298
Prosecutor v. Alfred Musema, 50, 56n28
Prosecutor v. Jean-Paul Akayesu, 34–41, 52–53
Prosecutor v. Clément Kayishema and Obed Ruzindana. See *Kayishema*
Prosecutor v. Georges Anderson Rutuganda, 45
Prosopon, 143, 144, 145, 146, 147
Proxmire Act. *See* U.S. Genocide Convention Implementation Act (1987)
Psychiatry, humanitarian, 26n7, 250–54
Pygmies: *citoyen*, 93, 97; economic contributions of, 93; as ethnic classification, 38; identified with nature, 20–21; in labor force, 93; marginalized in CAR, 93, 103–5, 114n19; on marital life, 101; in *Le silence de la forêt* (Goyemidé), 95, 97, 98, 100–101, 111

Rabeharisoa, Vololona, 16
Rabi Abdullah et al v. Pfizer, Inc., 276
Rabinow, Paul, 6, 16, 286n6
Race and racial identity: in *Akayesu* judgment, 38; antiracisms, 78–80; definition of, 34, 36–38, 45; Hamitic myth, 47–48; International Convention on the Elimination of All Forms of Racial Discrimination, 31; international jurists on, 31, 34, 38; objective approach to, 45, 46, 52; racial categorization

rejected by Rwandan tribunal, 38; as subjective category, 41; whiteblacks (*munjuvuko*) in *Le silence*, 98; whiteness, 126

Radiation therapy, 224, 225, 229, 237n6

Raffles, Hugh, 11, 19, 112n8

Rainforests, 88, 89, 301, 316

Rancière, Jacques, 149, 165

RCT (randomized control trial): acceptance of, 226; anthropologists on, 223–24; chemotherapy, 225; death as needed statistic in, 233–35; efficacy of results, 220, 224, 227; lifespan of, 235; media reports and, 225; mortal hierarchy in, 222, 227, 228, 231–36; objectification of the patient in, 220, 223, 224, 227, 229, 232–33; pharmaceutical funding, 224; phases of, 226–27; placebos, 223, 233; principal investigators for, 235, 281–82; science and, 230; statistical models, 224; statistics in, 227–28, 230; temporal paradoxes in, 220–21; terminology of, 228; treatment-naive populations for, 224

Recognizability, 118, 119, 143–44, 146

Recruitment of research subjects: competition in, 265–66, 279; consent forms for, 276, 281, 282–83; from disadvantaged populations, 271; in Eastern Europe, 265–66; exploitation of, 281–83; IRBs (internal review boards), 270, 275, 288n26; litigation and, 276, 277–78; minority populations and, 260, 279, 286n9, 286n15; prison populations and, 270, 278; of real-life patients, 261, 268; recruiting pamphlet for drug trial, 218, 219; selection biases in, 261, 268; shrinking pool of potential subjects, 267, 287n17; treatment-naiveté and, 224, 260, 266, 269, 271; of underrepresented groups, 268–69, 287n18

Redfield, Peter, 6, 13, 242

Regulatory communities. *See* Forest councils

Religious groups: protection of, 39, 42, 45

Remote surveillance, 293, 294, 296, 304, 305

Requiem for Nature (Terborgh), 291

Rettig, Richard, 286n12

Reverby, Susan, 286n9

Reverse engineering, 157, 170, 171

Reynolds, Pamela, 75

rhGM-CSF trials, 288n31

Richards, Paul, 63

Robbins, Bruce, 12, 13

Romanticism, 31–32, 48, 50, 61, 69, 88, 316

Rose, Nikolas, 16, 25n3, 91

Rothman, David J., 222, 223, 286n9

Rousseau, Jean-Jacques, 61–62

RPF (Rwandan Patriotic Front), 34–35, 55n14

Rubin, Gayle, 233

Russell, Edmund, 294, 318

Russia: Chernobyl nuclear crisis, 288n29, 288n31; drug trials in, 264, 265, 269, 274, 288n24

Rwanda: Arusha Peace Agreemant, 34–35; international intervention in, 35–36; peace talks with RPF (Rwandan Patriotic Front), 34–35, 55n14. *See also* Genocide; Hutu; ICTR (International Criminal Tribunal for Rwanda); Tutsi

Sadako and the Thousand Paper Cranes (Coerr), 66

Sagan, Carl, 19

Saint-Domingue, 8

San Antonio Breast Cancer Conference, 220, 230, 236n4

Sargent, Carolyn, 16, 63

Sasaki, Sadako, 66, 79

Sassen, Saskia, 5, 6

Scarry, Elaine, 233–34

Schabas, William, 40–41, 48

Scheper-Hughes, Nancy, 16, 63, 286n6

Schmitt, Carl, 12, 24, 26n9, 30–31, 128

Schürmann, Reiner, 119, 141, 149

Scott, David, 217n10

Scott, James, 217n8, 314

Scott, Joan, 8

Secular humanitarianism, 28–29

Sen, Amartya, 19

Sendak, Maurice, 68–69, 79

Sentiment: benumbedness, 140, 148; emergence of humanity as, 4, 14; of exclusion, 8, 10, 103, 181; hope, 218–19, 221, 222–23, 232, 236n2; innocence of children, 14–15, 60–69, 71, 73–74, 82–83, 84n2; limits of humanitarian aid, 2, 15, 238–39, 241, 243, 245–48, 253, 255, 277, 288n29, 288n31; material inequality and, 10, 11, 15; of perpetrators of genocide, 33, 44, 48, 49, 51–52. *See also* Humanitarian agents

September 11, 2001, 294, 306, 308, 317

Serra, José, 157, 169, 170, 171

Shachtman, Noah, 318

Shame, 138–39, 141, 144–45

Sharkey, Noel, 323n13

Schiller, Frederick, 290

Shrivastava, Aseem, 194, 200

Le silence de la forêt (Goyemidé): animality in, 98; baboon people (*un peuple de babouins*), 99; background of, 89; binary themes in, 94–95, 97; eel as icon of nationalist integrity, 98; elite readership of, 90; gender relations in, 96, 98, 101–2, 113n10; "going back" references in, 98; *Heart of Darkness* (Conrad) compared with, 94, 112n7; popularity of, 89–90; Pygmies in, 95, 96–97, 98, 100–101, 111; shifting of African and European identities in, 99–103; significance of *silence* in title, 95. *See also* Gonada (character in *Le silence de la forêt*)

Silent Spring (Carson), 309–10

Silva, Nanci, 179, 184

Singa Ndourou, Serge, 103, 104, 105, 106, 113n12, 114n19

Singer, P. W., 323n13

Sivaramakrishnan, K., 198, 273

Slater, Candace, 91

Slaves: ancient Greek terms for, 149n2; animalization of, 116; animal metaphors for, 149n2; antislavery movement, 28, 29; apprehension of meaning by, 121; attacks on citizens by, 133; as *instrumentum vocale*, 129, 130; lack of natality of, 132; struggle against exclusion, 8; transgenerational transcription into slavery, 132–33; will in relation to slave labor, 25n5, 129

Smithsonian Institution/Man and the Biosphere Program, 89, 112n3

Somerset v. Somerset, 28

South Africa, 116–17

Sovereignty, 128, 137, 141, 148, 241

Sparrowhawk (Easton), 323n14

Spivak, Gayatri Chakravorty, 8

Spurr, David, 90

State regulatory measures, 192, 197–98, 200

Stephens, Sharon, 60, 63, 69–70, 79, 80

Stoler, Ann Laura, 8, 83

Suffering, 28–29, 64, 65, 66, 67, 82

Sunder Rajan, Kaushik, 286n6

Surveillance: after September 11, 2001, 294, 306, 308, 317; insects as instruments of, 294, 296, 304, 305; military surveillance, 294, 301–2, 321n3; monitoring mechanisms, 112n3, 204–8, 258–59, 284, 288n33

Survival, 156, 181–83, 189n4, 218, 222, 228, 230

Sznaider, Natan, 12, 24

Takacs, David, 316, 324n25

Taussig, Michael, 92, 112n5

Technical essentialism, 324n30

Teitel, Ruti, 5, 6

Teixeira, Paulo, 167, 170, 171, 174

Terroir, 91, 92, 93

Terror, 94, 112n5, 316

Terrorism, 23, 24, 26n7, 247–48, 321n3

Testimony, 250–54

Thacker, Eugene, 324n28

Thanatopolitics, 120, 121, 122–23, 140, 141, 231

Threat: cyborg insects as, 22, 298–306, 316, 320, 321n3, 322n6; environmental degradation as, 2, 6; environmental toxicity as, 22–23, 311, 314; forest fires as, 20, 194–95, 208; humanity as, 6, 12, 21, 26n9, 204, 205–7, 214–15; modernity as threat to nature of humanity, 21, 97, 98, 111; Pygmies as threat to national identity, 20, 103–4; terrorism as, 23, 26n7, 247–48, 321n3; trophy hunting as, 86, 91, 105, 107

Ticktin, Miriam, 6, 13, 14

Titus, 147, 148, 150n12

Torture, 23, 26n7, 116–17

Toxic Feral Dog Release (Jeremijenko), 311

Traditional medicine, 323n12

Trauma: humanitarian psychiatry as testimony to, 252, 253–54

Tribunals. *See* Genocide; ICTR (International Criminal Tribunal for Rwanda); ICTY (International Criminal Tribunal for the former Yugoslavia)

TRIPS (Trade-Related Aspects of Intellectual Property Rights treaty), 168, 169, 171, 274

Trophy hunting, 86, 91, 105, 107

Trovan drug trials, 275–76, 281

Tsing, Anna, 3, 19, 87, 109, 112n5

Tuskegee syphilis study, 18, 261

Tutsi: *Akayesu* judgment and, 38–41, 52–53; categorization of, in *Kayishema*, 44–45; criteria of definition, 45, 47–48; deracialization of, 48; as employees of MSF, 249; ethnic classification of, 35, 38, 43, 45; group identification of, 39–40, 47–48; mass killings of, 35; as protected group, 37, 43; targeting of, 41

Twa. *See* Pygmies

UDHR (Universal Declaration of Human Rights), 9, 74

Umwelt, 138–39, 140

Uninhabited aerial drones, 302, 323n13

United Nations: Convention on the Prevention and Punishment of the Crime of Genocide, 33, 34, 37, 38; Convention on the Rights of the Child, 81; League of Nations, 50; relief operations of, 30; response of, to Rwandan genocide, 35–36; Security Council, 34, 36, 55n13; UNAIDS, 158, 171, 174; UNESCO, 89, 105; UNICEF, 59, 68, 74; United Nations Framework Convention on Climate Change, 9

United States: acknowledgement by, of genocide in Rwanda, 36; cancer in, 219, 236n2; experimentalization of everyday life in, 278; military surveillance by, 294, 301–2, 321n3; pill-taking lifestyle in, 267, 280–81, 287n17

Unit of Clinical Research of University Hospital in Porto Alegre, Brazil, 280, 281

Universal Declaration of Human Rights (UDHR), 9, 74

U.S. Genocide Convention Implementation Act (1987), 37–38

U.S. Public Health Service, 261

Valentine, Gill, 60, 62, 63

Vandergeest, Peter, 190, 198

Victims: humanitarian construction of suffering others, 253; Israeli victims of Palestinian bombings, 253; testimonies of, 250–54

Vietnam, 79, 246

Villagers of Kumaon, India: desire of, for self-government, 199; distribution of burden of regulation and, 191–92,

Villagers of Kumaon, India (*cont.*)
210–13; fires set by, 20, 194–95, 208;
forest guards hired by, 196–97, 204,
205, 206, 209–10; formation of environmental subjects, 193, 207–10, 213–
14, 217n10; monitoring mechanisms
for, 204, 205–7; responsibility of, for
forest management and use, 199–200,
209–10, 216n5; sanctions by, against
offenders, 203–4, 206, 208
Virilio, Paul, 293, 323n17, 324n30
Visibility: of animals, 139; in the Gnat
and the Sovereign (Talmudic story),
147–49; of HI-MEMS, 303–4; and the
human face, 143–44; of lethal environmental risks, 307–8, 309–10; nakedness, 136–38, 141, 143–44; natality as,
119, 127–34; *prosopon*, 143, 144, 145, 146,
147; recognizability, 118, 119, 143–44,
146; stealth, 22, 294–95, 317, 318, 322n7.
See also Gaze
Vivisystems: cyborg insects as, 298–306,
316, 320, 321n3, 322n6; DARPA research programs for, 296–97, 316; as
environmental sentinels, 297; HI-
MEMS, 297–98, 299, 300, 301, 302,
303–4, 324n28; private-sector development of, 296, 297; as undetectable,
295
von Karman, Theodore, 314
von Uexküll, Jakob Johann, 138, 139

Wade, Robert, 192
Wall, John, 60, 61, 76, 80, 84n2
Wallerstein, Immanuel, 5, 59
We Are the World, 78, 85n18

Weber, Max, 53
Weiss, Rick, 290, 305
Welsome, Eileen, 224
White, Hayden, 76, 136
WHO (World Health Organization),
158, 174
Whyte, Susan Reynolds, 175, 260, 271
Wiener, Norbert, 324n26, 324n29
Wilson, E. O., 294, 302–3, 316
Wilson, Richard Ashby, 14, 24
Wit (Edson), 232–33
World Bank, 157, 161, 169, 186–87, 215
World Conference on Human Rights
(Vienna, 1993), 67–68
World Trade Organization (WTO), 157,
158, 168–69, 171, 274
World Wildlife Fund, 108
WTO (World Trade Organization), 157,
158, 168–69, 171, 274

Xenophon, 133

Young, Iris, 165, 275
Yugoslavia. *See* ICTY (International
Criminal Tribunal for the former
Yugoslavia)

Zacharian, Rony, 56n21
Zana, Henri, 113n15
Zerner, Charles, 22, 24
Zimbabwe: Christian evangelism in,
75–76
Zoé/bios (bare life/political existence),
75, 113n16, 119–23, 125, 127–28, 131–32,
143–44, 149n3, 165, 244
Zoography, 116, 117
Zurr, Ionat, 309

Library of Congress Cataloging-in-Publication Data

In the name of humanity : the government of threat and care /
Ilana Feldman and Miriam Ticktin, eds.
p. cm.
Includes bibliographical references and index.
ISBN 978-0-8223-4810-8 (cloth : alk. paper)
ISBN 978-0-8223-4821-4 (pbk. : alk. paper)
1. Humanity. 2. Political ethics.
I. Feldman, Ilana, 1969- II. Ticktin, Miriam Iris.
BJ1533.H9.I53 2010
301—dc22
2010024238

31731724R00238

Made in the USA
Lexington, KY
23 February 2019